Short Fiction
A Critical Companion

by

Robert C. Evans
Anne C. Little
and Barbara Wiedemann

LOCUST HILL PRESS
West Cornwall, CT
1997

Library of Congress Cataloging-in-Publication Data

Evans, Robert C.
    Short fiction : a critical companion / by Robert C. Evans, Anne C.
Little, and Barbara Wiedemann.
    320p.   cm.
    Includes bibliographical references and indexes.
    ISBN 0-933951-73-6 (lib. bdg. : alk. paper)
    1. Short stories, American--History and criticism--Abstracts.
    2. Short stories, American--History and criticism--Bibliography.
    3. Short stories, English--History and criticism--Bibliography.
    4. Short stories, English--History and criticism--Abstracts.
    I. Little, Anne C.   II. Wiedemann, Barbara.   III. Title.
    PS374.S5E93 1997
    016.813'0109--dc21   96-52058
                                                                 CIP

Printed on acid-free, 250-year-life paper
Manufactured in the United States of America

for Robbie

with affection and respect

Dr. Robbie Jean Walker has both lived through and embodied a remarkable historical transition. Born the sixth of eleven children in rural Alabama, she attended a one-room schoolhouse for the first six years of her education. While going to high school during a period of segregation, she was bused fifteen miles each day past two closer schools. She graduated at the top of her high school class, attended college for two years, then had to postpone completion of her undergraduate education while she worked for ten years to save enough money to finish her degree. Once again she graduated at the top of her class (from Alabama A&M University), and then, at her first teaching job, instructed every student in grades nine through twelve at a small Alabama high school. In all, she taught for fourteen years in various public high schools, all the while working on a master's degree at Alabama State University and on a doctorate at Auburn University.

Dr. Walker joined the faculty of Auburn University at Montgomery in 1979 as an instructor in English, attaining the rank of full professor in 1992. Her extensive publication record includes articles on the teaching of writing and on African American literature. Her book *The Rhetoric of Struggle: Public Address by African American Women* (1992) has been used as a text at various colleges and universities. She is a frequent keynote speaker for the National Coalition for Equality in Learning, an organization in which she serves as a member of the national faculty. A member of various honor societies, she is also a frequent presenter at professional conferences.

Dr. Walker is currently working on a collection of her own essays and on a literary biography of Dorothy West, whose contributions to the Harlem Renaissance literary movement have not, to date, been appropriately celebrated.

A founder and for many years a director of the Auburn University at Montgomery Learning Center, most recently Dr. Walker served as dean of the university's school of Liberal Arts.

What no list of such achievements can convey, however, are the decency, kindness, compassion, and grace of Robbie Jean Walker. She is wise; she is good; she is generous; she is principled; and she is loved. She has a ready smile, a quick laugh, a large heart, and the immense respect of everyone who knows her.

We are honored to dedicate this book to Robbie Jean.

Contents

Acknowledgments

Anne Little thanks Alan Gribben for his efforts to create a departmental environment that encourages both effective teaching and scholarship and Susie Paul for her good-humored willingness to help sort through any number of complex ideas. She also thanks Matthew J. Bruccoli for teaching her to strive for accuracy in every detail. If she made any errors in this volume, she hopes he never finds out. Finally, she thanks Bob Little for his stability and laughter, both of which help keep her sane, and her parents, Anne and John Stewart, for always believing she could accomplish whatever she attempted.

* * *

Barbara Wiedemann would like to thank colleagues (and friends) at Auburn University at Montgomery for encouraging her in this project, Greg Glover for creating diversions, and Nichole Wiedemann for being Nichole.

* * *

Robert Evans wishes to thank his colleagues, friends, students, and teachers, especially Ann Depas-Orange, Eric Sterling, and Alan Gribben. He is grateful for the love of two wonderful aunts (Evelyn Somyak and Hazel Kovarik), two great sisters (Darla and Betty), two fine in-laws (Claramae and Carol Dunham), and one incomparable wife (Ruth).

* * *

All three compilers join in offering enthusiastic thanks and appreciation to Robbie J. Walker, who has no idea how much she means to so many people.

Preface

This book is intended as an aid to various readers, particularly students who are assigned to read short fiction and also members of the general public who choose to read of their own free will. The book focuses on nearly forty famous stories by English-language authors—the stories most frequently included in classroom anthologies. By providing summaries of some of the most interesting analyses these works have provoked, we hope to offer readers some jumping-off points for their own thinking. Some stories (such as Melville's "Bartleby" or Joyce's "The Dead") have been so frequently analyzed that our summaries can only begin to skim the surface of available discussions. Other stories, particularly by more recent writers, have not yet been thoroughly discussed, and so our summaries sometimes provide relatively thorough coverage of the available criticism.

In choosing criticism to summarize, we tried to keep several critieria in mind. We wanted to include a variety of theoretical perspectives, and we also wanted to include both older and newer voices. We wanted to include some of the most influential or most frequently debated approaches, but we also wanted to introduce readers to some of the most recent thinking. No one, probably, will be entirely happy with all of the choices we have made, but we hope that all readers will find something of value here. We have tried to make our summaries more detailed and lengthy than is usually the case in annotated bibliographies of this sort so that readers will have a fuller sense of the critics' various arguments.

Another innovative feature of this book is the lengthy introduction, which not only surveys a variety of critical approaches but also tries to make it as easy as possible for readers to understand, compare, and contrast some of the basic assumptions those approaches entail. Inevitably this survey simplifies its subject: the best way to understand any critic's particular ideas is still to study the unique expression of those ideas in particular essays or books. The present survey, however, attempts to impose some systematic order on the wide variety of currently available ways of reading literature. By examining some of the underlying assumptions that different kinds of critics tend to make (that is, by scrutinizing the kinds of ideas they tend to take for granted), we hope that this book will help to provoke thought, discussion, and understanding.

A further distinctive feature of this volume is presented in the Appendix. This section reprints Kate Chopin's famous (and famously brief) work "The Story of an Hour," and then it offers a number of different responses to particular portions of the work—responses written by actual students who were asked to use some of the critical approaches discussed in the present volume's Introduction. Chopin's story was selected not only because of its brevity but also because it lends itself so well to analysis from so many diverse perspectives. The brief analytical comments offered in this appendix, of course, are by no means intended to be definitive or exhaustive. Instead, they are intended to be suggestive, demonstrating how one *might* (rather than how one *must*) view a work from a particular point-of-view. We hope that this appendix, consisting as it does of work by students themselves, will help demonstrate to other students and "non-professional" readers how various critical theories can be useful in actually reading, comprehending, and enjoying short fiction.

Three indexes (prepared by John Burdett) follow the Appendix. The first, organized by critical approach, indicates which of the summarized discussions best illustrates a particular kind of theoretical perspective. This index does not attempt to include *all* of the summaries presented in the middle of the book. Some of the summarized discussions are not easily identified with one particular approach, and we have not sought to pigeon-hole any discussion by forcing a label onto it. However, when a critic's work does seem clearly to represent a particular approach (especially when the critic herself makes that emphasis obvious), we have listed her work under the appropriate category (or categories). For instance, an obviously Marxist approach to Shirley Jackson's story "The Lottery" would be listed in this index under the category "Marxism." An obviously feminist approach to the same story would be listed under the category "Feminism." And a "Marxist-feminist" approach would be listed under both categories. We hope that this index will thus help provide readers with a quick listing of books and articles that best exemplify particular *ways* of reading literature.

A more comprehensive topical index, covering a broader range of the ideas discussed in this book, follows. If a reader is interested in discussions of "women," for instance, she might check that entry in the index; if a reader is curious about the topic of "genre," he might consult that entry. This index is one of several features, then, designed to help make the book as "user-friendly" as possible. We hope, in the end, that this volume will satisfy the needs of various kinds of users: students who are just beginning their acquaintance with short fiction; veteran readers who want to discover what other thoughtful people have had to say about stories that intrigue them; teachers and students of both literature and critical theory; and anyone who is fascinated by the power of short fiction and with the variety of methods critics have used to try to explain its force.

The volume concludes with an Index of Critics.

The names of the individual contributors are abbreviated (as below) at the end of the section devoted to each short story writer, and an explanation of other abbreviations used in the book is provided immediately preceding the text.

R.C.E.

INTRODUCTION
Literary Theory and Literary Criticism: What's the Use?

Robert C. Evans

Although literary theory is often considered highly abstract and intellectual and therefore remote from the concerns of "ordinary" readers, any reader of a literary text inevitably uses a literary theory of some sort. Any reader, that is, inevitably makes assumptions about why and how a text should be interpreted, understood, or appreciated. Responding to a text inevitably involves applying these assumptions to the text, whether or not we are consciously aware of doing so. One goal of literary theorists, indeed, is to encourage us to be more conscious of the assumptions we make and use when we read. By being more conscious of these assumptions we can not only use them more insightfully but can also consider their strengths and weaknesses, their relative advantages and disadvantages. We can consider whether and in what ways they seem valid; we can make sure that we better understand their larger implications; we can determine whether we are applying them consistently; and we can help ensure that the theory we use is a theory we have freely chosen rather than one we have merely taken for granted simply because it is practiced by others. Studying literary theory, then, can not only introduce us to different ways of reading texts but can also encourage a fuller development of our minds by prompting us not only to think for ourselves but to make sure that we can explain why we have chosen to think and read as we do.

Studying literary theory, however, has become increasingly difficult as the number of such theories has itself increased, especially during the last century. So many theories now exist, and so many often seem so difficult to grasp, that it is little wonder that so many "ordinary" readers feel intimidated (or even repelled). Trying to make sense of a given theory, and then trying to determine how that theory can be compared and contrasted with others, is a genuinely daunting task. Different theorists seem not only to make fundamentally different assumptions but also, frequently, to speak fundamentally different languages—languages that often seem arcane and highly abstract. It is hardly surprising, then, that many readers, when confronted with the opportunity or need to expose themselves to theory, adopt the response of Melville's Bartleby and would simply "prefer not" to.

The Abrams Scheme

Understanding the assumptions that lie within and beneath various literary theories becomes much easier when we heed the advice of M.H. Abrams, himself a highly influential theorist. Abrams suggested a scheme that is both firm enough and flexible enough to make sense of just about any theory one can imagine.[1] By applying this schematic approach to different theories, we can better understand both how they are similar and how they differ, and because the Abrams scheme encourages a systematic approach to various theories, it also makes it much easier to remember both their common and their distinctive features. Any schematic approach, of course, inevitably involves some simplification; in the final analysis, the best way to understand a particular theorist's ideas will be to examine them with individual care and attention. The Abrams scheme, however, provides a useful way to begin the study of literary theory and to organize both the tactics and results of our thinking.

---

[1] Abrams has extended and updated his ideas since they were first published as the "Introduction" to his classic book *The Mirror and the Lamp: Romantic Theory and the Critical Tradition* (Oxford: Oxford University Press, 1953), 3–29. For more recent treatments see, for instance, the essay "Types and Orientations of Critical Theories" in the collection *Doing Things with Texts: Essays in Criticism and Critical Theory*, ed. Michael Fischer (New York: Norton, 1989), 3–30; and also the entry entitled "Poetry, Theories of (Western)" in *The New Princeton Encyclopedia of Poetry and Poetics*, ed. Alex Preminger and T.V.F. Brogan (Princeton: Princeton University Press, 1993), 942–54.

Briefly, Abrams argues that any literary theory that attempts to be complete will inevitably make certain fundamental assumptions about several basic aspects of literature. These aspects can be called the writer, the text, the audience, and "reality." To these four categories we can add a fifth: the critic. Any theory of literature, in other words, will tend to make assumptions about the role of the *writer*, the features of the *text*, the traits of the *audience*, the nature of "*reality*," and the functions of the *critic*. Moreover, assumptions in one category will almost inevitably affect, or be consistent with, assumptions in another. Take an obvious example: if a theorist assumes that "reality" is fundamentally structured by inherent or imposed differences between the sexes, that assumption will in turn affect how the theorist imagines the role of the writer (for example: male? female? sexist? liberationist? free? oppressed? etc.), the features of the text (for example: progressive? conservative? experimental? traditional? flexible? rigid? etc.), the traits of the audience (for example: men? women? repressed? tolerant? conservative? liberal? etc.), and the functions of the critic (for example: a supporter of liberation? an advocate for previously ignored writers? a student of "male" and "female" habits of thinking and writing? etc.).

Or take another example: if a theorist assumes that a literary text is a work of careful craftsmanship, he will automatically assume that the writer will (or should) be a craftsman, that the audience will (or should) appreciate such craft, and that the critic will (or should) help call attention to the highly crafted intricacies of the text. The relationship between these other ideas and the theorist's assumptions about "reality" are not, in this instance, inescapably clear. Thus the theorist may (for instance) assume that "reality" itself is highly complex and highly coherent and that the complex, coherent text therefore reflects reality; or he may assume that "reality" is complex or incoherent and that the text therefore provides either a satisfying or an illusory alternative. The category of "reality," in fact, is likely to be the most difficult category of the Abrams scheme to understand at first. For one thing, "reality" is likely to be defined differently by different theorists: some may emphasize individual psychological "reality"; some may stress social, economic, or political "reality"; some may focus on physical "reality"; some may even question the usefulness of the category (by suggesting, for instance, that an objective "reality" does not exist). Ironically, though, even theorists who doubt the existence of any independent "reality" will still need to use the concept. However, since "reality" can be defined so differently by so many different theorists, it seems best to highlight its debated, provisional status by placing the word in quotation marks. Most theorists can agree that literature involves texts, writers, audiences, and critics, but disputes about the nature of "reality" (or about how to understand it, if it *can* be understood) are often crucial to the differences between various theories. A Freudian critic makes different assumptions about "reality" than, say, a Jungian or Christian critic. Studying literary theory often involves studying different concepts of what is most fundamentally *real*.

Central Emphases in the Abrams Scheme

The Abrams scheme is useful as an analytical tool, however, not only because it breaks literary theories down into some basic component parts and suggests how those parts are interrelated. It is also useful because it suggests that each literary theory will tend to emphasize one component part as the crucial or most important. Some theories, for instance, will tend to emphasize the ways in which literature reflects, imitates, or mimics "reality." Abrams calls such theories *mimetic* (from the Greek word for imitation). In mimetic theories, the writer is judged by her ability to provide an accurate representation of "reality"; the text is judged by its success as such an imitation of "reality"; the audience expects the text to imitate "reality" and responds to it in those terms; and the critic thoroughly examines the work's relationship with "reality." Making one assumption (the need to imitate "reality") thus entails a whole series of related assumptions about writer, text, audience, and critic.

Some theorists, however, focus less on the text as an imitation of "reality" than on its function in affecting an audience. Abrams calls these kinds of theories *affective* theories, because they will tend to look at every other component of the scheme in terms of this emphasis on the audience. The writer will be judged by her skill in affecting an audience, as will the text. "Reality" in this case will be conceived mainly in social terms, and the critic will chiefly be interested in how (and how well) the writer uses the text to affect the audience.

Other theorists tend to focus less on the audience, however, than on the writer herself. Because these theorists tend to be interested in how the text is an expression of the writer, Abrams terms such approaches *expressive* theories. Instead of the text being seen mainly as a reflection of some external "reality" (as in mimetic theories), the text in expressive theories will tend to be seen as reflections of some important aspect of the writer (such as her mind, soul, values, emotions, or spirit). Expressive theorists will tend to assume that audiences are interested in such self-expression by writers, that the most important "reality" will be "reality" as perceived and expressed by the writer, and that the critic should mainly be concerned with examining the text as a form of the writer's self-expression.

Finally, Abrams notes that some theories tend to emphasize the central importance of the text itself. They think of the text not so much as an expression of the writer, as a reflection of external reality, or as an instrument for affecting an audience; rather, they think of it as having an independent existence of its own, as being an object interesting in its own right. For this reason, Abrams calls such theories *objective* theories, and for objective theorists the text is the most important aspect of literature. The writer is thought of mainly as the craftsman who creates the object; the audience is thought of as the persons who respond to the object; the critic is thought of as the person who studies the object most intently. The object may imitate reality or it may seem to reject such imitation; in either case, however, the focus of objective theorists is on the object (the text) itself.

Applying the Abrams Scheme

The Abrams scheme provides us, then, with a simple but surprisingly adaptable method for making sense of nearly any theory we might confront or wish to use. It offers a means of appreciating both the comparisons and the contrasts between competing theories, and it even gives us a means of studying literature itself. (Abrams assumes, for instance, that every literary work will tend to embody a particular theory of literature. We might therefore analyze a story by asking what the story implies about the role of the writer, the features of the text, the traits of the audience, the nature of "reality," and the functions of the critic.) The scheme makes it easier to grasp and remember the distinctive features of different theories, and it also functions as a tool for understanding both the most ancient and the most recent theories of literature.

This is not the place to apply the Abrams scheme to the scores of theories that have been used, over the centuries, to make sense of literature. Our focus, instead, will mainly be upon the most influential theories of the last hundred or so years. It seems worth beginning, however, by examining the assumptions that seem to underlay the thinking of four of the most important early theorists of literature: Plato, Aristotle, Horace, and Longinus. Examining these four theorists should be valuable for several reasons. First, doing so will help remind us that the most recent theories are hardly the only ways humans have used to think about literature. To the extent that the newer theories really are *new*, they may only be reflections of a very limited range of human experience and of a very distinct moment in time. Whether they will seem as valuable a hundred or a thousand years from now as they seem today, only time will tell. The ancient theorists, however, have in some sense already passed that test: Aristotle and the rest still have interesting and relevant things to say to us after many centuries, and some of the most basic issues of literary theory were confronted first by the first theorists. That, in fact, is a second reason for including them here. Many of the questions that stimulated Plato and Aristotle stimulate us still today, and many of the answers the ancients formulated have influenced recent theories and theorists. Although some recent theories seem distinctly modern (the Freudian approach, for example), others seem to build on earlier insights. The assumptions of modern "formalists," for instance, have much in common with the assumptions employed by Aristotle.

However, a third reason for examining a few of the ancient theorists is that those theorists themselves so powerfully influenced later critics and theories. Many of the most important critics of the Renaissance, for example, were very obviously influenced by their reading of Plato, Aristotle, and Horace (especially the last two), and the ideas of many Romantic critics have much in common with those of Longinus. Familiarity with the ancient theorists, then, can help us better grasp all the other theorists who followed them, including ones we have neither the space nor the time to study here. The ancient theorists provide certain paradigms and state certain basic positions that recur again and again in the history of literary theory. Once we recognize these basic patterns and ideas in Plato, Aristotle, Horace, and Longinus, we will be in a better position to recognize them in numerous later theorists.

Finally, one more reason for focusing on the four ancients suggests itself. As luck would have it, the thoughts of each one can be associated with a different central emphasis on the Abrams scheme. In other words, Plato tended to emphasize a *mimetic* theory of literature; Aristotle tended to present an *objective* theory; Horace tended to offer an *affective* theory; and Longinus tended to advocate an *expressive* theory. Studying the early theorists, then, can help us better understand some of the most basic arguments it is possible to make about literature and to see how those arguments compare and contrast.

Method and Abbreviations

The following brief descriptions of various theories attempt to present, as clearly and schematically as possible, the different assumptions each theory tends to make about the writer (**W**), the text (**T**), the audience (**A**), "reality" (**R**), and the critic (**C**). As explained above, assumptions in one category will tend to reflect and affect assumptions in the others. Inevitably there will be some repetition of phrasing, but this should have some value in highlighting the connections between different categories. Thus, if a theory regards the text (**T**) as a highly crafted object, it will tend to regard the writer (**W**) as a craftsman and the critic (**C**) as a student of craftsmanship. Laying out the assumptions of the different theories by using these five categories should make it possible to see the connections between categories *within a given theory* but should also make it possible to spot the comparisons and contrasts *between different theories*. Plato and Aristotle, for instance, tend to make fundamentally different assumptions about the nature of the audience; these different assumptions are readily apparent when one reads the summaries of their attitudes in the **A** categories of each scheme.

Although each category of each theory has generally been discussed in one paragraph each (labeled **W1**, **T1**, etc.), in some cases fuller descriptions have been provided and more paragraphs have been used (labeled, for example, **W2**, **W3**, etc.). Longer descriptions have been provided for theories that seem either unusually difficult, complex, or unfamiliar (such as deconstruction). Some of the most powerful theories, on the other hand, make intuitive sense to most readers (whether or not one accepts their assumptions) and therefore require less explanation. Feminism is a good example: few students have any difficulty understanding the implications and assumptions of feminist criticism.

Brief introductions to each scheme will attempt to provide extremely basic discussions of the sources and influences of each theory and of their historical significance and relations with certain other theories.

ANCIENT THEORIES

Plato

Ironically, Plato (ca. 427–347 B.C.) is not only one of the earliest and most influential commentators on literature but also one of its fiercest critics. Partly because he considered the influence of poetry on Greek culture excessive, and partly because he sincerely believed that society should operate according to standards of truth and virtue discovered and confirmed by philosophical reasoning, he was suspicious of the emotionalism and irrationality expressed and encouraged by many literary texts. Many later discussions of literature have been either explicit or implicit attempts to answer his objections, and in fact it has been famously said that the whole history of Western philosophy is a series of footnotes to Plato. Plato's attacks on literature (memorably expressed in the Ion *and in Book X of the* Republic*) are the logical result of his theory of REALITY, which is for him the most important component of the Abrams scheme.*

W1. Rather than being creative or possessing any true understanding of their own, writers are likely to be passive copiers or imitators of the external world. Writers are therefore likely to deal with the superficial appearances of things rather than presenting any genuine knowledge of what is truly real. Indeed, writers are often likely to be mere entertainers who appeal to (and thereby incite) the emotions and passions of their audience. Writers are likely themselves to be emotional, irrational, and illogical; they will tend to know how to manipulate words but not how to examine ideas seriously. Some writers will tend to rely on passive "inspiration" and will thus exercise even less rational control over their writings; in this sense such writers might fairly be described as inspired idiots. In general, then, writers will negatively influence society by encouraging irrationality. Some writers may have some social use, however, if their writings are used to help to make reason and virtue attractive to persons who are not capable of appreciating philosophical arguments on behalf of these ideals.

T1. A text should be judged mainly by how accurately it imitates or represents its subject matter; in this sense, a text's "content" is more important than its "form." However, texts created by poets and other "creative writers" are almost inevitably inaccurate and defective as imitations, partly because they imitate only the most superficial aspects of things. Since truth must mainly be defined in terms of logical propositions and philosophical rigor (rather than in terms, say, of emotional complexity or ambiguity), most "creative writing" is likely to fall short of such standards. To the extent that a text is philosophically untruthful or inaccurate, it is potentially dangerous. Rather than judging an artistic text in terms of the standards of its artistic genre (by asking, for example, whether it is a successful *tragedy*) and rather than judging a work in terms of its individual artistic excellence (by asking, for example, how all its parts fit together into a complex unity), Plato tends to focus on how accurately the text imitates philosophical *truth*. At best, artistic texts can merely present in attractive ways the truths already derived from philosophy. Truly thoughtful persons, however, will not need to rely on artistic texts in order to grasp those truths.

A1. Most members of most audiences are likely to be fascinated, deceived, and misled by the emotionally stimulating texts that creative writers concoct. Rather than using reason to search for genuine truth, most audience members will be content with the superficial appearances and appeals to passion that creative writers offer. Since such writers tend to be more interested in achieving popularity than in stimulating the minds of their audiences, and since most audiences tend to be more interested in being entertained than in truly learning, creative writers and their audiences will tend to encourage each other's own worst impulses. Audience members are unlikely to care that the writers actually know very little about the subjects discussed in their writings; instead, the audience will be satisfied if its emotions are aroused.

R1. True reality cannot be known by relying on the senses, which are almost inevitably deceptive. Instead, reality can only be known through the exercise of reason, intellect, logic, and philosophical inquiry. By using our senses we merely perceive particular physical objects; by using our reason we can discover general *ideas* or *forms* that explain and make sense of those objects. For example, in order to create any individual chair, there must first be a general idea of what constitutes a chair. Only after the *idea* of chair is known can an individual chair (an imitation of that idea) be created. In this sense, such philosophical *ideas* are more real than any individual, physical manifestation of those ideas. In addition, such ideas are eternal and universal: every physical chair that has ever existed (or can ever exist) has been (and will be) an imitation of the single, unchanging *idea* of chair (or "chairness"). Moreover, while individual chairs will inevitably decay and pass away, the *idea* of chair is immutable. Knowing such *ideas*, then, is far more important than knowing any particular imitation or manifestation of them. Unfortunately, however, creative writers tend to focus on just such imitations rather than focusing on the ideas themselves. Such writers therefore tend to distract audiences from the philosophical pursuit of truth. A philosopher, by using his reason, can come to know the "idea" of chairness; a carpenter can, in turn, possess a practical knowledge of that idea in order to create a physical chair; a poet or painter then will tend to imitate the individual chair created by the carpenter (and, to make matters even worse, can see that chair only from particular angles or perspectives). Artistic imitations, then, are inevitably several removes from genuine truth. In contrast, philosophical truth, because it is rooted in universal and immutable ideas or forms, is unambiguous, absolute, and non-relativistic: it does not depend on individual perspective. Plato's ideal model for knowledge tends to be mathematical knowledge. Thus, $2 + 2 = 4$ is true now, always has been true, and always will be true; it is just as true in France as in Nigeria or Nepal. It would be true even if no one were bright enough to realize its truth (it was true, for instance, even before human beings had evolved sufficiently to understand its truth, and it would still be true even if all humans vanished). This kind of *absolute truth* is the kind Plato most values, but he believes that it is a kind of truth that creative writing, almost by definition, cannot provide. Indeed, such writing cannot really provide "truth" in the best sense of the word; it can, at best, only make such truth palatable to persons who are either unable or unwilling to think philosophically.

C1. The critic should have a philosophical orientation; he should be a disinterested truth-seeker and should possess rational, disciplined knowledge. To the extent that the critic is a philosopher, he should work to expose the inadequacies of "creative" texts by demonstrating how they fall short of accurate, philosophical truth. To the extent that such texts can never be completely eradicated, the critic should examine their effects on society, particularly on the ways people think (or fail to think). The critic should act as a judge, condemning texts that undermine truth and encouraging texts that endorse truth. Aesthetics (the study of art) is not a separate realm for Plato; it is a branch of philosophy and, like any such branch, has an obligation to promote a true understanding of reality.

Aristotle

Aristotle (384–322 B.C.) was a student of Plato, but in his extremely influential treatise entitled The Poetics, *he offered one of the most cogent and systematic defenses of literature ever conceived. Although this treatise focuses mainly on tragedy, its implications are far-reaching because Aristotle (unlike Plato) assumes that literature can offer one way of knowing and understanding the world (rather than simply re-packaging knowledge derived from philosophy). Aristotle takes the literary TEXT itself far more seriously than does Plato; for this reason, he has been much admired by modern FORMALIST theorists.*

W1. The creative writer can be a discoverer of meaning; like the philosopher, he can be a truth-seeker, although in seeking truth he will use methods that differ somewhat from those of the philosopher, and he will also present the truths he discovers differently than the philosopher will. Therefore the creative writer should be judged according to the standards appropriate to his own field of endeavor. For instance, if he is a writer of tragedies, he should be judged by how well his work satisfies the requirements of tragedy as a genre or by how well he helps uncover the potentialities of that genre. In any case, the creative writer is, ideally, a conscious, deliberate artist, a skilled craftsman; he is not an inspired idiot or a merely passive imitator of external appearances. Because artistic skill is partly a result of in-born talent and because different writers will be drawn toward different genres (some being more inclined toward writing tragedies, for instance, while others are more inclined toward writing comedies), there will tend to be a definite connection between the character of the writer and the work he produces. At the same time, the successful writer will tend to possess some general insight into the nature of things, and especially into human nature, since human thoughts and actions will tend to be the focus of his art.

T1. The best artistic texts will be both complex and unified: every part of the work will be essential to it and will be linked to every other part. The connections between the different aspects of a successful text will seem natural and inevitable, and the quality of a text will be determined largely by how well it satisfies these combined criteria of *complex unity*. Every aspect of a text must be consistent with every other aspect; anything that is inconsistent is a defect. In the ideal Aristotelian text, everything fits; everything makes sense as part of a larger whole. In this sense, Aristotle places much more emphasis than Plato on the *form* of a text than on its content, although Aristotle also tends to assume that form and content (at least in great texts) are really inseparable: one cannot be discussed in isolation from the other. In judging a text, we must first determine the genre to which it belongs; it would be inappropriate, for instance, to judge a lyric poem according to the standards of a tragedy, or to judge a tragedy according to the standards of a comedy. Genres, however, are not mere artificial conventions; instead, they are logically necessary and natural ways of writing, natural ways of giving order to experience (or, rather, of perceiving the order that already exists in experience). In other words, experience itself is sometimes tragic, sometimes comic; therefore, tragedy can be a useful way of understanding experience, and so can comedy. Indeed, artistic texts help satisfy an innate and inevitable human desire for knowledge: all human beings have an instinctive need for knowledge; they want to perceive how individual facts relate to larger truths. The successful poem helps provide such knowledge and for that reason deserves respect and a valued place in society.

A1. Because the members of the audience have an innate desire to learn and to know, and because they take pleasure in learning and knowing, and because creative writing can be a form of learning and knowledge, art can have real philosophical and social value. The desire to learn is part of a general *human nature*; it is not confined to philosophers. Because human beings tend to learn through imitation, the fact that works of art are rooted in imitation is a potential source of their value; it is not a cause for condemnation. The most valuable works will therefore be those which best satisfy this innate human yearning for knowledge and understanding—works that reveal, for instance, how individual experiences relate to larger, universal truths. Because Aristotle assumes that a general human nature exists and that art can satisfy some of the most basic needs of that general human nature, he focuses on shared responses to texts rather than on individual, idiosyncratic, and relativistic reactions. The ideal member of the audience will be capable of appreciating the work's artistic unity, complexity, and structure (the arrangement of its formal features, the ways every part of the work contributes to the total effectiveness of the whole). In responding to a text, the audience will respond both to its form and to its content (which are, in any case, inseparable for Aristotle).

R1. Reality or nature consists of general forms, patterns, and coherent processes; the philosopher seeks to understand these, but the artist can also understand them and can help the audience know them as well. Whereas Plato tends to think of these forms as static and as somehow existing apart from or above actual things, Aristotle tends to think of these forms as dynamic processes that are inseparable from particular things. Aristotle's philosophy can therefore account for the way a thing can change while still remaining the same thing. As an acorn evolves into an oak tree, for instance, the plant actualizes the potential inherent in it from the beginning; in other words, it *achieves its form*. Every part of this process is related to every other part; the total process forms a complex and dynamic unity. One purpose (and need) of human life is to dis-cover the forms (the universal truths) that inhere within reality: those meaningful patterns already exist (they are not human concoctions), and philosophers and artists can help us come to know them more fully. Since Aristotle thinks of reality as dynamic, and since works of art (especially literary texts) tend to focus on human *actions* (i.e., meaningful patterns of behavior), literary texts can help illuminate human nature. For Aristotle, to know a particular aspect of reality is to perceive how it relates to some larger pattern or universal truth. Reality is a complex unity; to understand reality is to understand how all its parts fit together. Similarly, the work of art is a complex unity, and to understand it is to understand how all its parts contribute to the whole.

C1. Ideally the critic should have an integrated, systematic under-standing of the work of art, including the history of the art form, the particular genre in which the artist is working, and ways in which each part of the work relates to every other part and how the work as a whole satisfies both the requirements of its genre and the inevitable human need for meaningful knowledge. When examining a tragedy, for instance, she should ask such questions as these: how does this work meet the generic requirements of a tragedy? how does it perhaps reveal new potentials inherent in the tragic genre? how does the plot of the tragedy relate to its charac-ters or diction? Because the critic ideally possesses a systematic understanding of the art she examines, her responses are rational and objective rather than idiosyncratic or impressionistic. She should be able, that is, reasonably to explain why and how a work is successful. The critic is in some sense simply a more self-con-scious member of the audience as a whole: her response to a work of art will be similar to the response of the whole audience, but she will simply be able to explain that response more articulately. Just as the creative writer uses her art to help us see the meaningful patterns that exist within reality, so the critic uses her skills to help us see the meaningful patterns that exist within the individual text *and* how those patterns help illuminate reality as a whole. Because critics make it their business to think about art in general and spe-cific genres in particular, critics can even help suggest the as-yet unrealized potential of various genres. In this sense, critical knowledge can even help generate new works of art.

Horace

Horace (65–8 B.C.) was less a literary theorist than a practicing, profes-sional poet. Because he wrote during a period in Roman history when the value of literature was taken for granted, he felt no great need to defend literature from philosophical attacks or to ponder its underlying nature or purposes. His great statement about poetry, often called the Ars Poetica, *was in fact a poetic epistle addressed to members of an influential family interested in writing. In the epistle, Horace focuses mainly on giving very practical advice about how a writer should effectively appeal to an AUDIENCE (or at least avoid arousing their ridicule). Horace's ideas, which were influenced by Aristotle's and which were sometimes later even more explicitly combined with them by subsequent theorists, were extremely influential during the middle ages and Renaissance and into the eighteenth century. Some similarities exist between Horace's ideas and those of recent READER RESPONSE theorists.*

W1. The writer needs to keep the tastes and preferences of the audience in mind if he wishes to create an appealing work of art. In general he should follow customary practice, since custom is a generally reliable indicator of what the audience will accept. He can depart from custom if he does so moderately; extreme departures are likely to offend the audience. Moderate innovation, however, can please an audience by giving a touch of novelty to familiar themes or styles. The writer thus enjoys license within limits, and, in general, moderation is a worthy ideal: the writer should avoid taking on tasks to which his powers are unequal, since failure will result in public ridicule. The writer should be familiar with the customary practices and features of various genres, since these will affect his audience's expectations. He should know what is appropriate to each genre, and in general he should be careful not to violate decorum. If he depicts a young boy, for instance, the boy should act and speak as boys do. The writer should be a careful craftsman, and he should aim either to please his audience, to instruct them, or to do both. [Later interpreters of Horace tended to blend these goals, arguing that the writer should please *and* instruct or instruct *by* pleasing.] Although writers will need to depend on innate talents, they are also obligated to develop and refine those talents: here, as in much else, balance and moderation are important.

T1. The text should observe the basic rules of its particular genre—rules passed down by custom or tradition. It should be unified and not too complex, and it should be self-consistent. Violations of consistency (for instance, having a god suddenly appear on stage to solve problems in a plot) will seem ridiculous to the audience. The text should be carefully crafted; nothing should seem out of place. It should be a generally faithful imitation of real life and should use generally familiar language. It should convey wisdom, but it must also please. The most successful works tend both to please and to instruct (partly because they thereby appeal to the widest range of audience interests).

A1. Satisfying the audience is crucial; failure to do so will result in ridicule. The audience will be familiar with customary practices, social decorum, and the standards of real life. By violating any of these, the artist risks making a fool of herself. The audience will consist of different segments (the young and old, for instance, or those interested in entertainment and those interested in instruction). The writer who hopes to be successful should therefore try to appeal to as many audience interests as possible (without, of course, being inconsistent or violating custom). Because the audience will not tolerate mediocrity in a writer, the writer must seek to eliminate as many flaws as possible from his work. In general the writer should keep his potential audience constantly in mind and should do nothing that might provoke their ridicule.

R1. Horace tends to emphasize custom and tradition as reliable guides to "reality," and he also tends to stress the poet's need to imitate "real life"—i.e., the common standards of contemporary behavior. The writer should not depart too far either from what is customary or from what seems "realistic." For instance, she can create fictions and fictional characters, but these should seem real and credible. They should not wildly violate the audience's expectations. Similarly, the language the writer uses should be close to the language spoken in real life; it should not seem in any way excessive.

C1. The critic should act as an advisor, almost a father-figure, for the writer. He should give the writer honest advice about what will and won't work. He should try to help prevent the writer from making a fool of himself. In this sense the critic also acts as a spokesman for the audience in general: he articulates the standards by which the work will publicly be judged. The critic should be familiar with the requirements of various genres and with customary practice. He should be tolerant of minor failings and should not expect perfection, but he should judge how well the poet meets the requirements of his craft and the expectations of his audience.

"Longinus"

"Longinus" (first century A.D.) is the name traditionally given to the author of the important treatise entitled On the Sublime, *although the actual identity of the author is unknown. The treatise, written in Greek,*

was not printed until 1554, after which its influence became increasingly powerful. It became especially important in the late 1600s and had a great impact on eighteenth- and early-nineteenth century ideas about literature. Its strong emphasis on the crucial role of the character, spirit, and genius of the WRITER *makes it a central document in the history of "expressive" theories, particularly those associated with Romanticism.*

W1. The writer who hopes to achieve sublimity (an effect of heightened, almost irresistible power and force) must herself have a sublime mind and sublime character. She must be a good person whose thoughts and feelings are lofty, elevated, and exalted; she must transcend trivialities and strive to achieve ethical and artistic perfection. She must set ambitious goals for herself and for her art, and if her art occasionally falls short of absolute technical perfection, she will still win the respect of her audience by aiming high and achieving much. She should strive to embody, cultivate, and express a genius that will make her seem almost more than human. This same genius, however, will also make her an inspiring example of the best that human beings can achieve. Like an Olympic athlete, she should strive to surpass the accomplishments of her predecessors and contemporaries, not so much to achieve personal glory as to show the potential that humanity possesses and thereby give her fellow human beings goals for which to strive. Her achievements will thereby constitute not only personal triumphs but will also inspire artistic and ethical achievement in others. Again like an athlete, she must have natural gifts but must work diligently to develop those gifts to their highest pitch. She should not only imitate the works of sublime writers of the past but should thereby try to model her own character on theirs. Thus she should not only write as Homer would write but try to be the kind of person Homer was. The sublime writer has an important role in her culture: through her work and through her own example, she encourages her contemporaries to strive for spiritual and ethical perfection and to reject shallow, materialistic desires.

T1. The text will inevitably reflect the character of the writer; a debased writer cannot produce a lofty, powerful, or inspiring text. The sublime text will express the genius of the sublime writer, but it will also be the result of his trained and disciplined skills. The great work will express great and noble ideas in powerful, compelling, elevated language that is neither too ornate nor too colloquial, plain, or trendy. Unity and harmony contribute to the sublime effect of a work; the writer must know how to exploit and combine all the standard devices of rhetoric. A sublime thought, expressed in sublime language, will have an over-powering effect on an audience; they will feel themselves transported, uplifted, almost ravished by it. A sublime style will usually result only from long experience and practice, and especially from long exposure to the sublime writings of lofty predecessors. The truly sublime work will achieve a kind of immortality by appealing to intelligent readers always and everywhere. (Shakespeare, for example, might be taken as an example of a writer whose power transcends the limits of his own language, nation, and era.)

A1. Although human beings can become caught up in and enslaved by the trivialities of materialism and selfish pursuits, the sublime writer has the ability to inspire us, to remind us of our true spiritual and ethical potential, to encourage us to strive for elevation in our own souls. The truly sublime work appeals to yearnings that lie deep in our nature; it brings out the best in us; it transports and overwhelms us, allowing us to experience a kind of ecstasy that is closely associated with a feeling of immortality. We instinctively feel that the truly sublime work will cheat death, that it will appeal to the best in human beings everywhere and always, and we therefore feel a kind of awe in its presence. The fact that a human being has been capable of producing such a powerful work makes each member of the audience proud and joyful, and the work will have this powerful effect no matter how many times we experience it. The sublime work hits us with the force of a lightning bolt. The sublime simultaneously enthralls us and enhances our sense of freedom and power by showing us the excellence of which human beings are capable. An audience is usually willing to forgive small technical faults in a work that is otherwise powerful and grand.

R1. Human nature is fundamentally the same in all times and places. Although humans can allow themselves to become distracted by base desires (such as the pursuit of money or self-gratification), they are always capable of being roused and inspired by a truly great work. Such a work reminds them of what it truly means to be human in the best sense; it reminds them of the lofty potential human beings possess. Because such a work appeals to what is best in the human spirit, it achieves a kind of immortality, and it appeals to a fundamental human desire to transcend death—to create (and experience) something that is immortal. The appeal of the sublime transcends race, creed, sex, nationality, or other divisions; it unites us in a common sense of humanity's capacity for greatness.

C1. The critic will possess a sophisticated knowledge of the devices (metaphor, simile, etc.) on which a writer can draw, and she will evaluate how successfully the writer combines such devices to produce a unified, concentrated effect. Achieving that effect, however—specifically, the effect of sublimity—is the writer's most important goal, and it is her success in achieving this effect that determines the value of her work. Because the sublime is both an ethical and an artistic quality, the critic is inevitably a judge both of the writer's skill and of her character, just as she is also an advocate of what is ethically best for her society. The critic should try to help foster the kind of noble, elevated society in which noble, elevated writers can flourish; by the same token, she should try to encourage the production of noble, elevated works in order to help encourage society at large to achieve its fullest ethical and spiritual potential. In judging the worth of a work, the critic will attempt to function as a representative of humanity at its best; she will try to stand outside of her own class, sex, race, nation, and time and imagine how the work will be received by the best readers everywhere and always.

RECENT THEORIES

Traditional Historical Criticism

As the study of modern (as opposed to classical) literature became increasingly professionalized in the late nineteenth and early twentieth century, university departments of literature tended to emphasize the importance of understanding the historical contexts of writers, texts, audiences, and critics. Historical study of literature, which still is (and is likely to remain) one of the most central theoretical approaches, tends to emphasize social REALITY as the most important component of the Abrams scheme. A more recent brand of historical theory, usually called the NEW HISTORICISM (see below) makes some fundamentally different assumptions than the ones underlying traditional historical criticism.

W1. Because the writer's personality and values help shape the text, and because her personality and values are likely to reflect ideas, tendencies, or influences common during her time, historical study can help us understand not only those influences but also the writer and the text.

T1. Because the meaning of the text is likely to reflect meanings that existed (or were at least capable of existing) at the time the text was created, studying the era in which a text was produced can help us better understand the meaning(s) of the text. We will be in a better position to grasp the significance of the text if we know something about its historical contexts, because those contexts inevitably tend to exert a very strong influence on both the writer and the text.

A1. Audiences of the past differed in significant ways from audiences of today, and since the writer created the text partly with that past audience in mind, to understand the meaning of the text we must be able to look at it as its original audience(s) did. Past audiences often made different intellectual assumptions than we do; they often held different ideas and felt differently about important topics than do we. Studying and appreciating these differences can help us appreciate the text's original meanings and can help prevent us from imposing our own modern prejudices on old texts.

R1. People in the past tended to perceive reality differently than we tend to perceive it today; they often made significantly different assumptions than we do about what was real. Their view of reality was shaped (as every view of reality is shaped) by their particular historical circumstances, by what seemed true or important or meaningful at the time. To understand a text properly, we must try to recapture that earlier sense of reality; we must, in a sense, try to "get inside the heads" of the writer and her contemporaries.

C1. The critic is capable of learning about the past and of sharing that knowledge with us. She is a scholar who tries to discover the truth about the past by examining objective evidence. Her knowledge is disciplined and her reactions are informed; she is not a dilettante and does not express merely personal beliefs or idiosyncratic impressions.

W2. By studying surviving evidence from the author's life and lifetime, it is possible to gain knowledge about the author's beliefs, circumstances, connections, and general involvement with the ideas of his time and with his contemporaries. Such knowledge is important, because the more we know about the author and his times, the more likely we are to know what he intended his text to mean.

T2. The text cannot be understood apart from the context of ideas and other influences that helped shape it and that helped determine its meaning.

A2. In some respects, audiences that lived at the time a text was created were in the best position to understand a text, because they shared so many of the author's basic assumptions and so much of her basic understanding of the world. On the other hand, historical investigation can sometimes reveal aspects of the past that were not known at the time to all of the author's contemporaries but that nonetheless influenced the intended meaning of the text.

R2. Subsequent historical investigation can sometimes help us to achieve a valuable sense of perspective on, and therefore a rich understanding of, the past. For example, we may know, thanks to our hindsight, how one historical event led to another; we may be able to see connections between events that seemed to have no necessary connection to persons living at the time the events took place. Therefore, paradoxically, our understanding of their historical "reality" may be even more complicated (at least in some respects) than was their own understanding at the time. The possibility of gaining such knowledge is one justification for historical study in general and for the historical interpretation of texts in particular.

C2. The historical critic should ideally have some understanding of all the multifaceted contexts that may have affected not only the writer but also the creation and reception of the text. In other words, the historical critic ideally seeks to understand the text in as broad a context as possible, knowing as much as possible about all the influences that may have affected the original creation and meaning of the text. Only through such broad knowledge of different influences can a historical critic determine which particular influences were *most* important.

W3. No writer is likely to be able to stand completely apart from her own era. Even if she attacks or rejects that era's most basic values or assumptions, she is thereby influenced by them. What she is capable of thinking and feeling is likely to be influenced by the thoughts and feelings common during her time. In any case, her material circumstances—how much money she makes, how much freedom she enjoys, how much recognition she receives, how and where and why she is educated—will all influence her creativity, and these factors are all in turn matters for historical investigation.

T3. No text is likely to be completely unique; each text will tend to have been influenced by the texts that came before it and by texts composed at approximately the same time. In particular, the paraphrasable meaning of the text is likely to reflect what it was possible to think and say at the time the text was composed. Since the meanings of words change, and since new words come into the language over the course of time, historical investigation can help reveal much valuable information simply about the vocabulary a text uses and thus about what the text could have meant at the time it was written.

A3. By attempting to understand a text as it was (or could have been) understood by its contemporaries, we help to overcome (or get outside of or beyond) our own limited personal and present-day perspectives. In a sense we show our respect for the dead by trying to recreate, at least mentally, the world in which they lived. By doing so we can discover what we have in common with them but also how we differ, and both kinds of knowledge are valuable.

R3. Trying to discover the truth about past realities can help to explain the truth about the present; doing so can help us appreciate the factors that have helped influence the modern world. Past views of "reality" can be known by studying the various documents or texts or other pieces of evidence left behind.

C3. The historical critic will profit from the investigations of other kinds of historians—political, economic, social, cultural, etc. Historical investigation is ideally a cooperative enterprise in which each investigator tries to add some new piece of evidence to the total puzzle that comprises the past. By assembling the pieces and by being open to new evidence and to new interpretations of them, the historian can move closer and closer toward an "accurate" or "true" version of the past and of the texts that past helped influence.

Thematic Criticism

Thematic criticism is less a specific approach than a general tendency; there have been (and can be) many different types of thematic approaches. This is because thematic criticism tends to emphasize a view of literature as a means of expressing abstract ideas. Such criticism tends to look for the central theme, the controlling idea, of a work; for this reason, there tends to be a thematic component in almost every other theoretical approach, especially those (such as Marxism, Freudianism, myth criticism, etc.) which explicitly focus on abstract ideas. To the extent that thematic critics emphasize such ideas as highly important aspects of REALITY, they bear some similarity to Plato and to other theorists who measure a text by the value of the concepts it expresses.

W1. Whether he consciously intends to or not, the writer inevitably produces texts that can be understood in terms of abstract ideas. Most thematic critics tend to assume that the best writers are themselves interested in such ideas and that they use their texts to express or explore such concepts. Some thematic critics will explore a writer's consistent exploration of a particular idea over the course of his career, while others will tend to show how the writer's attitudes toward the idea change over time. In either case, thematic critics will tend to assume that the writer has some measure of control over the ideas he expresses and that writers will tend to explore the ideas that are personally most important to them.

T1. The text expresses, explores, examines (etc.) abstract ideas such as appearance vs. reality, the imagination, justice, prejudice, the nature of morality, etc. Such ideas help give the text its meaning, interest, and unity; the text is organized around such ideas. Texts that express such ideas are literally more significant or meaningful than texts that do not. Many thematic critics assume that one idea will tend to be the most important or defining focus of the text; this idea is often called the "central theme" or "central motif." In a sense, a text then becomes a way of making or exploring arguments about such ideas. Most thematic critics will assume that the text is intended to provoke thought about abstract ideas and that the most significant meaning(s) of a text will involve such ideas. Thematic critics tend to treat texts as (to some degree) philosophical or argumentative—i.e., as statements or explorations of different intellectual propositions or positions.

A1. Most thematic critics will tend to assume that the ideal audience will (or should) be interested in the abstract ideas a work explores. The audience will be less interested in the specific structure(s) or details of the text itself than in how the work relates to "larger" ideas that exist apart from the text itself. Indeed, they will be interested in how these larger ideas help to explain or make sense of specific details whose function is not immediately obvious.

R1. Thematic critics tend to assume that human beings have a tendency (and perhaps even a need) to understand their experiences in terms of large, meaningful patterns or abstract ideas. The richest experiences will be those that tend to disclose some larger meaning that can be applied to other experiences, whether in the past, present, or future. Abstract ideas help us to make sense of our lives, to understand our places in society or in the universe, and literary texts often deal implicitly with the most important of these ideas (for example, good vs. evil; right vs. wrong; the purpose of living; the nature of happiness; fate vs. free will; war and peace; crime and punishment; the nature of love, or of justice, or of duty, or of truth, etc.). Such ideas give us insight into the nature of human existence, and it is partly to gain such insight that we read literature.

C1. Thematic critics tend to emphasize the importance of abstract ideas; these ideas help to make sense of human life and therefore can also be used to help make sense of literary texts. Determining which idea(s) a text most emphasizes is one of the key tasks of the thematic critic. Ideally, such an idea should help explain the most important details of a work and the relations among and between those details. Because the idea will not be immediately apparent or strikingly obvious, the critic, by making the idea explicit and showing how it helps explain various details of the text, serves the useful task of making the text more comprehensible and therefore even more satisfying. Thematic critics will often assume that the best texts can help teach valuable lessons about (or at least provide valuable insights into) the ideas they explore. For this reason they often assume that literature has some social, intellectual, or even moral value above and beyond any value it may have simply as art.

Formalism (Anglo-American "New Criticism")

Formalism has been one of the most widespread and most influential kinds of criticism practiced in the twentieth century. As its name suggests, it tends to focus on the TEXT itself (and, in this respect, has much in common with Aristotelian theory). It was often called "new criticism" when it first began to exercise real influence (especially in the 1930s and 1940s). It was often considered opposed to TRADITIONAL HISTORICAL CRITICISM and to other kinds of theory which failed (in the formalists' view) to give sufficient emphasis to the literary text. By the 1950s and 1960s it had become perhaps the dominant approach in the professional study of literature, but almost from the moment it was born it was attacked by proponents of other approaches, including advocates for just about every other approach mentioned below. Although the "new criticism" is now considered by many to be distinctly old-fashioned, its central emphasis on texts and on the need for "close reading" is always likely to exert a strong appeal. Formalism is most vulnerable to criticism to the degree that it sees texts as being unified and harmonious wholes—complex unities. Many later approaches attack this central formalist assumption.

W1. The writer who creates complex, unified texts probably possesses a complex, unified mind or sensibility. However, although the text may reflect a complex unity already present in the writer's mind, what is in the writer's mind can ultimately never be known. All we can know is what the writer got down on paper—i.e., the text itself. Formalists therefore tend to be relatively uninterested in the psychology of authors.

T1. Formalists value texts that are both complex and unified—texts in which every part seems to "fit" or contribute to the larger whole. Therefore the text itself (specifically, how all its parts fit together) is the primary focus of formalist concern.

A1. The ideal audience takes pleasure in the text's complex unity, admiring the artistry with which the parts are arranged into a harmonious whole. Just as formalists tend to be uninterested in the psychology of writers, so they tend to be uninterested in the psychology of audiences. Their chief interest is in the arrangements and patterns of the words on the page.

R1. Reality itself is complex, but it is not chaotic; the writer, by composing complexly unified texts, helps us discern the meaningful patterns that can be found within reality. Appreciating the complexities of texts can thus help us better appreciate the complexities of the reality those texts reflect.

C1. The critic, like the ideal member of the audience, takes pleasure in appreciating the work's complex unity. The critic's job is to explain how all the parts fit into a harmonious whole. She helps illuminate the complex relations among the different parts of a text.

W2. The writer is highly skilled, and each text she creates is absolutely unique. A writer fails if her text fails to achieve complex unity.

T2. Each text is as individual as (for instance) each human being; no two texts are ever exactly alike.

A2. The audience should be willing to look for and appreciate the individuality of each text and should begin by assuming that everything in a text somehow fits. A text that *seems* to fail should be given some benefit of the doubt before it is dismissed. In trying to appreciate the text, audience members can benefit from the insights of other audience members. Ideally, they will participate in a genuine dialogue in order to appreciate the rich harmony of the text as fully as possible.

R2. Appreciating the uniqueness of each text should help encourage us to appreciate the uniqueness of other components of reality. Just as we contemplate the beauty of a text, so we can learn to contemplate the beauty of reality.

C2. Just as a priest helps us appreciate the intricacies of the divine, so the critic helps us appreciate the intricacies of a text. The critic serves the text by helping us appreciate its complex unity and harmonies.

Psychoanalytic Criticism

Psychoanalytic criticism is closely associated with the theories and influence of Sigmund Freud (1856–1939). Freud's approach to human psychology was strikingly original, especially in its emphasis on the personal unconscious and on sexual motivations. It was not long before Freud's ideas began to affect the interpretation of literature, and indeed Freud himself was quite interested in art and artists. In one sense the component of the Abrams scheme most emphasized by Freudian critics is the WRITER, for such critics are often fascinated by the psychological roots of creativity. More recent Freudian critics, however, have emphasized the ways each member of the AUDIENCE recreates the text in his or her own psychological image. Perhaps it is best to argue, then, that for Freudians the key Abrams component is "REALITY," because they focus on the central role of the psyche in perceiving and interpreting experience.

W1. The mind of the writer consists not only of her conscious awareness but of her unconscious drives and motives. The latter influence the former in numerous ways. The unconscious mind is therefore a powerful influence on a writer's creativity and on the texts she creates. Many of our strongest unconscious drives are sexual and are formed during our early development. Although many of these highly personal drives are often later repressed in the interests of social conformity, they are never extinguished; instead, they often find expression in indirect ways. Within the mind of each person, including each writer, three basic elements jockey for dominance: the *id* (strong instinctive desires dominated by the pleasure principle); the *ego* (conscious rationality, which helps organize and control and channel the impulsive *id* to useful purposes and which tries to accommodate the individual to external realities); and the *superego* (the expression of social values and expectations, which encourages moral behavior—behavior that works to the advantage of society at large). The *id* can be associated with the unconscious mind; the *ego* can be associated with the conscious mind; and the *superego* can be associated with the conscience, especially with the conscience as shaped and defined by social values.

T1. For some psychoanalytic critics, the text is inevitably an expression of the mind of its creator; attempting to study the text without knowing something about the writer is therefore misguided. The language and symbolism of the text will therefore often be full of psychological (especially sexual) significance. Just as a person's deepest unconscious motives will often be indirectly implied in the images and symbolism of his dreams, so the literary text functions in some ways like a dream: meanings are not obvious but are implied and must be interpreted by examining the clues provided by images and symbols.

A1. For some psychoanalytic critics, the unconscious motives, drives, and desires of the audience are at least as important as those of the writer. Such critics may focus on the unconscious desires of a large group of readers in a particular historical era; such a focus is often called "psychohistory." For example, Victorians may as a group have shared certain psychological motives that were not shared by "hippies" from the 1960s, and vice-versa. Similarly, seventeenth-century Puritans may have shared a set of psychological motives that differed from those of seventeenth-century "libertines." Different groups of people, then, may be motivated by particular sets of unconscious drives. However, some psychoanalytic critics would argue that each individual person is motivated by his or her own set of psychological drives or needs. For instance, Norman Holland argues that each person tends to have a particular "identity theme"—a particular way of interpreting experience based on his or her own psychic desires and repressions. Each reader will therefore tend to read a text in a manner that makes sense according to his or her own "identity theme" and will tend to overlook or reject interpretations that do not accord with that theme.

R1. Psychic reality is the most important kind of reality; our knowledge or experience of everything else (including the "external," "material" world) is filtered through our minds. Focusing on how the mind (or how individual minds) work, therefore, will be a main focus of psychoanalytic criticism.

C1. The psychoanalytic critic will focus on the psyches (especially the unconscious elements thereof) of such entities as writers, readers, and characters. Moreover, to the extent that a text itself may have hidden or submerged layers of meaning, the text itself may be said to have an "unconscious," and the psychoanalytic critic may therefore focus on analyzing the unconscious patterns latent within the text.

W2. According to some theorists (such as Harold Bloom), each author tends to be motivated by (partly) unconscious rivalry with other authors, especially with writers of the past. Each present-day writer is in creative conflict with his predecessors, and writers tend to follow certain patterns in attempting to deal with this "anxiety of influence." In attempting to establish their own independent identities as writers, they adopt various strategies, including denial, repression, and resistance and also an effort to surpass previous writers. The relationship between writer and audience can be similarly complicated.

T2. Some theorists, especially those influenced by the French psychoanalyst Jacques Lacan, argue that each text possesses an "unconscious"; therefore, interpreting the text will involve studying the complicated relations between the text's surface meaning and its underlying implications. According to Lacanian theorists, the various aspects of texts will tend to reflect the different stages through which humans ordinarily pass, including an initially strong identification with the mother (in which the mother is seen almost as an extension of the child, her only function being to satisfy the child's desires) and then a later loss of this sense of completeness as the child enters the social world, identified with language, law, and the father. Whereas some psychoanalysts seek to "heal" this split, others argue that such "healing" is by definition impossible and that healthy adults must accept and embrace their fragmentation and alienation, their conflictedness. For this reason, such psychoanalytic critics value texts which explore and expose fragmentation rather than pretending that it doesn't exist.

A2. Psychoanalytic critics tend to be especially concerned with issues of *gender*—i.e., with how not only writers but also readers come to adopt certain sexual roles or identities. Whereas some early psychoanalysts assumed that certain gender roles were "normal" or "healthy" and others not (or at least less so), more recent writers are likely to assume that particular gender roles are potentially fluid positions on a vast spectrum or continuum. For such writers, the simple opposition of "male" and "female" is too simple. Each writer, and each member of the audience, is likely to possess a far more complicated psyche than such a simple opposition can describe. In any case, the ways an audience responds to a text is likely to be strongly affected not only by the text's presentation of gender roles but also by each audience member's gender identity.

R2. Some psychoanalytic theorists believe that all human beings have the potential to confront the same basic stages of psychological development and encounter many of the same kinds of psychological influences, especially at the earliest ages. Some theorists believe that certain phases of development are healthy or "normal" and that others are self-destructive or unhealthy. Other (more recent) theorists are less likely to regard a particular psychological response as "normal" or "healthy." In either case, psychoanalytical theorists tend to stress that each individual's particular development is likely to be highly specific and distinct, depending on the influences or environment he encountered. Therefore, to assume that there is such a thing as a general "human nature" is to engage in a gross oversimplification. The psychological "reality" of each individual—whether he is a writer, a character, or an audience member—is likely to be highly personal and idiosyncratic.

C1. Psychoanalytic critics tend to focus on the psychological *complexities* of writers, characters, readers, and texts. They will assume that very little in any of these entities is simple or uncomplicated, and they will rely on larger theories, usually developed by theorists whose main interest is not literature *per se*, to help explain the ways these entities function. The psychoanalytic critic tries to penetrate beneath the surface of the entity he studies. Whether psychoanalytic criticism can ever provide "objective" or "scientific" analyses, or whether such criticism necessarily reflects the psychological complexities of the individual critic, is open to debate; different theorists have taken different positions on this issue.

Archetypal or "Myth" Criticism

Archetypal or "myth" criticism takes much of its inspiration from the work of the psychologist Carl Gustav Jung (1875–1961). Just as Aristotle was a student of Plato but later disagreed with his teacher in fundamental ways, so Jung was at first a follower of Freud but eventually rejected the latter's heavy emphasis on the personal and sexual unconscious. Instead, Jung tended to emphasize the common psychological habits and tendencies human beings share. He argued for the existence of a "collective unconscious"—a common reservoir of responses to common stimuli. "Archetype" is the term commonly used to describe a stimulus that provokes this kind of common, almost automatic response. Archetypal criticism is sometimes also called "myth" criticism, because certain basic stories or mythic figures are believed to structure the ways humans commonly try to make sense of their experience. In this sense, the aspect of the Abrams scheme most emphasized by myth critics is "REALITY." Like Freudian theorists, they tend to stress the interaction between the mind and experience, but because they emphasize the collective more than the personal unconscious, archetypal critics are more likely to be interested in the broader AUDIENCE than in the individual WRITER.

W1. The writer is able through her words to evoke universally shared thoughts and feelings that we cannot control or resist; she therefore exercises a kind of influence over her audience, but her power to exploit such feelings also suggests *some* measure of control or mastery over them. At the same time, the writer must be in tune with—or swayed by—these feelings in order to evoke them in others.

T1. The great text is highly complicated and possesses many levels of psychological significance and resonance. To describe only the surface level of the text (its "obvious" or paraphrasable meaning) is to give only a superficial account of it. The archetypal or myth critic is concerned with deeper levels of meaning; she explores patterns of imagery or of theme. These patterns, although not necessarily obvious on first reading, will probably deeply stir the reader's feelings.

A1. There *is* a general human nature; there are general habits of thought and feeling, typical human responses to certain basic stimuli. The successful text appeals to or stimulates these general and basic human responses. These responses are not necessarily ones of which we are consciously aware; indeed, they may be all the more powerful the more they are unconscious or preconscious. Fear of absolute darkness, for instance, is one common human response that a writer may exploit.

R1. Myth critics tend to be mainly concerned with general *psychological* reality, with "human nature." Our psychological responses, however, are largely the products of our interactions (as individuals and as a species through the eons) with physical nature. If artists can exploit references to darkness to suggest danger or evil, they can do so partly because human beings have always tended to respond fearfully to the dark. If springtime can be used to symbolize rebirth or to suggest comedy, that is partly because throughout the ages spring has tended to call up those kinds of associations in the human mind. Myth critics are very interested in the interactions between humans and nature, since those interactions are often at the root of our responses to literary works, no matter how "sophisticated" or "intellectual" those works (or our responses) may seem at first.

C1. Because the myth critic will tend to look for the deeper patterns in a work, he must be at home in, or at least have a profound interest in, numerous other disciplines, including psychology, anthropology, comparative religion, etc. He will be interested in any discipline which can help explain the underlying psychological traits or patterns of behavior common to all human beings.

W2. Although the writer exploits archetypal patterns or responses in her text, she need not consciously do so. Indeed, she probably cannot entirely or deliberately control the number or nature of the archetypal patterns the text reveals.

T2. Appreciating the archetypal patterns in a text can help us comprehend its deeper unity or coherence. Doing so may be especially useful when more obvious kinds of unity seem lacking or when the poem seems, on the surface, to be full of contradictions and incoherence. The significance of a particular image will largely depend on the specific description of it and on the larger context of the entire work. For instance, fire might be used in one work to symbolize destruction (as in a raging inferno) or it might be used in another work to symbolize security and comfort (as in a crackling fireplace). Similarly, a blizzard would suggest different meanings than a gentle snowfall. Thus, there is no simple, one-to-one correspondence between a particular archetype and a particular meaning; the context of the symbol and its specific features must be explored before the symbol's significance can be explained.

A2. Archetypal habits of mind are part of the deep structure of the human psyche; they are not thoughts or feelings we can easily or consciously choose either to have or to reject. Myths or archetypes appeal to or exploit our deepest collective fears and desires, our most tenaciously rooted instincts. Great texts tend to grapple with the worries and problems that trouble us most (e.g., death, alienation, powerlessness, etc.) or to celebrate those feelings that give us the greatest joy (love, security, community, etc.). The successful text appeals to us on an emotional, psychological level before it appeals to us intellectually. A text that lacks this kind of basic psychological power will be relatively unsuccessful, no matter how "cultivated" or "sophisticated" its superficial structure or phrasing or intention may seem.

R2. In a sense, our response to archetypes is pre-linguistic. A baby does not need to know a specific language in order to fear the darkness or to enjoy the sensation of suckling at its mother's breast or to take satisfaction in the feeling of warm water on its skin or to feel terror at being plunged into water that is either ice-cold or steaming hot. Presumably it also does not matter whether such a baby later ends up speaking Russian, Swahili, or English. Language is less important in determining our response to literature than these basic human reactions to common stimuli.

C2. The myth critic's familiarity with a wide range of texts (and not necessarily just "literary" texts, but also religious texts, folklore, etc.) will make it easier to appreciate both the uniqueness of any particular text *and* the general traits it shares with other texts.

W3. The writer should obviously be a conscious artist, but unless he is in touch and in tune with mythic patterns or with archetypal habits of mind, the text he produces will seem simple, sterile and superficial. Such a text may strike us as clever but not as moving, powerful, or profound. In a sense the successful text is as much the product of the collective mind of the whole human race as it is the result of any individual's conscious effort.

T3. A work achieves its individuality partly from the unique ways in which it exploits or combines mythic images or patterns of significance. The more one knows about the common patterns that underlie most works, the better equipped one is to appreciate the genuine uniqueness of any given text. The great text may exploit (indeed, probably must exploit) many of the very same patterns, symbols, etc. found in "common" or "popular" literature. By giving especially powerful expression to these archetypes, the great text achieves its greatness. Sometimes the best way to study archetypal images or patterns is in fact to study popular literature, because in such literature those features are likely to be most easily and obviously visible.

A3. The successful work appeals to psychological traits all humans share, not simply to traits confined to particular social classes, genders, or interest groups. The appeal of the successful text transcends particular eras and even, ideally, particular cultures, because the archetypal aspects of the text also transcend these limits. The great work touches chords that resonate powerfully in the hearts and minds of people everywhere and in every era.

R3. Myth critics tend to assume that some of the most important feelings or responses are the ones we can't ever quite put into words or that transcend the words we use in trying to describe them. The same basic myths and archetypes may be (in fact, almost inevitably *will* be) used by writers of different times, places, nationalities, races, genders, etc., because the basic patterns of human interactions with each other (social reality) and with nature (physical reality) almost always are, have been, and are likely to remain the same.

C3. Since any individual text involves a re-working or exploitation of images of patterns common to other works, myth critics greatly emphasize these commonly shared traits. They are less concerned with the absolute uniqueness of any individual work than with the features a work shares with many other texts. Thus they are much concerned with genres (different *kinds* of writing, such as comedy or tragedy). Paradoxically, the more one knows about the common patterns that underlie most works, the better equipped one is to appreciate the genuine uniqueness of any given work, especially if the work departs from or alters an underlying, expected pattern. Creating such changes may be one of the most effective ways for a writer to achieve maximum impact. Thus if we have been led with most of our past experiences with texts to expect that the sheriff will win the final gunfight (or that the daring knight will finally slay the ferocious dragon), but instead the sheriff bites the dust and the dragon eats the knight for dinner, we will know that the writer is deliberately toying with our expectations to achieve a particular effect.

Marxist Criticism

Marxist criticism is obviously indebted to the political philosopher Karl Marx (1818–1883), who emphasized the ways in which material or economic conditions affect every other aspect of human life. Marx not only sought to explain the historical rise of capitalism but also sought to explain why capitalism would necessarily give way to socialism and then to communism. His ideas became increasingly influential in the late nineteenth and early twentieth centuries; Marxist political parties, professing dedication to the interests of the working class, sprang up everywhere, and Marxist philosophy developed many subtle variations. The triumph of Lenin in Russia and the consequent formation of the Soviet Union made Marxism the official philosophy of a huge portion of the world's population—a proportion that became even larger when China and many countries in Eastern Europe also became officially communist following World War II. By the 1990s communist philosophy was no longer the official doctrine of the Soviet Union (which had now dissolved back into Russia and a number of other separate nations) or of the previously Marxist nations in Eastern Europe. Marxism in China, meanwhile, had become in some ways quite different from its former self. Marxist ideas, however, are still attractive to many persons and are always likely to have some appeal as long as conflicts exist between different economic classes. This emphasis on class conflict, indeed, is central to the Marxist understanding of "REALITY," which is probably the defining component of the Abrams scheme for Marxist theorists. In its heavy emphasis on changing social reality, Marxism has much in common not only with traditional historical criticism but also with the more recent "New Historicism." Important differences, of course, also exist.

W1. The writer himself, like the text he "creates," is the product of a particular set of social circumstances; he is implicated in a (class) power structure whether he is consciously aware of this or not. He is himself shaped by social pressures and social conditions, and there is a sense in which his role is just as much "written" and "pre-scribed" as the works he supposedly creates. This is one reason that the Marxist critic will tend to be less interested in either the text itself or in the writer himself than in the social circumstances that helped produce both. The Marxist critic is likely to ask, "what are the *practical, social* causes, functions, and conse- quences of any particular 'work of art'?"

T1. Marxist critics assume that no text can be understood apart from the historical and social conditions that helped shape its pro- duction. They are less concerned with studying the formal rela- tions among the parts of the "work itself" than with studying the ways in which the text reflects or implies or distorts or falsifies or criticizes or endorses (either tacitly or explicitly) the social (class) power-structure of its day or of the era in which it is being read.

A1. There is no monolithic "audience." The people who make up the audience for any text are necessarily members of particular (often different and conflicting) social classes. A given text will ei- ther help strengthen or help weaken the interests of a particular class. A given member of the audience is likely to value works which reflect or strengthen the interests of her class. By the same token, she will tend to dislike texts which seem foreign to her class interests or which threaten them in some way. Often, audience members may not be fully aware of the political reasons for their likes and dislikes. They may honestly believe that their tastes are "objective" or "disinterested."

R1. Marxist critics tend to be very suspicious of claims that any particular beliefs or social arrangements or values are "natural" or "eternal." It is usually in the interests of the dominant class to treat certain conditions or beliefs as if they were "natural" or "God- given" or "permanent," since doing so obscures the extent to which such conditions or beliefs serve their particular interests. A Marxist, however, will tend to believe that the conditions or beliefs of a certain society are shaped by its *history* and that they are therefore capable of being changed.

C1. Marxist critics will often attempt to "de-mystify" or undermine traditional beliefs and values, to rob them of their allure and mystique, to show that they are not neutral or "spiritual" or non- political or "objective" but to show that they are in fact rooted in power politics and class conflict. Marx, for instance, called religion "the opiate of the masses" because he believed that it tended to pacify the masses, to turn their attention away from the real (usually economic) problems of the real (material) world and from possible solutions to those problems. Any values or systems of belief that work (whether deliberately or not) to stifle or prevent or dilute radical progress can be seen as regressive or reactionary and should be opposed.

W2. Some Marxists believe that socially conscious (and conscientious) writers have an obligation to write works that will help to promote social progress. Others believe that a work can be made to promote such progress if it is properly interpreted, even if promoting progress was not the writer's explicit goal. Even a deliberately reactionary writer can provide evidence for diagnosing (and thus imply ways of remedying) a culture's social problems.

T2. A work can be seen either as reflecting a dominant ideology (system of beliefs), as undermining that ideology, or even as inadvertently doing the latter by doing the former. In other words, by *writing down* ideological assumptions and thus formulating them in a more explicit and noticeable way than is usually the case, the writer may (perhaps even without intending it) expose their vulnerabilities, contradictions, incoherences, etc. A text that is intentionally conservative or "reactionary" (or one written by a "reactionary" writer) may ultimately be more valuable than one that offers simplistic revolutionary propaganda, *if* the reactionary work exposes or inadvertently reveals the problems, contradictions, and illogic inherent in the system it endorses.

A2. Audiences, like writers, are the products of particular social circumstances. Social institutions (such as the school system) help to produce certain kinds of audiences; education, to a great degree, is simply indoctrination. All interpretation and reading is inherently political; to pretend otherwise is to be either deceptive or naive.

R2. Marxists will tend to reject the concept of an unchanging "human nature" as an invention of the dominant class to keep those beneath them more firmly under control. If people are led to believe that "human nature" is fixed and unchangeable, they will not be tempted to make a radical break with past or present social conditions.

C2. Some Marxists see the critic's role as exposing the ways in which literary texts are implicated in oppressive power arrangements. They may point out, for instance, how a given work expresses the class interests of its author or of the audience to whom it most strongly appeals. Every text necessarily has political implications, because every text necessarily either ratifies or challenges the existing social structure, or perhaps it ratifies the structure in some ways and challenges it in others, or perhaps it *seems* to ratify the structure but can actually be used to undermine it.

Structuralist Criticism

Structuralist criticism typifies the very strong interest in the twentieth century in the issue of language—in the ways in which our experiences of (and attempts to understand) "REALITY" necessarily involve coming to terms with language. As their name implies, structuralists assume that "reality" is structured like (or even by) language; therefore, the techniques used in studying how languages function can also help us understand how other systems of meaning operate. Just as a linguist studies the structures by which language achieves "meaning," so a structuralist anthropologist might study the structures by which a culture operates, and a structuralist literary critic might study the structures by which a text operates or becomes meaningful. In this sense, structuralism (like many other literary theories) is not chiefly or primarily a theory of literature, although it can be applied to literature. Structuralism began to influence English-language criticism in the 1960s and 1970s especially, but even as it began to gain influence it began to come under attack from so-called post-structuralist thinkers (especially deconstructors). These thinkers tended to express strong skepticism about the structuralist ambition to provide "true," "scientific," "objective" explanations of the subjects they studied.

T1. Just as an individual word only makes sense when it is seen in relation to the larger language of which it is a part, so an individual text only has meaning in terms of the larger structure(s) in which it participates. For this reason, knowing the structure of the larger system is crucial to understanding the individual text. The word "amo" will make no sense unless one knows Latin; similarly, *Paradise Lost* cannot be understood apart from knowledge of certain structures or codes, which include (for instance) the English language; the genre of epic poetry; the Christian religion; classical literature, etc. To interpret any specific text is to relate that text to the larger codes or structured languages of which it is a part. Whereas formalism focuses on individual texts, structuralism focuses on the larger structures in which individual texts are embedded.

W1. Knowing about the individual writer is less important than knowing about the larger cultural codes the writer used. Only in relation to those codes can the writer's work have meaning. In this sense, it is impossible to communicate an entirely personal or private meaning. Just as structuralists are less interested in individual texts than in the larger codes that allow those texts to have meaning, so they are less interested in individual producers of meaning (writers) than in the larger codes by which meaning is produced. The codes, in fact, are what give meaning to the work: meaning is not the product of a single mind but of larger cultural structures or patterns of meaning.

A1. In the process of interpretation, audiences relate individual texts to larger codes, just as they understand individual words because they know the larger language of which those words are components. Without an understanding of the larger language or code, it would be impossible to understand the single word. Because these codes are largely social and shared, structuralists tend to emphasize the larger codes or language-systems rather than the personal responses or "private psychology" of individual audience members.

R1. Reality is interpreted in terms of structures which are imposed by the human mind; meanings do not exist inherently in things or independently of the interpreting mind. However, individual minds will be structured by shared languages or shared cultural codes. The same "things" will have different significances according to these different codes or languages. There is no "natural" reason, for example, that a red light should signify "stop"; it could just as easily signify many other meanings (even "go"). In our culture a red light (often) signifies "stop" only because that meaning is part of a larger social code. Knowing that code is crucial to making correct interpretations; failing to know it can produce very serious mistakes. Our lives are structured in terms of numerous overlapping codes; the process of living is largely a process of learning these codes and then using them to interpret our experiences. In this sense, knowing the larger code is more important than having (or responding to) any single experience. Most codes will tend to function in terms of *differences* or in terms of *binary oppositions*. For instance, a red light is significant (that is, literally signifies something) partly because it is *not* a green light or *not* a yellow light. We respond differently to a novel because we can see that it is *not* a lyric poem; expecting a novel to function like a poem would simply make no sense because we would be using an inappropriate code.

C1. The structuralist critic focuses less on individual works than on the larger codes or languages in terms of which a work achieves meaning. The critic's job is to understand the intricacies of those codes—to understand how they work, how their component parts fit together, what rules govern them, how and when they are applied, etc. Since any individual work may be meaningful in terms of any number of possible codes, the critic should explore many different possible codes in seeking to interpret a work. In writing about the work, the critic will focus as much on explaining the larger codes as on interpreting the individual text, especially since knowing how the larger codes work can help one interpret numerous other individual texts. The critic's goal is to achieve objective knowledge of how the codes function. (Deconstructionists and postmodernists doubt that such objective knowledge can ever be achieved. Deconstructionists believe, for instance, that the structuralist can never get completely outside of the codes or languages by which he himself interprets meaning; therefore his interpretations can never be objective or neutral.)

Feminist Criticism

Feminist criticism has been one of the most influential of all recent theories, and its influence is unlikely to recede. Since half the population of the world is female, feminist criticism of one variety or another is always likely to have some relevance to the ways people write and interpret. Of course, many varieties of feminism are imaginable: Marxist feminism, Freudian feminism, Jungian feminism, poststructuralist feminism, multicultural feminism, etc. Feminist critics often disagree among themselves about specific issues and techniques, but almost all share the assumption that "REALITY" (whether social, psychological, political, economic, etc.) is structured in terms of sexual or gender differences. Whether these dif-

ferences are innate or culturally imposed, they are real, and whether a feminist seeks to erase them or emphasize them, they are always likely to be at the center of the feminist enterprise. In European and Anglo-American criticism, feminism became an increasingly important movement in the 1970s, 1980s, and 1990s.

W1. The writer will inevitably be influenced, in one way or another, by the assumptions his or her culture makes about sexuality and gender. The writer will tend either to accept or resist (or some combination of the two) the sexual and gender stereotypes that the culture prescribes for writers, readers, plots, characters, genres, etc. The opportunities a writer possesses may in fact be affected by the sexual stereotypes of his or her culture.

T1. The text will inevitably be influenced, for good or ill, by the sexual and gender roles common in the culture in which the text is created. A text will inevitably either affirm or subvert (or some combination of the two) the stereotypes taken for granted in that culture. The best texts will subject such stereotypes to scrutiny and perhaps even criticism, whether explicitly or implicitly. Even texts that are deliberately sexist or reactionary may be useful in exposing stereotypes to view and therefore to potential criticism.

A1. The audience will inevitably be influenced, in various ways, by its culture's gender and sexual assumptions. The audience is also inevitably divided into different interest groups, depending on the sexual or gender identities of the audience's members. A woman reader, for instance, will almost certainly approach a text differently than a male, because women and men tend to have different cultural experiences and to have been exposed to different kinds of conditioning. By the same token, a lesbian reader may respond differently to a text than a heterosexual woman, and an underprivileged African-American woman may respond differently than a prosperous white lesbian. The audience will inevitably consist of different audiences made up of different kinds of men and women with different kinds of experiences and orientations.

R1. Our experience of reality is inevitably affected by our culture, and our experience of our culture is inevitably determined in part by our sexual identities and gender orientations. "Reality" is not a neutral descriptive term; our experience of reality can never be completely "objective" or disinterested. Our views and experiences of reality are inevitably affected by our sexual roles or gender identities (among other factors). Literary texts inevitably influence these roles and identities and are influenced by them.

C1. One role of the critic will be to explore the various ways in which texts influence, and are influenced by, sexual roles and gender identities. If such influence is repressive, the critic will ideally use his or her criticism to help subvert such stereotypes and thereby help promote social progress and individual freedom. The critic is not merely an "objective" student of literature but is ideally a force for positive social change.

Deconstruction

Deconstruction is one variety of poststructuralism and therefore has a complicated relationship with structuralist thought. Often identified with the philosophy of Jacques Derrida (1930–), deconstruction accepts the structuralist emphasis on the importance of language but rejects the structuralist effort to achieve an objective, scientific understanding of language or of much else. To achieve such an understanding would necessarily require the ability to stand somehow outside of or apart from language, but such an objective position, by definition, can never be obtained. Paradoxically, then, deconstructors would tend to emphasize "REALITY" as the most important component of the Abrams scheme, but for them "reality" can never be grasped apart from the language(s) by which we attempt to grasp it. Language is a maze from which we can never really escape in order to achieve a "clear perspective" on something outside the maze. Deconstruction, then, is less a philosophy than a tactic or technique of interpretation—one that provides no final answers but, instead, one that keeps returning us to the insoluble problems posed by language. Deconstructive theory thus has implications for any aspect of human life involving language—which is to say, for nearly all aspects of human life. Deconstruction was especially influential in the late 1970s and 1980s and was considered by many to pose a devastating threat to formalism. Marxist and new historicist critics, however, saw deconstruction itself as a kind of formalism because of its alleged lack of interest in historical and social issues. Some Marxists and feminists, however, attempted to use deconstruction itself as a political tool, useful in undermining more traditional points of view.

W1. The writer who produces a text is himself the product of a larger language system. In this sense, it is that system rather than any particular individual that really produces the text. (Structuralists also tend to share this assumption.)

T1. Because the text is part of a larger language system that is full of contradictions, instabilities, irresolvable paradoxes, and gaps, the text itself can never be completely harmonious, stable, unified, or non-contradictory. (Structuralists are much less likely to emphasize contradictions and gaps; this is one important way in which deconstruction parts company from structuralism.)

A1. Since no real unity exists *within* the text, any unity or pattern of consistent meaning will necessarily be imposed by the audience. Ideally, the audience should realize that these patterns *are* externally imposed; they should not assume that the patterns are objectively present in the text. In other words, they should not assume that the patterns they impose reveal any real "truth" about the text. (This assumption directly contradicts a major tenet of formalism.)

R1. "Reality" itself can never be objectively known. All of our experience of "reality" is filtered through a language system (or "discourse"). Because many different language systems exist, many different versions of "reality" exist. We can never possess "true," "objective" knowledge of "reality"; deconstruction radically questions all of these standard categories. (Although deconstructors share with structuralists a belief that we interpret reality in terms of different "codes," deconstructors are much less likely than structuralists to assume that we can ever know or understand those codes objectively—that we can ever get fully outside them to see them from a neutral point of view.)

C1. Because the text possesses no inherent meaning or unity, the critic in a sense creates any meanings she finds in the text. In this sense, the critic herself is a kind of author, a kind of creator. By producing a critical, deconstructive reading of a text, she produces another creative text, which can itself be further criticized or deconstructed. (Whereas structuralism sees the critic as a kind of scientist who pursues objective knowledge of the codes she studies, deconstruction denies the possibility of such knowledge; the critic is less a scientist than a creative writer herself.)

W2. Whereas traditional theories almost all assume that the author is a unified, single subject with a unified, single sensibility, deconstruction assumes that the author is herself largely a product of the language system she happens to use. What an author is capable of thinking and writing is largely determined by the language system available to her, with which (and through which) she necessarily thinks and writes. Rather than individual consciousness determining language, individual consciousness is determined *by* a pre-existing (and unstable) language system. Deconstruction thus poses a radical challenge not only to conventional theories of interpretation but also to conventional humanistic notions such as individuality, the unified self, and personal creativity.

T2. Deconstruction emphasizes the paradoxes, contradictions, or gaps in texts (and not only in "literary" texts but in *all* texts). However, it does not attempt to resolve or harmonize or unify these contradictions. Rather, it tries to show how such contradictions exist at the heart of any work (indeed, at the heart of language in general and of any piece of language). A text can have no single, stable, unified pattern of meaning. Any patterns found in the text are not inherent *in* the text but are imposed by readers. Whereas traditional critical theories tend to eliminate or reduce multiple, conflicting, and contradictory readings of a single text, deconstruction acknowledges the inevitability of such a proliferation of meanings and indeed seeks to release it and make it possible.

A2. Each reader is himself the product of a language system (or of competing language systems). Therefore, the reader himself is less important than the language system(s) that influence(s) his responses to a text. Just as deconstruction undermines the common notion of an individual creative "author" who has "authority" over a text, so it also undermines the common notion of an individual reader who has personal control of his responses to a text.

R2. Almost all traditional literary theories assume that literature imitates (or "re-presents") a reality outside itself. Deconstructors assume that a text can never really get beyond or above the web of language to imitate an external "reality." The text's connections to "reality" are less interesting to deconstructors than are its connections to and with other texts, which are themselves largely responsible for shaping our notions of what "reality" is. Thus, deconstructors are very much concerned with the question of *inter-textu-*

ality—with the ways in which a particular text is a re-writing and revision of previous texts. The connection between the text and context ("history") is complicated for deconstructors because "history" is itself already textual: the only way we "know" history is through texts. "Historical events" are not simple givens (data) to be known; rather, "history" is itself constructed by, in, and through language ("discourse"). We cannot know "history" directly; we know only our *construction* of history. The problem of the relation between "text" and "history" suggests again that in interpreting one text, we must fall back on other texts, and to interpret them we must fall back on others, and to interpret them we must fall back on others, and so on and on in an infinite regress of textuality. Here as elsewhere, deconstructors focus on a hierarchical pairing (such as "history/fiction") in which one term ("history") is privileged over, or seems superior to, another ("fiction"). They then *subvert* or de-stabilize the hierarchy, showing how "history" is itself already a kind of fiction. Normally we try to suppress or escape this kind of paradox, but this is precisely the kind of puzzle which deconstructors look for and emphasize.

C2. The complexities a critic finds in a text will inevitably be irresolvable contradictions, not complex unities. The critic should look for (and tug on) these "loose threads," and he should also look for the ways in which one text re-writes (i.e., both replicates and alters) previous texts. Unlike the formalist critic, the deconstructor is less concerned with elucidating the author's *skill* in constructing a harmoniously unified work than with scrutinizing the text for those points at which its self-contradictions become most apparent. The critic is less concerned with *how* the text means than with showing how it implies something that seems to contradict or subvert its "obvious" or "intended" meaning.

W3. Whereas traditional theories almost all assume the author's control over his text and its meaning(s), deconstruction presumes that the text's operations and significances are largely determined by the functions of language itself. The author cannot control or suppress the contradictions embedded in the text because they are embedded in language itself. The best authors will be those who are aware of the inherently contradictory and unstable nature of language and who will highlight and emphasize those very features of language in their texts: they will emphasize the *literariness* of the text rather than offering the text as the accurate transcript of some supposedly external reality.

T3. The distinction between "literary" language (on the one hand) and "normal" or "philosophic" or "scientific" language (on the other) is a fiction. All language is, at root, "literary" (metaphorical, figurative). All language imposes structures on reality rather than discerning "true" or "objective" structures beneath or within "reality." We cannot stand outside of our system(s) of language ("discourses") and view "reality" with an "innocent eye." Deconstruction radically questions all of these concepts, all of these "hierarchies," in which (for instance) "philosophy" is presumed to be different from (and superior to) "literature," or in which "reality" is presumed to be distinguishable from (and more trustworthy than) "language." One typical deconstructive move or tactic is to take a standard hierarchy of concepts, such as

$$\frac{\text{philosophy}}{\text{literature}}$$

and reverse it, showing how the "inferior" concept infects or taints the "superior" one. Thus, "philosophy" normally pretends not to be "literature," but it cannot itself escape all of the ambiguous qualities or features it attributes to literature. Similarly, since literature is a way of using language in which the metaphorical, figurative, fictional aspects of language are most openly acknowledged and embraced, "literature" may, paradoxically, be the most "philosophic" (or "truthful") kind of language-use. The point of this deconstructive tactic is *not* to construct a *new* hierarchy, not to "privilege" the old "inferior" term and topple the old "superior" one. Rather, the point is to show how the hierarchy is *unstable*, and to insist on and preserve a sense of that radical instability. Once we realize that the hierarchy is wobbly, we do not try to pretend that it is stable; instead, we always look for the wobbling.

A3. On the one hand, deconstruction gives the audience a much more active and important role in determining the meaning(s) of a text. Since the text's meanings are not determined by the text itself or by the author, the reader has a much more prominent role to play in determining the meaning. On the other hand, since the individual reader is herself the product of discursive (linguistic) systems, since her very role as reader is something that is partly determined by the nature of the discursive system which she has imbibed and literally *embodied* since her earliest days, and since her individual consciousness is shaped and conditioned by the language by which that consciousness is constituted, the reader's autonomy and independence are radically problematized. Deconstruction is usually thought to undermine the hierarchy "text/reader," in which the text is presumed to present a determinate or definite meaning to the reader. But the deconstructive process can also work the other way. Thus, the hierarchy "reader/text," in which "reader" is the privileged term and which assumes that readers determine the meanings of texts, can be deconstructed by raising the issue of the extent to which readers are *themselves* "texts" constructed and constituted by language-systems. By deconstructing in both directions, we achieve not a hierarchy but an unstable pairing in which neither term is privileged.

R3. Just as the meaning of a text cannot be pinned down or delimited or controlled by appealing to the "intention" of the "author" (for reasons mentioned above), so that meaning cannot be pinned down by appealing to the "context" of the "text." For instance, it is not possible to ascertain the clear, unequivocal meaning of a Shakespeare sonnet by appealing to its "historical context" (such as "Elizabethan ways of thinking" or "Renaissance assumptions") because that context is not a neutral, objective, unquestionable description of an historical *reality* but is *itself* a constructed text which can itself be deconstructed. Such a "context" is a partial, incomplete, subjective selection of all the available data from the period in question. Notice again the typical deconstructive procedure: paired concepts (in this case, "text"/"context"), which seem simply neutral and descriptive, are actually shown to exist in a kind of hierarchy in which one part of the pair is implicitly assumed to be superior to and in control of the other part ("context" is assumed to control the meaning of a text). Once this hierarchy has been shown to exist, the deconstructor undermines it (shows how it wobbles), in this case by showing that "context" is actually "text," that what seems *real and objective* is actually *constructed, invented, imposed*. It therefore becomes impossible to stabilize the "meaning" of a "text" by appealing to its "context," since that "context" is itself a "text."

C3. If all language is inherently "literary" or "fictional" or "figurative," then criticism cannot distinguish itself entirely or absolutely from the literature which is ostensibly the object of its attention. Criticism is a kind of literature; literature can be a kind of criticism. The critic is no longer a sort of scientific, objective truth-seeker; instead, she should be aware of her own role as a kind of creative writer, someone who uses language in a creative, figurative, "literary" way. On the one hand this new view of criticism gives the critic a kind of new dignity and enhanced status, since she is no longer simply a kind of parasite on the literary text but is herself the creator of richly interesting texts of her own. On the other hand, this new view robs her of her pretensions to scientific objectivity. Her own texts are themselves susceptible to further deconstruction, by herself or by others. The patterns she once claimed she "discerned" in texts are patterns she herself *imposes*; the meanings she used to claim to "find" or "discover" in texts are meanings partly of her own invention. Rather than being embarrassed by this fact, however, she should freely acknowledge it and embrace it. The best critics are those who are aware of the contradictions inherent in what they are attempting to do.

Reader-Response Criticism

Reader-response criticism is one of the most obvious results (and causes) of the decreasing influence of FORMALIST theory. Whereas formalism emphasizes the text as a self-contained object in its own right, reader-response criticism, as the name implies, highlights the reactions of individual members of the AUDIENCE. To the extent that it assumes that each reader will tend to respond uniquely, it has much in common with PSYCHOANALYTIC criticism; to the extent that it assumes that responses will be broadly similar, it bears some resemblance to TRADITIONAL HISTORICAL criticism (this is especially true of so-called "reception theory," which studies how and why texts have traditionally been received or understood in different times and places). Reader-response criticism tends to share with DECONSTRUCTION a skepticism about the possibility of offering "neutral" or "objective" interpretations. Reader-response theory became especially influential in the late 1970s and 1980s and is likely to remain attractive to anyone who sees the audience's experience as central to literature.

W1. Writers have, at best, only a limited amount of control over how their texts are interpreted. Indeed, for some reader-response critics, there is a sense in which the author is himself the creation of the reader, because the reader inevitably makes certain assumptions about the author's values, intentions, and performance. The reader perceives the author through the text, but the reader also perceives the text through his own mind or consciousness. In a sense, the author is himself only another reader of the text he produces; the fact that he is the author does not guarantee that his interpretation of the text is "correct," and in fact it probably makes little sense to speak of "correct" interpretations at all. However, some reader-response critics (phenomenologists) argue that the reader can in a sense enter into the mind or consciousness of the author and perceive the text through the author's eyes; in this sense the text provides an opportunity to perceive from another's point-of-view. Still other reader-response critics see the author and reader as cooperative co-creators of the text, each contributing something to the reading experience, while other reader-response critics see the relationship between writer and reader as inherently antagonistic.

T1. Texts exist not as autonomous objects of study but rather as events in the minds of those who read them. In important respects, a text does not exist until it is read or perceived. Therefore the minds, perceptions, and responses of individual readers are the sources of textual "meaning." Reader-response critics disagree about the extent to which a text (or its author) can control the responses a text elicits, but they tend to concur that such responses are the most important subjects of critical attention. Some reader-response critics see the text as a fluid and dynamic *process* rather than as a static object; in this sense, the text is more like a piece of music (which unfolds in time) than like a painting (which in a sense can be perceived all at once). By breaking the text down into small unfolding moments of time, such critics enhance the possibility that different readers will perceive each moment (and therefore the total experience or event) in different ways. Some reader-response critics argue that the text itself shapes, moment-by-moment, our unfolding understanding of its meaning: by providing new information, by clearing up or creating ambiguities, the text shapes our response. Other reader-response critics would argue, however, that the text can never really control our responses to it; for these critics, the responses shape the text rather than vice-versa.

A1. Some reader-response critics focus on the specific reactions of individual readers; for critics who adopt this approach, no two readings of a given text (even if those readings are done by the same reader at different points in time) are ever exactly the same, so that no text can ever mean quite the same thing to different readers (or even to the same reader at different times in his life). Each reader brings to the text her own unique personality and consciousness, and because the text is filtered through her mind, each reading of a text produces, in a sense, a unique text. In this sense, the audience member is as much the "creator" of the text as the author. However, some other reader-response critics focus on the general or *shared* responses of large groups (or communities) of readers. These critics argue that no reader reads in complete isolation; rather, each reader is part of an interpretive community, whose informal and often unstated rules of interpretation she has learned. The existence of interpretive communities with shared rules of interpretation helps explain why different readers can largely agree about the "meaning" of a text.

R1. Reader-response critics tend to agree that there can be no neutral, objective perception of reality, especially of reality as embodied in literary texts. The perspective of the observer will always help determine what, exactly, the observer sees, and since different observers will look at reality from different (even, in some respects, unique) points of view, in a fundamental sense "reality" will be different for each observer. Any similarities in persons' perceptions of reality will result from prior similarities in the points-of-view from which they observe. The kind of "reality" emphasized by reader-response critics will tend to be a "reality" defined by individual or social *psychology*. Since both individual and social psychology are partly shaped by historical and cultural forces, some reader-response critics are interested in how different perceptions of "reality" are created by cultural conditions and institutions.

C1. Since interpretation is necessarily subjective to one degree or another, the critic should not pretend that his reading of the text is the only possible or the only valid reading. The best critics, in fact, will try to be as self-conscious as possible in their employment of interpretive strategies. In other words, they will never assume that their interpretations are perfectly "natural" or are dictated by the "text itself." Agreement with other critics should be seen as indicating that one shares (for whatever reasons) the same interpretive assumptions as those critics; agreement indicates not that objective truth has been discovered but rather that those in agreement are part of the same basic interpretive community and share the same basic interpretive paradigms. Some reader-response critics (particularly those with an interest in history) will try to study changes in interpretive communities over time. In studying a Shakespeare play, for instance, they might study the range of possible interpretations that were available to Shakespeare's contemporaries; they might study the actual recorded *reception* of the text—not in order to arrive at a "true" interpretation of the text but precisely to show, in part, how differing interpretations evolve and even co-exist.

Dialogical Criticism

Just as DECONSTRUCTION is inextricably linked with the work of Jacques Derrida, so dialogical criticism is inevitably tied to the work of its founder, Mikhail Bakhtin (1895–1975). Like many twentieth-century thinkers, Bakhtin was interested in the nature of language, but his emphasis on how language functions (as different voices within the TEXT) gives his theory some important connections with FORMALISM. However, his tendency to think of the text as a dialogue, cacophony, or polyphony of voices differs from the formalist emphasis on artistic unity, while his interest in the ways the text interacts with history makes his theory comparable, in some ways, to the NEW HISTORICISM. Dialogical criticism became especially influential in the late 1970s and 1980s.

W1. The writer is always engaged in actual or potential dialogue with actual or potential readers and also with the different "voices" that find expression in his work. These different "voices" may reflect different aspects of his own being, since the writer, like the text, is the result of and reflection of dialogue between different voices or discourses. Every work is inherently rhetorical; that is, it attempts to affect (and is therefore affected by) its audience.

T1. The text is less the expression of a single, authorial point of view than a site of dialogue, conversation, debate, and negotiation between different points of view. The voices of characters in a work, for instance, may be just as important as the voice of the narrator or author in determining how a work is interpreted. The best texts are rarely monological—i.e., rarely the expression of simply one point of view. In this sense, texts never possess absolute unity and coherence; rather than being static objects they are dynamic processes of dialogue.

A1. The audience is not simply external to the text; rather, the writer inevitably takes the potential reactions of potential audiences into account while shaping the text, so that the very process of writing the text involves a kind of dialogue with anticipated audiences. In this sense, the audience has a hand in the composition of the text, so that even before the text is read it has already been affected by points of view other than those of the author alone.

R1. Social reality is crucially important in influencing the traits of writers, readers, texts, and critics. All these entities are embedded in society and are necessarily engaged in dialogue, interaction, and negotiation with actual or potential audiences. Words are always *addressed*. Observing the interaction of points of view within a work can help us appreciate the complex interchange of points of view in society itself.

C1. The critic will not try to reduce the text to the expression of a single point of view but will show how the text articulates different, sometimes competing voices. The critic must pay attention not only to what a text explicitly says but also to what is left unsaid and/or to what is only implied. The critic will not try to force one monologic interpretation on a text but will keep her ears open for the different voices a text articulates.

New Historicism

Just as other recent theories have attacked the FORMALIST emphasis on unity and artistic harmony, so does the new historicism, but new historicism is also suspicious of unifying explanations generally, especially in literary history. Rather than finding sameness in the past (by claiming, for instance, that most people at a particular time tended to act or think alike), new historicism tends to focus on conflict, contention, domination, and resistance. In this sense it has much in common with Marxism; both tend to focus on changes in social "REALITY." However, new historicism tends to differ from Marxism in having a less obvious or consistent polit-ical agenda. New historicism was explicitly formulated mainly in the 1980s and became very influential by the end of that decade.

W1. Whereas traditional historical criticism tends to emphasize the writer as the most important influence on the text, new historicism tends to emphasize multiple and often contradictory influences. Traditional historicism assumes that by studying the historical context that influenced the writer, we can better understand the text the writer produced. New historicism tends to assume that there is no such thing as a single or coherent historical "context" that can help to explain either the writer or the text in any simple, single way. Rather, the historical forces that influence a writer and text are likely to be so numerous, so diverse, and so potentially conflicting that studying a writer or text historically will compli-cate, rather than simplify, our understanding of them.

T1. The text is not only influenced by contemporary forces but is itself also a social force that inevitably exercises some influences in return. In other words, the text is not so much a thing as an *act*, a social deed. Whereas traditional historical criticism tends to em-phasize the writer and text as the essentially passive objects of his-torical influences, new historicism is interested in exploring the dynamic relationship—the give *and* take—between the text, its own era, and even later eras. Once a text is created, it exerts multi-ple and largely unpredictable influences of its own. Because any text consists of elements of the larger codes a particular society uses to structure itself and to communicate, any text can poten-tially be useful in the attempt to understand any other text pro-duced by that culture. Therefore, even texts that seem to have nothing to do with literature can be useful as jumping-off points for the study of literary texts. Similarly, literary texts can offer points of departure for reflections on an entire culture.

A1. The text will inevitably reflect many of the influences that also affected contemporary audiences; for this reason, literary texts can be highly useful in studying past societies, since the codes or as-sumptions by which those societies operated are inevitably em-bedded in such texts. Contemporary audiences responded to liter-ary texts in ways shaped by larger codes of meaning, larger ide-ologies or fundamental assumptions. However, these codes them-selves are likely to have been diverse, multifaceted, incoherent, and even conflicting. For this reason, no single code or ideology is likely to explain the contemporary audience. Indeed, such a single entity—*an* audience—is unlikely to have existed; instead, it makes more sense to think of varied, conflicting, and unstable audiences. No single interpretation of a text is therefore likely to do justice to the complex responses of actual contemporary audiences.

R1. New historicist critics tend to assume that our experience of reality is inevitably social: that is, no individual exists in isolation or in a vacuum, and therefore one's experience of "reality" is never truly private. That experience instead is shaped by the larger codes and discourses by which one's society is structured. However, those codes and discourses are themselves numerous, unstable, and often conflicting. A culture is not a single or coherent entity but is instead a dynamic process of constant conflict and negotiation among different interests. For this reason, cultural questions are always in some sense questions of *power*. To a great degree, new historicists are interested in how texts affect and are affected by shifting relations of power. Every text (indeed, every aspect of culture) is in this sense enmeshed in politics (in the broadest sense of that term).

C1. The critic herself can never be a disinterested observer or a neutral investigator. Inevitably she is enmeshed in her own contemporary culture—in her own contemporary set of power-relations. Inevitably her own writing is influenced by political motives and has political effects, although neither these motives nor these effects are likely to be completely simple, entirely conscious, or entirely under the critic's deliberate control. Because the relations between a text and its surrounding culture are likely to be so complex and multifaceted, no field of study is irrelevant to a critic's work. Profitable insights can be gleaned from anthropology, sociology, philosophy—indeed, from any discipline that can offer insights into the ways a culture operates. Like any writer, the critic herself is caught up in a larger dynamic process of negotiation over which she can exert only *some* degree of influence. The best critics will be those who are as self-conscious as possible about the political dimensions of their work and who do not try to pretend that such dimensions do not exist.

Multiculturalism

Multiculturalism is less a particular critical theory (with a routine series of practices and methods) than a general orientation. Like a number of other recent approaches it emphasizes social "REALITY" as the key component of the Abrams scheme, and like them, too, it acknowledges the differences that exist within society, especially differences involving group identities. In Anglo-American criticism, multiculturalism has become increasingly important since the 1960s as different groups have asserted and explored their separate ethnic, sexual, and linguistic identities.

W1. The writer is not merely a person but is inevitably a member of a particular group; membership in this group inevitably affects how and what he writes and how his writing is received by others (who are also members of various groups). Is the writer black or white? Gay or straight? English-speaking or Spanish-speaking? A mulatto? A mestizo? Lesbian or bisexual? A black lesbian, a white lesbian, a chicana lesbian? The answers to such questions will inevitably affect the writer's experiences and thus also his work. Even a writer who seeks to write simply as a "human being" will thereby be adopting a position toward one or another group; no writer, then, can ever completely adopt a "neutral" or "objective" stance or transcend social differences or group identities.

T1. The text will inevitably reflect the experiences of the writer—experiences shaped by the writer's relations with the various groups that constitute her society. The text may express the values and perspectives of the minority group to which the writer belongs, or it may attempt to express the values and perspectives of the dominant or majority group, or it may challenge majority values, or it may try to accommodate or reconcile minority and majority values, or it may express any of a number of other possible relationships between the majority and minority culture. Inevitably, though, it will be affected in some way by the existence of these alternative cultures. In a society composed of different groups who adhere to different values, any text will have a political dimension; it will either affirm or undermine the values (and therefore the relative social power) of the group.

A1. Just as writers are inevitably members of various groups within a larger society, so the same thing is true of the audience.

Membership in such groups affects how a particular reader experiences or responds to a particular text. The reader, for instance, may value a text that affirms the values of her group, or she may disdain a text that seems to undermine the values of her group, or she may respond in less obvious ways. In responding to a given text, an audience member will inevitably be expressing her sense of her identity, particularly her degree of identification with one or another of the groups that compose society. A reader who assumes that her values are natural or inevitable or objective or neutral is either deceiving herself or is trying to impose her values on others.

R1. The most important kind of reality for multicultural critics is social reality—the existence of persons in society and particularly in social groups. These groups may *seem* natural and inevitable (for example, male/female; black/white; young/old) but they are to some degree *socially constructed*. For example, to be born as a woman in a sexist society is one thing; to be born as a woman in a "liberated" society is another. To be gay in a small, rural Southern town will probably involve a different set of experiences than being gay in San Francisco. Similarly, to be a young, attractive woman in a sexist society will probably involve a different set of experiences than being an elderly, unattractive woman in the same society. Multicultural critics assume that one's experience of "reality" is always shaped, to one degree or another, by the cultures to which one belongs or with which one is associated by others. Identity will often involve complex, overlapping membership in various groups: one might, for instance, be an elderly, attractive, Spanish-speaking black lesbian in a small Southern town.

C1. The multicultural critic is suspicious of the claim that there is a general "human nature." He will tend to examine how a writer's membership in a particular group (or groups) affects how he writes and how his writing affects (and is affected by) members of his own and other groups. He will tend to examine how texts explore (or attempt to ignore) human differences. He will tend to value works that take such differences seriously. He will be very interested in the *political* dimensions of texts—i.e., in how texts affect (and are affected by) the status and power of the groups to which their writers and readers belong. His approach will tend to be interdisciplinary—drawing, for instance, on history, psychology, anthropology, sociology, linguistics, or any other field that can help illuminate the differences between human groups.

Postmodernism

Postmodernism is less a well-formulated theory than a recent intellectual trend that has affected thinking about society, interpretation, and the arts. It is similar in important ways to POST-STRUCTURALISM or DECONSTRUCTION, especially in its skepticism about large-scale "truths" or "objective" interpretations of "REALITY." By its very nature postmodernism is fluid and difficult to define, and as one of the most recent of critical orientations, it is still in the process of evolution. It became a subject of widespread discussion in the late 1980s and 1990s.

W1. Ideally the writer adheres strictly to no stable system of thinking but actively explores (or is passively open to) a variety of positions, roles, attitudes, stances, often in the same work. While formalism would tend to seek an underlying order in such diversity, postmodernism is comfortable with and even celebrates complexities, contradictions, ambiguities, and the potential freedom they exemplify. Rather than nostalgically mourning for a lost sense of coherence and or for a stable system of larger values, then, the postmodern writer ideally embraces what might strike a formalist as incoherent and chaotic. Rather than being disengaged from or hostile to popular culture, the postmodern writer interacts with it, recognizing no rigid distinctions between "high" and "low" art.

T1. Whereas previous approaches to texts have often sought to find underlying patterns of unity or coherence (whether formal, psychological, thematic, social, etc.), postmodernism shares with deconstruction a belief that texts will be (and even should be) full of contradictions, gaps, incoherences, and randomness and will reveal unexpected, startling, and even unsettling juxtapositions of styles, genres, and modes of thought. Postmodernism also shares with deconstruction a belief that every aspect of reality is in some sense simply a "text" or "sign," so that a text's most important relations will not be with reality *per se* (which we can never truly or fully know) but only with other texts. The text can never accurately "mirror" the external world except insofar as the world itself is full of contradictions or incoherence. Since a text can never really imitate a coherent external reality (partly since no such coherent reality exists), the text will always in some sense be referring back to itself and will never really get "beyond" or "outside" itself.

A1. Rather than appealing to the audience's sense of logic or reason or to its beliefs in particular ideologies or world-views, postmodernism will implicitly undermine or subvert all these stable systems. Ideally the audience will cooperate in and welcome this sense of disruption; ideally audience members will find the confrontation with postmodern art liberating (even if disillusioning). Ideally the audience will not search for the "deeper, underlying" meanings of a text but will delight in its surfaces, in its ironic juxtapositions of apparently contradictory meanings. Rather than feeling threatened by the chaotic qualities of the postmodern text, the audience ideally will adopt the same playful, tentative, ironic attitude that helped produce the work in the first place. Just as the text is full of contradictions, so is the "identity" of each audience member; indeed, the notion of a coherent, stable "identity" is implicitly disrupted by postmodern art.

R1. Previous kinds of writing and thinking had placed great confidence in the possession of (or at least the search for) large "meta-narratives" that would make sense of diverse phenomena. Postmodernism is suspicious of all such totalizing (and ultimately reductive) explanations. Marxism, for instance, cannot explain all the phenomena it attempts to encompass; nor can Christianity or structuralism or Freudianism or Islam or science or any other coherent system of thought. Attempts to see the world in terms of such larger ideologies almost inevitably result in oppression of ideas, persons, cultures, works, etc., that "don't fit." Postmodernism is therefore suspicious of any large-scale ideology that tries to make sense of the world by *imposing* sense on it. Rather than trying to penetrate beneath the surface of things to disclose some more important underlying reality, the postmodern writer doubts the existence of such a reality and thus sees all things as in some sense ornamental, decorative, illusory. Giving up the search for "meta-narratives" means feeling comfortable with diversity, uncertainty, and toleration and also means accepting and even enjoying the contradictions one finds within oneself and others. Reality (or in any event our experience of reality) is inherently fragmented and incoherent.

C1. The postmodern critic will call attention to and revel in the (inherent) contradictions, (unintended) ironies, and (irresolvable) paradoxes in the texts she examines. Rather than faulting a text that is full of contradictions (as would a formalist), she will acknowledge the inevitability of such contradictions or tensions and will indeed value texts that highlight them or that do not attempt to disguise, ignore, or disparage such "incoherence." The critic will be at least as interested in how texts can be *used* by different persons as in what those texts "inherently" *mean*, since inherently they "mean" no single thing (i.e., have no stable significance). The critic will be suspicious of, and skeptical toward, any text that claims to set forth an all-embracing explanation; like the deconstructor, she will interrogate such a text to expose its heterogeneity—its lack of a simple, single, coherent meaning.

Pluralism

The most influential spokesman for critical pluralism has been Wayne Booth, who has been defending this approach since at least the 1960s. Like any critical theory, pluralism makes important assumptions about the nature of reality, but perhaps the most important component on the Abrams scheme for a pluralist involves the role of the CRITIC herself. This is true because pluralism is not itself an interpretive approach but rather a way of coming to terms with the vast variety of approaches that have been (and will undoubtedly continue to be) proposed. Pluralism assumes that each approach, by asking different questions about literature, will provide different kinds of answers and that each kind of answer is at least potentially valuable in its own right. Pluralism does not attempt to harmonize competing ways of thinking, nor does it radically doubt the validity of all ways of thought. Rather, it emphasizes that each separate theory can provide insights consistent with the questions the theory asks and the assumptions it makes. Pluralists encourage practitioners of a given theory to be as logical and consistent as possible in developing and applying their theories, and it also encourages practitioners of rival theories to give their rivals a fair hearing. Pluralism thus shares with POSTMODERNISM a suspicion of dogmatic, all-embracing explanations, but it encourages an intellectually responsible use of any particular interpretive approach.

W1. A writer can be viewed from multiple perspectives—as a craftsman, as an individual psyche, as a representative human being, as a member of a particular culture, as an advocate of a particular politics, as a member of a particular gender, etc. The kinds of questions we ask about a writer and the kinds of answers we find to those questions will therefore vary, depending on how we happen to be approaching the writer at any particular moment. Different kinds of approaches or questions will inevitably elicit different kinds of results or answers. We need to be careful, then, to understand exactly which approach we are adopting and need to realize that any single approach is not the only one that might be used.

T1. Everything just said about the writer is also true of the text. A text can be treated, for instance, as a formal object; as a historical, social, or political document; as a revelation of the author's psyche or of some underlying psychology of humans in general; etc. No single approach is either totally right or completely comprehensive; each is appropriate in its own way; each ideally reveals a different aspect or dimension of the text. A text can be seen to make or possess some coherent sense *within* the specific terms of a particular approach, but no single approach can tell us everything about the text's significance(s). Whereas formalists might seek to harmonize these approaches or find their common ground (thus producing an integrated or coherent, even if complex, reading of the text), pluralists feel no strong urge to harmonize or homogenize divergent readings. Indeed, there is real value in being able to ask fundamentally different kinds of questions of the same text.

A1. Ideally each audience member will be as conscious as possible of the kinds of questions she is asking of a text and of the larger assumptions those questions take for granted. Ideally each audience member will realize that the answers she elicits when interrogating a text will be only partial answers (answers that are relevant to and from one perspective), not absolutely complete or final explanations. Ideally, each reader will try to understand thoroughly the rules, procedures, and interpretive methods of whatever approach(es) she adopts and will be able to recognize when and how a particular interpretation either satisfies or falls short of the standards appropriate to that particular approach. The reader will try to provide as rigorous, logical, and intellectually responsible a reading as possible *according to the standards of the approach she adopts*. If she chooses a Marxist perspective, for instance, she should not simply assume that that perspective is, in and of itself, superior to any other. Rather, she should recognize that different Marxist readings of the same work will do fuller or lesser justice to the ideal potential of a Marxist reading of that work. Whatever approach a reader adopts, she should try to use it intelligently and thoughtfully and should be vigilant to avoid errors or mistakes. She should be aware of the premises from which she is arguing, should scrutinize those premises as much as possible, and, assuming that she still finds them valuable after scrutinizing them, should apply them with consistency and rigor to her reading of the work. Finally, she should avoid assuming that her way of reading is the *only* legitimate way.

R1. Reality can be approached only from particular perspectives or angles or assumptions or premises. A complete and impartial and thoroughly objective understanding of reality seems impossible. Our questions about reality, and our answers to those questions, make sense only in terms of the assumptions that underlay both the questions and the answers. Whereas a "monist" assumes that there is only one way of understanding reality, and whereas a skeptic assumes that there is no valid way of understanding it, and whereas eclecticism tries to pick and choose among different approaches in order to construct a comprehensive approach, a pluralist assumes that different approaches will spotlight different aspects of reality and that there is some value in using many different approaches.

C1. The pluralist critic does not believe that "anything goes." He does not assume that any particular interpretation is valid simply because it is unique. Rather, he tries to test each particular interpretation against the standards implied by the interpreter's own assumptions. He tries to determine whether a particular reading does justice to the potential inherent in that kind of reading. Some formalist interpretations, for instance, may be more thorough and exacting than other formalist interpretations. The same would be true of Marxist, deconstructive, structuralist, psychoanalytical approaches, etc. Within the terms of a given system of thought, it is possible to determine how close a particular reading comes to an *ideal* reading *within that system*. Thus, a pluralist critic is neither a complete skeptic nor a complete relativist: he does not assume that all interpretations are just as valuable as any others. Rather, he tries (1) to determine the premises from which a critic is working; (2) to decide whether those premises are coherent or contradictory (i.e., whether they are self-consistent); (3) to assess whether an interpreter using those premises has applied them rigorously and consistently and has seen as much with them as they will allow him to see. The pluralist critic assumes that no single perspective has any monopoly on the truth, and he is suspicious of systems that claim to be able to explain everything.

Abbreviations

Each bibliographical entry is identified by a number that follows the first three letters of the relevant author's last name. Thus the first entry on Ann Beattie is abbreviated "**Bea 1**," the second "**Bea 2**," and so on. The only exceptions involve the two authors who share the last name "O'Connor." In these cases, Flannery O'Connor is identified by the abbreviation "**O'Cfl**," while Frank O'Connor is identified as "**O'CFr.**"

The names of critical approaches discussed in the Introduction (and exemplified in the appendix) have also been abbreviated. These abbreviations, which generally follow each bibliographical entry, are designed to indicate which approach(es) a particular entry most seems to exemplify. Thus an entry followed by the abbreviations "**PSY**," "**MARX**," and "**THEM**," for instance, might be usefully understood in connection with the discussions (offered in the Introduction) of Psychoanalytic, Marxist, and Thematic theories. *These designations are in no sense meant to be either exhaustive or restrictive.* Rather, they are merely intended to help readers understand the kinds of basic assumptions that particular critics seem to be making in the specific essays summarized in this book.

The following abbreviations designate the particular theories or theorists discussed in the Introduction:

ARCH = Archetypal (or "Myth") criticism
ARIS = Aristotle
DECON = Deconstruction
DIAL = Dialogical criticism
FEM = Feminist criticism
FORM = Formalist criticism (Anglo-American "New Criticism")
HIST = Traditional historical criticism
HOR = Horace
LON = Longinus

MARX = Marxist criticism
MULT = Multiculturalism
NHIST = New Historicist criticism
PLAT = Plato
PLUR = Pluralism
POSTM = Postmodernism
PSY = Psychoanalytic criticism
READ-R = Reader-response (or "affective") criticism
STRUC = Stucturalist criticism
THEM = Thematic criticism

Short Fiction
A Critical Companion

"WEEKEND"

Bea 1. Beattie, Ann. "An Interview with Ann Beattie." With Steven R. Centola. *Contemporary Literature* 31 (1990): 405–22.

In the interview, Beattie mentions that while she is obviously a woman writer and thus gender would naturally enter into her writing, she does not see herself as focusing on gender issues; in fact, she contends that her male characters are as credible as her female ones (406–7). She points out that her fiction primarily concerns relationships (406). Her characters, often uncommunicative, frequently lead double lives, having both a private life and a public one (410). Unable to control their own lives, they harbor a secret existence (412). Denying that her fiction is autobiographical, Beattie contends that she writes only about situations that interest her (407–8). Acknowledging that she usually writes about the upper middle class, she nevertheless argues that she does not address a particular audience (415) but that all readers should be able to relate to her stories because of their universality (411). Her method is to describe a situation—like Hemingway, she allows a detail to create or suggest a character (419)—and then step back to allow the reader to come to his or her own understanding (417). She does not want to "presume ... [to] enlighten people" (417). Indeed, questioning the possibility of only a single reading or interpretation to a story, she suggests that there is a "counter narrative" at work in her stories (418). When asked what she wants to be remembered for, she responds for fiction that is "moving; that ... makes you think; that ... makes you wonder about something" (422). **HIST, THEM**

Bea 2. Beattie, Ann. "A Conversation with Ann Beattie." With Larry McCaffery and Sinda Gregory. *The Literary Review* 27 (1984): 165–77.

Commenting on her fiction, Beattie states that she frequently chronicles the breakdown of relationships, a result of the partners' inherent instability and their inability to communicate (165–66). She presents her characters and the situation without supplying much background information and without offering in her conclusions solutions or answers (168). In fact, Beattie says of her endings that they "impl[y] further complexity" (173). She defends her "emotionless" or flat style, suggesting that it mimics the short sentences people use in conversation (174). Mentioning that she works quickly without trying to express a particular philosophy, she says of her writing, "I just *do it*, the way I get my groceries" (177). **HIST, THEM**

Bea 3. Gelfant, Blanche H. "Ann Beattie's Magic Slate or the End of the Sixties." *Women Writing in America: Voices in Collage*. Hanover, NH: University Press of New England, 1984. Pp. 31–43. Reprinted in *The Critical Response to Ann Beattie*. Ed. Jaye Berman Montressor. Westport, CT: Greenwood Press, 1993. Pp. 21–29.

An examination of two collections of Beattie's short stories, *Secrets and Surprises* and *Distortions*, and a novel, *Chilly Scenes of Winter*, suggests that Beattie chronicles the end of an era, specifically the sixties, creating in her fiction a picture of the disillusionment that follows the abandonment of dreams (32–33). Similarities exist among the three works. The landscapes are often "desolate" and rain is frequent, trapping people inside their homes (33)—characteristics that are evident in "Weekend," from the collection *Secrets and Surprises*. Beattie's stories, comprised of trivia, detail the ordinariness of everyday life when dreams are gone and there is nothing left (34). The characters, unable to direct their own lives and often uncommunicative, cling to the trivia because facing the larger questions of life is too unsettling; in other words, the "pain of living for a useless death must be camouflaged" (35). Perhaps the only way to confront the nothingness is to be "simple," much as Lenore is in "Weekend": she finds comfort and even meaning in everyday tasks of cooking and caring for her children and her companion, George (41). Simpleness is perhaps the best defense against the madness that results from looking too closely at the nothingness (41). Beattie's stories "end in irresolution, suspension, irony, or erasure" (42): a story about the nothingness of life must end with nothing.

Beattie's dilemma is the difficulty of writing "interesting and significant stories" while writing about the ordinariness of life (37). But she exactly depicts contemporary culture (40) and creates a recognizable, though disturbing, world (43). **THEM, FORM**

Bea 4. Hammond, Karla M. "Ann Beattie: Still with the Sixties." *Denver Quarterly* 15 (1980): 115–17.

The stories in Beattie's second short story collection, *Secrets and Surprises*, present characters who seem trapped, sometimes by bad weather (as in "Weekend") and sometimes because they have nowhere to go (115). They also share a sense of quiet desperation, pessimism, and depression (115). The characters, often more attached to a dog or a car than to each other, do not have strong commitments, ambitions, or close relationships (115–16). They are children of the sixties (115). The strength of these stories lies in Beattie's sparse and economical style (115) and in her ability to create a believable and, at times, upsetting world through choosing the exact detail (115). Beattie "has gone to the heart of her own generation," and the portrait she paints "is at once compelling and thoroughly convincing" (117). **THEM, FORM**

Bea 5. Iyer, Pico. "The World According to Beattie." *Partisan Review* 50 (1983): 548–53.

Beattie's stories generally resemble the typical *New Yorker* story such as that written by Cheever or Updike, stories that "chronicl[e] the sad eccentricities, plaintive longings, and quiet frustrations of their generation" (548). Beattie's characters, from the sixties or influenced by the sixties, lack the conviction and commitment of that decade (549). They seem in a "limbo," with no destination, no control over their lives, no enduring relationships, no ambition, nor interests: "Their main activity is refining inactivity" (549). Beattie even reads her stories in a monotone, suggestive of the flatness of the narratives themselves (550). Although the stories lack variety in themes and mood (552), Beattie's ability to write is unquestioned. She can create a believable world with a few details (552); she is the chronicler of her generation (553). **THEM, FORM**

Bea 6. Mckinstry, Susan Janet. "The Speaking Silence of Ann Beattie's Voice." *Studies in Short Fiction* 24 (1987): 111–17.

Although several reviewers of Beattie's stories suggest that her typical non-endings are appropriate responses to the contemporary world, the stories often "tell two stories at once: the open story of the objective, detailed present is juxtaposed with a closed story of the subjective past, a story the [female] speaker tries hard not to tell. In the space between these two narratives lies the point of the story" (111–12). A knowledge of Seymour Chatman's discussion of resolved and revealed plots leads one to the realization that Beattie superimposes one plot on the other (112). Thus while one plot does not reach closure, the other does. The female protagonists, in trying to avoid the emotional and subjective story, focus on the present, but unintentionally reach a closure on the hidden story (112). Learning to recognize and then to understand the hidden plot, in other words learning to read the story that is untold, enables the reader to get beyond the surface and, like an analyst, understand the character (117). **THEM, STRUC, FORM**

Bea 7. Porter, Carolyn. "The Art of the Missing." *Contemporary American Women Writers: Narrative Strategies*. Eds. Catherine Rainwater and William J. Scheick. Lexington: University Press of Kentucky, 1985. Pp. 9–25.

Beattie's narrative technique, used in two short story collections, *Distortions* and *The Burning House*, helps explain why she "is known for a certain kind of story ... one marked by understatement, caustic dialogue, and an unsentimental view of social relations" (9). Beattie's world is one in which "Something has been lost, although no one can quite remember what" (10). Although there is much that Beattie does not include in her fiction (poverty, for instance), her sharp, accurate focus on white middle class life often makes one wince (10). Beattie's effectiveness is due partly to her narrative technique (11). Her stories, examining social groups more than individuals, are generally written in the present tense with little exposition (12). This rhetorical device enables Beattie to focus on the present, reduces the need or likelihood for exposition, and forces Beattie to reveal characters through dialogue and action (12). Supporting this minimalist approach is Beattie's reliance on metonomy instead of metaphor (12); her stories move from one association to another (25). Beattie's use of metonomy does not allow for the closure that is possible with symbols (15). At the conclusion of the story, the reader feels a lack of finality, producing a sense that something is missing (16). Beattie's stories "produce a vision of a world in a state of lack" (18). Beattie's work has matured. The early stories, lacking plot development, resemble photographs (18); the character is displayed in a series of pictures (18). *Secrets and Surprises*, which includes "Weekend," is transitional (19). But the stories in the later volume *The Burning House*, although they contain typical Beattie characteristics, have protagonists that develop and reach new levels of understanding (20). **FORM, THEM, READ-R**

Bea 8. Schapiro, Barbara. "The Culture of Narcissism." *Webster Review* 10 (1985): 86–101.

Coming of age in the sixties, Beattie's characters, bored and restless, can be defined in negatives; they cannot form lasting relationships, they have no control over their future, and they find no meaning in their lives (86–87). They illustrate what Christopher Lasch has called the culture of narcissism (86). Although Schapiro examines two novels, *Chilly Scenes of Winter* and *Love Always*, her observations apply to Beattie's short stories as well. The characters' inability to relate to others is due to pathological narcissism which is caused by "the failure to achieve a securely structured or integrated self," resulting from a traumatic loss in childhood (88–89). This early loss produces in the adult unexpressed anger, rage, and aggression which results in feelings of guilt and inadequacy (91–92). Occasionally women can supply some comfort, but often they also suffer fragmentation and disintegration (93). Beattie's fiction implies a world view in which the world, like the characters, is "unstable and untrustworthy" (93), a view which is complemented by Beattie's sparse and economical style (100). **THEM, HIST, FORM**

B.W.

"AN OCCURRENCE AT OWL CREEK BRIDGE"

Bie 1. Ames, Clifford R. "Do I Wake or Sleep? Technique as Content in Ambrose Bierce's Short Story, 'An Occurrence at Owl Creek Bridge.'" *American Literary Realism* 19 (1987): 52–67.

The "considerable impact of the story's close lies in the reader's abrupt discovery that he has somehow crossed over into the consciousness of the protagonist at the moment when all experience ends" (52). We suddenly recognize "that Farquhar's delusion has been our own" (53). The work thus "moves from being a story about an event to being the event itself" (54). Bierce subtly creates and then alters the narrative tone and point of view (55–59), and, just as Farquhar is deceived by the Federal scout, so are we deceived by Bierce (61). The "occurrence" of the title is not just the hanging but our participation in Farquhar's psychological experience of it (65). Although readers (like Farquhar) are suddenly hanged, "like him they err on the side of life and liberty and choose the world of life over the world of death" (65). **READ-R, FORM**

Bie 2. Cheatham, George, and Judy Cheatham. "Bierce's 'An Occurrence at Owl Creek Bridge.'" *The Explicator* 43 (1984): 45–47.

The name Peyton "is a variant spelling of Payton, the Scottish form of Patrick (from the Latin, meaning a patrician, a person of noble descent). Farquhar derives from the Gaelic *Fearachar*, meaning manly or brave, the name of an early Scottish king" (45). The name is thus appropriate to the background and aspirations of Bierce's character, who first plots a romantic escape, then imagines it happening—even concluding his vision with a reunion that is "the epitome of clichéd romance" (46). Bierce ends each section of the story "with a flat realistic statement to undercut Farquhar's preceding fantasies or romantic illusions" (46), and his careful choice of even such a minor detail as the name suggests the artfulness of his story (47). **HIST, THEM**

Bie 3. Davidson, Cathy N. *The Experimental Fictions of Ambrose Bierce: Structuring the Ineffable.* Lincoln and London: University of Nebraska Press, 1984. Pp. 45–54.

Peyton Farquhar combines three kinds of typical Bierce characters: "the sadder and wiser man who has learned the lesson of his previous limitation, the fortunate unfallen who survive through chance and their own short-sightedness, [and] the defeated protagonist whose death is a measure of his previous self-deceptions" (45). In this story, Farquhar both does and does not survive his moment of epiphany or illumination (45). "The military language of the first section ignores (implicitly, *denies*) feelings and sensations. It depersonalizes and ritualizes the processes of killing, so that those who order and those who act as ordered never need to evaluate" their behavior (48). Ironically, this depersonalized language is "the logical illogical extension" of the romantic but militaristic "language employed in the second section," which describes Farquhar imagining what it would be like to play a role in the war. Yet as Farquhar approaches death, both the language of heroic fantasy and the language of depersonalized ritual begin to give way to "new perceptions ... recorded in a new language *for* and *of* life" (49). The energetic involvement Farquhar had earlier sought is now achieved (mentally) just before he dies; in the imagined water, he experiences a "perceptual baptism" in which he is "born again into a world he had never before conceived, a world free from the death-dealing language of war and the misleading rhetoric of patriotism" (51). His mind moves from simple sensory reactions to more complex evaluations (51). "About to die, he finally begins to appreciate the values inherent in much of his previous life, the life his former rhetoric had led him to condemn" (52). As he mentally heads home, he rethinks his "earlier assumptions, language, and behavior" and now values life itself rather than military glory (53). However, just as Farquhar jumps to conclusions and sees what he wants to see, so Bierce encourages the story's readers to do the same (54–55). We initially misperceive, much as Farquhar does. **THEM, READ-R, FORM**

Bie 4. Grenander, M.E. *Ambrose Bierce*. New York: Twayne, 1971. Pp. 93–99.

In this work and in similar stories, Bierce makes the reader feel "an intense fear coupled with a bitter realization that it is cruelly inappropriate" (94). In such works the protagonist's responses are simultaneously "intellectual, emotional, and sensory"; the physical reaction is often emphasized by slowing the protagonist's sense of time (94). This tale is comparable in various ways to others by Bierce (94–99). **THEM, HIST, READ-R**

Bie 5. Linkin, Harriet Kramer. "Narrative Technique in 'An Occurrence at Owl Creek Bridge.'" *Journal of Narrative Technique* 18 (1988): 137–52.

By using shifts in time and points of view, Bierce makes his readers share Farquhar's experience, especially his sense of dislocation (137). Although the opening section gives us all the clues we need to understand what is really happening, we ignore them until the final sentence—like Farquhar's noose—yanks us back to reality (137). The narrator's diction accommodates both military and civilian perspectives, emphasizing facts rather than hypotheses (138) while also making us share Farquhar's perspective (139). The objective tone momentarily breaks down when the narrator looks into Farquhar's eyes, thus foreshadowing the story's larger plunge into Farquhar's perspective just as we are becoming familiar with the narrator's point of view (140). Sometimes the narrator shifts pronouns ambiguously; elsewhere he fails to provide commentary when we expect it; then he suddenly shifts to flashback; in these and other ways, he makes us share Farquhar's disorientation (141–45). "Critics who insist only careless readers fail to recognize the third section as hallucination ignore how brilliantly Bierce tricks the reader through silence" (145). Ironically, it is in section three that Farquhar seems most alive (146), although eventually the narrative voice begins to displace his perspective (reversing the earlier process [146–49]). "Sharing more than Peyton Farquahr's time frame, we learn of our own susceptiblity to rhetoric" and "fall victim to easy belief in narrative consciousnesses possessing partial truths" (150). **FORM, READ-R**

Bie 6. Logan, F.J. "The Wry Seriousness of 'Owl Creek Bridge.'" In *Critical Essays on Ambrose Bierce*. Boston: G.K. Hall, 1982. Pp. 195–208. Reprinted from *American Literary Realism* 10.2 (1977): 101–13.

This finely crafted story is "a speculation on the nature of time and ... abnormal psychology, particularly on processes of abnormal perception and cognition," and also on ways of knowing (196). Bierce satirizes tritely heroic war stories and the inattentive, imperceptive readers they satisfy (196). Farquahar is not heroic but is actually rather stupid; an opening allusion to his "unsteadfast footing" links him ironically to Shakespeare's impulsive warrior, Hotspur, in *1 Henry IV* (198). Bierce uses overblown romantic rhetoric to mock Farquhar while describing him; any sentimentality belongs not to Bierce but to his protagonist (199). However, Bierce makes Farquhar somewhat sympathetic by humanizing him, whereas the Union soldiers are inhumanly anonymous robots who seem mere "extensions of their weapons" and who are described in extremely simple language (201). The military language associated with Farquhar is exaggerated, whereas the language associated with the soldiers is mechanical and extremely understated (202). The story's narrator can be ironic and possesses military knowledge, and the narrative point of view alternates between detached omniscience and empathetic identification (203). Bierce effectively uses such poetic devices as meter and alliteration (203); he suggests that even a quick death may not be painless because normal schemes of time may not apply (204). The story explores two competing logics; in one, time can be infinitely subdivided; in another, time inevitably ends (207). The story recounts a hallucination, not a tragedy; it satirizes war and suggests what death may be like (207). The abrupt ending is not a trick or surprise but an inevitable fulfillment of the irony the story everywhere exhibits (207). **FORM, THEM**

Bie 7. Morris, Roy, Jr. *Ambrose Bierce: Alone in Bad Company.* New York: Crown, 1995. Pp. 215–18.

Careful reading shows that "the ending is no trick—except on the unfortunate and dull-witted Farquhar" (216). Even the title implies that the real story takes place *at* the bridge, not downstream (216). Farquhar is the kind of fool who could mentally concoct this kind of escape (217). He may originally have been excused from military duty because he owned more than twenty slaves (217). Farquhar's strange shout, "Put it back! Put it back" may actually be either an expression of his wish that the board be put back in place or an echo of the officer's command that Farquhar's hands be re-tied (217). Several analysts have suggested that Farquhar's rise through the water parallels the process of being born; the rope may thus be a kind of ironic umbilical cord (218). Farquhar's experiences resemble those described by students of near-death experiences, which may themselves be repressed memories of being born (218). This story may in fact reflect Bierce's own near-death experience in 1864 in the Civil War (218). He certainly drew on other personal memories to write this story, including war-time familiarity with a real Owl Creek, service as a railroad sentry, and hangings he witnessed while in San Francisco (218). Like Farquhar, we believe that the escape is happening because we want to believe (218). **FORM, THEM, HIST**

Bie 8. Owens, David M. "Bierce and Biography: The Location of Owl Creek Bridge." *American Literary Realism* 26.3 (1994): 82–89.

Although control of Southern rail lines was indeed a cause of much fighting as the Civil War drew to a close, and although Bierce uses historical details to give his story an air of accuracy, the real Owl Creek bridge was in Tennessee, not in Alabama (82). Owl Creek borders the Shiloh battlefield where Bierce's regiment fought fiercely in 1862 (82). Union soldiers used the creek for bathing and swimming (82). Bierce's regiment spent some time guarding and repairing railroads, and Bierce himself was a skilled map-maker (82–83). In late 1862 or early 1863, he witnessed the hanging of two union soldiers convicted of murder (83). Bierce later drew maps as part of Sherman's march to Atlanta; after being wounded, he travelled to northern Alabama, where he worked after being discharged from the army (83). Perhaps Bierce did not set the story in Tennessee because readers familiar with that area would have known that there was no railroad near the real Owl Creek; he may thus have created a fictional Owl Creek in Alabama, equipped with a railroad bridge (84). Struggle for control of rail lines did occur in northern Alabama, so that setting is appropriate (84). Farquhar's personality makes it possible to read the story as "emblematic of the death of romanticism and its trappings" (85). "Given such a reading, the owl becomes an important symbol" because it was traditionally associated with "darkness and death as well as wisdom" (85). Ironically, Farquhar's wisdom comes at the cost of his death (85). **HIST, FORM**

Bie 9. Palmer, James W. "From Owl Creek to *La Rivere du Hibou*: The Film Adaptation of Bierce's 'An Occurrence at Owl Creek Bridge.'" *Southern Humanities Review* 11 (1977): 363–71.

Robert Enrico's film adheres closely to the story's events, but his deletion of Bierce's exposition makes Farquhar seem less ironic (363). Comparing and contrasting film and story can help reveal the ways in which the two arts are both alike and distinct (363). By using both realistic and expressionistic techniques, Enrico creates perhaps even greater suspense and ambiguity than in the story concerning whether Farquhar is really already dead (364). "The film flash[es] Farquhar's escape before our eyes with a kind of immediacy that works with the speed of our imagination and still seems rooted in a concrete reality" (364). "Enrico uses slow motion, distorted sound, repeated sequences that expand time, and overexposed lighting to convey Farquhar's inner life and to suggest the unreality of the events of the 'escape'" (364). By circling Farquhar as he swims, the camera seems to suggest that he is going nowhere (365). Yet the film, much more than the story, encourages us to identify with Farquhar and with his will to live (365). Both Farquhar and the viewer share a renewed appreciation for life and of natural beauty (365), although Enrico errs by including a sentimental and too-explicit song (366). The film's ambiguous point of view skillfully blends objectivity and subjectivity (366). By deliberately making Farquhar more sympathetic, Enrico offers "a more generalized indictment of mankind's calculated cruelties" (366). Whereas Bierce's irony is more specifically aimed at the deluded Farquhar, Enrico's irony more generally satirizes war (366–67). The film nowhere implies that Farquhar is a slave-owner (367), nor does the film emphasize either the treachery of the northern scout nor Farquhar's self-delusions (368). Much of Bierce's irony is missing from the film (368). The film emphasizes barren trees when focusing on the hanging and leafy trees as Farquhar runs through the woods toward his home, thus reinforcing the symbolic contrast between death and life (369). "The branches that obscure our view convey the difficulties in seeing and understanding what is happening" (369). In the final shot of the film, the "birdsongs on the soundtrack that ironically proclaim the sunrise and signal the hanging, the sentry's dutiful march back and forth on the bridge, the tangle of branches that nearly obscures the hanged man—all these elements elicit a number of possible reflections from the viewer, among them the general indifference of nature to man, the ritual efficiency of man's inhumanity to man, and the final insignificance of any one man's death" (370). **FORM, THEM, READ-R**

Bie 10. Powers, James G. "Freud and Farquhar: An Occurrence at Owl Creek Bridge?" *Studies in Short Fiction* 19 (1982): 278–81.

Farquhar obviously "was from a structured background, born into an ordered world where formalities counted much among the gentry" (279). Because he thus felt constricted and inhibited, he longed for the release of egoistic, libidinous energies (279–80). His plunge into the water is equivalent to a descent into the dream-world of the *id* and provides him with "a thrilling experience [that is] non-rational in nature" (280). "The reader too, with the surprised hero, has been introduced to that hidden domain of Farquhar's personality, passionate in nature— his unconscious world, alien to anything rational and clamoring for spontaneous expression" (280). While earlier his wife had been described in unexciting, domestic terms, his final vision of her is charged with sexual energy; she becomes "the apotheosis of feminine loveliness and gratification" who is "tantalizing [and] entrancing" (280). Although the end of the story returns both Peyton and Bierce's readers to a mundane reality, Farquhar's "lively sally into the dream world, albeit brief, permitted him to taste emotions long sublimated, but undeniably vibrant and powerful" (280). **PSY, READ-R**

Bie 11. Stoicheff, Peter. "'Something Uncanny': The Dream Structure in Ambrose Bierce's 'An Occurrence at Owl Creek Bridge.'" *Studies in Short Fiction* 30 (1993): 349–58.

The detailed, dream-like description of the "escape" actually hints at the details of the hanging that is really taking place (349–51). The brief moment of dying "divides itself into infinite units of experience, saturating the mind with stimuli"; ironically, the swinging body becomes a kind of pendulum (351). Many details in Farquhar's dream suggest the physical details of the hanging. For instance, in his dream Farquhar is in motion (like his falling body); the cracking and smashing sounds in his dream actually mimic the sound of his neck breaking; and his sense of upward movement reflects the brief jump of a hanged body (352). Yet the dream is also shaped by Farquhar's deep desire to feel heroic and be victorious (354–55), and his desire to escape death is symbolically depicted as a kind of birth in which he breaks free from an attached cord (355). Bierce's story thus reflects and anticipates psychological accounts of the functions of dreams (356). **THEM, PSY**

R.C.E.

"THE DEMON LOVER"

Bow 1. Austin, Allan E. *Elizabeth Bowen: Revised Edition.* Boston: Twayne, 1989. Pp. 73–75.

Bowen's evocation of setting and mood emphasizes Mrs. Drover's growing hysteria and contributes to the story's tension (73). The abandoned house is symbolically linked to her subconscious (73). Whether the haunting is real "hardly matters: to Mrs. Drover it is real and her fear-driven energy gains [from the reader] a willing suspension of disbelief. However, a subtle undertext provides a psychological explanation" (74). At the beginning of the story, Mrs. Drover is already psychologically vulnerable (74); she thus illustrates Bowen's tendency to "put into situations the characters who will be most sensitive to them" (74). Even when she first knew her fiancé, Mrs. Drover sought security and safety more than love; perhaps she felt unattractive to other men (75). By the end of the story she is terrified by the possessiveness that at first made her fiancé appealing (75). **FORM, THEM, PSY**

Bow 2. Calder, Robert L. "'A More Sinister Troth': Elizabeth Bowen's 'The Demon Lover' as Allegory." *Studies in Short Fiction* 31 (1994): 91–97.

Nothing suggests that Mrs. Drover is unhappily married; the lover is not technically sadistic or a psychopath; and realistic, rational interpretations of the story fail (92–93). The lover is not individualized or made sympathetic; instead he symbolizes the violence of war (94–95). His return represents the return of war; the taxi, normally a symbol of safety, becomes a symbol of mechanized brutality (96). This allegorical story appears in a collection focused on wartime experiences; it suggests the links between the two world wars, and Kathleen's helplessness symbolizes the feelings of millions of Europeans in 1941 (97). **THEM**

Bow 3. DeVitis, A.A. "The Demon Lover." *Masterplots II: Short Story Series.* Ed. Frank N. Magill. 6 vols. Pasadena, CA: Salem Press, 1986. 2: 565–67.

Although the story "can be read as a modern retelling of the folk legend and the ballads concerning the return of a lover from the dead to reclaim his earthly bride," this may not be the most fruitful interpretation (566). In a postscript to the volume in which the story appeared, Bowen emphasized the whole book's focus on "'life, mechanized by the control of war-time ... emotionally torn and impoverished by change'" (566). In this story, pressures generated by World War I are reignited by World War II, so that the work's main focus is "a nervous collapse" (566). Bowen is unusual in dealing with the war-time experiences of civilians rather than with combatants (566–67). Bowen uses third-person narration and effective juxtaposition, especially of past and present, thus implying that the past always lies mentally latent (567). The fact that Kathleen does not marry for so many years after losing her initial lover partly implies "the decimation of a generation by the machine of war" (567). Now in her forties, she faces another change of life, so that the letter, itself signed "K.," may be a hallucination by which she recaptures part of her past (567). **FORM, HIST, THEM**

Bow 4. Fraustino, Daniel V. "Elizabeth Bowen's 'The Demon Lover': Psychosis or Seduction?" *Studies in Short Fiction* 17 (1980): 483–87.

Douglas Hughes's psychological reading of the story is unconvincing and depends on assumptions the story does not support (483). The tale, a "well-wrought mystery of high suspense" (483), does not imply that Mrs. Drover suffered a complete, traumatic mental collapse after her fiancé was lost in the war (483–84). Instead, her reaction to the empty house (associated with images of "age and death, of repetition and stagnation") represents her reaction to an empty, unsatisfying marriage (484). Rather than depicting Mrs. Drover as deluded, Bowen emphasizes the clarity of her thinking; she shows no signs of "incipient mania" (484–85). In the published collection, this story follows another that emphasizes the theme of desertion (485). The same theme is prominent in the English ballad from which Bowen derives her story's title, as is the theme of dissatisfaction with a marriage (485). Both facts suggest that Mrs. Drover also has an unconscious desire to leave her marriage (486). The man in the taxi really is Mrs. Drover's former fiancé, whose death was only presumed. Bowen had depicted him during the courtship as a sadist, and now she depicts him as a psychopathic killer (486). Although such an interpretation cannot pretend to offer a realistic explanation for every detail of the story, it makes more sense than seeing Mrs. Drover as deranged (486–87). The fact that not every detail can be realistically explained is related to the fact that "the story's thrilling suspense seems almost to depend on the reader's own sense of dislocation, on the interruption of logical cause and effect" (487). Hughes's flawed reading depends on something for which the text provides no evidence: "a fluctuating narrative point of view—one moment an objective third person, the next the centered consciousness of an hysteric" (487). **THEM, PSY, READ-R**

Bow 5. Green, James L., and George O'Brien. "Elizabeth Bowen." *Critical Survey of Short Fiction*. Ed. Frank N. Magill. Revised ed. 7 vols. Pasadena, CA: Salem Press, 1993. 1: 261–68.

The deserted house symbolizes Kathleen's empty existence as a wife; by marrying William Drover, she betrayed both her lover and herself (265). Motivated by unconscious desires to visit the house, she finds the letter she herself had written, while the sound of the "intruder" leaving the house is a projection of her own repressed identity seeking to escape the marriage (265). Symbolically, her marriage represents England's rejection of its own ideals; archetypally, Kathleen and her lover are comparable to Adam and Eve, as their meeting in a garden beneath a tree implies (266). By making the pact with the soldier, Kathleen suffers the same kind of alienation as Eve, and the story ultimately suggests that the "failure of love condemns Kathleen—and by implication humankind—to insanity and damnation in the modern wasteland" (266). **THEM, PSY, ARCH**

Bow 6. Hughes, Douglas A. "Cracks in the Psyche: Elizabeth Bowen's 'The Demon Lover.'" *Studies in Short Fiction* 10 (1973): 411–13.

The story is "a masterful dramatization of acute psychological delusion, of the culmination of paranoia in a time of war" (411). The point of view is restricted to that of the disturbed Kathleen Drover, whose loss of her fiancé during World War I plunged her into a serious emotional collapse from which she never fully recovered (411). As she returns to her house and sees evidence of the new loss of her most recent past, she feels a growing awareness of time and death (411–12). "For Mrs. Drover, psychologically maimed and predisposed to a sense of loss, the return to the house is a shattering revelation, a threshold experience that activates her dormant hysteria" (412). Her guilt over the loss of her lover and her subsequent remarriage made him seem "a cold, ominous figure in her diseased imagination"; the flashback is filtered through her presently disturbed mind (412). Her guilt and paranoia eventually lead her to hallucinate about the letter and its imagined message (412). "The paper on the bed may well exist but the message is a fabrication of her own mind" (413). In the taxi she finally crosses over into madness as she imagines herself being kidnapped (413). The story is "a pathetic psychological drama" (413). **FORM, THEM, PSY**

Bow 7. Lassner, Phyllis. *Elizabeth Bowen: A Study of the Short Fiction.* New York: Twayne, 1991. Pp. 64–67.

The story, effective because of its brevity, uses "psychological horror" and "sex antagonism" to show "how rage transcends time and space" (64). The politely worded letter is nonetheless extremely egocentric; it presumes a "male fantasy of total devotion" (65). Kathleen is trapped whether she waits for her lover or whether she marries (65); the final capture simply makes explicit the domination her lover had always exercised (66). Even in their earlier final meeting he had been ghost-like and cruel; although a soldier, he is evil and nonheroic (66). He is the product of larger historical forces, and his uncertain death symbolizes the havoc war can wreak (66). "This ghost is not terrorizing the woman because she fails to fill the emptiness in his life. Terrorized himself by historical forces he cannot redirect, much less understand, he imposes a promise on his fiancée that will provide the one stabilizing element in his life and death" (66). Even his signature—"K"—suggests that Kathleen may become merely his reflection (66–67). **THEM, FEM**

R.C.E.

"PAUL'S CASE"

Cat 1. Arnold, Marilyn. *Willa Cather's Short Fiction*. Athens: Ohio University Press, 1984. Pp. 60–65.

Paul seems eccentric, "maybe even half-crazy" (61), and the structure of the story itself is bold, abruptly juxtaposing the first and second parts (61). "Paul's Case" provides an appropriate conclusion to the theme of the whole collection of stories; he is a "hungry forest child" who cannot resist "the luscious appeal of the garden" (61). Yet he also typifies Cather's focus on aliens: he rejects mere human love and falsely assumes that his problems can be solved by changing his environment (62). Because he cannot see reality clearly, he alienates himself from everything (62). Cather's view of Paul's neighborhood seems more sympathetic than his; in any case the materialistic values he pursues in New York do not really differ from those he thinks he rejects (62). He lacks knowledge of true art; the real artists in the story work hard and are not deluded (63). For Paul, "[a]rt equals shine; shine equals wealth" (63). He is like the hothouse flowers with which he surrounds himself; he cannot survive in the real world (64). **FORM, HIST, THEM**

Cat 2. Carpenter, David A. "Why Willa Cather Revised 'Paul's Case': The Work in Art and Those Sunday Afternoons." *American Literature* 59 (1987): 590–608.

Cather's revisions make the story more subtle, de-emphasize heredity, and instead stress "an extremely bleak" environmental determinism (591). She deleted phrasing that linked Paul's problems to his mother (592) and that had given his and his parents' experience with the West (593). Far from being an artist, Paul reveals a "pretentiously fraudulent temperament" (597), and Cather disdains both Paul and his constricted home environment (598). He lives in illusion and achieves no self-discovery (607). Cather depicts a determinism "even more extreme than Calvin's" since it is controlled by an essentially amoral industrial society" obsessed with wealth (608). Paul never really escapes the values this environment dictates. **HIST, THEM**

Cat 3. Daiches, David. *Willa Cather: A Critical Introduction.* Ithaca, NY: Cornell University Press, 1951. Pp. 144–47.

The story's rather conventional purpose is to explore "the strange shapes the desire for beauty can take where an atmosphere of genteel ugliness removes all normal opportunities for aesthetic growth and stifles and distorts all natural sensitivities" (146). The work is part of Cather's attempt to justify her role as artist, but "although she displays a fine sense of atmosphere and considerable skill in describing interiors, ... these are not yet wholly put at the service of her art" (146). Like some other early stories, this one is a bit too propagandistic (146–47). **THEM, HIST, FORM**

Cat 4. Myering, Sheryl L. *A Reader's Guide to the Short Stories of Willa Cather.* New York: G.K. Hall, 1994. Pp. 184–92.

Topics covered include publication history; circumstances of composition, sources, and influences; relationship to other Cather works; and interpretations and criticism. The story's original subtitle was "A Study in Temperament"; variously revised versions of the work have appeared, but most recent editions use the original 1905 text (184). The story was composed between 1901 and 1903 (184), and Paul's experiences parallel, in some respects, Cather's own in Pittsburgh, especially her attraction to the symphony and the theater (185). Like Paul, she also visited New York in the winter and was attracted by the arts and by the idea of escaping from dreary circumstances (185). James Woodress has claimed that a youth in one of Cather's Latin classes provided a model for Paul, and an early reviewer asserted that the story reflected a real event, well known in Pittsburgh, in which two boys absconded to Chicago with $2000 (186). Erik Thurin has compared Paul to Narcissus and has likened his New York bathing to Roman baths that Cather associated with decadence (186). "Paul's Case" has not been as easily linked to the epigraphs for *The Troll Garden* as have some other stories from that collection, although the story has been connected thematically with other works in that volume (186–87). One reason for the story's wide appearance in anthologies may be "that it was the only story Cather would allow to be reprinted during the last years of her life" (188). Some critics have read it as an indictment of materialistic mediocrity, but other interpreters have been less sympathetic to Paul, claiming that he is not a true artist and that he is largely responsible for his unhappiness (188). John A. Weigle even diagnosed him as a schizophrenic (188). Other critics have suggested that Paul lives out common human fantasies, while some see biographical connections with Cather's own early life—especially her rejection of standard sexual roles (189). Homosexuality is a theme stressed by Larry Rubin and Claude J. Summers, while Cynthia Briggs argues that the story typifies

Cather's tendency to describe enclosed rooms offering panoramic perspectives (191). **HIST, THEM, MULTI, PSY, PLUR**

Cat 5. O'Brien, Sharon. *Willa Cather: The Emerging Voice.* New York: Oxford University Press, 1987. Pp. 282–85.

This well crafted story, an improvement on Cather's earlier fiction, explores the mind and temper of a romantic (282). Cather here achieves an ironic distance from her protagonist that had been missing in some earlier works, which tended to be too autobiographical. Psychological and social observations are here effectively blended, and the story offers social commentary without being too heavy-handed (282). Appearing last in Cather's collection *The Troll Garden*, this story sums up motifs and other aspects from the works that precede it (282). Paul shares Cather's own love for music and theater and her impatience not only with middle-class conventions (symbolized by the pictures of Washington and Calvin) but also with prescribed gender roles (283). Nevertheless, Cather implies that his outlook is not entirely healthy; he is a kind of "parasite-vampire greedily drawing life from an external source" (283). Ironically, Paul's temperament is not that of an artist; he is passive rather than creative, and he is egotistically satisfied with mere physical comfort (283–84). He seeks escape rather than challenge; his choice of death is linked to the earlier "forms of self-dissolution he has pursued" (284). Yet Cather nevertheless presents Paul with some sympathy, and she seems especially sympathetic to his rejection of "polarized sex roles" (285). **FORM, THEM, HIST, FEM, MULTI**

Cat 6. Page, Philip. "The Theatricality of Willa Cather's 'Paul's Case.'" *Studies in Short Fiction* 28 (1991): 553–57.

Theatricality is important to the story's plot and theme: Paul is repeatedly depicted as a sort of costumed actor whose various roles and self-consciousness fragment his life (553–55). Attracted by theatricality but aware of its limits, Cather uses the theatrical metaphor to "portray Paul as intimately as she wants, and yet ... remain aloof" (556). **THEM**

Cat 7. Pitcher, Edward W. "Willa Cather's 'Paul's Case' and the Faustian Temperament." *Studies in Short Fiction* 28 (1991): 543–52.

Like Faust, Paul sells his soul for temporary pleasures (543). The wild boy from San Francisco bears some resemblance to Faust's Mephistopheles (549). **THEM, HIST**

Cat 8. Rubin, Larry. "The Homosexual Motif in Willa Cather's 'Paul's Case.'" *Studies in Short Fiction* 12 (1975): 127–31.

Because the story was first published during the height of Victorian prudery, Cather merely drops obvious hints about Paul's sexuality, which intensifies his sense of alienation (127–28). Paul dresses as a dandy, seems effeminate, fears his father, and has only two significant relationships in the story—both with boys his own age (128–30). The fact that Paul's departure from the Yale student is unfriendly suggests that the latter rejected Paul's sexual interest in him (130). Paul's pervasive sense of fear (especially of his father) suggests the secret Cather implies (130–31). **HIST, MULTI, THEM**

Cat 9. Salda, Michael N. "What Really Happens in Cather's 'Paul's Case'?" *Studies in Short Fiction* 29 (1992): 113–19.

Throughout the story, Paul fantasizes and day-dreams, especially after moments of excitement (114). Is it therefore possible that Paul, while alone in the basement, only *imagines* his escape to New York? (115). The escape seems almost too good to be literally true (117), and when Paul at the end drops back "into the design of things," Cather suggests that his fantasy has burst—not that he literally commits suicide (118). **THEM, PSY**

Cat 10. Sedgwick, Eve Kosofsky. "Across Gender, across Sexuality: Willa Cather and Others." *South Atlantic Quarterly* 88 (1989): 53–72.

Just as Cather the English teacher at first rejected Oscar Wilde's sexuality and art, so Paul is rejected by his own English teacher (64). Perhaps "Cather, in this story, does something to cleanse her own sexual body of the carrion stench of Wilde's victimization" by identifying with Paul's complicated sexuality (65). **HIST, MULTI**

Cat 11. Summers, Claude J. "'A Losing Game in the End': Aestheticism and Homosexuality in Cather's 'Paul's Case.'" *MFS: Modern Fiction Studies* 36 (1990): 103–19.

Seeing the story as a response to aestheticism and the Oscar Wilde scandal helps clarify its treatment of homosexuality (104). At first Cather's attitudes to Wilde and aestheticism were negative, but "Paul's Case" reveals her changed opinions (104–7). Paul resembles Wilde, and although his homosexuality is not openly stated, it is frequently implied (107–9). Yet "the cause of Paul's unhappiness and suicide is not his homosexuality but his inability to integrate his homosexuality into real life. This inability is itself the result of the homophobia that pervades his society and that he himself internalizes" (110). The omniscient narration contributes to the story's complexity, creating sympathy for Paul without completely endorsing his perspective (110). Although his society deserves blame, his own lack of imagination helps lead to his tragedy, just as Wilde was partly responsible for his own fate (110). Paul lacks the imaginative sympathy and empathy he needs to be successful as an artist and human being (111–12). Cather criticizes both dull social conformism and the aesthetes' disdain for the ordinary, yet the story also shows a growth in Cather's ability to sympathize with Wilde and his ideas (117). Cather sees imagination and agape love as possible "antidotes to alienation and anomie" (117). She implies that homosexuals need social integration (not separation) and self-acceptance rather than self-hatred (117). Although Cather can perhaps be accused of blaming the victim, her story evokes the kind of imaginative response it implicitly values (118). **HIST, MULTI, FORM**

Cat 12. Thurin, Erik Ingvar. *The Humanization of Willa Cather: Classicism in an American Classic.* Lund: Lund University Press, 1990. Pp. 134–37.

In this story Cather subtly alludes to the classics rather than offering many obvious references (134); in this sense it foreshadows her later writing, and the allusions contribute to the story's success (134). Paul's bathing at the Waldorf recalls a custom Cather associated with Roman decadence (134–35). The theme of homosexuality is linked to allusions to the self-loving Narcissus (135), and Oedipal overtones emerge in Paul's fear that his father will kill him ("which can easily be taken as a suppressed desire to kill his father" [136]). Symbolism associating the Mediterranean with "a free and Dionysian approach to life" is also important in the story, and such symbolism, like everything else, is "perfectly integrated" (136). **HIST, THEM, PSY, FORM**

Cat 13. Wasserman, Loretta. *Willa Cather: A Study of the Short Fiction.* Boston: Twayne, 1991. Pp. 21–26.

Cather said that Paul was based both on a boy she had taught and on her own first impressions of New York City and its stately hotels (22). While some critics think the story emphasizes the powerful influence of a person's environment, others see Paul as an emotionally immature boy who rejects a normal if unglamorous community (24). Perhaps Cather was influenced by the psychologist William James, who described persons paralyzed by their over-indulgence in artistic pleasure (24). The fact that the story lends itself to divergent readings suggests its beautiful tension and complexity, especially in its latter half, which appeals to a basic human desire "to win without desert or guilt" (24). Even in death Paul feels no remorse or regret; Cather refuses to rig the story in favor of sentimental moralism (25). Paul lives out a basic human dream of unfettered self-indulgence (25). **HIST, FORM, THEM**

R.C.E.

"THE OPEN BOAT"

Cra 1. Adams, Richard P. "Naturalistic Fiction: 'The Open Boat.'" In *Stephen Crane's Career: Perspectives and Evaluations.* Ed. Thomas A. Gullason. New York: New York University Press, 1972. Pp. 421–29.

Realism, naturalism, and symbolism all developed within a general romantic tradition (421). The narrative framework of Crane's story involves "a loss of safety, an approach to safety, a retreat from safety, and a flawed achievement of safety" (422). The sense that nature is alien to human emotions (the distinguishing trait of naturalism) is best symbolized in this story by the cold, distant star (423). Yet much of naturalism's emotional power derives from "a submerged but still vital belief in the romantic world of warmth and relatedness" (424): the correspondent sounds like a "frustrated romantic" (424), and the story is full of "contrast and tension" (425) between the naturalistic and romantic views of nature. Crane's animistic imagery suggests, ironically, that nature is indeed alive and willful (424), and Crane uses "nearly a hundred more or less distinct terms" suggesting color—a typical trait of his style (425). Such imagery, like the animistic language, heightens "the contrast between the [colorful] world of man's desiring and the [bleak] world of so-called objective reality" (426). Whereas a naturalistic view might seem to reduce everything to "material cause and effect," Crane (like most naturalists) is unwilling or unable to make this sacrifice: "his men ... remain in possession of their souls. Indeed, as a result of their experience, and quite in the traditional romantic fashion, they find or save their souls; that is, they grow stronger, wiser, broader, and more mature" (426). The story thus follows a romantic pattern of death and rebirth; facing death deepens the men's mutual love and understanding of life (426). "Crane apparently wants some stable certainty in human character to oppose to the deadly certainties of science" (427), suggesting that because nature is indifferent, humans should be true to one another (427). Although naturalism is a defensive (and perhaps inevitably defeated) position, Crane makes great art from his ambivalent, conflicting views (427–28). **HIST, FORM, THEM**

Cra 2. Billingslea, Oliver. "Why Does the Oiler 'Drown'? Perception and Cosmic Chill in 'The Open Boat.'" *American Literary Realism* 27.1 (1994): 23–41.

Crane's emphasis on lived experience forestalls any effort to discern any large, general "truths"; he shows how our emotions affect and alter our perceptions (23–24). The story emphasizes "contraries, especially between the object perceived and the temperament of the perceiver," thus highlighting "acts of seeing, both literal and metaphorical, on the part of the persona, characters, and reader" (26). "What is most important in our reading of the story is the process of deciphering, repeating the process the men undergo as they try to be interpreters—readers of their own experience" (28). Crane is as interested in acts of perception and presentation as in experiences themselves since all three are inseparable (28). In trying to decide why the oiler, of all the men, is the one who drowns, various explanations suggest themselves, including greater exhaustion from all his work (28) and failure to hold on to part of the boat when he enters the water (31). Moreover, if "Darwin's explanations help clarify the oiler's death (he did not adapt), so too do Marx's (he willingly sacrificed himself, perceiving it his place)—so too does the Newtonian mechanistic indifference of the universe (he was simply in the wrong place at the wrong time)" (36). Finally, though, the story shows "the failure of the imagination to confront the forces of the universe relativistically. As an impressionist work, it denies, as it must, the transcendental, except as an illusion in the theatre of the mind" (39). The story concerns both physical adventure and the nature of consciousness (39). **THEM, READ-R, HIST**

Cra 3. Cady, Edwin H. *Stephen Crane.* Revised ed. Boston: Twayne, 1980. Pp. 150–54.

Although many critics have interpreted the story autobiographically, its great artistry deserves more emphasis, especially its masterful control of three points of view—of the group, the narrator, and the correspondent (151). The perspectives of the men are most important. Crane should not be simply identified with the correspondent, who tends to see nature as indifferent and man as pitiable or absurd (153). Another view of the human condition, however, is implied in the Christ-like conduct of Billy, who does most to create the solidarity that makes man seem anything but absurd (153–54). The story implies "that man by courage and complicity can rise superior to the pathos of his situation; he can understand it and answer it with the magnificence of his defiance, his acceptance, and perhaps even his use of it to achieve a classically tragic elevation" (154). **FORM, THEM, LON**

Cra 4. Gordon, Caroline, and Allen Tate. *The House of Fiction: An Anthology of the Short Story with Commentary*. New York: Scribner's, 1950. Pp. 308–12.

"H.G. Wells called 'The Open Boat' 'the finest short story in English'" (308). Crane's writing generally offers "a stronger illusion of reality than any of his contemporaries were able to offer" (308), and he is especially effective in creating narrative authority (309). The opening paragraph of this story "brought about a revolution in the writing of fiction, at least in the English speaking world" (310), and in general it is "hard to find a more masterly use of the Roving Narrator" method, since the "correspondent functions dramatically throughout" (310). Crane convincingly describes sensations, in part by constantly shifting points of view (311), not only among the men but between panoramas and close-ups, thus contributing to the work's unity of tone (312). "On one level the Complication ... of the story is the correspondent's facing death, the Resolution his escape from it"; in the process he "attains heroic stature" (312). **FORM, ARIS**

Cra 5. Kissane, Leedice. "Interpretation Through Language: A Study of the Metaphors in Stephen Crane's 'The Open Boat.'" In *Stephen Crane's Career: Perspectives and Evaluations*. Ed. Thomas A. Gullason. New York: New York University Press, 1972. Pp. 410–16.

Crane uses physical encounters to symbolize psychic adventures; all humans are adrift in an open boat (410). The story's interest resides in the narrator's eventual acceptance of life's struggle and his ability to find solaces that make it endurable (410). Ironically, Crane uses language "drawn from domestic routines he knew as a boy" (411) to describe the unfamiliar experience of a shipwreck (411). Such language describes the men's actions while also providing insight into the correspondent's consciousness (412). However, the childhood memories implied by the lowly metaphors also suggest man's smallness in relation to nature (412). At first nature seems hostile, then merely indifferent; through his own sufferings the correspondent learns to empathize with the larger human predicament (413–14). Crane's language, especially toward the end, associates women with hospitality, love, and nurturing. This implied emphasis on the need for (and power of) love prevents the story from ending pessimistically (416). **THEM, HIST, FORM**

Cra 6. LaFrance, Marston. *A Reading of Stephen Crane*. Oxford: Clarendon Press, 1971. Pp. 195–205.

Whereas Crane's newspaper account of the actual ship's sinking conveys facts, the story conveys "moral truth" (196). Crane emphasizes the threat by sometimes switching from the point of view of the men to that of a detached narrator (196). At least fifteen references to the hazardous surf help foreshadow the experience the men will undergo (196). However, "this is the only Crane story in which both the protagonist's fears and illusions are dissipated, in which he attains the full awareness typical of the intelligent man after the fact of experience, before the feared unknown is undergone" (197). He realizes nature's indifference early in section six (197), and before the end the men overcome their fear (198). The survivors maturely, calmly accept the oiler's death (198); they already know the indifference of amoral nature and respond with a "stoic humanism" typical of Crane. Any imagined transcendental union with nature is an illusion (200); Mordecai Marcus correctly shows that as the men come to see nature less as hostile than as indifferent, their brotherhood and companionship deepens (200). At first the men are committed to each other's survival; then they realize how their situation typifies the plight of man in general; then they achieve a moral awareness of the need to help others (202–3). "The human commitment to brotherhood in this story enlarges from the immediate group to universal mankind to the social forms man has created for communicating his humanity to other living men" (204). The ending does not symbolize a "romantic death and rebirth" (204), nor is Billy particularly virtuous (or a Christ figure); "Crane's humanism is realistic, neither romantic nor sentimental" (205). Finally, the correspondent *is* a reliable spokesman for Crane; no irony undercuts his narrative authority (205). **FORM, THEM**

Cra 7. Metress, Christopher. "From Indifference to Anxiety: Knowledge and the Reader in 'The Open Boat.'" *Studies in Short Fiction* 28 (1991): 47–53.

The story deals with problems of knowing (47). At first, both reader and characters lack knowledge but seem undisturbed (48); later this lack becomes a source of anxiety for both (49). For a moment the reader briefly gains knowledge the characters do not possess (i.e., that no lighthouse is nearby), but then the glimpse of the mysterious man waving the coat plunges both back into ignorance (50). Finally, in the story's frustrating last sentence, the characters possess a knowledge the reader lacks: they know how they will interpret the experience (51). Crane thus suggests that direct experience provides greater insight than mere reading (51). "This failure of reading alone, without the aid of experience, to open up and create a more profound and perfect understanding engenders further anxiety in the reader, for while the characters can listen to the 'great sea's voice' and achieve interpretation, the reader can listen only to the text—not experience —and thus now feels necessarily limited in the quest for meaning" (52). The story forces us to feel and share the anxiety of not knowing. **THEM, READ-R**

Cra 8. Metzger, Charles R. "Realistic Devices in Stephen Crane's 'The Open Boat.'" In *Stephen Crane's Career: Perspectives and Evaluations*. Ed. Thomas A. Gullason. New York: New York University Press, 1972. Pp. 417–20.

Although Crane uses an omniscient narrator to make the story convincing by introducing much factual detail, the narrator never tells us too much; we often learn from the dialogue (417–18) and see from limited, individual perspectives, frequently discovering new facts gradually, as the characters do (418). Crane also presents "multiple perspectives, multiple interpretations, and the commission and correction of error" (418); often the characters move from hopeful inaccuracies to disappointing, frustrating realities (419). Repetition is used to foreshadow events and to emphasize obsessive thoughts (419), and although irony is sometimes used too blatantly, in general Crane is convincingly realistic (420). **FORM, DIALOG**

Cra 9. Wolford, Chester L. *The Anger of Stephen Crane*. Lincoln and London: University of Nebraska Press, 1983. Pp. 129–34.

The famous opening sentence suggests that the men are battling the unconscious (the sea) and are deprived of the "light, knowledge, and consciousness" the sky would symbolize (130). The opening passages perhaps allude to classical epics (like the *Odyssey*) also concerned with voyages home, but only in Crane's story "does the quest seem futile" (131). Neither the men nor the readers know which character(s) will survive (131). The ending is paradoxically both lyrical and ironic, and the idea that the men may afterwards serve as "interpreters" may be absurd (132), since there is no larger meaning to learn or interpret. Although the last paragraph is ambiguous and may not be ironic, the endings of other works by Crane preceding it suggest that an ironic reading cannot be excluded (134). **THEM, FORM, HIST**

R.C.E.

"BARN BURNING"

Fau 1. Billingslea, Oliver. "Fathers and Sons: The Spiritual Quest in Faulkner's 'Barn Burning.'" *Mississippi Quarterly* 44 (1991): 287–308.

"Sarty's discovery of self-reliance underscores a maturation, existentialist in nature" (287), and in his escape he "immerses himself in the world of nature" (288). The closing image of the constellations may symbolize Sarty's past and future wanderings, while his closing hunger recalls the opening scene (289). Meanwhile, the fire associated with his father is finally replaced by the rising sun (291). "The synaesthesia of the opening paragraph indicates not just hunger or deprivation but the extent to which Sarty's subconsciousness attempts to distance him from the court's proceedings" and typifies (like the description of Sarty's final run) the flowing prose Faulkner uses in this tale at "points of great pressure" (291). However, in contrast to such pressure-points, "the final passage possesses an incantatory, idyllic, lyrical style which suggests a freedom and peace" (292). Although recent critics have attempted to depict Ab as an almost heroic figure, he is associated more with anarchy, pride, and paranoia than with a struggle for working-class advancement (292–93). Indeed, he "owns his own family, demanding their absolute obedience to his own patriarchal instincts. There is a kind of legalism to his demands," and he consistently demeans women (293). "What Abner Snopes has done—is doing—to his family is to stifle each member's individuality" (293), and his protest against the aristocracy is compromised by his own racist and sexist language and conduct (295). In contrast, Sarty's growing "self-reliance and sense of self-worth may have been stimulated by the ax which his aunt and mother gave him for Christmas, and by their own kindnesses" (297). Sarty may also be motivated by sibling rivalry (with his older, conformist brother) and by the inspirational power of his own name (297). Whatever the cause or causes of his revolt, Sarty eventually realizes that he must escape from Ab's "increasing denigration of the self" if he is "to realize his own humanity" (299–300). Unlike his father's conduct, "Sarty's acts are always on behalf of another" (303); even when he defends his father in the fight, his "concept of justice is a fair confrontation between opponents,

27

each man honorably facing his opponent in the open" (303). Abner, on the other hand, acts secretly and selfishly and seems not to care how his behavior affects his family (303–5). Paradoxically, "it is this complete denigration of human ties on the part of his father that finally sets [Sarty] free" (307). **THEM, FORM, MARX, FEM, MULTI**

Fau 2. Bradford, M.E. "Family and Community in Faulkner's 'Barn Burning.'" *Southern Review* 17 (1981): 332–39.

The end of the story provides "a remarkable release of tension—almost a catharsis—which is a consequence of the reader's participation in the internal conflict of Sarty, the unnatural and hyperbolic choice he is forced to make" (338). Although familial and social ties are normally inseparable, the father's unbending pride leads his son to a rejection of the father that is also an embrace of social, ethical values (338–39). **FORM, THEM, READ-R**

Fau 3. Cackett, Kathy. "'Barn Burning': Debating the American Adam." *Notes on Mississippi Writers* 21.1 (1989): 1–17.

In his book *The American Adam*, R.W.B. Lewis classified American writers as tending to endorse either optimism, pessimism, or a more balanced irony when assessing human nature and the possibilities of American progress (1–2). The optimists rejected the past and external authority and put great faith in the individual, but Ab exemplifies the unbridled egotism such ideas can produce (4–5). "Faulkner shows that Abner Snopes is far from achieving any individuation, completeness, or god-like wholeness, as might be believed by Emerson, Thoreau, or Whitman: rather, he is a narrow, rigid man, actually bordering on being bestial" (7). Although Ab would like to reject both the past and any sense of sin (8–9), Faulkner shows that such escape is impossible (11). "For Faulkner, the American Adam's isolation, individuality, stoicism, and detachment from tradition and law is nothing more than a monstrous license to perpetuate havoc and failure to face the reality that humanity is cast into an imperfect world and forced to assume responsibility to alter that world as best as possible" (15). As Sarty comes to realize this truth, he rejects his father's self-centeredness. **THEM, HIST**

Fau 4. Carothers, James B. *William Faulkner's Short Stories*. Ann Arbor: UMI Research Press, 1985. Pp. 60–64.

The opening paragraph already suggests the multiple levels of awareness the story explores (60). In choosing to disobey his father, Sarty must make a decision that is attractive in theory but personally negative in its practical results, and his choice is even more difficult "because Ab Snopes is not a complete villain" (62). "Ab always behaves in a fashion consistent with his own notion of how he can best preserve his integrity. He is a stern father and husband, but he becomes violent only when he believes that he has been threatened. There is something admirable in his spirit (63). Sarty's final emphasis on his father's bravery is not completely unreliable (63). Yet while Ab is static, Sarty is in the process of development (63), and although the story is partly a tale of initiation, it also offers a "fictional rendering of the Oedipal crisis" (64). **THEM, PSY**

Fau 5. Comprone, Joseph. "Literature and the Writing Process: A Pedagogical Reading of William Faulkner's 'Barn Burning.'" *College Literature* 9.1 (1982): 1–21.

Reader-response theories suggest ways to integrate the teaching of literature with the teaching of writing (1–6), especially by stressing the process of "writing as discovery" to "help students learn how to *read* literature before they attempt to *interpret* it" (6). Faulkner's story can be used as the basis for a series of step-by-step writing assignments that will first encourage students to respond subjectively and then encourage them to formulate objective explanations they can share with others (6–15). The effect of reading a literary text is disruptive and disorienting, whereas the effect of reading exposition should be the opposite (15). By moving through the series of proposed exercises, students should learn not only how to respond to literature but also how to explain their responses clearly (15). "A story such as 'Barn Burning' thus becomes the reader's means of learning to question and revise hypotheses while involved in the acts of reading. Writing a final interpretive response, on the other hand, becomes the means of organizing in-process responses into a 'final' communicable form" (17). **READ-R**

Fau 6. Fowler, Virginia C. *College Language Association Journal* 24 (1981): 513–22.

Because most critics tend to focus on Ab or on Sarty, or on Ab versus de Spain, they fail to emphasize the internal conflict within the boy (513–14). Sarty's choice, however, is not between a wholly negative Ab and a wholly positive de Spain, because de Spain and his cohorts do not themselves live up to the values with which Sarty associates them (514–15). Ab himself became disillusioned with Southern aristocrats (516). Similarly, if "Sarty's belief were simply in the Southern aristocracy, as represented by Major de Spain, then that belief, because based in part on illusion, would be at some point in the future, like Abner's, shattered. But in fact it is on precisely this point that Sarty differs from his father" (517–18). Although he (somewhat mistakenly) associates the aristocrats with the moral values he respects, the source of those values is within himself (518). Ironically, by trying to teach Sarty loyalty to blood ties, Ab introduces him to the abstract concept of loyalty, and although Sarty is strongly bound by emotional ties to his father and family, he ultimately chooses to be loyal to higher values (518–19). However, "for Sarty, Abner and the rest of the family represent the sole emotional bonds he has, and it is only by recognizing the strength and importance of these ties that we can fully appreciate his sacrifice of them to moral responsibility" (519). Paradoxically, Sarty turns on his father only when his father, by failing to warn de Spain, seems to betray his own code of moral conduct; Sarty runs to warn de Spain partly to preserve his own sense of Ab's morality (520). Sarty's cries at the end indicate his recognition that he has lost not simply a loved one but also a person whom he had tried to idealize; his "attempt to convince himself that Abner is brave, is good, is pitiably unconvincing, even to himself, and thus represents his recognition of what his father really is" (520). "Sarty's actions at the end of the story thus spring from his own innate moral impulses, and his new 'loyalty' is ultimately not to de Spain and the Southern aristocracy but to those impulses" (520). **THEM**

Fau 7. Franklin, Phyllis. "Sarty Snopes and 'Barn Burning.'" *Mississippi Quarterly* 21 (1968): 189–93.

Although previous critical approaches have tended to underemphasize Sarty's importance, his experience is central to the story (189). Sarty's first reactions to the de Spain house are partly naive, and in the first confrontation with the de Spains it is Ab who seems in control (190). Only when Sarty feels that Ab has violated his own code does he fully reject his father, and Faulkner artfully makes us see events from Sarty's point of view and thus participate in his development and dilemmas (191). Sarty's growth toward maturity is Faulkner's main focus, and over the course of one week the boy goes from siding with his father (and sharing some male bonding with his father and brother) to rejecting his father, in part because Ab puts him under the control of the women (192). The moral struggle the story explores is less a struggle between the Snopes family and the rest of society than a struggle within Sarty (193). Perhaps the "timid morality" of Sarty's mother is one source of the boy's own growing strength; if so, then the story is not so much about the pull of blood versus the pull of larger ethical values than about the conflict between two aspects of Sarty's own background (193). **THEM, FORM, FEM**

Fau 8. Grimwood, Michael. *Heart in Conflict: Faulkner's Struggles with Vocation.* Athens and London: University of Georgia Press, 1987. Pp. 137–38.

Faulkner sympathized with Sarty and highly valued "Barn Burning" itself, perhaps in part because the story reflected aspects of his own life (137). "Faulkner may have projected his own 'limp,' his own ineffectual father, and his own overly solicitous mother into Sarty's situation. The tone of the story is grim and its style is highly literate" (138). **HIST, PSY, FORM**

Fau 9. Hiles, Jane. "Kinship and Heredity in Faulkner's 'Barn Burning.'" *Mississippi Quarterly* 38 (1985): 329–37.

"Sarty's seeming interruption of the antisocial pattern established by his father is actually a continuation of it, and the ostensible resolution of his moral dilemma [is] actually no resolution at all" (329). Ab rebels against society because he considers his clan to be threatened and potentially exploited by it (331), and just as, during the war, "his sole allegiance to the clan justifies his adoption of the life of an outlaw, independent of society, so his illegal activities necessitate his dependency on the clan for protection from society at large" (332). He is bound to his clan by the same ties that bind Sarty, and he never deserts his family (332). Faulkner himself expressed sympathy for clannishness, a fact which suggests that Sarty's abandonment of his clan may be more ambiguous than is usually assumed (333). The opening scene of the story suggests Sarty's confusion of emotions and intellect and his "failure of understanding" (334–35), and indeed neither the narration nor the presentation of characters is unambiguous (335). Ab himself is torn between "authoritarianism and anarchy" (335), while Sarty's "repudiation of family follows the pattern of alienation, aggression and escape established by his father" (336). He gives loyalty neither to his family nor to De Spain "but turns instead to the woods, a scene reminiscent of his father's fugitive hideaway during the war" (337). His very break with his father implies their connection (337). **HIST, NHIST, MARX, THEM**

Fau 10. Johnston, Kenneth G. "Time of Decline: Pickett's Charge and the Broken Clock in Faulkner's 'Barn Burning.'" *Studies in Short Fiction* 11 (1974): 434–36.

The time on the broken clock in Abner Snopes' wagon alludes to the start of Pickett's charge at the Battle of Gettysburg—a foolishly romantic assault that Faulkner saw as the high-water mark of Confederate hopes and power (434–35). Major de Spain represents this old aristocratic tradition, but time is on the side of the rising class represented by Snopes (436). **THEM, HIST**

Fau 11. Jones, Diane Brown. *A Reader's Guide to the Short Stories of William Faulkner.* New York: G.K. Hall, 1994. Pp. 3–32.

Topics covered include publication history; circumstances of composition, sources, and influences; relationship to other Faulkner works; and interpretation and criticism. The story was rejected five times before being accepted for publication; it was placed first in the *Collected Stories*, although Faulkner at one point had not planned to include it (3).

Most commentary on the textual evolution of the work focuses on its relationship with the later novel *The Hamlet* (3). "Comparisons of manuscripts, typescript, magazine text, and *Collected Stories* versions" of the story "reveal numerous early modifications" (4). Faulkner's ancestors had themselves been troubled by arsonists (4), and critics have suggested other parallels with Faulkner's own life (4–5). Suggested literary parallels for Ab Snopes have included Achilles, Prometheus, the Fisher King, Spenser's Talus, Milton's Satan, and Shakespeare's Iago (5). Sarty's sisters, stirring the boiling pot, have been compared to the witches in *Macbeth*, while the imagery comparing Ab to tin has been traced to Conrad's *The Nigger of the "Narcissus"* (5). Ab has also been compared to Hawthorne's "Black Man," to Melville's Ahab, and to Fitzgerald's Gatsby (5–6). Sarty has been compared and contrasted to Twain's Huckleberry Finn (5–6). Critics have scrutinized the relationship between "Barn Barning" and *The Hamlet*, offering many explanations of their differences (6–9); in the novel the tone shifts from tragic to comic (an unusual transformation for Faulkner), and the focus shifts from the father-son relationship to a contest of wits between Ab and de Spain (8). Critics have also studied the similarities and differences between this story and other works by Faulkner, focusing particularly on how Ab and Sarty appear differently in different works (9–10). Thematic studies of the story have concentrated on such themes as initiation, family loyalty, and matters of class (11–13), and the story has been admired for its complex story-telling, its use of point-of-view, its sophisticated use of language and dialect, and its patterns of imagery (including dwellings, timepieces, injured limbs, and horses [13–16]). The relationship between this work and other tales in the *Collected Stories* has been studied in order to determine how the story fits into (and contributes to) the larger volume (16–17). Interpretations of the story have tended to emphasize either Ab or Sarty as the main character (18). Irving Malin compares their conflict to the tension between the Freudian ego and super-ego; ultimately Sarty gives his allegiance to the latter (18). James Bowen and James Hamby focus on Sarty's development of an independent sense of self (18–19), while Jane Hiles argues that Sarty actually repeats his father's "cycle of 'alienation, aggression, and flight'" (19–20). Critics have differed in their views of Ab. Irvin Howe associates him with envy (20); William Stein links him to Satan (20); Charles Mitchell stresses his will-power and unfettered avarice (20–21); Karl F. Zender focuses on Ab's efforts to teach Sarty (21–22); and Richard C. Moreland offers a relatively sympathetic view of Ab (22). Critics have debated Faulkner's attitude toward the upper classes as described in the story and have also debated whether Sarty's ethics are inspired by society or are inherently personal (23–24). Discussions of the story's narration have focused on Sarty's maturation, on the use of progressive verbs, on multiple voices and manipulations of time, and on combinations of sensations (as in the first paragraph [25–26]). Discussion of imagery has centered on eyes, Ab's stiffness, and symbols of death (26). The critical attention the story has received indicates its significance in the Faulkner canon (26). **HIST, THEM, FORM, PSY, PLUR, ETC.**

Fau 12. Mitchell, Charles. "The Wounded Will of Faulkner's Barn Burner." *Modern Fiction Studies* 11 (1965): 185–89.

Abner's wounded foot is used symbolically to suggest his ruthless but wounded will (185). Unlike his son, he excludes rather than embraces emotion; he is amoral and self-centered. "His will's godlike freedom from moral restrictions was stopped when the representative of moral authority, the military policeman, wounding him in the heel, judged and punished him" (186). His wounded heel links him with the similar limits imposed on Achilles and on Meville's Ahab, while his directionless, stubborn, proud defiance links him with Satan (186). Just as Satan is linked with fire and sought to destroy God's garden, so Abner burns barns (187). To Sarty the de Spain plantation is almost Edenic; his father, however, burns barns repeatedly because he tries to relive and reverse the moment when his freedom of will was first limited (187). Ironically, his self-assertion becomes a kind of self-degrading self-imprisonment, and the fenced-in pig symbolizes his reluctantly fenced-in appetite (187). Abner rejects reciprocity and relationships, the foundations of morality; when he arrives at the de Spain plantation he repeats his earlier mistakes by reasserting his untrammeled freedom and his rejection of authority (188). Although frequently tried, Abner always also functions as accuser, judge, and executioner, using fire (an ancient symbol of will, linked with Prometheus, who stole fire from the gods [188]). Unlike his father, Sarty links his will with his heart or emotions; he tries to achieve freedom within moral limits (189). In the final scene, his harmony with external nature suggests the inner harmony of this man-child, and he knows that the rising sun will cause the stiffness in his own legs to relax (189). **THEM, FORM**

Fau 13. Moreland, Richard C. *Faulkner and Modernism: Rereading and Rewriting.* Madison: University of Wisconsin Press, 1990. Pp. 3–22.

"Revisionary repetition" involves incremental growth, change, learning, and development; "compulsive repetition" is static and resists change (4–5). Faulkner's own development shows that he was capable of (and interested in) repetition that involved revision and learning, and "Barn Burning" occurs at a pivotal moment in his career, poised between compulsive and revisionary repetition (7). Ab Snopes becomes a more humorous, more sympathetic figure in *The Hamlet* (8), but even in "Barn Burning" Ab is a provocative figure who threatens social conformity and exposes the violence by which it preserves itself (12–13).

Even if Sarty cannot appreciate his father's impertinence, Faulkner encourages us to do so (13). When Ab smears excrement on the rug at the plantation, he exposes the plantation as a place of exploitation and exclusion for blacks and poor whites (13–14). As in his use of oxymorons, Faulkner refuses to reconcile or smooth over contradictions (14–15). Sarty, however, "finally cannot appreciate Ab's unaccountable difference from his society's dominant dialectics of master and slave, planter and tenant, white and black, clean and filthy, legal and criminal; unable to read Ab's difference as a potential criticism of the exclusive terms of those dialectics, Sarty reads it more simply as a condemnation of Ab and perhaps of Sarty himself" (17). Even when, at the end, Sarty imagines Ab as once having been heroic, he accepts conventional, conservative definitions of heroism (18). **THEM, HIST, MARX, DECON, NHIST**

Fau 14. Parr, Susan Resneck. *The Moral of the Story: Literature, Values, and American Education.* New York: Teachers College Press, 1982. Pp. 131–36.

Sarty's choice raises the question of the extent to which any individual can exercise free will, especially since Sarty has begun to imitate some of his father's behavior—for example, by showing disdain for his mother (131). Although the story shows that an individual choice can make a difference, it also shows the painful and enduring consequences such choices can involve, and it makes Sarty's decision all the more difficult by refusing to make Ab a complete villain (132). Yet Ab does reveal his cruelty by ordering his wife to hold Sarty, thus making her an accomplice (134–35). Although Ab has some notion of equity (as when he cuts the sandwich into three equal pieces), he usurps the law and dehumanizes others by over-valuing material possessions (136). Paradoxically, however, in the story's final moments de Spain behaves in much the same way (136). **THEM, FEM**

Fau 15. Phillips, Gene D. *Fiction, Film, and Faulkner: The Art of Adaptation.* Knoxville: University of Tennessee Press, 1988. Pp. 174–79.

Sarty knows that it is wrong to destroy a person's barn, "and with it the individual's harvest or livestock, because of some petty grievance" (175). In the story, Sarty never discovers his father's shameful conduct during the war, though the reader does; in the PBS film, however, Sarty's discovery of this fact finally destroys his false image of Ab and helps motivate his rebellion (177). Whereas Sarty is not actually bound with rope in the story, in the film his struggle to loosen the ropes symbolizes his whole internal struggle (178). In the film (as opposed to the story), Sarty knows that his father has survived; his decision not to return to his family, therefore, is motivated not by guilt but by the knowledge that he cannot go back (178). By beginning and ending the film with shots of the family travelling by wagon, with Ab's hands firmly grasping the reins, the director implies Ab's dominance as well as the recurrent patterns of their lives (178). Some scenes in the film were shot in and around Faulkner's own Mississippi home, and Faulkner's nephew Jim was cast as Major de Spain, whose house represents the stability Sarty's family lacks (179). **THEM, FORM, HIST**

Fau 16. Reed, Joseph W., Jr. *Faulkner's Narrative.* New Haven and London: Yale University Press, 1973. Pp. 43–46.

Generally Faulkner's first-person stories narrated by children present the main character as static; by using third-person narrative in "Barn Burning," Faulkner successfully depicts a child's psychological growth (43). "A first-person solution would have severely limited 'Barn Burning'; instead the third-person with a strong point of view is combined with rhythmic interruptions of objective narration and dramatic dialogue, and all of this is set within an elaborate series of time devices" (43). By combining many intense thoughts and sensations, the opening sentences make us empathize with Sarty (43). Sarty's own italicized comments, which move from simple to complex, reflect his maturation (44–45). Stylistically, the "long run-on flows of prose come at points of great pressure. The final passage moves into [an] incantatory, idyllic prose style ... to deal with freedom, the peace which lies outside the frantic circle of recurrence" [i.e., of repeated crimes and relocations]. It contrasts with the claustrophobic, hungering, sensual run-on paragraph which begins the story, making clear the line between imprisonment and freedom" (46). Similarly the boy moves from being passive to being active (46). **FORM, READ-R, THEM**

Fau 17. Rio-Jelliffe, R. "The Language of Time in Fiction: A Model in Faulkner's 'Barn Burning.'" *Journal of Narrative Technique* 24.2 (1994): 98–113.

The story "interweaves two points of view and voices or styles, each with its own distinct time frame" (102), counterpointing "the contrary views and voices of the bewildered child and the knowledgeable man he becomes twenty years later" (103). "Time tilts back and forth from one sentence to the next, or even within a single sentence, when the child's inarticulate groping breaks through the man's skilled cadences" (103). The two voices qualify, subvert, and ironize one another (104). For example, "the older narrator relates what the boy cannot articulate, and also what he apprehends but would deny. When the boy raises false hopes against what he knows to be true, the narrator exposes the self-deception, instantly bringing the future to bear upon the present" (107). On the other hand, when the narrator seems to explain or justify

Abner, he seems morally less impressive than Sarty (109). **FORM, DIA-LOG, THEM**

Fau 18. Ross, Stephen M. *Fiction's Inexhaustible Voice: Speech and Writing in Faulkner*. Athens and London: University of Georgia Press, 1989. Pp. 13–15.

"Barn Burning" exemplifies Faulkner's (and other writers') use of distinct "voices" in fiction. These include a *"phenomenal"* voice (which refers to the acts of speech or writing in a story); a *"mimetic"* voice (which imitates different patterns of speech); a *psychic* voice (which expresses the internal discourse going on in a character's mind); and an *intertextual* voice (the more omniscient voice of the author or narrator). In "Barn Burning" and in other works of fiction, these voices are intermingled and entangled (15). Faulkner discriminates between different characters (such as Sarty and Ab) by distinguishing how they talk (13). Moreover, both the word "voice" and also different examples of distinct voices repeatedly occur in the story, and Faulkner skillfully uses different kinds of dialect (13). Additionally, some of the most important events in the story take the form of different "speech-acts"—different ways of speaking (or of refusing to speak). For instance, at first Sarty refuses to speak out against his father, but by the end of the story his decision to do so constitutes his major act of rebellion (14). Much of the story focuses on the inner voice of Sarty's own mind (often represented by italicized passages) as the boy struggles to decide which outer voices he should obey (14). The story's narrative voice (which provides, for example, information about Ab about which Sarty is ignorant) is recognizably Faulknerian in the extravagant nature of its figurative language and its sentence structure (15). **DIALOG, FORM**

Fau 19. Stein, William Bysshe. "Faulkner's Devil." *Modern Language Notes* 76 (1961): 731–32.

Ironically, Abner's name literally means "Father [God] is light," and Faulkner gives him various characteristics of Satan (731). Thus he seems as insubstantial as tin (731), has a wounded heel and a claw-like hand (731), is associated with fecal matter, possesses a "diabolical hatred that is as consuming as God's love" (732), and reveals "a tormenting yet immovable regretfulness that leads to the motiveless malignity sometimes assigned to [Shakespeare's] Iago" (732). His "robotlike perversity" and "contempt for tradition and order" foretell the modern world's "depraved mechanization of all values" (732). **FORM, HIST, THEM**

Fau 20. Trilling, Lionel. *The Experience of Literature: A Reader with Commentaries. Fiction.* New York: Holt, Rinehart, and Winston, 1967. Pp. 321–24.

Faulkner seems to have enjoyed depicting persons like Major de Spain, who are "principled," "magnanimous," and "incapable of acting for their own advantage," and who seem to represent "the ideal of personal honor" (321). However, although by "every ethical, social, and personal standard Faulkner condemns and despises [such characters as] the Snopeses, ... it is plain that they fascinate him" and "he seems to take as much pleasure in their contemptibleness as in the admirable traits" of characters such as Major de Spain (322). The reader is torn, like Sarty, for Ab "has much more at stake" than Major de Spain and is "the more morally serious of the two" (324). "In this story, indeed, the magnanimous Major de Spain does not show to the best advantage. His rage over the rug ... is of course wholly justified, yet it sinks to a kind of childishness before Abner Snopes's passion for independence, even though that is virtually an insanity" (324). Snopes exhibits "integration and definiteness," and his criticism of the major's wealth has some justice (324). **HIST, THEM, READ-R**

Fau 21. Volpe, Edmond L. "'Barn Burning': A Definition of Evil." In *Faulkner: The Unappeased Imagination: A Collection of Critical Essays.* Ed. Glenn O. Carey. Troy, NY: Whitston, 1980. Pp. 75–82.

Class conflict is not central in this story; Sarty's egotistical father disdains rich and poor alike (76). Whereas the father is rigid and metallic, the imagery of the final paragraph emphasizes Sarty's union with the natural world (77). Because Sarty's struggle for psychological growth at first occurs "far below the level of his intellectual and moral awareness," the adult narrator helps translate and interpret the moral significance of the boy's experiences (77). "Like the stopped hands of the inlaid clock which was her dowry, the mother is a figure without life or power"; she is a mere extension of her husband—the kind of extension Ab would like to make of Sarty (78). The fact that Ab walks with a limp, casts no shadow, and is associated with fire makes him seem almost Satanic—an embodiment of egotism and will-power whose pride refuses to accept any authority besides his own (79). Sarty's growing rebellion indicates not only his own developing individuality but his respect for the individuality and rights of others (80). Although for a brief time after the second court hearing Ab appears almost human and generous, this interlude only emphasizes his final return to his grim destructiveness (81). "Whether Ab is actually killed [at the end] we do not know. The detail is unimportant. For Sarty, Ab is dead. Significantly, the boy feels grief but no guilt.... His nightmare ended, Sarty, appropriately, falls into a dreamless sleep, from which he awakens whole and at peace, ready for the future" (81). As this story shows, Faulkner is greatly interested "in exploring the complex combinations of social and psychological forces that produce blindness to the individuality and rights of others" (81). **THEM, FORM**

Fau 22. Wilson, Gayle Edward. "'Being Pulled Two Ways': The Nature of Sarty's Choice in 'Barn Burning.'" *Mississippi Quarterly* 24 (1971): 279–88.

The anthropologist Ruth Benedict distinguishes between the paranoid and Apollonian ways of life; the first is rooted in lawless egotism, the second in cooperation and community (280). Because Ab represents the paranoid style, he is part of no community; by using pieces of fence to light his fires, he shows "his rejection of any societally imposed limits" (281). The family's wagon symbolizes their transient life, just as the identical shacks in which they live suggest their lack of a permanent home (281). "On the other hand, the Harris and de Spain barns represent productivity and fertility, permanence and continuity, because they house the equipment, stock, and seed by which a society produces the goods to sustain and perpetuate itself." A barn and its contents are the effects of a society which is built upon the willingness of men to subordinate their unfettered desires to a communal consensus in order to develop a permanent community" (282). Sarty associates the de Spain house with the law that allows a community to function (282), and the farmers in Faulkner's story try to deal justly even with Ab, as when the judge demands proof of Ab's crimes (283). The attractive male characters are often associated with military service—another indication of their commitment to order and cooperation; ironically, Ab himself bears the same name as a Biblical military leader (283–84). Just as Ab refused allegiance to a higher cause during the war, so he refuses allegiance to anyone other than himself in later life (285). The Apollonian characters in the story know the appeal of blood loyalty, but they choose to give their allegiance to higher values, and this is a choice Sarty must also make (286). Although Sarty shares some physical traits with his father, the two characters seem increasingly different, and Faulkner perhaps presents Ab as a kind of mythological Fisher King who represents death and barrenness (286–87). **THEM, ARCH**

Fau 23. Yunis, Susan S. "The Narrator of Faulkner's 'Barn Burning.'" *The Faulkner Journal* 6.2 (1991): 23–31.

Faulkner's narrator often seems "more intent upon explaining and justifying Abner's barn-burning than in registering the pain his family suffers in the context of these fires" (23). The narrator often seems "as capable of neglect and abuse as the Snopes men are," and if we pay too much attention to "the narrator's instructions on how to read Abner, we fail to hear the voices that the narrator and the men he speaks for abruptly silence" (24). Yet most readers still respond to Ab's abuse of Sarty and resist the narrator's efforts to control their responses (25). Both the narrator and Ab engage in strategies of control (26–27), and just as "Sarty and Abner struggle to control their own emotional responses and those of their enemies, so they control any expression of feeling by the females" (28), and the narrator "silences the emotional women just as Sarty and Abner do" (29). "The narration is a deliberate focusing upon the abuser, not the feelings of the abused. The narrator is the voice of Sarty's evasion of pain through identification with the oppressor instead of the oppressed as a technique of survival, but also as a means of detaching from pain" (29). Indeed, Faulkner himself may have identified with Ab's desire to reject imposed authority (30).**READ-R, DIALOG, FORM**

Fau 24. Zender, Karl F. "Character and Symbol in 'Barn Burning.'" *College Literature* 16 (1989): 48–59.

Sarty in effect kills his father because he fails to see Ab's full complexity (49). However, the story encourages us not to see simply from Sarty's limited perspective (52). "Vengeful, tyrannous, Ab is nonetheless governed by a desire for his son's affection, a desire which he characteristically expresses not in its own form but aggressively, as something Sarty must learn" (52). "Allowing us to inhabit Ab's point of view is an act of artistic courage on Faulkner's part. It is a striking example of how much of the human condition lies inside the pale of his imaginative sympathy" (54). When we come to realize the love and sense of social injustice that motivate Ab, we cannot view him as Sarty finally does (54). Although Sarty finally embraces abstract moral values, "we have no reason to believe that a truth and a justice so casually alluded to can encompass the after-trauma of inadvertent father-slaughter or the *in*justice of Sarty's family's subjection to the quasi-slavery of turn-of-the-century tenant farming" (55). In this sense Sarty is naive and the story lacks a fully complex engagement with reality, and the same is true of Faulkner's expression of abstract moral principles in his Nobel Prize acceptance speech (56–57). "Where is narrator sympathy invested in 'Barn Burning'? Everywhere and nowhere. It is invested in Sarty, and in Ab, but never, sadly, in the two of them together" (58). **THEM, MARX**

R.C.E.

"A ROSE FOR EMILY"

Fau 25. Allen, Dennis W. "Horror and Perverse Delight: Faulkner's 'A Rose for Emily.'" *MFS: Modern Fiction Studies* 30 (1984): 685–96.

Faulkner's imagery makes Emily seem both "grotesquely fat and excessively thin, living and dead, male and female"—a "copresence of opposites" (686). Appropriately, her story "is concerned with the mutation and corruption of bodies, with violations of the line between life and death, and with the differences and relations between the sexes" (686). Critics have tried to explain her conduct by attributing it to "sexual repression, Oedipal fixation, [or an] evasion of change and death," and her appearance helps make sense of all three explanations (688). Paradoxically, although aristocracy depends on erecting distinctions, "Emily's incestuous relationship with her father is an appropriate metaphor for the closed aristocratic world in which one deals only with one's own kind" (689). Yet this kind of incest is also an attempt to deny sexuality, and Emily's "reproduction is limited to painting" (690). Sexuality and death, being common, both threaten aristocratic distinctions (691), and democracy itself is "a violation of social boundaries and a blending of social classes for which intercourse is an appropriate metaphor" (692). The story pits the democratic "we" against the aristocratic Griersons, but both the townspeople and Emily feel ambivalent about their own motives and thus illustrate yet another way the story blurs distinctions (693). Similarly, Emily's crime is ambivalent: it at once denies and acknowledges both sexuality and death (693–94). Full of paradoxes and oxymorons, the story explores the simultaneous human impulses to create and deny distinctions (695). Even our own reaction to the story is an ambivalent mixture of shock, fascination, horror, and delight (695). **THEM**

Fau 26. Birk, John F. "Tryst beyond Time: Faulkner's Emily and Keats." *Studies in Short Fiction* 28 (1991): 203–13.

Critics have demonstrated Keats's great influence on Faulkner, and in structure, theme, and imagery this story seems clearly modelled on the poet's "Ode on a Grecian Urn," one of Faulkner's favorite works (203).

Both poem and story have five similar sections and both emphasize the endurance of art (203–4). **HIST, FORM, THEM**

Fau 27. Brooks, Cleanth. *William Faulkner: Toward Yoknapatawpha and Beyond.* New Haven and London: Yale University Press, 1978. Pp. 152–165, 382–88.

"A Rose for Emily" reveals interesting similarities and differences with another early Faulkner story, "Miss Zilphia Gant." Although Emily is victimized by her domineering father (153), as she grows older she adopts many of his willful characteristics (155). Like Zilphia, she takes "a partial truth to be her whole truth" and thus becomes grotesque (156). Yet they are not merely individual or even regional freaks; instead, their experiences have a larger significance (156). By placing Emily so precisely in a particular community, Faulkner paradoxically gives her story a larger, universal dimension (157). Faulkner communicates the complexity of the community by creating a distinctive narrator—one who not only speaks for himself and for the community but one who also indicates the distinctions that exist within the community, especially distinctions involving the different generations (158). The narrator is not a member of the older generation, but neither is he very sympathetic to the younger; he has "not only a sense of community but also a sense of history" (159). Although Emily is in some sense insane, the narrator is also capable of seeing her as both a pathetic and a tragic figure (160). By focusing on a few important episodes in Emily's life, the narrator also highlights her struggle with traditions and conventional expectations (161). Like the community at large, he is fascinated by her behavior and responds in complex ways (162). The more thoughtful members of the community—whom the narrator represents—would have considered Emily as "more sinned against than sinning. She had not willed the great warping of her life; it had been imposed upon her. They would have felt, too, that her insistence on meeting life on her own terms had something heroic about it" (163).

Although various chronologies have been proposed for this story, Emily seems to have been born in 1852 and to have died in 1926; Homer's death occurred in 1885/86 (383–84). Critics have misread the story in various ways—arguing, for instance, that Emily had help in sealing up the upstairs room, whereas an early version of the work implies that Tobe could have provided all the assistance she needed (385). Common sense can help confute some readings of the story's "symbolism" (386), nor should the story be read as reflecting specifically on "Southern" culture (386). Faulkner's story differs from recent newspaper accounts of similar incidents because Faulkner endows his story with larger meanings and significance (387). Some interpretations of his work contradict not only his intended meanings but (more important) the text of the story itself (388). **HIST, FORM, THEM**

Fau 28. Brooks, Cleanth, and Robert Penn Warren. *Understanding Fiction*. New York: Crofts, 1943. Pp. 409–14.

Although the story emphasizes horror and psychological abnormality, it must have some moral significance to be truly meaningful (410–11). Such meaning derives from the town's attitude toward Emily; her strong will and detachment lead them to treat her both with admiration and condescension (412). Emily's "independence of spirit and pride" and her "refusal to accept the herd values" exhibit "a dignity and courage" that make her simultaneously intimidating, pitiable, and admirable (413). Her madness manifests "her refusal to submit to ordinary standards of behavior" (413). Her defiance and self-sufficiency are typical of tragic heroes (414). **THEM, FORM**

Fau 29. Fetterley, Judith. *The Resisting Reader: A Feminist Approach to American Fiction*. Bloomington: Indiana University Press, 1978. Pp. 34–45.

The ending is shocking not only because of the suggestion of necrophilia but because the possible perpetrator is a murderer who is female; both details seem unnatural and hence grotesque (34). The story deals with "the patriarchy North and South, new and old, and of the sexual conflict within it" (35); it shows how oppression begets violence (35). Emily reflects "the culture that has produced her," and her "furious isolation is in direct proportion to the town's obsession with her" (35). When the men break into the locked room at the end of the story, "they find that Emily has satisfied their prurience with a vengeance," and just as she had been turned into a symbol, so has Homer (36). The crayon drawing ensures that Emily's father remains a presence even after his death, and although his violence seems aimed outward (at suitors), it is really directed at Emily's feminine freedom (37). She is imprisoned by her status as a lady, as a "Miss" who is regarded with both veneration and envy (37–38). "The violence implicit in the desire to see the monument fall and reveal itself for clay suggests the violence inherent in the original impulse to venerate" (38). Even apparent kindness is constricting: "Sartoris's remission of Emily's taxes is a public declaration of the fact that a lady is not considered to be, and hence not allowed or enabled to be, economically independent" (38). The town takes on the controlling role earlier filled by her father, and the male narrator's sexism is revealed both in his disdain for women's "gossip" and in his indulgence of Emily's oddness (39). However, neither he nor the townspeople see Emily as a true individual, preferring to see her as a "lady," and Emily uses the stereotype to her advantage (40). Paradoxically, "by defining a lady as a subhuman and hence sublegal nonentity, they have created a situation their laws can't touch," even becoming criminals themselves (by sneaking on to her property to deal with the smells [41–42]). Her treatment of Homer mirrors the violence done to her (42), and although her vengeance shows a kind of power, it is a kind that is severely limited (43–44). She kills Homer because she feels compelled to have a man, but the town's stereotyped conception of her as a "lady" allows her to get away with murder (43–44). **FEM**

Fau 30. Hays, Peter L. "Who Is Faulkner's Emily?" *Studies in American Fiction* 16 (1988): 105–10.

Although critics have argued that Emily was based on a poem by John Crowe Ransom, she seems instead to resemble one of Faulkner's cousins, who had married a Yankee named Jack Barron (105). However, Emily also resembles Emily Dickinson, a subject of great publicity during Faulkner's youth (106). Both Emilys dressed in white, had over-protective fathers, were denied marriages, became recluses, and were fascinated with death (109). The story may pay tribute to Dickinson (109). **HIST**

Fau 31. Jones, Diane Brown. *A Reader's Guide to the Short Stories of William Faulkner.* New York: G.K. Hall, 1994. Pp. 87–141.

Topics covered include publication history; circumstances of composition, sources, and influences; relationship to other Faulkner works; and interpretation and criticism. This tale was Faulkner's first short story published in a national periodical, although it had been rejected before being accepted (87). Although it may have been written as early as 1927, the earliest record of its existence is dated October 7, 1929 (87). Scholars have offered different accounts of its relations with another Faulkner story, "Miss Zilphia Gant" (87–88). Manuscript sources permit study of the author's revisions and improvements, including the elimination of abstract phrasing and of a long discussion between Emily and her servant before Emily's death (88). The final version is less gruesome and more ambiguous, especially in chronology (88–89). Scholars have sought real-life models for the characters and events, including a similar courtship that really occurred in Faulkner's hometown (89). Perhaps Faulkner was influenced by "Emily and the Baron," a popular historical tale at the time (90). Other scholars have found literary parallels in the works of such writers as Hawthorne, Dickens, Poe, George Washington Cable, Browning, Keats, Blake, Sherwood Anderson, and T.S. Eliot, and in the tradition of Gothic writing (90–94). Marion Barber and Paul Levitt revealed strong parallels between the story and a poem by John Crowe Ransom entitled "Emily Hardcastle, Spinster" (94). The story has also been discussed in connection with Mark Twain, Carlos Fuentes, Henry James, and Irvin S. Cobb (95). It has been frequently discussed in connection with two other Faulkner stories—"Dry September" and "Miss Zilphia Gant" (95–96)—and Emily has been compared and contrasted with other Faulkner women (97–100). In this respect, themes of sexual desire, of fantasy projections, of feminine authority, of generational conflict, and of oppression and repression have been stressed (99). More general parallels between Emily and other Faulkner characters have discussed her in terms of modernity, perversion, incest, psychopathology, and lack of being mothered (100–1). Homer Barron has been compared to other Faulkner characters (101), but special interest has focused on the story's narrator, whose story-telling role, knowledge, and relations to the rest of the community have been much discussed (101–2). Critics also have focused on the settings, themes, and images this story shares with other works by Faulkner (103), and they have also considered how the tale fits into the larger *Collected Stories*, which it introduced (104–5). Interestingly, Faulkner himself never alluded to Emily's story again in his later fiction (106).

Interpretations and criticism have ranged from formal to psychological to historical to feminist, to name just a few types; Faulkner himself saw Emily as a victim of repressed desire (106) and even saw her as pitifully torn between God and Satan (107). She has been seen as an aristocrat; as a female too much influenced by her father; as someone who commits murder to atone for her own violation of social and religious standards; and as an isolated, visionary artist (107). Norman Holland has stressed how both she and the narrator use the psychological strategies of denial and incorporation (108), although Wayne Tefs has argued that Emily cannot be psychoanalyzed (109). Judith Fetterly has seen her as a "lady" whose patronizing, patriarchal culture allows her to get away with murder (109–10), while Barbara Lupack emphasizes the parallels between Homer and Emily's father (110). Jack Sherting stresses her Oedipal relationship with her father and notes how much she eventually resembles him (110), while Victor Strandberg emphasizes such Freudian themes as "oedipal fixation, trauma, regression, narcissism, and sexual perversion" (111). Other critics have claimed that she resists change; that our images of her are both fluid and fixed; that she uses Homer as a substitute for her father; that she murders him to punish him for using their courtship to hide his homosexuality; that she represents Faulkner's critique of the unfair treatment of spinsters; that she is crazy; that she is a necrophiliac; that she is not a necrophiliac; that she is both idolized and scapegoated by her community; that she is heroic; that she murders Homer for violating her honor because no gentlemen are left to do so; that the community's attitude toward her is very complex and unstable; and that Colonel Sartoris represents either old-fashioned graciousness or racist and sexist repression (111–15).

The narrator has been seen as either objective or subjective, singular or plural, male or female (or neither), sympathetic or predatory, and sensitive or voyeuristic, among other things (115–17). Tobe has been seen as healthy and active (unlike Emily); or as one of the three most important men in her life; or as an accomplice in murder; or as a man interested in self-possession (117–18). Critics have also debated the importance to the story of such themes as time; resistance to change; conflicts between North and South; conflicts between past and present; and conflicting ideologies, especially of race and gender (118–21). Discussions of style have highlighted Faulkner's use of such qualities as suspense, surrealism, comedy, and satire (121–22). Numerous critics have discussed the significance of the story's title; the rose (a word not mentioned in the work itself) has been seen as a symbol of love; as an ironic allusion to lines in *Romeo and Juliet*; as a symbol of victory over time; as a tribute to Emily by the narrator; as a symbol of secret (or *sub rosa*) events; as a symbol of mutability; and as an ironic symbol of the carefully preserved Homer (122–23). Disagreements about the narrative point-of-view are relevant to discussions of the story's structure and chronology; the latter issue has been much debated (123–27). Floyd Watkins has argued that the story's different sections reflect a symmetrical pattern "of one intrusion, two intrusions, isolation, two intrusions, and one intrusion" (127). John V. Hagopian notes that each intrusion is linked with death (127). Structuralist analyses have been offered by William Hendricks and John Skinner; reader-response analyses have been offered by Menakhem Perry and by Norman Holland (127–29). James Mellard has explored the story's Gothic elements; Mary Arensberg and Sara Schyfter have compared the text to a mind; Austin Wright has emphasized the interpretive resistance provided by the story's ending; Suzanne Brown has seen the story as an exploration of linear and spatial modes of patterning; Eric Montenyohl has explored parallels with folk legends; and James Ferguson emphasizes the story's highly complicated treatment of time (130–32). The (implied) dialogue among the many different critics is often the most interesting aspect of their work (133).**HIST, THEM, FORM, PSY, PLUR, ETC.**

Fau 32. Moore, Gene M. "Of Time and Its Mathematical Progression: Problems of Chronology in Faulkner's 'A Rose for Emily.'" *Studies in Short Fiction* 29 (1992): 195–204.

Although eight different chronologies have been proposed for the story, Faulkner's manuscript solves some difficulties by establishing the date of death for Emily's father (195). The competing chronologies have resulted from differences concerning various kinds of internal and external evidence (196). In the original manuscript, Emily's "taxes were remitted not in 1894 but in 1904, 16 years after the death of her father in 1888" (198). This chronology (detailed in an appendix) differs from the one proposed by Perry "by only one year," although problems still remain in determining precise dates for the story's events (202). **HIST**

Fau 33. Reed, Joseph W., Jr. *Faulkner's Narrative.* New Haven: Yale University Press, 1973. Pp. 12–20.

As a ghost story, the tale depends on suspense, order, empathy with the first-person narrator, death and decay as subjects, and the reader's desire for horror (13). Related traits include "simplicity, verisimilitude, and precision in suspense" (14). Although Faulkner tempts us to agree with the interpretations of Emily offered by competing sub-groups in the community, we retain allegiance to the narrator, who seems tough-minded and objective and who promises us horror (15). We empathize with the community in resenting the aristocratic Emily and thereby participate in her isolation (16–17). Faulkner makes her seem increasingly distanced and objectified (17). The final description of her room is "perhaps the most brilliantly economic instance of Faulkner's exercise of stopped-action description, [in which] the things we see are frozen each for a moment like stills spliced into a movie" (18). Our earlier empathy with the narrator is suddenly replaced by empathy for Emily (19), and we feel some guilt for having participated in violating her "tragic isolation" (19). **FORM, THEM, READ-R**

Fau 34. Roberts, Diane. *Faulkner and Southern Womanhood*. Athens and London: University of Georgia Press, 1994.

Emily's hidden sexual desires undermine not only her status as a "spinster lady" but also the whole conventional structure "of southern class and history" (158). She exemplifies Faulkner's interest at the time in how "the denial or misdirection of the middle- to upper-class white woman's sexuality becomes the obsessive focus of her being. Where class absolves the Confederate Woman from desire, it implicates the spinster in repression and destruction. Class is the reason for Miss Emily's spinsterhood" (158). Although her culture teaches her to repress her bodily desires, her refusal to do so becomes an act of asserting what is usually unspoken (159). Homer's corpse symbolizes not only a still-born love but also Emily's determination to achieve and preserve some dominance over men (159). In a sense, the citizens violate her when they finally penetrate her room and subject her to their judgment (160), yet Emily herself is "an interrogation, a parody, and a celebration of the Confederate Woman" (160). Homer's room/tomb symbolizes Emily's womb/tomb—a place of stilted desire, dominance, and death (160). **FEM, MARX, NHIST, THEM**

Fau 35. Rodman, Isaac. "Irony and Isolation: Narrative Distance in Faulkner's 'A Rose for Emily.'" *Faulkner Journal* 8.2 (1993): 3–12.

Although the narrator is usually seen as representing his community, he is as isolated as Emily and the young Faulkner (3–4). He keeps an ironic distance from the townspeople; his literary language implies his uncommon perceptiveness (4). The confused chronology of the story mirrors the way the townspeople "compartmentalize their thoughts" (8); their "perceptions do not threaten their preconceptions" (9). The narrator, while of the town and partly speaking for it, keeps a distanced, lonely, sane, and literary perspective (11). **THEM, FORM**

Fau 36. Schwab, Milinda. "A Watch for Emily." *Studies in Short Fiction* 28 (1991): 215–17.

Time is an important theme in this story, and by "wearing [her] watch in her pocket ... Emily demonstrates her effort to subjugate the clock to her own will" (215). Many of her actions result from her desire to stop time and resist change, which she associates with loss (215–16). For her, time "merely drones on in endless repetition, like the absurd tick, tick, tick of her invisible watch" (216). Nevertheless, she is literally chained to the time-piece she tries to control, and Emily herself resembles a "living corpse" (216–17). The story's unusual structure implies Emily's repetitive experience of time (217). The narrative itself takes little actual time since it consists mostly of flashbacks; only after her funeral does time, in this sense, stand still for Emily (217). **THEM**

Fau 37. Skei, Hans H. *William Faulkner: The Novelist as Short Story Writer: A Study of William Faulkner's Short Fiction.* Oslo: Universitetsforlaget, 1985. Pp. 108–12.

The story is told only partially from the point of view of the whole community; Faulkner's pronouns often shift (109). The tale (which consists of four parts, roughly equal in length, plus a shorter fifth part) is told in fragments which are not in chronological sequence (109). The voice behind the narrative "we" may be a member of Emily's own generation (110). "In contrast to [the situations in] most gothic fiction, Emily and her house are very much in and of this world, although she has felt compelled to end all association with her fellow men" (112). **FORM**

Fau 38. Stafford, T.J. "Tobe's Significance in 'A Rose for Emily.'" *Modern Fiction Studies* 14 (1968): 451–53.

Emily's relation with Homer is perverse and is thus unworthy of the pride she displays (452). Ten references to the black servant, Tobe, meaningfully contrast him with Emily (452). His actions are "purposeful and altruistic," whereas she is immobile and eventually violent (452). He represents her possible link with humanity and is himself a healthy human; yet she alienates herself from everyone and ignores him specifically (452). His name suggests the potential "to be" once he is free of Emily (452). He is strong and enduring, like Dilsey in *The Sound and the Fury* (453). Faulkner implies that Emily's pride needs to be tempered by the kind of "humility, patience, endurance, courage, and pity" represented by Tobe (453). **THEM, MULTI**

Fau 39. West, Ray B., Jr. "'Atmosphere and Theme in Faulkner's 'A Rose for Emily.'" *William Faulkner: Four Decades of Criticism.* Ed. Linda Welshimer Wagner. N.p.: Michigan State University Press, 1973. Pp. 192–98. Reprinted from *Perspective* (Summer 1949): 239–45.

As in most stories, the first indication of Faulkner's meaning is implied by the contrasts he immediately establishes—in this case, the strong contrast between past and present, which creates an atmosphere of "distortion" and "unreality" (192). This atmosphere—established already in the first sentence—"prepares us for Emily's unnatural act" (193). Contrasts between past and present dominate the story, but also important are contrasts between reality (represented by Homer) and withdrawal (represented by Emily). Although at first it seems that reality may triumph, this conflict is not resolved until the very end (195). "Emily's resistance is heroic. Her tragic flaw is the conventional pride: she undertook to regulate the natural time-universe" (197)—which inevitably leads to defeat. The story seems to imply that people "must come to terms with both the past and the present; for to ignore the first is to be guilty of a foolish innocence, to ignore the second is to become monstrous and inhuman, above all to betray an excessive pride (such as Emily Grierson's) before the humbling fact of death" (198). Like much great literature, the story suggests that "man's plight is tragic, but that there is heroism in an attempt to rise above it" (198). **THEM, FORM**

R.C.E.

"ABSOLUTION"

Fit 1. Allen, Joan M. *Candles and Carnival Lights: The Catholic Sensibility of F. Scott Fitzgerald.* New York: New York University Press, 1978. Pp. 44–45, 93–101, 111.

In "Absolution" and other works Fitzgerald reverses the traditional symbolism of light ("the essence of all that is good") so that it "represents the essence of evil" (44–45). He also uses "the Augustinian antithesis of sacred and secular, spirit and flesh, the City of God and the City of Man, candle and carnival light" (45). "Absolution" fills in Jay Gatsby's early life by showing his "midwestern Catholic background" and the "boyhood spiritual crisis" that shaped "his mature dream" (94). Similarities between the story and *The Great Gatsby* can be noted in the "compressed style," "ritualistic tone," the identification of light with evil, and images of light and the amusement park (94–95). The priest is tormented by the sensual sights, smells, and sounds outside his window, and Rudolph is tormented by his "'sins of dirty words and immodest thoughts and desire'" (96–97). But Rudolph suffers most after he lies in the confessional, as Fitzgerald had done (97). Rudolph's father is somewhat similar to Fitzgerald's father, who had once hit his son, though not with the "savage ferocity" of Carl Miller (98). Like Gatsby, Rudolph feels "shame" over his lack of money, a trait both characters share with their creator (99). Toward the end of the story, after Father Schwartz's "repressed sexuality" has driven him mad, he describes a "'glittering'" amusement park with its "'big wheel made of lights turning in the air'" (100). An obvious reference to a ferris wheel, the image also suggests "the vision of Ezekiel, which prefigured the destruction of the holy city of Jerusalem" and "prefigure[s] Rudolph's fall from grace, his rejection of God and His City, and his being blinded by the carnival lights of the secular world he chooses" (100). The amusement park is Fitzgerald's "metaphor for the active secular world," "the earthly paradise, the City of Man," the "'something ineffably gorgeous somewhere that had nothing to do with God'" (100). Later, as Jay Gatsby, Rudolph "will try to create his own amusement park," becoming "a knight in pursuit of the grail he imagines Daisy Fay to be" (101). "Absolution" closes "with a celebration of sensuality and fecundity" as Rudolph "looks squarely at 'the heat and the sweat and the life' with the imagination of the artist" (101). Having been "failed" by his father's materialism and "cruel piety" and by Father Schwartz's "diseased imagination," Rudolph will never be able to attain the City of God, but must forever dwell in the City of Man (101). **FORM, HIST, THEM**

Fit 2. Brondell, William J. "Structural Metaphors in Fitzgerald's Short Fiction." *Kansas Quarterly* 14.2 (1982): 95–112.

Like many Fitzgerald stories, "Absolution" has a traditional five-part superstructure (Exposition, Rising Action, Climax, Falling Action, and Denouement), but critics looking only at that structure have found a flaw in the "'split character focus'" between Father Schwartz and Rudolph (95–97). Closer examination, however, reveals a substructure built around a central metaphor presented in the headnote to Section V: "'*Sagitta Volante in Dei*'" ("'Arrows flying by day'"), a misspelled reference to a verse from Psalm 90, "'His faith will surround you as a shield; you will not fear the terror of the night, nor the arrows flying by day ...'" (97–98). This metaphor, which "appears at a critical moment, just before the climax" to "signal the impending crisis," traces the "psychological motion" of the story and shows that the apparently flawed "shift in focus" is in fact "a virtue and a strength" (97). Both Father Schwartz and Rudolph are afraid: the priest fears life as it is represented in the sights, sounds, and smells outside his window, and the boy fears "the consequences of his ... 'terrible sin'" (99). But worse than their fear is their imperfect faith that prevents them from trusting in God to provide "the refuge and comfort they sought" (102). **FORM**

Fit 3. Bruccoli, Matthew J. *Some Sort of Epic Grandeur: The Life of F. Scott Fitzgerald*. New York: Harcourt Brace Jovanovich, 1981. Pp. 191–92.

Because Fitzgerald claimed in 1934 that he had originally planned "Absolution" as "a picture of [Gatsby's] early life," much discussion of the story has focused on the relationship between the story and the novel (191–92). But Fitzgerald had also told his editor Maxwell Perkins that the story "was salvaged from a discarded version before he approached the novel from 'a new angle'—by which he meant a new plot" (192). The main characters of both the novel and the story have "a romantic disposition" but few other similarities (192). Rudolph Miller is most likely "a preliminary treatment of the figure who developed into Jay Gatsby" (192).

Fit 4. Christensen, Bryce J. "The Mystery of Ungodliness: Renan's *Life of Jesus* as Subtext for F. Scott Fitzgerald's *The Great Gatsby* and 'Absolution.'" *Christianity & Literature* 36.1 (1986): 15–23.

In his portrait of Jay Gatsby, Fitzgerald draws parallels to Jesus, especially by calling him "'a son of God'" who tended "'His Father's business'" (15). Fitzgerald's omission from *The Great Gatsby* of the material that became "Absolution" might even have resulted from his wish to draw another parallel by imitating in Rudolph Miller's background the Bible's "almost total silence" about Jesus's early life (15). But the portrait of Jesus that underlies Gatsby is more likely that of Ernest Renan's *The Life of Jesus* than the Biblical one (16–17). The Biblical Jesus is surrounded by "the sacred Christian mystery of the Incarnation ... God appearing in the flesh of the perfect Word entering the imperfect world—and yet remaining perfect" (16). Gatsby, like Renan's Jesus, more likely represents "the secular mystery of the romantic ideal struggling (but inevitably failing) to find adequate embodiment in the harsh truth of reality" (16). Using language related to the Incarnation to create the mystery of Jay Gatsby, Fitzgerald, like Renan, challenges the idea of "any genuine intersection between the ideal and the real, any truly valid incarnation" (16–17). Those who know Fitzgerald's admiration for Renan's book and have learned Gatsby's background through Rudolph in "Absolution" know that the novel is not Christian (21). Rudolph's lies and failure to confess before communion are decidedly unchristian, but the story is most "at odds with ... Christianity" when it suggests "that the creations of the imagination are irreconcilable with and superior to the reality they defy" (21). Rudolph finds "'something ineffably gorgeous somewhere that had nothing to do with God'" and begins his "idolatrous pursuit of a 'radiant and proud' romantic ideal" to counter "the 'dinginess' of factual truth" (22). Although he should have had help from Father Schwartz, the priest himself is a romantic idealist whose madness shows "the inevitable consequence of repudiating the Christian Incarnation in favor of romantic idealism" (22). Similarly, Gatsby's pursuit of "an incarnation of his [own] romantic ideals" results in "disenchantment and destruction" (23). **HIST, THEM**

Fit 5. Cushman, Keith. "Scott Fitzgerald's Scrupulous Meanness: 'Absolution' and 'The Sisters.'" *Fitzgerald/Hemingway Annual* (1979): 115–21.

One can see evidence of the influence of James Joyce's "Two Sisters" on "Absolution" (116). Both stories concern "the relationship between an innocent young protagonist and a priest who has lost his vocation" (116–17). In both stories the priest has a "nervous breakdown" that is evident in his "mad laughter" (117). Joyce described his style as "'scrupulous meanness,'" which could refer to a "sour attitude" or, more likely, "'strict economy, a passion to make the smallest detail carry its full burden'" (117). The impact of Joyce's work "depends on the dark resonances concealed just beneath the surface" (118). In "Absolution" Fitzgerald achieves a similar depth of meaning, particularly in the communion scene, which shows Rudolph's fears and reveals that they are unnecessary because he "is merely the innocent victim of his savage religious upbringing" (118). Like Joyce's "paralyzed" characters, Rudolph "is a prisoner ... of his father's tyranny and of the fanatical Catholicism beaten into him" (119). Unlike Joyce's character, though, Rudolph "escapes the paralysis into the romantic fantasy-world of Blatchford Sarnemington" and by the end of the story "has begun his journey toward the 'glimmering' ... and the 'glittering' ... that was to lead to the kingdom of Jay Gatsby" (119). Fitzgerald learned from Joyce how to show the barrenness of Rudolph's life but was able to "evok[e] the glimmering and glittering" on his own (120). **HIST, FORM, THEM**

Fit 6. Hagemann, E.R. "Should Scott Fitzgerald Be Absolved for the Sins of 'Absolution'?" *Journal of Modern Literature* 12 (1985): 169–74.

Fitzgerald's "Absolution" is weakened by "loose diction, violated point of view, flawed characterization, and even faulty grammar" (169). For example, even though what happens in the confessional is central to the story, we never actually hear Father Schwartz absolve Rudolph Miller (169). Words like "'staccato'" and "'cobalt'" in the description "'staccato eyes, lit with gleaming points of cobalt light'" are imprecise (169). And Fitzgerald does not prepare the reader for a reference to Rudolph's "'inner convictions'" or offer anything in the characterization of Rudolph to explain his knowledge of such military terms as "'cuirasiers'" or "'pennon'" (173). Although the reader feels "a vague admiration" for the story because "its structure is sound," Fitzgerald should have worked harder to make the story easier reading (174). **FORM**

Fit 7. Kuehl, John. "A la joyce: The Sisters Fitzgerald's Absolution." *James Joyce Quarterly* 2.1 (1964): 2–6.

Fitzgerald admired James Joyce's work and admitted the influence of *A Portrait of the Artist as a Young Man* on *This Side of Paradise* (2). Joyce's influence is also evident in the similarities between "Absolution" and "Two Sisters," a story from *Dubliners*, a volume that Fitzgerald regarded as one of the "'great English classics'" (3). Although the stories differ in point of view and narrative pattern, they are similar in theme (4–5). Both examine "the betrayal of the child by the adult," but Joyce's treatment is more "subtle" than Fitzgerald's, where "Rudolph's father merely bullies him" (5). Fitzgerald also "dissipates" some of the intensity of his story by offering two betrayers instead of the one in "The Sisters" (5). In Joyce's story the priest's homosexual attraction to the boy is conveyed through one character's "enigmatic statements, iterative oral imagery and, above all, the boy's thoughts, dreams and actions" (5). In "Absolution," "vestiges of homosexuality" appear in "a few equivocal references," but the story deals primarily with heterosexuality, with the "priest and boy becoming secret sharers" (6). Although the priest is at first Rudolph's confessor, he later "finds himself confessing Rudolph's sin of 'immodest thoughts and desires,'" his "betrayal" of the boy finally resulting from his inability to provide the guidance a priest should offer and ending like Joyce's priest in madness (6). **FORM, THEM, MULTI**

Fit 8. Malin, Irving. "'Absolution': Absolving Lies." In *The Short Stories of F. Scott Fitzgerald: New Approaches in Criticism.* Ed. Jackson R. Bryer. Madison: University of Wisconsin Press, 1982. 209–16.

Although not "orthodox" in any way, Fitzgerald is "a religious writer" who "can never completely remove himself from the Catholicism of his youth" (209). Through "structural (and thematic) opposition," "Absolution" explores many typical Fitzgerald conflicts and examines "the attempt to escape from this world, to transform routine experience and to enter other complete worlds" (209). The story "asks whether art itself—that is, imagination, dream, romance—can be as sufficient, helpful, and necessary as religious belief" (209). The opening paragraph establishes the "alternation" between opposites in its rhythm, tone, structure, images of sight and sound, and the contrast between the priest who is "'rundown'—like an 'old clock'" and the "'beautiful, intense'" boy sitting in "'a patch of sunshine'" (210–11). The pattern of opposition continues throughout the story in the contrasts between father and son, "light and dark, youth and maturity, earth and Heaven, lie and truth" (211–16). Fitzgerald, "a conscious, disarming ironist," creates distaste for his characters (the priest, the boy, and his father) while also causing us to "admire their search for absolution" (215). The story clearly reveals Fitzgerald to be "a religious writer" as he explores his "own conflicts between 'romance' (magical transformation) and absolution" (216). Fitzgerald offers no resolution to the conflict but rather demonstrates the longing for one: "some vision in which wounds are healed, souls united, and lies transformed into truths" (216). He presents the story's "thematic tensions in the subtle, 'overlooked' patterns of imagery" to create "a satisfying labyrinth, a religious (and artistic) triumph which *contains* contraries" (216). **FORM, THEM**

Fit 9. Martin, Robert A. "The Hot Madness of Four O'Clock in Fitzgerald's 'Absolution' and *Gatsby*." *Studies in American Fiction* 2 (1974): 230–38.

In June 1924 Fitzgerald published as the story "Absolution" the discarded prologue of what later became *The Great Gatsby* (230). Although no manuscript survives to show the relationship between the story and the novel, one can see "numerous parallels" between the two (230).

Fitzgerald made major changes in "style, structure, and narrative method," but in the central characters' similar Midwest origins, their fathers' admiration of James J. Hill, their "desire to escape" their backgrounds, and their "disillusionment," one can see that Rudolph is a young Jimmie Gatz (231). Also important are the less noticeable correspondences between the story and novel in the references to "'four o'clock,' the number four, and several associated images" (231). Rudolph's first visit to the priest takes place in the "hot madness of four o'clock," and the scene of the last meeting when Father Schwartz collapses seems reminiscent of the earlier one (232). Four o'clock becomes a significant time in *Gatsby*, as three key scenes occur in the heat of four o'clock in the afternoon and three at four o'clock in the morning: for example, when Daisy comes to tea, when Gatsby and Tom argue at the Plaza, and when Gatsby dies (233–34). The number four also becomes significant because of many key scenes of four people and many references to the number "four" (232–33). Images of heat and clocks also recur throughout the novel (232–37). The "hot madness of four o'clock" becomes "the structural and possibly metaphorical center" of the novel and shows "a continuing and in many ways symbolic connection between 'Absolution' and *The Great Gatsby* and Fitzgerald's own career as a writer" (237). **HIST**

Fit 10. Miller, James E., Jr. *The Fictional Technique of Scott Fitzgerald.* The Hague: Martinus Nijhoff, 1957.

The Great Gatsby represents an important step in Fitzgerald's development as he moved from a looser form like that Henry James denigrated as the "novel of saturation" to the tighter, more controlled form James labeled the "novel of selection" (1–2). In "Absolution," originally intended as a prologue to *Gatsby*, one can see some of the techniques used so successfully in that novel (88). By "splitting the final episode of the narrative" into two parts, one at the beginning and one at the end, Fitzgerald creates a "compact structure" with a frame that is "integral" to the story (88). This "rearrangement of the chronology" allows Fitzgerald to introduce Rudolph through the priest's consciousness, which "colors" what follows "and establishes the probability of the confirmation of Rudolph's 'own inner convictions'" (88). By examining an essential transforming event in Rudolph's life, Fitzgerald "suggests much more than is explicitly stated about Rudolph's character and future," thus attaining one of the main qualities that set *Gatsby* apart from Fitzgerald's earlier novels, what Conrad labeled in his own writing "the art of 'magic suggestiveness'" (80, 88–89). **FORM, HIST**

Fit 11. Morse, J.I. "Fitzgerald's *Sagitta Volante in Dei*: An Emendation and a Possible Source." *Fitzgerald/Hemingway Annual* 4 (1972): 321–22.

The last word in the headnote to Section V (*"'Sagitta volante in Dei,'"* "'An arrow flying into God'") is in the wrong case to follow *"in"* (321). Although the error could be corrected as *"Deum,"* Fitzgerald probably simply reversed the last two letters of *"Die,"* which would have made the line "'the arrow that flieth in the day,'" an allusion to Psalm 90: 5–6 (321). The latter correction achieves a "flat, Joycean irony" that matches the story's beginning (321).

Fit 12. Piper, Henry Dan. "The Untrimmed Christmas Tree: The Religious Background of *The Great Gatsby*." In *The Great Gatsby: A Study*. Ed. Frederick J. Hoffman. New York: Charles Scribner's Sons, 1962. Pp. 321–34.

Fitzgerald initially planned for his third novel, *The Great Gatsby*, to be set in "'the Middle West and New York of 1885'" and have "'a Catholic element'" (322). "Absolution," which he called the abandoned "prologue" to *Gatsby*, is essential to a full understanding of the novel, especially "the religious considerations that served ... as a basis for [its] moral judgments" (324). "Absolution" explores "a ten-year-old boy's first encounter with evil," while *Gatsby* offers the "consequences" (324). Rudolph Miller becomes Jimmie Gatz in the novel, Rudolph's imaginary friend Blatchford Sarnemington becomes Jay Gatsby, and Rudolph's moment of illumination when he realizes he can "exist apart from God" is the moment when Jimmie Gatz is transformed into Jay Gatsby (325–26). The story originated from the agony Fitzgerald experienced as a child after telling a lie during confession, and Fitzgerald uses it to examine his own failing romantic idealism against the Catholic faith of his youth (327–28). Because Fitzgerald had not quite worked out his new moral system, however, "Absolution" is not as successful as *Gatsby* (327–28). Using Nick Carroway as narrator and judge, Fitzgerald solves the problems of "Absolution" (328) so that in *Gatsby* Fitzgerald was able to save the moral values of the Catholic faith "without the sectarian dogma" (333). **HIST, THEM**

Fit 13. Perosa, Sergio. *The Art of F. Scott Fitzgerald*. Ann Arbor: University of Michigan Press, 1965. Pp. 59–60.

In "Absolution" Fitzgerald introduces two techniques he later uses in *The Great Gatsby* (59). First, much of the story is presented in "a long flashback sequence" like that describing "Gatsby's and Daisy's past in the novel" (59). Second, Father Schwartz's crisis "is not properly analyzed but rather suggested by a careful correspondence of symbols" (59). Although the story does not explain "Gatsby's 'mystery,'" it does foreshadow "the technical and stylistic maturity of the novel" (60). **FORM, HIST**

Fit 14. Stewart, Lawrence D. "'Absolution' and *The Great Gatsby.*" *Fitzgerald/Hemingway Annual* 5 (1973): 181–87.

Fitzgerald claimed that he dropped the prologue to *The Great Gatsby* "'to preserve the sense of mystery'" surrounding his title character (181). Examining "Absolution," the story made from that prologue, however, shows that despite "a few superficial similarities," the story and the novel "are basically irreconcilable" (181). The two protagonists share a disbelief in their parentage, "each having invented an alter ego"; both stories have "imagery of rundown clocks and falling leaves" and at times seem to share "the same voice as storyteller" (182). But Rudolph seems unlikely to grow up to have Gatsby's uniqueness or ability to dream (182–83). Although Rudolph fears God, Gatsby is "'a son of God'" whose "dreams develop in Biblical imagery" (183). In fact, Gatsby seems more like Father Schwartz than Rudolph, and examining the story as a prologue to the novel has minimized the importance of the priest (184). Father Schwartz is a "tragic, dream-haunted man" who transforms the amusement park into a symbol of "his yearning for God" just as Gatsby is a "tragic, dream-haunted man" who transforms "a girl ... into a manifestation of the Divine" (185). Fitzgerald allows us to see both men with "a double vision," recognizing the beauty of the dream as well as the limitations of the object (185). "Absolution" hardly seems the prologue to Gatsby except as "the destruction of the priest foreshadows what must inevitably happen to Gatsby and his more intense dreams" (185). **HIST, FORM, THEM**

A.C.L.

"BABYLON REVISITED"

Fit 15. Baker, Carlos. "When the Story Ends: 'Babylon Revisited.'" In *The Short Stories of F. Scott Fitzgerald: New Approaches in Criticism.* Ed. Jackson R. Bryer. Madison: University of Wisconsin Press, 1982. Pp. 269–79.

"Babylon Revisited" was written in 1930, a year Fitzgerald saw as a turning point with Zelda's confinement to a sanitorium (269), and the story reflects his shifting "from false romanticism to a firmer realism in his life as a writer" (277). The story involves "the double theme of freedom and imprisonment, of locking out and locking in," developed through images of bars, keys, and locks (269). The story also has two opposing motifs: "Babylon, ancient center of luxury and wickedness in the writings of the fathers of the Church," and "the quiet and decent homelife that Wales wishes to establish for his child" (270). These motifs are introduced through the contrasting exterior scenes showing Paris streets at night and interior scenes in the Peterses' living room (271). Although Charlie has rebuilt his life, apparently freeing himself from the excesses of his past, a series of mistakes establishes the bars of the prison which will lock him out of his daughter's life and lock him into the prison of his loneliness and isolation (270–74). **HIST, THEM, FORM**

Fit 16. Brondell, William J. "Structural Metaphors in Fitzgerald's Short Fiction." *Kansas Quarterly* 14.2 (1982): 95–112.

In "Absolution," "The Freshest Boy," and "Babylon Revisited" Fitzgerald provided "a map, [a] structural metaphor," to help show the inner lives of his protagonists. The structural metaphor of "Babylon Revisited" is the image of his dead wife, Helen, in a swing (109). Here a kind of messenger from the past, she acts as a check on his "'exultation'" over Marion's agreeing to his custody of Honoria, and later other elements from the past swing into the present, curbing his hope (109). Yet Charlie's responses to each difficulty are balanced like the motion of a swing and reveal he has indeed developed the self-control that will insure his success in getting his child (111). **FORM, THEM**

Fit 17. Bruccoli, Matthew J. *Some Sort of Epic Grandeur: The Life of F. Scott Fitzgerald.* New York: Harcourt Brace Jovanovich, 1981. Pp. 308–9.

In "Babylon Revisited," Fitzgerald examined "the collapse of his [own] life" through the account of Charlie Wales (308–9). Despite the "self-pity" evident in the portrait, Fitzgerald obviously suggests that Wales's dilemma resulted from "the abandonment of traditional values," his "'selling short'" in personal rather than financial terms (309). **HIST**

Fit 18. Butterfield, Herbie. "'All Very Rich and Sad': A Decade of F. Scott Fitzgerald Short Stories." In *Scott Fitzgerald: The Promises of Life.* Ed. A. Robert Lee. London: Vision, 1989. Pp. 94–112.

Ten of Fitzgerald's short stories that "chart the course" of the twenties are "small masterpieces of art and imagination" (108). In "Babylon Revisited," the best of these, Fitzgerald offers his "definitive review both of his and Zelda's expatriate years and of the American 1920s and their collapse" (108). Although sad, the story is "far less depressing" than the other nine because "it ends with an understanding of and commitment to, not romance, but love" (109). "Babylon Revisited" surpasses the other stories "in its emotional concentration and in its rare fusion of intensity and reticence," but all offer "a voice ... at once awed (in the tradition of wonder and enthusiasm) and ironic (in the tradition of discrimination and judgement)" and a "style" at once sumptuous and melancholy, and, always marvelously cadenced" (110). They offer both "self-criticism" that is "oblique and severe" and a "highly charged and well founded critique ... of the world of the rich, or of the adventures of the capitalist economy" (110). **HIST, THEM, FORM, MARX**

Fit 19. Cowart, David. "Fitzgerald's 'Babylon Revisited.'" *Lost Generation Journal* 8.1 (1987): 16–19.

A central theme of "Babylon Revisited" is "the ambivalent consequences of having money" (16). Although Charlie Wales had "had both home and money," he is now a homeless "exile" like Bonnie Prince Charlie, the Prince of Wales; Napoleon III, alluded to in Charlie's association of the "'cab horns'" of Paris to "'the trumpets of the Second Empire'"; and ghosts, permanent exiles referred to in many ways throughout the story (16). Charlie's locking his wife out of their home parallels his own "present situation, when he is himself figuratively locked out" of the home he wants to make with his daughter (16). The contrast between what he has and what he wants—but what Fitzgerald strongly suggests he will never get—is emphasized as "images of coldness, exile, and solitude counter images of hearth, home, coziness, and security" (16). Charlie seems about to understand that money cannot buy back what he has lost, but his decision to "'send Honoria some things ... a lot of things'" when he cannot take her with him suggests he has not (17). Images of "time and entropy" show that, somewhat like Gatsby, he also fails to realize "the irretrievability of the past" (18). Despite other critics' arguments to the contrary, Charlie becomes a tragic figure "when, defeated by forces vastly larger than himself, he keeps intact his sobriety and his new-found integrity" (18). Fitzgerald elevates Charlie's story to the level of tragedy through his five-act structure, his depiction of Charlie's "'tragic flaw'" in "his inability to perceive the limitations of money," and his links of Charlie to mythical deities and ritual rebirth (18–19). The hope implied by the rebirth myths, however, is not present for Charlie Wales (19). **THEM, HIST, FORM, ARCH**

Fit 20. Gross, Seymour L. "Fitzgerald's 'Babylon Revisited.'" *College English* 25.2 (1963): 128–35.

The Ritz bar, where "Babylon Revisited" begins and ends, is "one of the story's chief symbols of the relentless impingement of the past on the present" (129). That Charlie Wales can return to the bar without fear of a moral relapse seems to suggest he has separated himself from the excesses of his past, but by the end of the story it is evident that he can never fully escape (129). Charlie has reformed, but unjustly will continue to pay for his sins (129). The first scene in the warmth and comfort of the Peters home "is the symbolic obverse of the opening scene at the Ritz bar" (130). Yet in both places Charlie is an outsider, suggesting that he will not be allowed to make a home with his daughter in the future (130). In the "tender and loving" conversation of Charlie's lunch with Honoria, Fitzgerald shows "the absolute rightness of Charlie's desire to be reunited with his daughter" (131). The scene also suggests Honoria's loss if she cannot live with her father (132). Past and future come together when Lorraine Quarles and Duncan Schaeffer meet father and daughter (132). Although Charlie knows he is stronger than they, these "'ghosts out of the past'" will destroy "the promise of [his] tomorrow" (132). The final scene in which Honoria waves goodbye "framed in the window" reveals symbolically the distance between Charlie and the life he hopes to make with her (133). Although Marion Peters' objections seem "motivated solely by a concern for Honoria's welfare and duty to her dead sister," she is jealous of the money her sister had had and resentful of Charlie's success (133). She seems to represent "middle-class values and virtues—home, responsible job, hard work, the respect of the community"— yet her behavior suggests limits to those virtues, as she "unwittingly [allies] herself with [Duncan and Lorraine] to destroy Charlie" (134). When Duncan and Lorraine intrude on Charlie's final meeting with the Peters, Charlie tries to push them—and his past—"backward into time," but Lincoln's "'swinging Honoria back and forth like a pendulum from side to side'" evokes the past, which "has set the pendulum of the future in motion" as Honoria gets symbolically farther from her father (135). Back at the Ritz bar Charlie remains strong in his commitment to change, but he is fully aware of what he has lost (135). Fitzgerald's final sentence destroys all hope as Charlie seeks comfort in his dead wife "for whom time has also stopped" (135). **FORM, THEM**

Fit 21. Hagopian, John V. "A Prince in Babylon." *Fitzgerald Newsletter* 19 (1962): 99–101.

"Babylon Revisited" is "a Catholic, Dantesque story which shows Charlie Wales's suffering in purgatory and suggests his "eventual redemption" (99). Images outside the Ritz Bar and in Montmartre suggest purgatory (100). Charlie's behavior suggests his rebirth (100). And Helen, who comes to him in a dream, is his Beatrice (100). **THEM, FORM**

Fit 22. Kuehl, John. *F. Scott Fitzgerald: A Study of the Short Fiction.* Boston: Twayne, 1991. Pp. 80–86.

As has been noted, the limited omniscient point of view allows the reader to see the conflict between the profligate Charlie Wales and the reformed Charles J. Wales, a conflict represented by the struggle between Lorraine and Duncan and Marion and Lincoln and by the contrast between pre- and post-war Paris (80–81). When the story begins, Charlie is already a reformed sinner (82). Although the story is bracketed by a framework of scenes in the Ritz bar, the geographical progression "confirms rather than transforms [Charlie's] identity" (82). In the opening scene Charlie asks about Duncan, but from then on, Charlie renounces Lorraine and Duncan (82). After his failure to regain his daughter, Charlie still takes only one drink, thus proving that his reformation is complete (82). Fitzgerald's success at blending "autobiographical and historical phenomena" is evident in his use of stock market allusions to relate "public financial and private moral transactions" so that the "first is a macrocosm of the second and the second is a microcosm of the first" (83). The pattern of Charlie Wales's life is similar to Dick Diver's in *Tender Is the Night*—"work, success, inaction, dissipation, illness"—but the story is finally more optimistic than the novel because Charlie has begun to work again, proving he "possesses 'character'" (84–86). **FORM**

Fit 23. Male, Roy R. "'Babylon Revisited': A Story of the Exile's Return." *Studies in Short Fiction* 2 (1965): 270–77.

Since "Babylon Revisited" is not a difficult story to understand, few articles have been written about it (270). Still, it can be profitably examined in new ways, including "generic, historical, and biographical" (270). Fitzgerald's story has several themes in common with others like

"Rip Van Winkle" and "Ethan Brand" which deal with "the Exile's Return": the theme of mutability, or "the sense of permanence and change," which is similar to "the *ubi sunt* formula in poetry"; the search for a reunion with "some form of the feminine principle"; "the loss of identity"; and "freedom and responsibility" (Charlie "maintain[s] that he is now a responsible person but den[ies] responsibility for his wife's death") (271–74). Although similar in themes to other stories of the Exile's Return, "Babylon Revisited" is different with its modern techniques of dramatic presentation, "restricted point of view," "skillful transitions," and "dialogue ... both realistic in tone and radiant with meaning" (274). The story is successful because Fitzgerald could see so clearly that he "was writing about the end of an era, not just some changes in a corner of tourist France" and because he was able to write with the "double vision" Malcolm Cowley recognized, serving as participant and judging observer who sees Charlie "with both sympathy and ironic detachment" (274–75). Although the story examines the conflict "between Charlie and Marion," the more important conflict "is between Charlie Wales (who presumably takes his last name from the prince who was the epitome of the goodtime Charlies in the twenties) and 'Mr. Charles J. Wales of Prague,' sound businessman and moralist, between the regally imaginative but destructive past and the dull, bourgeois but solid present" (275). Charlie knows his old ways led to "dissipation," but he still follows his longing for them and goes to the Ritz bar, where he meets Lorraine and Duncan, a grave error that costs him his daughter (276). Charlie is in fact a man "caught between two worlds" with Lorraine on one side and Marion on the other. He thinks "'they couldn't make him pay forever,'" but it is clear they will keep him in exile (277). **HIST, THEM, FORM**

Fit 24. Mangum, Bryant. *A Fortune Yet: Money in the Art of F. Scott Fitzgerald's Short Stories.* New York and London: Garland, 1991. Pp. 96–98.

"Babylon Revisited" is one of Fitzgerald's most artistically successful stories but also has the elements to make it entertaining to a popular audience (96). Through Charlie Wales the reader sees both "the Paris as it existed for expatriate wanderers before the Depression and the now-dimmed Paris to which [he] returns" (96). The story appeals to a popular audience through their "ambivalent feelings toward Charlie," while avoiding sentimentality created by too much sympathy for Charlie (96–97). Although Fitzgerald leaves the element of hope that the *Saturday Evening Post* audience would have expected, he shows the careful reader that Charlie's second chance may come too late (98). **FORM, READ-R**

Fit 25. Perosa, Sergio. *The Art of F. Scott Fitzgerald.* Trans. Charles Matz and Sergio Perosa. Ann Arbor: University of Michigan Press, 1968. Pp. 95–98.

Although Charlie Wales seems to have reformed, his sister-in-law Marion Peters fears he has not and, after the return of his former acquaintances suggests he has not escaped the past, she refuses to give him custody of his daughter, Honoria (96–97). Marion's stance is partially influenced by "personal resentment for his past happiness and wealth" and is "both selfish and cruel" (97). Having proved his transformation through his behavior with his daughter and shown his resolve by not falling into his old pattern of drinking, Charlie will eventually triumph (97). Near the end of the story Honoria becomes "a symbolic light of redemption and eventual salvation" (97). **THEM**

Fit 26. Slattery, Sister Margaret Patrice. "The Function of Time in *The Great Gatsby* and "Babylon Revisited."" *Fitzgerald Newsletter* 39 (1967): 279–82.

Both *The Great Gatsby* and "Babylon Revisited" have circular time structures, but while the novel moves from present to past to present, the story moves in the opposite direction, from past to present to past (279). Likewise, the protagonists' attitudes are reversed (279). Gatsby rejects the present as he tries to regain the past, and Charlie denies the past as he tries to make a new life in the present (279). Although Charlie wants to regain his daughter in the present, his inability to break away from the past is evident in his beginning his quest for his daughter at the Ritz Bar, which represents his past; his failure to admit responsibility for his treatment of his wife; his maintaining a pattern of drinking; and his constant recall of events from the past (280–81). As in *Gatsby*, the clashing of past and present illuminates the internal conflicts of the characters (281). Charlie cannot relinquish his hold on the past and will therefore jeopardize his hope for a future with his daughter (281). **THEM, FORM, HIST**

Fit 27. Toor, David. "Guilt and Retribution in 'Babylon Revisited.'" *Fitzgerald/Hemingway Annual* (1973–74): 155–64.

Roy Male is correct in stating that Charlie Wales brings about his own downfall by visiting the Ritz bar but is incorrect in saying this "'is a story of suspension between two worlds'" (155). In fact, Charlie is tormented by "his own inner sense of guilt and his inability to expiate it" (156). He seems to be facing his problems when he allows himself one drink a day, but by going to Prague where he is not known, he has simply escaped or avoided dealing with them (156). At times Charlie seems to acknowledge his guilt "to himself—and others," but then he issues "a denial, a shifting, or a sharing of the blame," as when he hopes

Honoria avoids the combination of his and Helen's traits which "'had brought them to disaster'" (158). He even excuses himself for her death and denies responsibility for the visit from Lorraine and Duncan (159–62). Charlie Wales's story is "not ... about the inability of the world to forgive and forget, or even about a man drawn back to the past and therefore unable to come to terms with the present" (162). Instead, it "is ... about self-destruction, about the human mind's ability to delude itself into thinking that what it does is based on logic and reason" (162). **THEM**

A.C.L.

"THE YELLOW WALLPAPER"

Gil 1. Berman, Jeffrey. "The Unrestful Cure: Charlotte Perkins Gilman and 'The Yellow Wallpaper.'" In *The Talking Cure: Literary Representations of Psychoanalysis.* New York: New York University Press, 1985. Pp. 33–59.

The Living of Charlotte Perkins Gilman: An Autobiography discusses events in Gilman's life that are relevant to understanding "The Yellow Wallpaper." Her father, soon to become a prominent librarian, deserted the family upon learning that his wife, for health reasons, was advised not to bear more children. Gilman's mother withheld affection from Charlotte, one of two surviving children out of four, reasoning that if the girl did not expect affection then she could not be hurt in the future (34–35). In response, Charlotte created a dream world that sustained her until her mother told her it was wrong to fantasize; the thirteen-year-old girl obeyed (36). Even though she had misgivings about the institution of marriage, she, at twenty-three, wedded Charles Walter Stetson (37) and ten months later bore a daughter and immediately entered into a severe depression (38). Seeking a change, she left for California and improved. Upon arriving home and feeling the depression returning, she sought the help of the well-known neurologist S. Weir Mitchell, who prescribed a rest cure (39). For months she complied. Realizing, however, that her condition was deteriorating and that marriage and motherhood were the sources of her affliction, she divorced her husband (39). Motherhood for Gilman represented "weakness and passivity" (39) and was "the ultimate human sacrifice" (40) Gilman's life affected her writings, both the nonfiction, which gained her fame, and the fiction, especially "The Yellow Wallpaper." Especially relevant to the development of her theories concerning women and their relationship to the culture was the trauma caused by her parents' actions (40–45). S. Weir Mitchell, a well known psychiatrist (author of numerous standard medical texts) and fiction writer (nineteen novels), introduced the rest cure, with its components of bed rest and minimum stimulation (46). Although most of his patients were women, he held conservative views concerning them and their roles (47). Information concerning Mitchell's treatment of Gilman comes from her own autobiographical writing (49).

Turning to Mitchell after three years of depression, she entered into the rest cure confident that it would alleviate her problems (49). After a month, Mitchell sent her home with explicit directions, among which was "never touch a pen, brush or pencil as long as you live" (50). After three months, she rejected Mitchell's advice and began writing, immediately making gains toward a recovery (50). Perhaps the rest cure failed with Gilman because although Mitchell supported the idea of motherhood, she did not: "She was attempting to flee from the domestic prison of the mother's world—the parasitic world of abject dependency upon men, the depressing routine of endless drudgery, screaming babies, intellectual impoverishment, and helpless resignation. Mitchell's paternalistic therapy locked her into the mother's role" (50). As Gilman herself acknowledges, "The Yellow Wallpaper" is a fictionalized version of her breakdown and treatment, with the ending suggesting the outcome for Gilman had she continued Mitchell's regimen (51). Comparing the autobiographical account of the breakdown and cure with the fictional version suggests that the short story is more direct and honest (52). In the autobiography, Gilman describes her husband as being without fault, but in the story the narrator's husband, insensitive and patronizing, forbids her to write (52). For Gilman writing leads to salvation; when the fictional narrator is denied writing, her recovery becomes impossible (53). The home, both for Gilman—as evident in her later tome *The Home: Its Work and Influence*—and for the narrator, is seen as a prison, as is suggested by the bars on the nursery (53). The wallpaper, a projection of the narrator's fears, symbolizes her conflicting emotions about motherhood and marriage (53–55). Indeed, "the wallpaper recreates the mother's inescapable horror of children and her regression to infancy. The pattern and sub-pattern mirror her terrified identification with the abandoned child and abandoning mother" (55). The wallpaper also suggests the narrator's uneasiness about sex, an uneasiness also seen in her desire to sleep downstairs in a room with a single bed (56). Stating that she wrote the story "to convince him [Mitchell] of the error of his ways" (58), Gilman sent him a copy and later discovered that he subsequently changed his treatment (58). **HIST**

Gil 2. Feldstein, Richard. "Reader, Text, and Ambiguous Referentiality in 'The Yellow Wall-Paper.'" In *Feminism and Psychoanalysis*. Eds. Richard Feldstein and Judith Roof. Ithaca, NY: Cornell University Press, 1989. Pp. 269–79.

In the manuscript of the story the word "wallpaper" appears three different ways: wall paper, wall-paper, and wallpaper. Editors, however, without justification, have imposed consistency in publication (270). Feldstein argues that the ambiguity is intentional, for the word refers to something that "resists analysis" (270), much as the narrator

resists her husband's anaylsis. She "produces a feminist counterdis-
course" (271) that opposes his traditional, patriarchal one. Many critics
argue that because the narrator succumbs to madness (as is indicated,
for instance, by her gnawing of the bedframe and her crawling around
the room), she cannot be a feminist (271). However, the ending seems
ironic, and the narrator's madness seems questionable (273). The narrator's actions provide an ironic alternative to the world view of John
(273). Although he treats her as a young girl, she responds by resisting
his authority in many ways, feigning sleep at night, pretending not to
write, and refusing to respond to his treatment (273). Reading the story
as a narrative of the mental breakdown of a woman is to accept the authorities' view. But reading it as a narrative of a woman's resistance
brings into question the culture's assumptions about madness and
women (274). The narrator identifies with other oppressed women as
represented in the wallpaper (275). Her creeping is a form of resistance
and revenge (275). If the narrator and protagonist are identical, the ending takes on additional meaning, for the protagonist must have recovered sufficiently from her madness in order to write an account of it
(277). **HIST, FEM**

Gil 3. Golden, Catherine. "'Overwriting' the Rest Cure: Charlotte
Perkins Gilman's Literary Escape from S. Weir Mitchell's Fic-
tionalization of Women." In *Critical Essays on Charlotte Perkins
Gilman*. Ed. Joanne B. Karpinski. New York: G.K. Hall, 1992. Pp.
144–58.

Charlotte Perkins Gilman was just one of many well-known writers,
such as Walt Whitman, treated by S. Weir Mitchell, a famous neurologist and novelist, or treated according to his rest cure therapy, such as
Virginia Woolf (144). Gilman not only rejected Mitchell's therapy and
his orders not to write but also created a story that criticized his methods and included him in it (145). Gilman "'overwrote' Mitchell's efforts"
to make her into a compliant female patient (145). The rest cure relies on
secluding the patient for six to eight weeks during which time the
patient is allowed no stimulation such as visits from friends, diversions,
such as sewing or exercise, and is given a high fat diet (147). Even so,
Mitchell's treatment was more progressive than others which relied on
ovariotomies to relieve depression (146). Although Mitchell did not
write about Perkins in his fiction, his protagonists, most often passive
females who depend on strong males, frequently suffer from mental
problems and are treated by the rest cure (145–47). "The Yellow Wallpaper" takes the same themes and situations found in Mitchell's fiction
but suggests different results and conclusions (151). Gilman's protagonist at the outset is as passive and submissive as Mitchell's heroines, but
through her madness she gains strength (151). John, her husband, has
the confidence and authority seen in Mitchell's male characters (152),

but his fainting at the conclusion illustrates his failure to understand his wife (152). The narrator, at first, resists his orders: she secretly writes in her journal and pretends to sleep (153). However, because she is entrapped within the house, her recovery is doomed, and she chooses madness over becoming the submissive woman that John and Mitchell in his novels and practice prefer (154). The story thus illustrates the damage done to women who accept the patriarchal view (154). Literature offered Gilman "an opportunity to challenge the restrictions imposed upon women" (155). **FEM, HIST**

Gil 4. Hedges, Elaine R. "'Out at Last'? 'The Yellow Wallpaper' after Two Decades of Feminist Criticism." *Critical Essays on Charlotte Perkins Gilman.* Ed. Joanne B. Karpinski. New York: G.K. Hall, 1992. Pp. 222–33.

An overview of the criticism of Gilman's story since its re-publication in 1973 shows that the work is now firmly established in the literary canon and has been the subject of numerous critical studies with often widely divergent interpretations (222). The two prime areas of contention concern the symbolism of the wallpaper and the meaning of the conclusion, in which the mad narrator creeps over her husband (who has fainted). The first critical studies considered the story as a woman's attempt at achieving autonomy while facing limitations set by society. The wall paper, then, becomes a symbol of oppressive traditional gender roles (223) and the conclusion, then, is seen as a victory since the narrator escapes from them (224). The mid-eighties saw readings based on the ideas of Jacques Lacan. In these, the narrator does not achieve a semblance of autonomy but instead is oppressed by male discourse, from which she escapes only by moving from the Symbolic realm back into the Imaginary one of an infant (224–25). These readings consider the color and odor of the wallpaper; both relate to the culture's repression of female sexuality, resulting in the narrator's inabilty to accept her sexual nature (225). The conclusion is seen in a negative light. The narrator is unable to accept her sexuality, or (if one considers the organic quality of the wallpaper) she is unable to accept motherhood (226). The nineties brought articles that, challenging the earlier critics, argued that "The Yellow Wallpaper" should not be read as containing a message for women. Such a reading, which assumes that all woman share certain characteristics, is essentialistic (226). Rather, the story should be read as a product of the culture in which it was produced. Thus, the wallpaper with its yellow color and strange smell symbolizes the fear at that time of overwhelming immigration from southern Europe and Asia (227). Other critics discover in the story an indictment of capitalism (227). No longer is the narrator seen as on a journey towards selfhood; instead, she is a victim of the "culture of consumption" (227). The changing interpretations reflect the different historical periods of the critics themselves. The year that "The Wallpaper" was reissued was the year of the *Roe v. Wade* decision, a period in which women's fight for autonomy was achieving some victories (229). Thus, reading the story as a woman's attempt at creating an identity seemed natural (229). The more recent critical approaches come out of changes in the political and intellectual climate (230). The failure of the Equal Rights Amendment, among other events, helped create a climate of "skepticism or disillusionment about women's power to create and sustain significant political and social change," and the new (post-structuralist) critical theories question the concept of identity and the ability to control one's life (230). While some recent critics read the conclusion as the defeat of the narrator, most see the text as succeeding in its critique of the culture (230). **FEM, PSY, PLUR, NHIST, HIST**

Gil 5. Hume, Beverly A. "Gilman's 'Interminable Grotesque': The Narrator of 'The Yellow Wallpaper.'" *Studies in Short Fiction* 28 (Fall 1991): 477–84.

The narrator becomes a grotesque figure, representing the general state of women in the nineteenth century (477). Although the narrator fights the social forces that oppress her, ultimately she is defeated (477). One source of oppression is John, the narrator's husband, who maintains traditionally paternalistic views (478). Although the narrator rebels against him, her rebellion does not lead to freedom but to defeat and insanity (480). Ironically, when John realizes the extent of his wife's madness, he faints, a stereotypic response of a nineteenth-century woman (478). The narrator, untraditionally for women, uses writing to try to understand her difficulties, which she sees as stemming from a situation with gothic qualities (479). The narrator's writing and the wallpaper have certain commonalities: they are both seemingly random at first reading but on a deeper inspection have a grotesque pattern (480). The narrator wants to interpret the pattern in the wallpaper, but it is difficult to comprehend the grotesque, with its "elements of humor and horror" (483). Eventually in her attempt to unravel the wallpaper's design, she "merges into it, and in effect, becomes it—as the woman in the wallpaper" (481). Through her intense desire to understand the grotesque, the narrator becomes part of it herself (482). **THEM, HIST, FEM**

Gil 6. Jacobus, Mary. "An Unnecessary Maze of Sign-Reading." *Reading Woman: Essays in Feminist Criticism.* New York: Columbia University Press, 1986. Pp. 229–48.

Gilman wrote a gothic tale that "tapped male hysteria about women" (235). The female body is seen by the culture and John as "repugnant," and thus female desire is oppressed (235). Therefore, when John finally confronts his wife and the feminine other she represents, he faints (236).

Madness, which John will not accept, is attributed to women by the culture: knowledge is the province of men, while subjectivity (with its closeness to madness) is the province of women (237). Gilman links the gothic, the oppression of women, and the repression of the feminine in the story (239). The narrator illustrates the oppression by first accepting her husband's authority and then literally by creeping (239). The gothic or uncanny is incorporated into the story by the questions it raises. Was it the narrator or a previous tenant who gnawed the bedstead? Was the room used as a nursery or as a prison for another mad woman? Is the past being repeated by the narrator? (240). John faints because he is confronted by "an embodiment of the animality of woman unredeemed by (masculine) reason" (241). The narrator represents male fears about femininity and female sexuality (242). Represented in the story by the color yellow and the smell of the wallpaper, female sexuality is a subject not allowed in literature of the late nineteenth century (242–43). Although the wallpaper suggests female sexuality, it also represents a text that cannot be read, even though the narrator attempts to do so (245). And at the conclusion, she becomes a figure in her own reading of the text: she sees herself as the woman imprisoned behind the bars of the wallpaper (247). **FEM, HIST, THEM**

Gil 7. Johnson, Greg. "Gilman's Gothic Allegory: Rage and Redemption in 'The Yellow Wallpaper.'" *Studies in Short Fiction* 26 (1989): 521–30.

"The Yellow Wallpaper" contains several elements of a gothic tale: "the themes of confinement and rebellion, forbidden desire and 'irrational' fear ... the distraught heroine, the forbidding mansion, and the powerfully repressive male antagonist" (522). Gilman uses gothic conventions to relate her tale of the oppression encountered by a nineteenth-century woman (522). The narrator, caught between the practical world of her husband and her own imaginative one, attempts to save herself through writing, detailing her journey inward to discover her selfhood (523). Because her husband John has no tolerance for the narrator's imagination, he represses her, treating her like a child (524). She, however, "creat[es] a Gothic alternative to the stifling daylight world of her husband and society at large" (524). Her imaginative growth and developing selfhood are seen in her growing awareness of the wallpaper (524). At first, in daylight, she sees the suggestion of a pattern in the wallpaper; then, at dusk, the pattern becomes clearer; finally, in the moonlight she discerns a woman trapped beneath the paper (524–25). She then identifies with the woman and realizes that the source of her own power lies in her imagination (525). Neither the imaginative nor the practical world can comprehend the other. Since the rational cannot comprehend the imaginative and vice versa, the narrator must supply her own text in defiance of John (527). She does this by writing her journal, an act of disobedience (527). Another text in the story—the wallpaper—tells the story of oppression, with which the narrator comes to terms in her journal (528). The conclusion, in which she has liberated the figure imprisoned within the wallpaper, seems positive. The narrator's crawling suggests "insistent growth into a new stage of being" (529). Developing from a helpless individual in bed (similar to an infant), she has progressed to a crawling child (529). John, in a reversal of the roles typical of a gothic tale, faints at the sight of her (529). **HIST, THEM, FEM**

Gil 8. Kasmer, Lisa. "Charlotte Perkins Gilman's 'The Yellow Wallpaper': A Symptomatic Reading." *Literature and Psychology* 36 (1990): 1–15.

Unlike the male editors and readers who disapproved of the story in the late nineteenth century (1), contemporary feminist readers have canonized it (2). Recent feminist critics see the narrator's husband's inability to understand her as typifying earlier readers' inability to understand the story, and the narrator's search for freedom, which she finds by pulling down the wallpaper, as representing women's search for freedom (2–4). The text reveals feminine "moments ... that disrupt the male desire, allowing the desires of the woman to emerge" (4). The moments are found in the "symptomatic points, or the impasses of meaning, in [the narrator's] journal" (4). The narrator, although slightly questioning John's prescribed treatment for her, acquiesces to his diagnosis on the basis of his authority; in doing so, she accepts his discourse, which considers her as a child who must be protected and cared for (4–5). According to Jacques Lacan, a child, entering into language, acquires the prevailing discourse, even though it does not completely represent the child (6). The language that the narrator has accepted is a patriarchal discourse that assumes male as the standard and female as the other and that typifies the nineteenth-century view of women as inferiors who need guidance and protection (6). The feelings that the narrator is unable to express in the patriarchal language are evident in her journal as symptomatic points, such as when she conjectures that perhaps the reason that she is not improving is related to the fact that John is a doctor (7). After failing to convince John of her condition, she focuses on the wallpaper as if it holds a key to understanding herself (7). On one level the wallpaper represents the oppressiveness of her marriage; on another level it offers freedom from such oppression (8). The wallpaper, suggesting *écriture feminine* as discussed by Helene Cixous, represents a discourse that is not contained by male discourse and is opposed to it (8). Because of the connection between the wallpaper and the narrator, the implication is that the narrator is disrupting male discourse and is doing so in a discourse that arises from her desires and her body (9). The emotions she attributes to the wallpaper are ones that

John would have her deny (10). Her language begins to change as she describes the wallpaper. Instead of using short declarative sentences, she employs complex ones filled with phrases (11). Her description of the wallpaper also aptly describes herself imprisoned in an oppressive marriage (11). However, instead of seeing the wallpaper as a symbol, she sees it as reality; she has regresssed to the state of a child, leaving the symbolic realm behind (12). The conclusion does not imply liberation; instead, the narrator is trapped in the imaginary realm, without access to the symbolic, and thus has lost the ability to communicate (12). However, Gilman, unlike the narrator, does communicate successfully (through her use of symbols) information about her own mental breakdown (13). **FEM, READ-R, PSY**

Gil 9. Shumaker, Conrad. "'Too Terribly Good to Be Printed': Charlotte Gilman's 'The Yellow Wallpaper.'" *American Literature* 57 (1985): 588–99.

"The Yellow Wallpaper" was rejected by one editor because of its possible impact on the audience; later it was included in a collection by William Dean Howells with the comment that it is "too terribly good to be printed" (588). What the readers were objecting to was the subject: mental breakdown in a middle-class woman (589). More contemporary readers find the story to be a condemnation of gender roles (589). The story presents a particular world view (589): women represent imagination whereas men typify rationalism and realism, conflict and tension being created by the opposing forces (590). Gilman, as a young girl, was ordered by her mother to forego daydreaming; she complied. Likewise, the narrator in "The Yellow Wallpaper" is ordered by her husband John to rest; she, however, mentally begins to explore the wallpaper (590). John does not understand, nor can he accept that work (or in her case writing) can be theurapeutic and that rest can be detrimental (591). He fears her imagination and sees madness as a result of too much imagination (591–92): "Imagination and art are subversive because they threaten to undermine his [John's] materialistic universe" (592). John's attempts to have the narrator ignore her imagination ironically result in her destruction (592). Traditional gender roles promote fear of the imagination because it is assigned to women, who are considered to be inferior (593). The narrator understands John's stance, but she is unable to communicate her position and instead uses her journal to discusss what she cannot discuss with him (593). Because he represents reason as opposed to her imagination, the narrator doubts herself and is not capable of questioning John or the society that supports his position (594). But he is as much a prisoner of society's views as she is (595). Gilman uses the structure of the story to emphasize her themes. Foreshadowing suggests that the narrator is mad (even though she is unaware of it) and suggests that she is separating herself from the traditional role of wife

(595). The pattern of the wallpaper and the bars on the window suggest the trapped nature of female gender roles (596). The window symbolizes freedom, but her only freedom is to creep (597). Madness also affords another type of freedom; she has freed herself from her roles as wife and mother, and no one "not even Jane—the wife she once was—can put her back" (597–98). The unpopularity of the story when it was first published can be attributed to the sharp criticism it contains of nineteenth-century attitudes (598). **THEM, FEM, FORM, HIST**

B.W.

"RAPPACCINI'S DAUGHTER"

Haw 1. Brenzo, Richard. "Beatrice Rappaccini: A Victim of Male Love and Horror." *American Literature* 48.2 (1976): 152–64.

"Rappaccini's Daughter" tells of a woman who is "destroyed" by the three men in her life, despite her essential innocence and their apparent concern for her (152). Because she is female, Beatrice is exploited by Giovanni, her father, and Baglioni, all of whom "'project'" their own evil upon her (153). From the first moment he sees her, Giovanni is attracted to her, but, influenced by Baglioni, he also finds her threatening (153–54). His imagination is so stimulated by her that he has trouble discovering the real Beatrice (154). When he meets her in the garden, he finds her "'so human and so maidenlike,'" but he continues to idealize her, although this time in a positive way (156). His assessment of her moves "between the two classic extremes of ... woman as demon or as saint," so that he never knows what kind of woman she really is (157). When Beatrice shrinks from his touch, for example, he assumes she does so because of the poison in her, never considering her actions to be prompted by morality (157). He himself in fact seems "to desire sexual union, while fearing its dangers," not only the obvious possibility of losing his life if she is poisoned but also of losing control of his life to her (157). What he really wants is "to possess Beatrice, to change and control her," and "to shape her into his personal image of the divine woman" (158). His motive becomes apparent when he uses Baglioni's antidote to test Beatrice (158). Suspecting that her poison has infected him, he wishes his breath could kill her, thus projecting onto her the "deadly intent" he himself feels (159). Surprisingly, although Dr. Rappaccini is ultimately responsible for the poisoning, Giovanni never blames him, but instead lashes out at Beatrice, who is "willing to sacrifice her life for him" while still recognizing that he had "'more poison in [his] nature'" than she did (159). Although Baglioni seems a kindly man, he too punishes Beatrice for the sins of her father, in part out of fear (without foundation, it becomes clear) that she will replace him at the university (160–61). The evil he projects onto Beatrice is his own ambition (162). By making his daughter poisonous, Rappaccini gives her power over others that he would wish to have himself (162). She has no desire for power, though, and ironically his experiments make her more, not less, "vulnerable" (162). Had she been a man, Beatrice would not have been treated as she was (163). But because the three men see her as a danger, they act to destroy her (163). Because of the poison in her body, Beatrice at first seems a "femme fatale"; however, it is "the hommes fatals" who bring her death (164). **FEM, THEM**

Haw 2. Bunge, Nancy. *Nathaniel Hawthorne: A Study of the Short Fiction.* New York: Twayne, 1993. Pp. 67–71.

"Rappaccini's Daughter" examines the conflict "between the detached intellectual knowledge of the scientist and the emotional knowledge love produces" (67). Love, as represented by Beatrice, seems the more valued, although she is presented in a somewhat negative light when she fails to consider her effect on Giovanni (68–69). If one is not convinced of the narrator's attitude toward Beatrice (and thus his stance in the conflict of the intellect and the emotions), however, other stories can offer clues (69). "The New Adam and Eve" implies approval of what Beatrice signifies by openly "condemn[ing] intellectual knowledge as incomplete and dangerous in large part because it presents itself as true" (69–70). "Little Annie's Ramble" uses images of water like those associated with Beatrice to suggest refreshment and nourishment (70). Despite Hawthorne's focus in "Rappaccini's Daughter" on "the human tragedy created by intellectual arrogance," the other two stories draw attention to the kind of love Beatrice offers as an antidote (71). "Rappaccini's Daughter" remains ambiguous, however, leaving the reader aware, as Beverly Haviland notes, "'that truths are many, not one'" (71). **THEM, FORM**

Haw 3. Crews, Frederick C. *The Sins of the Fathers: Hawthorne's Psychological Themes.* 1966. Berkeley: University of California Press, 1989. Pp. 3–7, 117–35.

Biographers who find "repose" (4) in Hawthorne's work and critics who see Hawthorne as a Christian allegorist have overlooked his "ambivalence" (7). "Rappaccini's Daughter," in particular, invites an allegorical reading ("Giovanni renders himself unworthy of the Christian redemption embodied in Beatrice"), but a "literal" interpretation of Giovanni's sexual confusion is "more workable" (118). Although Beatrice is unaware of her "allure," Hawthorne draws attention to "her voluptuous beauty [that] sets off the wildest fantasies in" Giovanni (120). But as he is drawn to her sexually, he remembers her "poisonousness" and recoils (121). Beatrice's garden also "has strong sexual connotations" (121), and she seems "erotically" attracted to its flowers (122). Lisabetta "functions as a pander," helping Giovanni gain entrance to the garden in a way that is described in language suggesting intercourse (123). Giovanni is much like Rappaccini, whose "fiendish passion for knowledge" (125) is fueled by "sexual disgust" (127). After Giovanni learns that Beatrice has contaminated him, he lashes out at her "with a sadistic longing to destroy the woman who has both inspired and inhibited [his] lust" (130). For all her deadly attractiveness, however, Beatrice maintains "her purity of soul" to the end (131). If Beatrice's garden is a kind of Eden, the fall comes with Giovanni's "inability to assimilate the discovery of sexuality in" Beatrice and Beatrice's being "victimized by the consequences" (131). Religion comes into the story through heavenly images of Beatrice when Giovanni is deluding himself into believing that Beatrice is pure (132). But his faith is based on an untruth (133), and when he loses his faith in her, "he achieves the height of blasphemy" (133). His loss of faith has been caused by a "'father'" who has created this perverted "new Eden," "committed a kind of incest by" contaminating Beatrice, and is promoting a marriage that will be "vicariously incestuous" (133). The portrait of Giovanni seems an *"almost* ... pitiless symbolic anatomy of an adolescent mind" until one realizes how close Giovanni is to Hawthorne (134–35). **PSY, THEM**

Haw 4. Dauber, Kenneth. *Rediscovering Hawthorne.* Princeton: Princeton University Press, 1977. Pp. 25–35.

Although Crews's interpretation is different from Male's, both critics are trying to unify the apparent inconsistencies in the characters in "Rappaccini's Daughter" (28). Allegory, which we assume this story to be, implies layers of meaning that nevertheless have "unitary force" (30). "Rappaccini's Daughter," however, contains actual "contradictions": it "is the story of an innocent ... girl destroyed by a faithless love, and it is the story of a dangerous woman enticing an innocent boy" (30–31). Both stories exist within the tale, but Aubepine focuses on one, then the other, to keep attention on both (31). Although "Rappaccini's Daughter" contains "two incompatible expositions," neither is "ambiguous" (31). Baglioni is at one moment the "true friend of Giovanni's father" and then "a meddling, selfish academic" (32). Dame Lisabetta acts as "a simple, God-fearing peasant" then "a pandering, gold-grubbing go-between" (32). In the "innocent-boy-enticed story," Baglioni and Giovanni are "the positive figures"; Beatrice and Rappaccini, "the negative" (33). In the "deserted-girl story," Baglioni and Giovanni are "negative"; Beatrice, and maybe Rappaccini ("heartless and coldly intellectual" but also "loving if misguided father"), is positive (33). Hawthorne intentionally leaves the two opposing readings unresolved (34). His purpose in doing so becomes apparent by examining the progression of his work as a whole, in particular as it is revealed through the prefaces to his novels and introductions to stories like "Rappaccini's Daughter" (18). The appeal of Hawthorne's work cannot be demonstrated through historical criticism or New Criticism but rather through his attempts to create intimacy with the reader (221–24). By offering more than one interpretation, he is attempting to "engage the reader" (13); he is issuing an "invitation to his audience to interpret itself in his work" (50). **DECON, READ-R**

Haw 5. Dunne, Michael. *Hawthorne's Narrative Strategy.* Jackson: University of Mississippi Press, 1995. Pp. 70–78.

Like Robert Coover and John Barth in the twentieth century, Nathaniel Hawthorne experimented with different "narrative levels" that challenge what is now considered the "doctrine of [authorial] impersonality" (70–71). One can examine Hawthorne's method in "Rappaccini's Daughter" using the twentieth-century narratological approach outlined in Gerard Genette's *Narrative Discourse* (71). "Rappaccini's Daughter" has several narrative levels, for example, "diegetic," "when a narrator tells us about the actions of fictional characters who live in a fictional world—the narrator ... telling us about Signor Pietro Baglioni"; the "metadiegetic," [w]hen one of this narrator's fictional characters, Baglioni, tells a tale about Alexander the Great"; and the "extradiegetic," when a narrator "exists apart from the diegetic narrative, as in the fictional critical essay framing 'Rappaccini's Daughter'" (71). Hawthorne also uses "metalepsis," a "'transition from one narrative level to another'" (59). Hawthorne refers to himself in the original title of the story, now a subtitle, with "*Aubepine*," "French for *hawthorn*," and "intensif[ies] this self-referentiality" as the "extradiegetic narrator" discusses Aubepine and his works using French titles for Hawthorne's own stories (72–73). The narrative that focuses on Giovanni and Beatrice is distanced from the reader by its "remote" setting, literary allusions connecting the characters to "the world of literature," biblical allusions linking them to the Garden of Eden, and such references as those that emphasize Beatrice's "exotic" beauty (73–75). Baglioni's "metadiegetic" tale about a poisonous woman that draws an obvious parallel to "the 'real' diegetic Beatrice" enhances the distancing (75). Hawthorne offers many possible explanations for events in the story but is "characteristically careful" to keep "the diegetic narrator" from telling what is true (75–76). In fact, the reader cannot know the truth on "any single diegetic level" because even the extradiegetic narrator "lie[s]" when he tells who wrote the story (77). At one point the "diegetic narrator" seems to offer proof that Baglioni is deceiving Giovanni, but it must be confirmed by consulting the medical department of the University of Padua, "an extradiegtic library" (77–78). Since Hawthorne has already shown that the diegetic level is a fiction, the "validation cannot take place" (78). Hawthorne's metalepsis that seemed able to decrease "the level of fictionality" instead increases it, but "without compromising the authority of his diegetic narrator" (78). **STRUC**

Haw 6. Male, Roy. *Hawthorne's Tragic Vision*. New York: Norton, 1957. Pp. 55–71.

Like later Hawthorne women, Beatrice in "Rappaccini's Daughter" represents the "dual promise" of "tragic involvement with sin" and "the consequent possibility of redemption" (54–55). The complex mixture of good and evil found in her is also evident in the purple shrub that has a central place in her garden (56). Nourished by life-giving water ("spirit") that flows from the broken earthly fountain ("matter"), the shrub combines poison with beauty (56). Other characters in the story also "embody in various ways this dualism of good and evil" (57). Rappaccini is an obvious villain who has nevertheless developed cures with his science (58). Baglioni seems good, but under scrutiny also emerges as a villain (59). Although the story shows that Beatrice's purity finally outweighs her evil, her real importance lies in how Giovanni responds to her (60). Himself a mixture of good and evil, Giovanni is tested like Dante (alluded to in the opening paragraph) to see whether he can achieve something higher than "his ardent earthly passion" (61). At times he intuits the truth of Beatrice's goodness that he sees in her eyes, but more often he allows his senses and Baglioni's promptings to create doubt in his mind (63–66). In his confusion he offers the antidote to Beatrice, thus failing his own test as he submits her to one (66–67). **THEM**

Haw 7. Miller, John N. "Fideism vs. Allegory in 'Rappaccini's Daughter.'" *Nineteenth-Century Literature* 46 (1991): 223–44.

At first "Rappaccini's Daughter" seems an "unmistakable erotic allegory" that presents Beatrice as a woman with both "potent sexual allure," like the purple flowers in her father's garden, and an "angelic spirit," like the "pure fountain water" found there (223). Hawthorne undercuts the allegory, however, by having the narrator and even Beatrice argue for "a fideistic denial" [one based on faith] of those erotic qualities suggested by the sensory evidence associating her with the flower (223). The two readings, the empirical that leads to the erotic allegory and the fideistic that asserts Beatrice's purity, remain "incompatible" (223). Despite possible connections between the story and people in Hawthorne's life, critics overlook a biographical interpretation in trying to deal with the contradictions (224). The story's "false leads, superfluous ambiguity, and internal contradictions" may be explained, though, by examining "Hawthorne's emotional and personal relationships" (226). His use of too many conflicting allusions that "cancel out one another" may arise from his attempts to conceal the link to these relationships (226–27). Some critics find the conflict "between faith or fideistic intuition and empirical rationalism" to be "central" to the story, "with Hawthorne or his narrator opting for faith and shallow-hearted Giovanni reverting to an unregenerate empiricism" (230). According to this reading, Giovanni fails because he does not disregard the sensory evidence of Beatrice's dual nature and take her purity on faith (230). But examination shows too many "inconsistencies" to make this interpretation valid (230). The narrator, Giovanni, and even Beatrice contradict themselves in assessing what happens (230). For example, Beatrice asks Giovanni not to believe his senses, which suggest her deadly nature, and then implies that the danger he perceives in her is real by admitting the deadliness of her sister-shrub (229–31). Hawthorne may denounce Giovanni's inability to "[maintain] an idealized, fideistic view of Beatrice" because of similar tendencies in himself toward women in his own life (235). A biographical link may also explain why Hawthorne undercuts the allegorical reading of Beatrice (235). Like the "evidence" offered to prove "*literary* antecedents for fictional characters," references in the story can support the claim of biographical antecedents (235–36). Edenic allusions connect the story to two real places Hawthorne had compared to Eden, the place where he spent idyllic vacations with his mother and younger sister, Louisa, and the Old Manse, where he spent the first three years of his marriage and wrote "Rappaccini's Daughter" (236). The portrait of Beatrice could have been based on Louisa and their mother, both of whom Hawthorne was very close to, and his wife, Sophia, who was surprisingly similar to Louisa (238–41). References to Sophia in Hawthorne's letters suggest her resemblance to Beatrice, including a dual nature that might have generated Giovanni's internal conflict over the spiritual and physical qualities in Beatrice (239). In appearance, however, Beatrice is a "'dark temptress' ... mysterious, seductive," more like Hawthorne's older sister (243). The portrait of Beatrice may very well result from his feelings for his wife, both sisters, and mother, his awareness of their sexuality and his own attraction to them (243). And his call for faith in Beatrice's purity that challenges the allegorical reading admitting her sexuality may result from Hawthorne's desire to keep his image of Sophia pure and not to expose his "ambivalences about the women closest to him" (244). **HIST, THEM, PSY**

Haw 8. Newman, Lea Bertani Vozar. *A Reader's Guide to the Short Stories of Nathaniel Hawthorne.* Boston: G.K. Hall, 1979. Pp. 256–70.

"Rappaccini's Daughter" was published as "Writings of Aubepine" in December 1844 in the *United States Magazine and Democratic Review* and then under its current title in 1846 in *Mosses from an Old Manse* (257). The preface, removed in 1846, probably because it seemed too "partisan," was restored in the 1854 edition of *Mosses* (257). On first hearing the unfinished story, Hawthorne's wife, Sophia, asked whether Beatrice would "'be a demon or an angel,'" to which he responded, "'I have no idea!'" (258). Sophia might also have offered guidance on making the Italian names suggestive (258). The exploration of "the estrangement of the individual" and other elements of "Rappaccini's Daughter" may have some autobiographical origins, but the "earliest germ for the story" is an anecdote from Sir Thomas Browne's *Pseudodoxia Epidemica* that Hawthorne recorded in his notebook and then has Baglioni tell Giovanni (258). Hawthorne's notebook suggests other possible sources, and the story itself alludes to *The Divine Comedy*, the Bible, and Spenser's *Faerie Queene* (259–61). One can also note similarities to nineteenth-century Romantic and Gothic works like Keats's *Lamia* and Mary Shelley's *Frankenstein*, Hawthorne's own stories (especially "The Birthmark" and "The Artist of the Beautiful") and novels (*The Scarlet Letter*, *The Blithedale Romance*, and *The Marble Faun* [261–63]). Because of the complexity of the story, readers often disagree about its meaning (263). For example, the four characters have been "judged alternately as admirable or reprehensible, heroic or villainous, or as fancifully ideal or ironically grotesque" (263). The difficulty in interpreting the story arises primarily from three "attributes" (264). First is the "subtle yet highly significant shift" from Giovanni's perspective to "an authoritative, omniscient point of view" (264). Second is the allegorical complexity of the story with its "multitude of conflicting literary allusions" that some readers find confusing and others enriching (265–66). One reader sees the story as a fairy tale allegory with the roles ("prince and princess, a good fairy and an evil one") confused, and another reader finds it "an allegory of science" (266–67). The third attribute that provokes varied readings is "the ambivalence in Hawthorne himself," especially toward women and sex (267). Beatrice's nature (angelic yet poisonous), the sexual connotations of some words, the "clearly incestuous innuendos," "Giovanni's confusion" over Beatrice's sexuality—all contribute to the ambiguity of the tale (267–68). Also confusing is Hawthorne's attitude toward "[s]cience, faith, and morals" (268). All the characters have positive and negative traits, a fact which one reader says makes them more human (269). Despite the confusion, however, most readers praise the story, some for its symbolism, in particular, "the poison and the fountain as central symbols for man's corrupted nature" (269). Looking at criticism from 1950 to 1974 suggests that readers respond to the story according to their "own values and concerns" (270). Feminist readers see Beatrice "as a victim of male exploitation" (270). The story has influenced writers as diverse as Henry James and Octavio Paz, and critics continue to see the story's relevance to twentieth-century dilemmas (270). **PLUR, HIST**

Haw 9. Rosenberry, Edward H. "Hawthorne's Allegory of Science: 'Rappaccini's Daughter'" (1960). In *On Hawthorne: The Best from*

American Literature. Eds. Edwin H. Cady and Louis J. Budd.
Durham: Duke University Press, 1990. Pp. 106–13.

"Rappaccini's Daughter" is confusing until one sees that the story is
an allegory of science (106). Giovanni, gazing into Rappaccini's garden,
is the "impressionable young student discovering ... an exciting
laboratory of experimental science" (107). The water in the garden is
"intellectual energy"; the deteriorated fountain, "transitory uses, forms,
and disciplines"; the purple shrub, "the crowning product of a potent
but lawless force of mind" (107). Rappaccini, moving fearfully through
the garden, is Hawthorne's typical scientist, but Beatrice is a new breed,
at home in the garden yet possessing the charm to attract Giovanni
(107–8). Although sometimes "contemptible," Baglioni is the
"humanitarian" who challenges Rappaccini's devotion to pure science
(109). Beatrice's real significance in the allegory becomes clear when her
breath conveys death and she responds by crossing herself and then
casually "'arrang[ing] the fatal flower in her bosom'" (110). Through her
actions Hawthorne shows "both the awful power of modern science"
and her acceptance of the "regrettable" consequences "of technological
progress" (110). She is "the innocent victim of Rappaccini's experiments," but she is also "without the least loss of personal innocence, the
transmitter of them to a foolish and unwary society to which her
training has made her effectively a stranger" (113). **THEM**

Haw 10. Ross, Morton L. "What Happens in 'Rappaccini's Daughter.'" *American Literature* 43 (1971): 336–45.

Despite attempts to dismiss "contradictions, implausibilities, and
absurdities" as unimportant to allegorical readings of "Rappaccini's
Daughter," the story has a "major flaw in [its] literal surface" (336–37).
The story concerns how Giovanni examines "conflicting evidence"
about Beatrice's character and tries to determine whether she is "angel
or demon" (337). In their first meeting Beatrice and Giovanni discuss
how she should be evaluated, and she asks that he trust the words she
speaks (338). By this time Hawthorne has already raised doubts about
evidence provided by the senses as Giovanni questions what he thinks
he has seen (338). Following his "familiar formula of alternative
possibilities," Hawthorne then offers the evidence of intuition, as
Giovanni seems able to see into Beatrice's soul (339–40). While
Hawthorne had at first carefully controlled the point of view, the
narrator becomes more and more "intrusive" in telling the reader which
kind of evidence to believe, moving from a limited omniscient to a fully
omniscient perspective (340–41). Although "the reader has been
systematically made to empathize fully with Giovanni's very human
point of view" as he tries to determine Beatrice's character, now
"attention is suddenly diverted to" establishing what kind of man
Giovanni is (341). When Giovanni tests Beatrice with the antidote, the

reader knows the test is unnecessary, but the narrator states what should now be obvious: that Giovanni suffers from "'a certain shallowness of feeling and insincerity of character'" (342). Hawthorne's failure to allow the reader to examine conflicting evidence to assess Beatrice's character is "a betrayal of the human condition we initially and naturally share with Giovanni" and a significant flaw that inter-feres with any allegorical reading one might attempt to make of the story (345). **FORM, READ-R**

Haw 11. Shurr, William H. "Eve's Bower: Hawthorne's Transition from Public Doctrines to Private Truths." In *Ruined Eden of the Present: Hawthorne, Melville, and Poe: Critical Essays in Honor of Darrel Abel.* Eds. G.R. Thompson and Virgil L. Lokke. West Lafayette, IN: Purdue University Press, 1981. Pp. 143–69.

One can see in *Mosses from an Old Manse* a "transitional moment" for Hawthorne when "[h]is values suddenly clarify" (144). The transforma-tion reflected in that volume came about during the three "honeymoon" years he spent at the Old Manse with his new wife and is recorded in the preface, "The Old Manse," and the two Garden stories (144). In the preface Hawthorne shows his awareness of the heritage of both the Calvinist ministers who previously inhabited the house in which he is living and the theological books around him (145–46). Although con-nected to "the older Calvinist tradition," he identifies more fully with transcendentalism (147). He also conveys "the sense ... of having arrived at his private inner garden," however (147), reflecting a move away from the "public solutions" offered by both Calvinism and transcenden-talism (144). Although aware of the limitations of "allegorizing on the garden in the present stage of human history," he does so in "Rappac-cini's Daughter" and "The New Adam and Eve" (148), as well as the three novels that follow, *The Scarlet Letter*, *The House of Seven Gables*, and *The Blithedale Romance* (160). The allegory of "Rappaccini's Daughter" is much clearer when "seen in the context of New England Calvinism, es-tablished by the place where he wrote it and the preface to the collection in which he published it" (149). In this reading Beatrice and Giovanni are Adam and Eve; Rappaccini is Satan, who only in a Calvinist allegory could control the garden; and Baglioni is "an ineffective Christ in a fallen world" (150–52). The acknowledgment that Rappaccini "'was generally thought to have gained the advantage'" over Baglioni could make sense only in a Calvinist reading (152). The story may also reflect "the bitter fight between Galenic and Paracelsan medicine," with Rap-paccini representing the side that advocates herbal cures and Baglioni, "drugs derived from chemical experiment" (152–53). The controversy led to the cultivation of botanical gardens, the earliest of which was planted at the University of Padua, where the story is set, in 1545, a sig-nificant date in Calvinist history (152–53). In this story Hawthorne is

"the new bridegroom cultivating the Garden of his Calvinist predecessors," although whether as parody or "savage stereotype" of Calvinism
is not clear (153–55). In writing the story Hawthorne "found the
groundwork of values, symbols, and narrative patterns for the three
great novels that follow" (155). "The New Adam and Eve," shaped by
the bliss of Hawthorne's new marriage, shows an innocent Adam and
Eve "corrupted" by man's Art (156). In this story "the natural world is
still the unfallen Garden" controlled by a benevolent Nature, but Adam
and Eve find answers to their questions, not in Calvinism or transcendentalism, but the "private truth" of "love" (159). The three novels written after the "enlightenment experienced at the Old Manse" reflect
Hawthorne's understanding of how "the basic myth (the Garden) and
the longer vehicle (the romance)" could be used to examine the questions raised by "the historical clash" between Calvinism and transcendentalism and his abandonment of both "for purely private solutions"
(169). **HIST, THEM**

Haw 12. West, Ray B., Jr., and Robert Wooster Stallman. *The Art of
Modern Fiction.* New York: Rinehart, 1949. Pp. 28–33.

To minimize the improbability of "Rappaccini's Daughter," Hawthorne leaves some details unclear and sets the story in a distant time
and place (28). By doing so, however, he also suggests more than a literal reading (29). His references to Rappaccini's garden as "'the Eden of
the *present* world'" invites an association of Rappaccini's garden with
the Garden of Eden, but the details of the story will not allow a strict
allegorical correspondence to the biblical story (29–30). If Dr. Rappaccini
is Adam, for example, Beatrice is an unlikely Eve (30). If Giovanni is
Adam and Beatrice is Eve, Dr. Rappaccini becomes Satan, but with that
pattern one wonders why Beatrice should be Satan's daughter (30).
Very likely Hawthorne intended a symbolic rather than an allegorical
reading, leaving room for both the "inconsistent and ambiguous" (30).
Evil in this new Eden, though, is like that in the biblical garden: a variation of "original sin" or "the desire for excessive knowledge" (32). And
like the consequence the original Eve brought to humanity through her
sin, the "only antidote" for evil in the new Eden is death (32). **FORM,
THEM**

A.C.L.

"YOUNG GOODMAN BROWN"

Haw 13. Colacurcio, Michael J. "'Certain Circumstances': Hawthorne and the Interest of History." In *New Essays on Hawthorne's Major Tales*. Ed. Millicent Bell. Cambridge: Cambridge University Press, 1993. Pp. 37–66.

Although "the historical dimension" is an obvious element of Hawthorne's works, few readers are interested in exploring it (37). Some approaches, for example, "source studies" and psychological readings, have even discouraged examination of the relevance of history (38–39). However, Puritan tales like "The May-Pole of Merry Mount" that one would expect to emphasize the spiritual questions are surprisingly political when placed in the context of history, and study of historical allusions that add particularity to "My Kinsman, Major Molineux" and "Roger Malvin's Burial" reveals that Hawthorne was critiquing events in American history (41–49). In "Young Goodman Brown" the historical context can explain Brown's loss of faith that at first seems all too sudden, and this can in turn lead to an understanding of what Hawthorne was saying about the Puritan community (49–50). In the Puritan church of the New World, people were allowed full membership if they were judged sanctified on the basis of visible evidence available to the congregation (51–54). The people of the church were thus joined together in a community in which they in effect sanctioned one another's election (54). When he enters the forest, Brown is part of this kind of community, but when he sees evidence that the people from his church are aligned with the devil, his whole system of community collapses and he falls into despair. His rapid descent is not so surprising, however, when one realizes what he has lost (51–55). Ironically, though, if one examines the evidence the devil offers to challenge Brown's faith, one notes that it is all spectral, the same kind of evidence used to convict people of witchcraft in Salem. Although Brown "sees" his fellow Puritans in the forest, the visible evidence may be false (57). The devil might have assumed their shape in order to persuade Brown that all people are evil and that their covenant of virtue is a delusion (58). What knowledge of the historical dimension of the story can finally reveal is "that the discovery of Saints and the detection of

witches were parts of the same problem, that specter evidence was simply the negative test case of visible sanctity" (58). The Puritan need to
judge the sanctification of others led quite easily to its perversion in
hunting for witches, and Brown's rapid descent—"from believing in
those who have believed in him to doubting all virtue but his own"—
seems to be Hawthorne's way of showing "this definitive Puritan
dilemma" (58–59). **HIST**

Haw 14. Crews, Frederick. *The Sins of the Fathers: Hawthorne's Psychological Themes.* 1966. Berkeley: University of California Press,
1989. Pp. 98–106.

Young Goodman Brown is dramatically changed by his "dreamlike
or dreamed" journey into the forest (99), where he goes after his wife
urges him to "'sleep in your own bed'" (100). The "sensual overtone" of
her request and his manner of refusing suggest that his "meeting with
the Devil" is related to "his flight from his wife's embraces" (100), and
the prize Satan offers is "[k]nowledge of sin," especially "sexual sin,"
about which Brown has a prurient interest (102). Phallic imagery emphasizes the sexual nature of the forest gathering, where Brown seems
concerned about "parental, not wifely sexuality" (103). The "Oedipal
theme" is suggested by Brown's response to learning the sins of his
grandfather and father (103): "aligning himself with unscrupulous male
authorities," Brown is freed from constraints on his own behavior (104).
Although Brown's mother seems to escape censure, his "attitude toward womankind is violently ambivalent," as can be noted in his subsequent relationship with his wife (104–5). His "uncertainty," one finally understands, had originally derived from "his insistence upon
seeing Faith more as an idealized mother than as a wife" (105). It does
not matter whether Brown actually experienced the meeting in the forest because he has been shaped by his "initiation into human depravity," even if it came from "indulging [his] fantasies" (106). **PSY**

Haw 15. Easterly, Joan Elizabeth. "Lacrymal Imagery in Hawthorne's 'Young Goodman Brown.'" *Studies in Short Fiction* 28
(1991): 339–43.

After Young Goodman Brown cries out to Faith to "'resist the Wicked
One'" (339), he finds himself alone: "'He staggered against the rock and
felt it chill and damp, while a hanging twig, that had been all on fire,
besprinkled his cheek with the coldest dew'" (339). Although
Hawthorne does not comment directly on Brown's actions, the image in
this passage reveals "a young man who has faced and failed a critical
test of moral and spiritual maturity" (339). Tears on Brown's face would
indicate his sorrow and compassion for the sinners he has seen in the
forest, his awareness of his own guilt, and his readiness for moral and
spiritual growth, but instead of tears Hawthorne provides the cold,

damp rock and "'the coldest dew'" to reveal the "emotional barrenness" of Brown's heart (342–43). **THEM**

Haw 16. Eberwein, Jane Donahue. "'My Faith Is Gone!': 'Young Goodman Brown' and Puritan Conversion." *Christianity and Literature* 32.1 (1982): 23–32.

"Young Goodman Brown" is an allegory of "Everyman's crisis of faith" in a Calvinist context (23). According to Puritan doctrine, man is innately depraved because of Adam's sin and can be saved only through God's grace bought by Christ's death (24). Faith comes through this grace, as man is sanctified (24). The early stages a Puritan might typically go through in the process of conversion are learning church dogma, becoming aware of his sins, and praying for grace (24–25). If he is one of the elect, then he would "find faith and accept the covenant of redemption," struggle to overcome his sins, and perhaps finally feel assured of his salvation (25). Although no one could be certain, the convert's continued hope of salvation or his benevolent life might suggest his conversion was true (25). Hawthorne's story begins in the middle of this process, after Brown has married Faith (25). Hawthorne deals with the struggle that could finally reveal whether Brown has actually "achieved faith and experienced grace" or has only had the kind of awakening that Jonathan Edwards observed to mimic real conversion (25). Like the self-scrutiny revealed in Samuel Sewall's diary, Brown's allegorical self-examination might have been prompted by the doubt related to his first communion, permitted only to those whom the church had admitted to full membership after evidence of grace (26–27). When he is tempted by the devil, Brown seeks guidance from church members, but he is disillusioned by their behavior (27). He has forgotten that everyone is sinful and that behavior provides no real evidence of whether a person is saved (27). Brown resolves to resist the devil but discovers that his faith is too weak (28). Although he does remove himself from temptation, he has not saved himself because salvation comes only through God's grace, not through man's resistance to sin (28). Brown presents himself to the community as a saint among sinners, but his later life gives little evidence that he has been redeemed (29). The struggle in the forest might have been only a "season of awakening" (29), however, and the outcome might not indicate his damnation (29). Yet after that night he does not renew his spiritual journey (29). Instead he isolates himself from those who could help him grow (29). Like many of Hawthorne's other Puritan characters, Brown "got lost halfway in the conversion process" (31). **HIST, THEM**

Haw 17. Hostetler, Norman H. "Narrative Structure and Theme in 'Young Goodman Brown.'" *Journal of Narrative Technique* 12.3 (1982): 221–28.

In "Young Goodman Brown" the discrepancy between the narrator's point of view and that of Goodman Brown allows Hawthorne to critique Brown's behavior (221). Hawthorne establishes early that the narrator's and Brown's perceptions do not agree (222). Brown never questions his own perceptions, but Hawthorne makes clear that the narrator's are more accurate. For example, what the narrator describes as "'something [that] fluttered lightly down through the air and caught on the branch of a tree,'" Brown sees as a "'pink ribbon'" (223). Yet when Faith is seen the following morning, she has not lost the ribbon, as the narrator notes (223). An "extreme Lockean," Brown believes he can know truth through his senses and never realizes that his perceptions are influenced by his mind (223). He looks for evil in the external world and fails to see that evil exists in "all human nature" (224). The devil becomes a "false guide" (225), persuading Brown to reject the brotherhood of human beings, the one thing that would ultimately make possible Brown's salvation (226). **FORM, HIST, THEM**

Haw 18. Levy, Leo B. "The Problem of Faith in 'Young Goodman Brown.'" *Journal of English and Germanic Philology* 74.3 (1975). Reprinted in *Modern Critical Views: Nathaniel Hawthorne*. Ed. Harold Bloom. New York: Chelsea, 1986. Pp. 115–26.

At first "Young Goodman Brown" seems to be a traditional allegory of the temptation of an innocent Everyman by the Devil (116–17). However, Goodman Brown is a complex character who struggles to resist (117). When he believes Faith has abandoned him, he falls into despair (118). The story can also be read as a psychological study of the repression of Brown's id by his ego and superego and the subsequent projection of his guilt onto his wife Faith (118–19). This approach to the story, however, ignores the theological elements that explore the power of evil (119). A third interpretation suggests that the story is not simply about Brown's loss of faith but instead examines faith's more terrible abandonment of Brown (120). The purpose of allegory is to demonstrate an abstract truth, but in "Young Goodman Brown" Hawthorne does not allow the reader to find a system of truths in which to take comfort (123–24). In particular, by not revealing a way to reconcile the dual elements of Faith as allegorical figure and literal character, Hawthorne "disrupts the allegory" (124) and shows "there is no necessary connection between our critical need for faith and the responsiveness of faith" (125). **THEM, PSY, READ-R**

Haw 19. Male, Roy R. *Hawthorne's Tragic Vision*. New York: W.W. Norton, 1957. Pp. 76–80.

The night Young Goodman Brown spends in the forest introduces him to "the ambiguity of good and evil" embodied in his wife Faith, "both pure and poisonous, saint and sinner" (77). The scene he encounters "is essentially sexual," as is emphasized by "images of penetration," and he "qualifies" for the ceremony because of his marriage (78). As a result of what happens in the forest, Brown is stunned by the pervasiveness of evil, and the rest of his life is shaped by his inability "to attain a tragic vision, a perspective broad enough and deep enough to see the dark night as an essential part of human experience" (79–80). **PSY, THEM**

Haw 20. Martin, Terry. "Anti-allegory and the Reader in 'Young Goodman Brown.'" *Mid-Hudson Language Studies* 11 (1988): 31–40.

Hawthorne obviously invites the reader to read "Young Goodman Brown" allegorically, but also challenges the notion that allegory can provide "a cognitive system of understanding" (31). While allegory aims at a reassuring and certain moral, "Young Goodman Brown" raises and leaves unanswered a number of questions prompted in part by the "fallibility of Brown's senses and of his reasoning" (32–33). If we fail to see the discrepancy between Brown's perceptions and Hawthorne's, however, our reading suffers from "the same naiveté" as Brown's (35). In response to his Calvinist heritage that is "allegorical in its antithetical division of the world into [the domain of] God and [the domain of] the devil," Brown expects to be able to distinguish the elect from the damned (35–36). The reader, confident that Hawthorne has provided the signals for an allegorical reading, likewise expects to be able to decode them (36). But Hawthorne "undermines" that reading by "calling attention to its arbitrariness," by suggesting the ambiguity of the signs, and by showing how much Brown's "perceptions" are influenced by his "desires" (36). Like Brown, we want to find the hidden meaning in the signifiers in front of us, but to do so, we must ignore the "contradictory evidence" (38). Hawthorne uses a "subtle" interplay between the "framework of traditional allegory and the narration of an ironic and skeptical modern consciousness" to reveal "the potentially fatal flaw of the allegorical reader" (38). **READ-R, HIST, DECON**

Haw 21. Morris, Christopher. "Deconstructing 'Young Goodman Brown.'" *American Transcendental Quarterly* 2.1 (1988): 23–33.

Historicist critics, examining the "Calvinist dilemmas" of "Young Goodman Brown," believe that what ultimately happens to Brown proceeds inevitably from the beginning of the story (23). Those who follow "newer critical approaches" believe that the "theme concerns reading" (23). A third possibility arises from the two theories together: "that the necessity articulated in the story is the inevitability of misreading" (23). Although readers tend to assume the identity of certain characters in the story, the assumptions often cannot be confirmed (24). For example, critics often refer to the traveller as the devil; however, the text suggests but does not confirm that he is (24). Brown thinks he hears the deacon and the minister in the forest, but the narrator does not clearly identify them as such (25). Later in the story the narrator does mention these characters, but his reliability is challenged by the implausible claim that the fellow-traveller's staff was actually used by the Egyptian magi (25). The contradictions apparent in the narrator's attitude toward the Puritan era also create doubt about his credibility, further tending to "subvert the authority of narration in general" (26). Throughout the story the reader struggles to distinguish what is signified and what is signifier: words like "'young'" and "'goodman'" appear as both proper and common nouns so that the reader cannot tell what Brown's real nature is (28). Other issues are, likewise, "undecidable"; for instance, one cannot be sure that Brown is correct in seeing a pink ribbon as evidence that Faith has given herself to the devil (30). Because "all signifiers are ultimately undecidable," the reader misinterprets as Brown does (30). The "'dark figure'" that speaks to those gathered in the forest is also the text or figures on the page that speak to the reader (31). Like Young Goodman Brown, we have been interpreting the story and may react as he did when we discover "that the betrayal of our faith was inherent in our first act of 'suspending belief,' of extending faith to the storyteller, narrator, or author" (31). **DECON, READ-R**

Haw 22. Newman, Lea Bertani Vozar. *A Reader's Guide to the Short Stories of Nathaniel Hawthorne.* Boston: G.K. Hall, 1979. Pp. 333–48.

   Probably intended for Hawthorne's abortive collection *The Story Teller*, "Young Goodman Brown" was published in April 1835 in *New-England Magazine* and in 1846 in *Mosses from an Old Manse* (333). Readers have suggested various historical sources for the story, many related to the Salem witch trials: oral accounts handed down in Salem, where Hawthorne grew up, and various written accounts including court records; Cotton Mather's *Wonders of the Invisible World*, a kind of justification of the trials; and Robert Calef's *More Wonders of the Invisible World*, which severely criticizes the Puritans (334–35). Many names in the story come from these sources (334–35). Works by Spenser, Milton, Shakespeare, and others are cited as possible literary sources (337). Readers have also seen similarities in such things as theme, characterization, and symbols between "Young Goodman Brown" and many other Hawthorne works like "The Minister's Black Veil" and "Rappaccini's Daughter" (338–40). Comparisons to *The Scarlet Letter* are most numerous, however, because both use the "symbolic" method and explore "the effect of sin on individuals in the Puritan community" (337–41). Although one of the most frequently discussed stories in American literature, "Young Goodman Brown" poses "fundamentally simple questions": "Why does Brown go into the forest? What happens to him there? Why does he emerge a permanently embittered man?" (341). Hawthorne's "ambivalence" allows many possible answers, but the responses are determined by whether the reader blames Brown or sees him as "a victim of Puritanism" (342). Psychological critics think him "a sick man with a diseased mind who cannot help what he sees" or does (343). Freudians explore the "sexual overtones" of Brown's experience and see Brown as failing to deal with Faith's sexuality or having a "mother fixation" (343–44). Other readers, though, find Brown "an evil man who is solely responsible for all that happens to him" (344). Still others believe he "emerges a troubled man not because he succumbs to evil but because he resists it" and thus fails to "complete the initiatory cycle" necessary for rebirth (344–45). The story has also been read as "a historical allegory in which Brown represents 'young America'" encountering "the fiery ordeal" in "the unexplored territory" (345). Many discussions of the story focus on "[s]tylistic concerns," with some readers finding that the "method" conflicts with the "message," while others think the opposite (345). Fogle, whose stylistic analysis is the "best and most complete," argues that "Hawthorne combines ambiguity of meaning with clarity of technique to achieve 'that reconciliation of opposites which Coleridge considered the highest art'" (346). The significance of Faith's pink ribbons has been interpreted in various ways, representative of her "sinfulness," her "innocence," her "feminine passion," and "the psychological state of man between the scarlet of total depravity and the white of innocence" (347). To a few readers the ribbons are an ineffective symbol, but most find them "an example of Hawthorne's artistry" (347). Although Hawthorne suggests the issue is unimportant, a number of studies seek to determine whether Brown only dreamed what happened in the forest (347). The story is generally regarded as Hawthorne's best and by many is even considered the greatest American story or one of the world's best as it "transports each reader simultaneously to seventeenth-century New England and to the unexplored depths of his own soul" (348). **HIST, PSY, FORM, THEM, PLUR**

Haw 23. Ponder, Melinda M. *Hawthorne's Early Narrative Art.* Studies in American Literature. Vol. 9. Lewiston, NY: Edwin Mellen, 1990. Pp. 52–61.

"Young Goodman Brown" shows the influence of such eighteenth-century writers as Joseph Addison, James Thomson, and Edmund Burke. Adopting the theories of Addison in *The Spectator*, Hawthorne offers "a kind of extended simile" to demonstrate how "a good man's loss of faith feels" (52). Following the practice of Thomson in *The Seasons*, Hawthorne uses a narrator to show how the sublime in nature (the majestic and powerful landscape) can create terror in a human being (52). From Burke, himself influenced by Addison, Hawthorne learned

the importance of using the narrator to convey Brown's "sublime terror" as well as his own reaction to Brown's experience in the forest and
subsequent behavior (53). Hawthorne thereby insures the reader's sympathy for Brown and horror over his reaction (53). Hawthorne sets the
tale in a specific time and place that have special meaning because of his
ancestor's unrepented participation in the Salem witch trials, but the
story also raises issues of universal significance (53). The story begins at
sunset in the forest, where the increasing darkness and obscurity (two
elements Burke had identified as sublime) prevent Brown from seeing
clearly and contribute to the kind of terror and "'astonishment'" that
Burke says "'anticipates our reasonings, and hurries us on by an irresistible force'" (54–55). This type of response is evident in Brown, who
interprets the sounds he hears as his own wife and townspeople he respected (55). What matters to the narrator is not whether the sounds are
real or imagined, but how Brown reacts to them (55). When he sees
what he thinks is Faith's ribbon, Brown is so full of "sublime terror"
that he flees, believing "there is no good on earth" (55–56). Using much
of what Burke says produces sublimity—"darkness, vacuity, solitude,
vastness" and so on—the narrator has created "a scene of sublime terror" for Brown and in turn prompts terror in the reader by showing
Brown after his loss of faith to be worse than any horror he has seen
(56). Hawthorne demonstrates "the effects of terror on the mind of its
victim in order to give the reader an experience of terror" (57). Gradually lessening the "ironical distance" he had established from Brown in
the beginning of the story, the narrator creates sympathy for him by
having the reader experience Brown's fear and confusion (58–59). But
the narrator also comments on Brown's behavior so that finally the
reader can judge Brown for not "questioning the testimony of his
senses" and for believing "that evil is the only condition of the world"
(59–60). Through his own responses to Brown's behavior, the narrator
enables the reader to see "the complexity of moral life" that Brown fails
to understand and shows that the sublime, although sometimes
"terrible," can be "a means for giving moral enlightenment" (60–61).
HIST, READ-R, FORM, THEM

Haw 24. Tritt, Michael. "'Young Goodman Brown' and the Psychology of Projection." *Studies in Short Fiction* 23 (1986): 113–17.

Critics tend to agree that Young Goodman Brown's experience in the
forest results in his believing "all men ... evil" and suggest that his actions derive from his awareness of his own guilt (113–14). Another reading is also possible: that Brown projects onto others the guilt he cannot
bear to recognize in himself (114). Brown goes to the forest with an
"'evil purpose'" and while there "is transformed into a 'demoniac'"
who feels "a kinship with those he meets" (114). On his return his behavior suggests that he sees only the guilt of others, not his own (115).

In the classic manner identified by Freud, Brown is only subconsciously aware of his own guilt and as a "mechanism of defense" projects his guilt onto the people in his community, including his wife, because he cannot face the evil in his own heart (116). He believes he is fighting forces in the outside world but in reality is "an unwary prisoner of forces acting from within" (117). **PSY, THEM**

A.C.L.

"THE SHORT HAPPY LIFE OF FRANCIS MACOMBER"

Hem 1. Baker, Carlos. *Ernest Hemingway: A Life Study*. New York: Charles Scribner's Sons, 1969. Pp. 284–85.

Ernest Hemingway asserted that the characters in "The Short Happy Life of Francis Macomber" were based on people he had known (284). The model for Macomber was "a wealthy young international sportsman—a 'nice jerk'" and for Margot, an attractive society woman who was "'the worst bitch I knew (then)'" (284). Robert Wilson, with "his enviable combination of courage and judgment," was drawn from white hunter Philip Percival, who had told Hemingway a less elaborate version of what became the short story (284). Percival thought the characters to be close to their models, but he was pleased that Wilson was unlike himself on two key points, the gun Wilson used and the liaisons he had in his tent with female clients (285). Percival also stated that he did not know of a client who "'ever succeeded in shooting her husband as EH describes'" (285). **HIST**

Hem 2. Baym, Nina. "Actually, I Felt Sorry for the Lion." In *New Critical Approaches to the Short Stories of Ernest Hemingway*. Ed. Jackson J. Benson. Durham: Duke University Press, 1990. Pp. 112–20.

Critics have long seen Ernest Hemingway's fiction as "deeply anti-woman in its values," although some stories, including "Hills Like White Elephants," have recently been shown to offer a sympathetic view of women (112). Based on the perspective of Wilson, the white hunter whose moral code seems close to Hemingway's, the traditional interpretation of "The Short Happy Life of Francis Macomber" makes Margot Macomber a classic "example of the 'bitch' stereotype" (113). According to Wilson (and Hemingway himself in his later years), Margot is the emasculating wife who shoots her husband rather than face the possibility that he has acquired courage (113). Careful examination, however, shows that Margot Macomber did in fact try to kill the charging buffalo and not her husband (113). Further, one notes that instead of a single narrative voice (Wilson's), the story has five—Wilson's, the lion's, Margot's, Francis's, and an omniscient narrator's—each presenting a different interpretation, but all except Wilson's finally silenced (113).

The lion's voice is heard first; he "takes almost half the narrative space to die" and "continue[s] to exert his presence on the story" (113). Through Margot's point of view we see a different side of Wilson from the one he conveys (114). He presents himself (and many critics see him) as a skillful white hunter with a strict moral code that makes him superior to his clients, but in reality he makes mistakes that endanger his clients, hunts from an automobile knowing it is illegal, and uses a very large unsportsmanlike gun to injure the animal so that his client can make the kill and feel courageous (115–17). Through watching Wilson exercise his talent of "blowing things' heads off," Margot has by the end of the story come to realize how one-sided the confrontation between hunter and animal really is (118). She has also seen how much like Wilson Francis is becoming, but she still shoots to save her husband (118). **FEM, FORM**

Hem 3. Beck, Warren. "The Shorter Happy Life of Mrs. Macomber." *Modern Fiction Studies* 1.4 (1955): 28–37.

After Margot Macomber shoots her husband, the white hunter Wilson tells her, "'That was a pretty thing to do. He *would* have left you too'" (28). Readers tend to accept Wilson's version of what happened, but Wilson may be an unreliable witness who fails to recognize the complexity of the Macombers and their relationship (28). After his initial stereotyping of the couple, Wilson is "repeatedly confused" by Francis's behavior (28). Wilson does not understand a man who admits his fear and therefore tries to insult Macomber to provoke him into behaving the way he thinks Macomber should (29). In assessing Margot, Wilson is equally puzzled (29). He sees and understands the "'enamelled' surface" that fits his perception of her type, but he does not understand the complexity underscored by Hemingway's references to her as "Margot," "Margaret," and "Mrs. Macomber" (29). The subtle variations implied by the use of all three names "delineate a volatile but not altogether malevolent personality" (30). The narrative reveals the complexity of both characters that Wilson cannot fathom (30). Francis is at first hampered by fear, "naiveté and confusion" that cause him to make a number of mistakes, but he does not succumb to the temptation of allowing Wilson to hunt the wounded lion alone (30). Although Hemingway exposes the Macombers' "shallow fashionableness," Margot's infidelity, and Francis's weakness, the portrait also reveals a "veiled, understated compassion" for the two (31). Because of Wilson's "code of bravery," which critics have offered as something to be admired in both Hemingway and his characters, Wilson is seen as the standard by which to measure the Macombers and as the character who sees most accurately (32). But his code is an inadequate guide for either Wilson's behavior or his assessment of others and does not represent Hemingway's values as they can be seen in his other works (32).

Margot responds to her husband's suddenly found courage by with-drawing and seems intimidated by the growth it implies, but at the moment his life is threatened she acts to save him (34–36). The text itself contradicts what Wilson believes, as it states: "'Mrs. Macomber ... had shot at the buffalo ... as it seemed about to gore Macomber'" (36). Had she wanted to get rid of her husband because he had changed, she could simply have allowed the buffalo to kill him, as it seemed about to do (36). But she also had a "happy moment" when she responded with "that access of recognition and penitence and hope in which love can renew itself" (37). Looking at a broader perspective than Wilson's, one can see a "more profound story, more humane in substance, and a larger and more subtly executed story than Hemingway has been cred-ited with by those who have taken Wilson's word for it," and Heming-way himself can be judged as less limited than is often supposed (37). **THEM, HIST, FORM**

Hem 4. Bender, Bert. "Margot Macomber's Gimlet." *College Litera-ture* 8 (1981): 12–20.

Like several other good Hemingway stories, "The Short Happy Life of Francis Macomber" begins with a paragraph that reveals much about the characters and action to follow (13). Francis asks if Wilson will "have lime juice or a lemon squash" (13). As soon as Wilson chooses a gimlet, Margot and Francis echo his choice (13). Wilson thus becomes an authority figure to Margot and guide to Francis, whose mention of a lemon squash had suggested "cowardice and defeat" (14). Wilson's choice of a gimlet (which, according to *The American Heritage Dictionary*, also means "'a small hand tool for boring holes, having a spiraled shank, a screw tip, and a cross handle'") likewise associates him with "sexual violence" and foreshadows his liaison with Margot (14). Mar-got's requesting a gimlet suggests her need "to be dominated sexually, physically, psychically" (14). Other images reinforce the sexual impli-cations of the gimlet: Wilson's "'big-bored'" gun, his "'double size cot,'" and the reference to Wilson's being "put 'out of business'" if his illegal chase is reported (15). Even his red face, which Virgil Hutton calls "a red badge of shame," suggests "a kind of blood-engorged sexual readi-ness" (15), the significance of which is underscored by Margot's refer-ences to his red face whenever "she makes sexual advances toward him" (16). Wilson's "'Topping'" to describe how well he slept is, to Francis as well as the reader, an obvious pun that emphasizes Heming-way's two themes, "male sexual dominance as it is related to male au-thority and courage" (16). Francis must learn "the meaning of Heming-way's violent puns" (16) to achieve the kind of male dominance that brings "primitive regenerative power" (18). Although many critics have debated whether Margot intended to kill her husband, the question fi-nally seems "unresolvable" and irrelevant (18). The story shows that the "threatening woman ... must be subdued" with violence (19). From the opening sentence to Margot's submissive "'please stop it,'" Hemingway unifies the work so that it reflects his "style and vision" and "values" (19). **THEM, FORM**

Hem 5. Blythe, Hal, and Charlie Sweet. "Wilson: Architect of the Macomber Conspiracy." *Studies in Short Fiction* 28 (1991): 305–9.

Wilson is usually seen either "as a competent judge of" the shooting of Macomber or as too limited or unethical to determine what happened (305). A third view is more accurate: "that Wilson deliberately engineers the death of Francis Macomber in order to gain leverage on Margot Macomber and protect the only thing in life Wilson truly values, his job" (305). Despite his professionalism, Wilson makes two mistakes: he chases the buffaloes in the car and then admits to the Macombers that he can lose his job if he is caught (306). Realizing that his candor has put him in jeopardy, he decides he must get rid of his clients before they report him (306). The first step in his plan is to give Macomber the larger gun and leave the smaller one in the car with Margot (307). Then he tells Macomber the most difficult way to kill a buffalo, knowing the insecure Macomber must try but will probably fail (307). Wilson takes only one bearer on the hunt so that Margot will have a clear shot at her husband (307). Finally, when the injured buffalo charges, Wilson misses "more than once" (307). For a professional like him not to hit his target suggests that he misses intentionally (308). Because he has watched the deterioration of his clients' relationship, Wilson believes Margot will shoot Macomber if given the opportunity, and after she does, he makes clear to her that she not he is now the one in danger of prosecution (308). **FORM**

Hem 6. Carpenter, F.I. "Hemingway Achieves the Fifth Dimension." In *American Literature and the Dream.* New York: Philosophical Library, 1955. Reprinted in *Ernest Hemingway: Five Decades of Criticism.* E. Lansing: Michigan State University Press, 1974. Pp. 279–87.

Hemingway believed that a writer could achieve what he called the "fourth and fifth dimension," but critics have not agreed on what he meant by the terms, especially the latter (279). Hemingway reveals most fully what he means by the fifth dimension in *For Whom the Bells Tolls,* as Robert Jordan and Maria experience during love-making a moment outside of time, in "the perpetual now" (280), or a moment of "perfect union" when "time has stood still" (284). The moment has been so intensified that it becomes a kind of mystical experience of "ecstasy transcending the traditional limitations of time and of self" (285). A similar moment comes for Francis Macomber immediately before his death as he realizes he has found courage (286). In "The Snows of Kilimanjaro,"

Harry has his moment of transcendence in his "ecstatic vision of supreme success" right before he dies (286). **HIST, THEM**

Hem 7. Flora, Joseph M. *Ernest Hemingway: A Study of the Short Fiction*. Boston: Twayne, 1989. Pp. 74–81.

One of Hemingway's best works of the thirties, "The Short Happy Life of Francis Macomber" is a "study of a fortunate death," immediately after Macomber's triumphant moment but before the glory fades (75). Atypical in its presentation of "external" rather than "internal action" (75), the story begins by plunging "in medias res" (78) and moves rapidly (75). It explores "the power of the emasculating woman," a concern related to F. Scott Fitzgerald, who is evoked through the title character's name, and Hemingway himself (77). Margot Macomber is more complex, however, than the label "emasculating" suggests (78). Although the reader never knows Margot's thoughts, she is presented somewhat sympathetically as one who "'had done the best she could'" in her marriage (78). Even Wilson early in the story acknowledges her ability to "'understand'" and "'be hurt for'" her husband (79). And when she shoots the gun at the end of the story, she aims "'*at* the buffalo'" because "at least a large part of Margot wants Francis alive" (79). In this scene the narrator refers to the two characters as "'Mrs. Macomber'" and "'her husband,'" emphasizing their relationship (79). Wilson's final view of her, which influences the reader's, is colored by Wilson's awareness that Margot knows he has unlawfully hunted from the car (79). The fact that he mistakenly has said the buffalo is dead before it kills Macomber also calls his credibility into question (80). Although Margot probably did not consider the consequences before she slept with Wilson, her action does prompt the hatred of Wilson that results in "Macomber's transformation" (80). The final scene between husband and wife shows Francis "reaching out" to Margot (81). She is fearful of the change she sees ahead, "but not because she fears Macomber will leave her" (81). After she misses the buffalo, she becomes "the victim of a hunting accident, crouched and crying in the corner of the car" (81). **THEM, FORM**

Hem 8. Hutton, Virgil. "The Short Happy Life of Macomber." *The University Review* 30 (1964): 253–63. Reprinted in *The Short Stories of Ernest Hemingway: Critical Essays*. Ed. Jackson J. Benson. Durham: Duke University Press, 1975. Pp. 239–50.

Critics have begun to challenge Mark Spilka's favorable portrait of Wilson; for example, William Bysshe Stein sees Wilson as a representative "'of the ruthless and selfish philosophy of British imperialism'" (239). In fact, Hemingway satirizes Wilson as "an unwitting hypocrite who harshly judges others on the basis of various strict and false codes that he himself does not follow" (239). One of Wilson's features—his

"'very red face'"—is "a perpetual badge of shame"; another feature—
his "'extremely cold blue eyes,'" or "'machine-gunner's eyes,'"—conveys a "deficiency of human warmth" (239). Although critics often cite
Wilson's courage, Hemingway actually portrays him as a brutal killer
while creating sympathy for his prey, the lion (240). Wilson presents
himself as a man who lives by a code, yet his behavior suggests he follows instead "the opportunistic requirements of his flesh" (242). While
the Shakespeare quotation Wilson lives by sounds noble, the fact that it
was originally spoken in *Henry IV, Part II*, by the comic figure Francis
Feeble conveys Hemingway's satiric purpose (243). If Wilson is not a
"reliable interpreter" of the action, then one must question whether Macomber triumphs at the end (245). Macomber's fear of the lion was, as
the Somali proverb indicates, natural rather than cowardly, but because
Margaret and Wilson see Macomber as a coward, he is prompted into
"foolishly and futilely attempting the almost impossible nose shot,"
which he misses (248). Instead of heroism he demonstrates a careless
acceptance of "Wilson's false creeds concerning bravery and death"
(248). Unlike the other two characters, however, Margaret Macomber
learns from her experiences (248). Although she had tried to be a good
wife, she reacts badly to her husband's fear (249). Nevertheless, she
later comes to understand fear and see the ugliness of the killing (250).
Finally, as the buffalo charges, she also realizes the danger her husband
is in and tries to save him (250). **THEM, HIST**

Hem 9. McKenna, John J., and Marvin V. Peterson. "More Muddy
Water: Wilson's Shakespeare in 'The Short Happy Life of Francis
Macomber.'" *Studies in Short Fiction* 18 (1981): 82–85.

Virgil Hutton correctly explains that Wilson's Shakespearean quotation was originally spoken by a fool in *Henry IV, Part II* (83). However,
Carlos Baker's *Hemingway: A Life Story* shows that Hemingway learned
the passage from an English officer during World War I and valued it
without reference to its context (84). In his introduction to *Men at War*
Hemingway praised the lines as sufficient to live by and passed them
on to his son (85). By giving the lines he esteemed to Wilson, Hemingway makes Wilson "the ethical center of the story" (85). But because
Wilson is "a rather discreditable character," placing him in that position
mars the story by creating a discrepancy between "the text" and Hemingway's "intent" (85). **HIST, THEM, FORM**

Hem 10. Nagel, James. "The Narrative Method of 'The Short
Happy Life of Francis Macomber.'" *Research Studies* 41.1 (1973):
18–27.

The narrative voice of "The Short Happy Life of Francis Macomber"
is not Hemingway's, as many critics believe, and the term "omniscient
narrator" applies only in certain places (18). Most of the story is told

through a "shifting third-person limited" point of view, and what the reader learns at any moment is shaped by the bias of the character whose perspective is conveyed (19). The information provided should thus "be regarded with caution and intelligent skepticism" (19). Most of the first section of the story is narrated through Robert Wilson's mind (20). Therefore, the reader sees the Macombers as Wilson does and judges them by Wilson's standards (20). As "in the traditional manner of the dramatic monologue," Wilson also reveals much about himself, in particular, that he is, according to Virgil Hutton, a "'hypocrite'" who does not follow the "'code'" to which he would hold others (20). At the end of the section, a shift to Macomber's perspective allows one to see how he feels after running from the lion (21). In section 2, the action of which precedes section 1, the reader learns about Macomber's fear through his point of view, although an omniscient narrator conveys that Macomber did not know the Somali proverb that acknowledges brave men's fear of lions (21). Twice in that section the narrative "shifts to the perspective of the lion" (21–22). After one passage told from the lion's consciousness, another passage "covers ... the same event" through Macomber's eyes in what is called "'reduplicate time'" (22). The "lion's bravery" is thus contrasted with "Francis' fear" (22). The charge of the lion is also presented in "'reduplicate time'" (23). The third section of the story shows the action through the eyes of each of the three main characters, Macomber's revealing "his growth and transformation" and Wilson's and Margot's confirming that the transformation is real (24). Examination of the shifts in point of view can settle the debate of "whether Margot shoots Francis intentionally" (25). The shooting is shown partially through Macomber's perspective and then through Margot's (25), and we are told through her point of view that "'she had shot at the buffalo'" (26). Wilson, whose assessment shapes the portraits of Margot and Francis in the beginning of the story, is the one who labels Margot a murderer, not Hemingway (26). **FORM, READ-R**

Hem 11. Nahal, Chaman. *The Narrative Pattern in Ernest Hemingway's Fiction.* Rutherford, NJ: Fairleigh Dickinson University Press, 1971. Pp. 95–101.

When Ernest Hemingway stressed the necessity "'to put down what really happened in action,'" critics failed to see that by "action" he also meant "moments of passivity as an essential component of any given total action" (18–19). One of his innovations in fiction was "to use inactivity—physical or mental—as part of the structure of" a work, offering a kind of "'suspended movement'" or a "'moment of pause'" in which a character reacts in "shock and recognition" to "a certain situation from which there is no way out" (21–25). The pattern of the narrative is similar to the human heartbeat, "the systolic, the active action, and the diastolic, the passive action" (25–26). "The Short Happy Life of Francis Ma-

comber" moves from systolic action to diastolic as Hemingway attempts to answer such questions as "What is man? What is he made
of?" (95–96). Like other Hemingway heroes, Francis Macomber is existing "at a very limited level" while searching for "some ideal life" (96).
The systolic part of the story depicts the hunt in which Macomber runs
from the lion, and shows the conflict between Macomber and his wife,
which is the primary focus (97). This portion ends when Margaret admits her infidelity with Wilson then refuses to discuss it (99). In the diastolic portion that follows, Macomber is stunned by his wife's actions
into the realization that he does not need her and has "a duty to himself" (99). He had been living in fear but is suddenly freed from it and
transformed (99–100). Although Macomber cannot articulate his "new
awareness," Hemingway reveals it in Macomber's actions, particularly
when he stands his ground the next day during the hunt (100). Margaret senses what has taken place and kills her husband (100). But what
matters most in this and other stories is that in the "stillness" of the
"diastolic" moments "revelations take place, ... new selves are discovered, ... and life acquires a meaning which includes the physical but
transcends it" (101). **THEM, FORM**

Hem 12. Oldsey, Bernard. "Hemingway's Beginnings and End-
ings." *College Literature.* Reprinted in *Ernest Hemingway: The Pa-
pers of a Writer.* Ed. Bernard Oldsey. New York: Garland, 1981.
Pp. 37–62. Also reprinted in *Ernest Hemingway: Six Decades of
Criticism.* Ed. Linda W. Wagner. East Lansing: Michigan State
University Press, 1987. Pp. 113–38.

The manuscripts of Ernest's Hemingway's "Indian Camp," "Big Two-
Hearted River," and "The Short Happy Life of Francis Macomber"
show relatively few changes in the body of the stories but substantial
revisions in their introductions and conclusions (113). The changes in
"The Short Happy Life" can address questions raised in the critical debate about that story (125). Hemingway's early versions reveal more
about Mrs. Macomber than the story does, and some of the information
is contradictory, suggesting that Hemingway was having difficulty "in
bringing her into proper narrative focus" (126). However, in an unpub-
lished typescript, "The Art of the Short Story," written twenty years
later, Hemingway claims to have drawn her from "'the worst bitch I
knew (then)'" (Item 251, quoted in Oldsey 127). In the second
manuscript (item 690) Macomber is an excellent shot, and Mrs. Macomber is "'one who could hit them fine and miss them just as well and
didn't know why she did either,'" a description that could have
"foreshadowed" the ending in the final version (129). How the
manuscripts would have ended is impossible to tell, but they do reveal
how Hemingway moved from an "awkward first-person narrator" to a
"technically intricate and subtle" story that offers "various angles of vi-

sion and perception" (129). Hemingway's "point-counterpoint technique" shifts primarily from Wilson to Macomber, with Margot Macomber's perspective offered at the beginning and end (129–30). In the
first instance she seems to see Wilson as superior to Macomber; in the
second they appear to her as "comrades in arms" (130). The story
avoids her perspective of the shooting, and later in "The Art of the
Short Story" Hemingway says that he himself does not know whether
she meant to shoot her husband (130–31). Hemingway implies that she
did, however, thus suggesting that Beck's reading of the killing as accidental is incorrect (130). From stereotypes in the early manuscripts
Hemingway moved to more realistically "flawed" characters in the
story, where he is able to show, through the "mainly ... contrapuntal
viewpoints" of Wilson and Macomber (131) and "a sometimes obscured
catechism of direct and indirect questions and answers" how Wilson
teaches Macomber "to face up to life" (132). The list of proposed titles
written probably near the completion of the story suggests that Hemingway was trying "to fuse the matter of matrimonial struggle with the
hunt and the temporary emergence of a self-respecting man" (133).
HIST, FORM

Hem 13. Seydow, John J. "Francis Macomber's Spurious Masculinity." *The Hemingway Review* 1.1 (1981): 33–41.

Critics have challenged the reading by Carlos Baker and others that
"The Short Happy Life of Francis Macomber" is a story of Francis Macomber's "ascendancy to manhood," but have not examined Macomber's behavior to provide evidence (33). Although Macomber seems
to find courage as he faces the charging buffalo, he has in reality suc-
cumbed to Wilson's false image of manhood and dies a failure (34). Macomber had gone on the lion hunt to prove himself and followed the
wounded animal to conceal the fear which began, understandably, as
he listened to the lion's all-night roaring (36). His confrontation with the
charging lion, however, exposes him to the scorn of Wilson and the
taunting of his wife, Margot, who calls him a coward (36). The reactions
of Wilson and Margot and their subsequent liaison on Wilson's double
cot drive Macomber to further attempts to demonstrate his courage (36).
If Wilson had been a proper guide, Macomber's fear of the lion, which
was natural for someone as inexperienced as he, would have prompted
Wilson to help Macomber prepare for the hunt (37). Instead, Wilson's
behavior provokes Macomber to hatred of Wilson that replaces the fear
and then to "an envigorated sense of masculinity" that ultimately leads
to overconfidence (37–38). Macomber dies thinking he had achieved
courage but in fact has been deluded into a false bravado that abruptly
ends his life (41). **THEM**

Hem 14. Smith, Paul. *A Reader's Guide to the Short Stories of Ernest Hemingway.* Boston: G.K. Hall & Co., 1989. Pp. 327–348.

The four surviving manuscripts from the composition of "The Short Happy Life of Francis Macomber" (very early undated fragments and the original and carbon setting copy) unfortunately offer little to show the development of the story's "unusual ... narrative strategy" (327). Critics have used the manuscripts, however, to interpret the ending of the story; help date its inception; show how *Cosmopolitan* magazine, which first published the story, eliminated "'bitch,'" "'bitchery,'" and "'bastard,'" likely to offend its female audience; and reveal that *Scribner's* accidentally deleted around one hundred words (327–28). Critics also examined Hemingway's two lists of titles as a way of understanding his intentions (329–30). Although R.S. Crane connected Macomber to "'a long literary tradition'" of "'cuckolds in subjection to their wives who are also ... cowards,'" most early critics focused on autobiographical sources (331). Other critics found literary influences in *The Red Badge of Courage*; *The Land of Footprints*, a 1912 book on hunting in Africa; and Tolstoy's "The Death of Ivan Illich" (331). Several critics examined similarities between "The Short Happy Life of Francis Macomber" and Hemingway's nonfiction *Green Hills of Africa* (332). "The Short Happy Life" has received more critical attention than any other Hemingway story, with examination of such details as the animal imagery, which suggests that Macomber grows from a "'rabbit'" to a "bull"; the guns Francis and Margot use; and the name "Macomber," which one critic noted is similar to a Swahili word meaning "'leader'" or "'superior'" (334). Most of the critics of the sixties and seventies lined up on either side of the Spilka-Beck controversy [see Spilka below and Beck above] in an attempt to prove that Margot does or does not intend to kill her husband or to determine whether Wilson is a reliable witness (335–45). Some psychological readings cited the story as a milestone in Hemingway's career, signaling, for example, a "'return'" to "'his early commitment to art'" (339). Robert W. Lewis showed how the three kinds of love (romantic, erotic, and agape) often merge and shape the relationships among Wilson, Macomber, and Margot (342). Robert Holland argued that critics fail to exonerate Margot because "'the stereotype of the Hemingway Bitch has become a critical commonplace" (342), and Anne Greco found Margot to be a strong woman whose adultery "'causes Francis to submerge his fear in a hatred that enables him to perform an act of great courage'" and whose action at the end is an attempt "to save him from a very real danger" (343). J.F. Kobler finally attempted to end the debate by saying that Hemingway's artistry prevents the reader from knowing the "'absolute truth'" about Macomber's death (344). The debate sparked by Spilka and Beck, however, raised the larger question of whether "the general vision of experience" evident in the body of a writer's work should influence the reading of a single work and stimulated criticism of all Hemingway's work to reach a higher level much faster than it otherwise would have (345). **FORM, HIST, PSY, PLUR**

Hem 15. Spilka, Mark. "The Necessary Stylist: A New Critical Revision." *Modern Fiction Studies* 6 (1960–61): 283–97.

Among the limits of the New Criticism in its attempt at objectivity is the failure to recognize the significance of the writer's style in a literary work: the "characteristic use of language," the "characteristic way of arranging experience for aesthetic ends" (287), and even his "total vision" (288), which includes "his favorite themes and methods" (288). How the New Criticism encourages even the "sensitive and intelligent critic" to ignore the writer's style is seen in Warren Beck's "The Shorter Happy Life of Mrs. Macomber," an analysis of a story by a writer whose work invites a New Critical approach (289). Beck's reading is much like others except on three points: "Mrs. Macomber's nature, the guide's reliability, and the events at the end" (290). The end of the story does little to support Beck's interpretation: a gunshot, her "crying and the repetition of 'Stop it' and 'please stop it'" do not suggest Mrs. Macomber's renewed love for her husband (290–91). Although Beck finds Wilson limited, Wilson is, like some other Hemingway men, a kind of "'frontier'" hero (292) who follows his own code "to counteract the ugly meaningless life of modern civilization" (291). Wilson is not narrow but, again like other Hemingway characters, keeps an emotional distance "because wasteland life has badly hurt" him (292). Instead of offering evidence that Margot wants to change, the story reveals that "her deepest feelings have rigidified: she now cherishes her power and wants to keep it" (293). Beck ultimately bases his interpretation on the sentence that says, "'Mrs. Macomber ... had shot at the buffalo ... and hit her husband,'" but like Macomber, who suddenly ran from the lion, she "is seized and betrayed by inner impulse" that overcomes her original intention (294). However, Hemingway's style cannot adequately convey her reaction because he "is notably weak in depicting women" and cannot show his characters' complex motivations (295). Still, Hemingway's work is valuable for offering an "authentic" vision of "masculine pride" (297). **HIST, FORM**

Hem 16. Spilka, Mark. "A Source for the Macomber 'Accident': Marryat's *Percival Keene*." *The Hemingway Review* 3.2 (1984): 29–37.

The novels of Victorian writer Captain Frederick Marryat probably influenced Hemingway's "The Short Happy Life of Francis Macomber" (29). In *Masterman Ready* three boys "fear roaring lions at night, run from one in daytime panic, and inadvertently wound one who exacts deadly revenge" (30). *Percival Keane* contains three allusions to the Shakespeare line that Wilson quotes—"'a man can die but once ... '"

(31). The novel also includes a conflict involving "vengeful anger" and attempted killing (31) and another "accidental" shot to a man's skull that later appears to have been deliberate (32–33). *The King's Own* offers a description of courage that Hemingway might have used to shape the portrait of Francis Macomber, in particular, that men are "'naturally cowards,'" that courage may be "'acquired from the fear of shame,'" and that wealth inhibits courage (34). If Hemingway's story was influenced by the probably intentional killing in *Percival Keene*, then the interpretation that Margot Macomber accidentally shot her husband may be dismissed (35). Her complex emotions also seem to be a more fully developed version of the "vengeful anger" in Marryat's story (35). Evidence in the story suggests that she deliberately shoots her husband because she cannot face the possibility that her husband's newly found courage will lessen her power over him, is afraid he will leave her, and perhaps wants to retaliate "for those painful years when his mental cowardice first initiated and then perpetuated the terrible conflict between them" (36). The opening of the story shows how "the public exposure of Macomber's cowardice" affects their marriage (36). Reading the story as one in which Margot has a sudden change of heart underestimates the strength of the hostility acting on her (37). **HIST, THEM**

A.C.L.

"THE SNOWS OF KILIMANJARO"

Hem 17. Baker, Carlos. "The Slopes of Kilimanjaro." *American Heritage Magazine* 19.5 (1968): 40+. Reprinted in *Hemingway's African Stories: The Stories, Their Sources, Their Critics.* Ed. John M. Howell. New York: Charles Scribner's Sons, 1969. Pp. 55–59.

The theme of "The Snows of Kilimanjaro" seems much like Thoreau's wish in *Walden* "'to live deliberately'" so that he would not learn too late that he "'had not lived'" (55). Realizing he is about to die, Harry must confront the knowledge that he had failed "to set down the results of his experience in the forms of fiction" (55). A discarded epigraph and the one Hemingway retained allude to the great height of Mount Kilimanjaro, the ascent of which requires the "ability to withstand the high altitude" (56). Harry knows that he has not even made the attempt to climb his own Kilimanjaro (56). Hemingway claimed to have conceived the story after a rich woman offered to take him and his wife to Africa (56–57). The story became his way of considering the consequences had he accepted the proposal and allowed a wealthy lifestyle to undermine his commitment to writing (57). The "stream-of-consciousness monologues" which convey the experiences Harry failed to write about contain places and events from Hemingway's life as well as fabrications (57). Harry's early memories recall the house in Michigan where Hemingway spent his boyhood summers (57). Another memory evokes Hemingway's first flat and neighborhood in Paris (58). The scene in which the airplane rescues Harry suggests Hemingway's emergency flight out of Nairobi when he was ill (58). Other real places and events are blended with those Hemingway invented (58). Through the story Hemingway confronted the fear that he would "die without having completed his work or fulfilled his unwritten promise to his talents" (59). **HIST, THEM**

Hem 18. Dussinger, Gloria R. "'The Snows of Kilimanjaro': Harry's Second Chance." *Studies in Short Fiction* 5 (1967): 54–59. Reprinted in *Hemingway's African Stories: The Stories, Their Sources, Their Critics.* Ed. John M. Howell. New York: Charles Scribner's Sons, 1969. Pp. 158–61.

With its "autobiographical intensity" Harry's story in "The Snows of Kilimanjaro" becomes Hemingway's "professional manifesto" (158). Most critics fail to understand the story's significance because they "[founder] on the two symbols," the mountain and the leopard, and do not see that Harry's dream-death reveals he has "earned the redemption" suggested by the symbols (158–59). The beginning of the story shows a detached man who can "easily ... deceive himself" with "the familiar lie ... that symbolizes his lost integrity" (160). In the second and third sets of reminiscences "the real Harry" emerges, as he longs to write and becomes more aware of "sense impressions" (160). As he moves deeper into the past, he acknowledges what he has become and rejects what is false in the present (161). He is finally given a second chance and takes it, treating Compton and the woman with "sympathetic understanding," honestly facing the past waste of his talent, and "record[ing] faithfully and in precise detail the sensory impressions of his journey" (161). Harry's flight "conveyed in the incisive Hemingway prose style" shows "the restoration of the seeing eye" and "announces Harry's victory" (161). **HIST, FORM**

Hem 19. Elia, Richard L. "Three Symbols in Hemingway's 'The Snows of Kilimanjaro.'" *Revue des Langues Vivantes* 41 (1975): 282–85.

The leopard and the mountain "are important archetypes, which symbolize the aspirations and actions of" Harry, the protagonist of "The Snows of Kilimanjaro" (282). The leopard is symbolic of Harry's lust and love of luxury that "diminish his moral character" (283). The hyena is a mocking symbol of "Harry's artistic failure and his aspiration to be atop of Kilimanjaro," as well as a symbol of death (284). When the hyena approaches the camp near the end of the story, Harry knows he is about to die, and when Harry dies, the animal sends out a cry that mocks Harry's "unheroic and humiliating death" (284). The mountain symbolizes "'the House of God,'" "the great artistic heights" Harry sought but did not reach, and death, prepared for by the many "snow, frost, and white images" throughout the story (284–85). **ARCH, FORM, THEM**

Hem 20. Evans, Oliver. "'The Snows of Kilimanjaro': A Revaluation." *PMLA* 76 (1961): 602–7. Reprinted in *Hemingway's African Stories: The Stories, Their Sources, Their Critics.* Ed. John M. Howell. New York: Charles Scribner's Sons, 1969. Pp. 150–57.

Much of the debate over "The Snows of Kilimanjaro" has centered on what its symbols mean, but they can best be interpreted by seeing how they illuminate "the conflict between idealism and materialism" with which Harry struggles (150). The first symbol, Africa, stands for "the mysterious nature out of which man comes and into which he returns at

last" (151). Africa is an ideal place of creativity and "moral regeneration," a place where Harry can regain the "integrity" he "lost" when he
stopped writing (151). Another ideal place that is also a part of nature,
"the snow-covered mountaintop," is a key symbol, not of death, as Tate
and Gordon suggest, but of "life-in-death" (151). It becomes a "means of
achieving eternal life" (151). The plain, on the other hand, symbolizes
"death-in-life," the empty, meaningless life Harry finds himself living
(151). The vulture, hyena, and even his wife are also emblems of that
life (153–54). Gangrene, the disease of "rotting flesh" from which Harry
is dying, suggests the decay of Harry's soul and contrasts with the body
of the leopard in the epigraph "preserved immaculately and eternally"
in the snows of the mountain (152). Harry's moral deterioration began
when he lost the ability to love, but at the end of the story he triumphs
by "gain[ing] the mountain top" in death and being "reunited" with
what is "ideal and permanent" (156). **THEM, FORM**

Hem 21. Gordon, Caroline, and Allen Tate. "'The Snows of Kili-
manjaro': Commentary." In *The House of Fiction*. New York:
Charles Scribner's Sons, 1950. 419–23. Reprinted in *Hemingway's
African Stories: The Stories, Their Sources, Their Critics*. Ed. John M.
Howell. New York: Charles Scribner's Sons, 1969. Pp. 142–44.

In *A Farewell to Arms* Hemingway's opening paragraph establishes
the tone of the entire novel, creating the kind of "unity of effect" Poe
advocates in his review of Hawthorne's *Twice Told Tales* (142). Also, the
end of the novel is anticipated in the beginning, as Chekhov advised
(143). For all its strengths in realistically examining a man facing his
death, however, "The Snows of Kilimanjaro" does not succeed as well
as the novel because "the snow-covered mountain of Kilimanjaro,"
which Hemingway offers "as the symbol of death," is not fully integrated into the story (143). Introduced at the end rather than the beginning, it cannot pull together the three layers of the story: "the man's intercourse with his wife, his communings with his soul, and the background of Enveloping Action, the mysterious Dark Continent" (144).
FORM

Hem 22. Herndon, Jerry A. "'The Snows of Kilimanjaro': Another
Look at Theme and Point of View." *South Atlantic Quarterly* 85
(1986): 351–59.

A closer examination than critics have previously given "The Snows
of Kilimanjaro" confirms that Harry's "dream of flight" is not a "self-
indulgent delusion of a failure" but "a vision of redemption" (351). Harry's thoughts as he re-examines his life focus on pain and loss, his own
as well as others' (352). He thinks of the retreat of the Greeks during the
Greco-Turkish War and the repatriation plan for Greeks and Turks

which resulted in so many deaths in the snow after World War I (352). Although Harry does not dwell on the suffering of the civilians, Hemingway very likely saw it as one of those elements which, according to his "iceberg principle," could be omitted but would still be felt in the story (352). That Harry's first memories are related to Christmas Day suggests he is seeking to understand "the relevance of the supposed truths of Christianity to the savagery of man's life" (354). The second, third, and fourth meditations contain some pleasant memories like "the delights of trout fishing" and the beauty of the Wyoming mountain that suggests a parallel to Mt. Kilimanjaro (355). But the meditations focus primarily on the "loss and pain inseparable from life," problems with his wives, Greeks killing their own men during battle, the burning of Harry's grandfather's house, and the arrest of a "'half-wit chore boy'" who thought he was doing "his duty" (354–55). As Harry believes one can, he captures "the essence of life" in a single paragraph, in the meditation, which includes "all the pain and the questioning" (355). Although he will never actually be able to write his words, he has "redeemed himself as an artist" (356). He also redeems himself as a man, moving "from the bitter verbal brutality directed against" his wife to an awareness of her "thoughtfulness" and his own responsibility for his failure to feel "compassion" and "pity" for her losses, the death of her first husband and one of her children (356–57). With the shift in point of view from Harry to Helen at the end of the story, Hemingway reveals Helen's awareness of the "bitter reality" of life that comes with Harry's death (359). **THEM, FORM**

Hem 23. Johnston, Kenneth G. "'The Snows of Kilimanjaro': An African Purge." *Studies in Short Fiction* 21 (1984): 223–27.

"The Snows of Kilimanjaro," written during a period when Hemingway was creating little fiction, was probably composed "to exorcise his guilt feelings for having neglected his serious writing, and to re-dedicate himself to his craft" (223). Like the gangrenous leg, Harry's artistic self has been slowly dying, and the safari had seemed a means of recovering (224). What he creates, however, are only fragments in his mind, not stories nearly ready for publication as he had thought (225). With his talent he had had the ability to achieve immortality, as the leopard had done, but Harry had not had the courage "to risk" climbing to new heights (225). In parallels to Thoreau's work, Hemingway's story "call[s] for Spartan simplicity," offers a "quest for self-knowledge," and explores "the limitations of wealth" (226). The vultures at the end reveal that Harry is dying, but the hyena "becomes the main symbol of death," coming near the camp at night and howling after Harry dies (226–27). **HIST, FORM**

Hem 24. Montgomery, Marion. "The Leopard and the Hyena: Symbol and Meaning in 'The Snows of Kilimanjaro.'" *Hemingway's African Stories: The Stories, Their Sources, Their Critics.* Ed. John M. Howell. New York: Charles Scribner's Sons, 1969. Pp. 145–49.

Hemingway's three symbols, the mountain, the hyena, and the leopard, develop his theme of "heroic perseverance," but with varying degrees of success (145). The leopard, which appears only in the headnote, seems to contrast with the hyena, a fully drawn symbol of the life of "moral decay" Harry had been living, but is insufficiently developed as a symbol (146–47). The "positive code" the leopard seems to represent can be construed only by comparing it to the negative code represented by the hyena and by associating it to the "heroic" acts Harry remembers (145–47). The mountain, also introduced in the headnote, recurs at the end of the story, but its symbolic significance is not adequately developed either (149). Although the mountain is connected to the "'House of God'" in the headnote, one cannot tell whether Harry's trip to the summit means he has "gained salvation" by "renouncing the hyena's way for the leopard's" or simply regained "the soothing balm of the snows of yesterday ... through the force of desire" (149). Because it is "not justified by Harry's nature," his end is more "sentimental" than "metaphysical" (149). The reader expects the leopard to reappear to suggest answers to questions raised by the headnote, but Hemingway has not used his symbols of the leopard and the mountain effectively (149). **FORM**

Hem 25. Nahal, Chaman. *The Narrative Pattern in Ernest Hemingway's Fiction.* Rutherford, NJ: Fairleigh Dickinson University Press, 1971. Pp. 17–27, 109–18.

When Ernest Hemingway stressed the necessity "'to put down what really happened in action,'" critics failed to see that by "action" he also meant "moments of passivity as an essential component of any given total action" (18–19). One of his innovations in fiction was "to use inactivity—physical or mental—as part of the structure of" a work, offering a kind of "'suspended movement'" or a "'moment of pause'" in which a character reacts in "shock and recognition" to "a certain situation from which there is no way out" (21–25). The pattern of the narrative is similar to the human heartbeat, "the systolic, the active action, and the diastolic, the passive action" (25–26). This pattern is especially effective in "The Snows of Kilimanjaro," where Hemingway uses italics to distinguish most of the sections of diastolic action (109–10). Although similar to flashbacks, the sections are not "'memories'" but Harry's attempts to deal with his impending death and his knowledge that "'now he would never write the things that he had saved to write'" (110–13). In the systolic passages he agonizes over the reasons he had failed, but in the diastolic passages he has a "wider vision" of "the vaster potentialities which remained unfulfilled" because he is dying (113–14). Toward the end of the story the diastolic action begins to take over as Harry feels death as a real presence (114). But he is not afraid (115). Rather, he experiences a "diastolic peace," a sense of "joy, an expectancy," that enables him to regain his creativity (115). With that, though, he moves back into the systolic mood where, wanting to write, he fights death (116). In something of "a nocturnal dance," he alternates frequently between the two moods until finally rendering himself to death "in diastolic acceptance" (116–17). At last he is "at peace with himself," aware that he is accompanied by death in the shape of Compie, "who is taking him to the mountain of life" (118). The epigraph of the story, which includes the "snow-covered mountain and the carcass of the leopard"—"Life-and-Death, *not* taken separately but *together*" (111)—becomes the "epitaph" for Harry (118). Like other Hemingway heroes, Harry "derives his sensitivity from his ability to be in tune with the spirit of the universe" (118). With his "capacity of true religious awareness of life," he becomes during moments of calm "more like a mystic than a man of action" (119). **FORM, THEM**

Hem 26. Santangelo, Gennaro. "The Dark Snows of Kilimanjaro." In *The Short Stories of Ernest Hemingway: Critical Essays.* Ed. Jackson J. Benson. Durham: Duke University Press, 1975. Pp. 251–61.

A central issue in interpreting "The Snows of Kilimanjaro" is whether Harry is redeemed at the end (251). Is the plane ride a triumph for Harry, or does it simply offer an "ironic counterpoint to his wasted life" (251)? Critics have sought to answer the question by examining a number of contrasts (for instance, between life and death), but equally important is "the contrast between projected art and accomplished art," or "fantasy and reality," made visible in the contrast between the pleasant imagined dream of flight and the reality of Harry's rotting leg (252). Harry is not redeemed in the end because he has "neither character nor faith" (252). The parallels between the story and Hemingway's own life reflect his fear of not fulfilling his potential as a writer (252). The contempt he expressed elsewhere for those who only talked about writing suggests that Harry's reminiscences should not be taken as art (254). The memories are "too close to life" (255) and "lack ... coherent structure" (256). The narrator's "satiric report" of Harry's "consciousness" and the focus on Harry's leg at the end of the story confirm that the airplane ride was fantasy contrasted with his real death as a "failed artist" (256–57). Harry's memories throughout reveal the "selfish," "self-indulgent" man he had been, and his "cruelty" toward his wife suggests that he has not changed (258–59). Although the image of the leopard preserved in the snow might suggest Harry is redeemed in a cold, clean death, the leopard's "striving" to reach the heights contrasts sharply with Harry's easy imagined flight (260). Ironically, though, Harry's memories presented in the story are not art that can redeem his wasted life, but the story about Harry's failure is a triumph for the creator, Hemingway, who faced the fear that he might waste his own talent (261). **THEM, FORM, HIST**

Hem 27. Smith, Paul. *A Reader's Guide to the Short Stories of Ernest Hemingway.* Boston: G.K. Hall, 1989. Pp. 349–61.

The earliest extant manuscripts of "The Snows of Kilimanjaro" (some typed and some handwritten) show a working title, "The Happy Ending," and many revisions, but no epigraph (349). The "third and final typescript" contains what probably came late in the process: the published title and two epigraphs, one of which Hemingway deleted (350). The story was first published in *Esquire* in August 1936 and named "Scott Fitzgerald" as a writer awed by the rich (352). In the collected version, published in *The Fifth Column and the First Forty-nine Stories* (1938), Hemingway changed the writer's name to "'Julian,'" still a recognizable allusion to an autobiographical Fitzgerald character (352). Biographers Carlos Baker, Jeffrey Meyers, and Kenneth Lynn, along with other critics, have noted parallels between the story and Hemingway's life (352–53). Critics have also found "literary analogues": Ambrose Bierce's "An Occurrence at Owl Creek Bridge," Conrad's *Nostromo,* James's "The Lesson of the Master" and "The Real Thing," possibly Beryl Markham's *West with the Night,* and more tenuously, Thoreau's description of two mountains and Tolstoy's "The Death of Ivan Illich" (353). Several critics have named possible sources for the epigraphs, the most convincing of which describes the remains of a leopard found high on the mountain, dead from the cause "that Harry believes corrupted him, the instinctual desire to feed well" (354). Many studies center on the controversy over the function of the title, epigraph, and symbols in establishing the meaning of "Harry's dream-flight to the mountain" (355). Critics have called the leopard "a symbol of Harry's 'fundamental moral idealism' triumphing over the 'aimless materialism'" of the 1920s, found a contrast between the hyena (Harry's "'present ignoble situation'") and the leopard ("'the memory of a more heroic past'"), and seen the hyena as the writer's "audience" "'weeping for the dead artist'" (355–56). Examining the weather throughout Hemingway's work, Bernard Oldsey argued that "snows" is plural to suggest more than one meaning: the snow in Harry's dream, the real snow on the mountain, "destroying" snow and "preserving" snow, and snow that implies an *ubi sunt* theme ("Where are the snows of yesteryear?") (357). Some critics have examined the narrative structure of the story, finding in the reminiscences "a thematic pattern of 'flight, retreat, and betrayal'"; "an archetypal pattern" leading "'to a kind of redemptive

Avalon'"; a progression to an "'impersonal state' ... in which one can create the 'pure and concrete and permanent'"; and a complex pattern of "love relationships governed by eros, agape, or romantic love" and "the recurrent images of death" (357–58). In this reading Harry's dream flight is not "transcendent" because he is "too strongly fixed in the erotic and its association with death" (358). Jackson Benson saw in the story Hemingway's "typical rituals of avoidance," but thought "the dream flight a 'slick magazine exit'" (358). Arthur Waldhorn found no redemption except "in Hemingway's 'remorseless honesty'" (358). Scott MacDonald argued that Hemingway's use of italics suggests "'a contrast between the fate of a fictional character who has lost his moral and artistic integrity and the achievement represented by his own story" (358). MacDonald also noted Harry's distinction between his first four reminiscences (material he "'had saved to write'") and his "'writing'" in the last section, raising the question of how to interpret the passage (358–59). **HIST, FORM, ARCH, THEM**

Hem 28. Whitlow, Roger. *Cassandra's Daughters: The Women in Hemingway.* Westport, CT: Greenwood, 1984. Pp. 68–74.

Like Margot Macomber in "The Short Happy Life of Francis Macomber," another story set in Africa, Helen in "The Snows of Kilimanjaro" is usually labeled a "bitch" by critics who associate the two stories, while Harry is considered "the Hemingway hero" (68–69). Although Harry himself calls Helen a "'rich bitch'" (69), he is in fact "weak, cowardly, dishonest, and cruel" to his wife while she "is strong, considerate, and deeply loving" (70). Harry blames his wife and her money for his "decline," but the story offers no evidence of her guilt (70–71). Moreover, he later admits that he "'destroyed his talent by not using it'" (71). Blaming Helen for her "'corrupting' influence" has allowed him to avoid writing or facing the possibility that he could not (72). Readers may tend to believe Harry's accusations of Helen as they do Wilson's assessment of Margot and Francis Macomber, but Harry's criticism should be trusted even less than Wilson's because Harry himself acknowledges that Helen is in reality "'a fine woman'" (72), and her actions confirm that she is (73). Despite the tragedies she has endured, Helen has had the character to rebuild her life to become an admirable woman (74). **THEM, FORM, FEM**

A.C.L.

"THE LOTTERY"

Jac 1. Brooks, Cleanth, and Robert Penn Warren. *Understanding Fiction.* 2nd ed. New York: Appleton-Century-Crofts, 1959. Pp. 72–76.

Although the story may seem to lack dramatic conflict, rich suspense, complex characters, and complexity in general, ultimately it exerts a forceful effect, to which its plotting and characterization contribute (72). The story is a kind of tale or parable, but it lacks the neat, simple moral associated with those forms (73–74). It does comment on "the all-too-human tendency ... to visit upon the scapegoat the cruelties that most of us seem to have dammed up within us" (74) and explores "the general psychological basis for such cruelty," showing how we tend to ignore misfortunes unless we ourselves are their victims (75). "'The Lottery,' then, deals indeed with live issues and with issues relevant to our time. If we hesitate to specify a particular 'point' that the story makes, it is not because the story is vague and fuzzy, but rather because its web of observations about human nature is too subtle and too complex to be stated in one or two brief maxims" (75). Jackson's realism makes the final terror and shock more effective and also reinforces our sense of "the awful doubleness of the human spirit—a doubleness that expresses itself in the blended good neighborliness and cruelty of the community's action" (76). **FORM**

Jac 2. Church, Joseph. "Getting Taken in 'The Lottery.'" *Notes on Contemporary Literature* 18.4 (1988): 10–11.

Summers, as "the owner of the coal business, ... is the most powerful figure in the community, and has the 'time and energy'—a leisure gained by the labor of others—to direct all the town's social programs" (10). Along with the other businessmen (Martin and Graves), he arranges, and presumably rigs, the lottery, which helps explain why he does not seem anxious (10). "Nor does he join the others in stoning Tessie, for apparently in his secure position he doesn't experience the frustrations they vent on the victim" (10). Tessie may be selfish in her reaction, but her claim that the lottery is not fair may still be true (10). Whereas the common villagers are described as "taking" their slips, the businessmen "select" theirs—a subtle implication that the results have been rigged (11). **THEM, MARX, NHIST**

Jac 3. Friedman, Lenemaja. *Shirley Jackson.* Boston: Twayne, 1975. Pp. 63–67.

Because modern man rejects the ancient practice of scapegoating as evil and outmoded, Jackson's story shocked its first readers (63). Jackson herself called the story an indictment of meaningless violence and inhumanity (64). Although some characters' names (e.g., the sunny Mr. Summers) suggest their nature or function, the story's power derives partly from the surprising darkness that underlies its initially pleasant surface (64). The objective narrative tone reflects the characters' lack of emotion, conscience, and compassion, and both features make the story finally more shocking (65). Although Mr. Summers in some ways seems progressive, he is basically conservative: he wants merely to modernize the lottery (66). The Adams family seems more willing to consider abolition, but they are weak and finally hypocritical (66). Mr. Warner is especially unbending because he views the lottery almost religiously; ironically, he also links it with civilization (66). Even Tessie resists only after she herself becomes a victim, and she is even willing to put her own daughter at risk to save herself (66). Although it may seem strange that none of the villagers seeks to evade the lottery, "the story proceeds by way of realism to grimly realistic fantasy. As such, the lottery may be symbolic of any number of social ills that mankind blindly perpetuates" (67). **THEM, FORM**

Jac 4. Gibson, James M. "An Old Testament Analogue for 'The Lottery.'" *Journal of Modern Literature* 11 (1984): 193–95.

Although Jackson's story invites comparison with Joshua 7:10–26, the story's irony contrasts with the idealized, romantic scriptural analogue (194). Whereas the biblical story emphasizes justice, Jackson stresses amoral chance (195). **THEM, HIST**

Jac 5. Hall, Joan Wylie. *Shirley Jackson: A Study of the Short Fiction.* New York: Twayne, 1993. Pp. 48–53.

Like many other stories in the volume it concludes, this work ends with a woman's defeat (48). Critics have stressed the story's mythic elements, and Jackson was familiar with James Frazer's famous study of myth, *The Golden Bough* (43). However, Jackson's husband stressed the story's contemporary relevance (49), and recent critics have seen the story as commenting on matters of class, social injustice, stage-managed democracy, and the effects of (and muted resistance to) patriarchal oppression (49). Although such readings seem unconvincing, Jackson does elsewhere tend to make females the victims of loss (49–50). She probably finished the story earlier, and revised it more fully, than her own later account suggests; the revisions were mainly in the interests of clarity (50–51). Although "most critics view the story as either an indictment of unthinking adherence to outmoded ways or a critique of an unjust class system," its emphasis on a woman as victim reflects a pattern also found in other stories by Jackson (52). Tessie is less passive than other such characters, but she finally shares with them "the bleak epiphany that she is lost" (53). **FEM, ARCH, MARX, NHIST**

Jac 6. Heilman, Robert B. *Modern Short Stories: A Critical Anthology.* New York: Harcourt, Brace, 1950. Pp. 384–85.

The sudden transition from innocuous realism to shocking symbolism may be too sudden to make the story an enduring success. Unfortunately, "the story gives us the sinister *after* the innocuous, instead of the two simultaneously. It might have been better if the symbolism had been implied more clearly earlier so that a reader would not have to go back and look for it (385). **FORM, THEM**

Jac 7. Jackson, Shirley. "Biography of a Story." In *Come Along with Me: Part of a Novel, Sixteen Stories, and Three Lectures,* by Shirley Jackson. Ed. Stanley Edgar Hyman. New York: Penguin, 1995. Pp. 211–24.

Jackson wrote "The Lottery" early in June 1948, having thought of the idea while walking home after shopping for groceries (211). She wrote the tale quickly after returning to her house; in fact, "when I read it over later I decided that except for one or two minor corrections, it needed no changes, and the story I finally typed up and sent off to my agent the next day was almost word for word the original draft" (212). Neither her agent nor the editors at *The New Yorker* particularly liked the work, although the magazine did accept it, asking simply for one alteration— "that the date mentioned in the story be changed to coincide with the date of the issue of the magazine in which the story would appear" (212). Shortly after the story was printed, Jackson received more than 300 letters from readers—only thirteen of them friendly (213). "Judging from [most of the] letters, people who read stories are gullible, rude, frequently illiterate, and horribly afraid of being laughed at" (213). Most letters expressed "three main themes"—"bewilderment, speculation, and plain old-fashioned abuse" (214). Some writers even "wanted to know ... where these lotteries were held, and whether they could go there and watch" (214). Quotations from many letters illustrate the wide range of responses (214–24). A few of the more thoughtful reactions include the following: one reader suggested that the story illustrated the habit of persecuting minority scapegoats (217); another saw it as depicting innate human cruelty (218); one suggested that it allegorized "the perversion of democracy" (219); someone else saw it as symbolizing "how village gossip destroys a victim"; another person thought that the story showed "that people will accept any evil as long as it doesn't touch them personally" (219); one suspected Jackson of communist sympathies (219); and still another suggested that the work demonstrated the often amoral and irrational power of society over individuals (220). **HIST, THEM, READ-R**

Jac 8. Kosenko, Peter. "A Marxist/Feminist Reading of Shirley Jackson's 'The Lottery.'" *New Orleans Review* 12.1 (1985): 27–32.

The lottery functions ideologically to instill fear, reinforce capitalist and male hierarchies, and encourage the townspeople to work for the benefit of those who run both the town and the lottery, especially Summers, who owns the town's main business (27–28). Because the "villagers believe *unconsciously* that their commitment to a work ethic will grant them some magical immunity from selection," they fail to understand that "the lottery's actual function is not to encourage work *per se* but to reinforce an inequitable social *division* of labor" (28). Significantly, the "'heads of households' are not simply the oldest males in their immediate families; they are the oldest *working* males and get their power from their insertion into a larger economy" (29). The fake democracy of the process discourages the villagers from criticizing those in power; Summers may wear jeans to seem a member of the common folk, but he also wears an elitist white shirt (30). Tessie is in some ways the logical victim of the lottery because she shows signs of rebellion in speaking both to Summers and to her husband (31). Although other villagers seem to have misgivings about the system, "ultimately these rebellious impulses are channeled by the lottery and its attendant ideology away from their proper objects—capitalism and capitalist patriarchs—into anger at the rebellious victims [such as Tessie] of capitalist social organization" (31). In the end, Tessie comes back under the control of her husband and also serves as an example of the dangers of disobeying (31). Although the lottery seems random, this problem vanishes "once we realize that the lottery is a metaphor for the unconscious ideological mechanisms of scapegoating. In choosing Tessie through the lottery, Jackson has attempted to show us whom the village might have chosen if the lottery had been in fact an election. But by presenting this election as an arbitrary lottery, she gives us an image of the village's blindness to its own motives" (32). Depressingly, the young males of the village follow the lead of Bobby Martin (the one boy whose father is identified as a member of the ruling class) in gathering the stones and fighting over them as if they were cash; meanwhile, the girls significantly stand aside, as passive as their mothers (32). However, by presenting the innocent Davy Hutchinson, Jackson shows that evil impulses are not innate but must be taught and learned (32). Although the depiction of capitalism may be too simple and exaggerated, the story does show that capitalism functions in part by "accusing those whom it cannot or will not employ of being lazy, promoting 'the family' as the essential social unit in order to discourage broader associations and identifications, offering men power over their wives as a consolation for their powerlessness in the labor market, and pitting workers against each other and against the unemployed" (32). **MARX, FEM**

Jac 9. Nebeker, Helen E. "'The Lottery': Symbolic Tour de Force." *American Literature* 46 (1974): 100–7.

Understanding the deeper implications of the story helps explain the faults some critics have found with the work (100–2). Jackson implies that man "is not at the mercy of a murky, savage *id*; he is the victim of unexamined and unchanging traditions which he could easily change if he only realized their implication. Herein is horror" (102). Symbolism of seasons and sacrifice is already present in the first paragraphs and thus helps prepare for the ending (102). The box symbolizes past traditions (103). However, whereas those traditions once had meaning, now they are burdensome and outmoded (104). The names of nearly all the characters are symbolic (102; 105–6). The three-legged stool on which the box rests symbolizes unexamined traditions (the tripod of the Delphic oracle; the Christian trinity; Hebraic tradition) that support "meaningless and perverted superstition" (106). Jackson shows how rituals formed to make the universe meaningful can degenerate into irrational horror (107). **THEM, FORM**

Jac 10. Oehlschlaeger, Fritz. "The Stoning of Mistress Hutchinson: Meaning and Context in 'The Lottery.'" *Essays in Literature* 15 (1988): 259–65.

Interestingly, the selection process "gives each woman a very clear incentive to produce the largest possible family. Each child she has gives her a better chance of surviving" (259). Thus "the story can be seen as the depiction of a patriarchal society's way of controlling female sexuality" by "the encouraging of fertility within marriage, along with the patriarchal domination that accompanies it" (259). Indeed, a "conflict between male authority and female resistance is subtly evident" throughout the story (259). While women tend to be the ones who express misgivings about the lottery, it is the men who control it (260). The whole story is reminiscent of the almost-completed stoning of a woman in the Gospel of St. John; in both cases "a priestly caste made up of men seeks to use its spiritual authority to control female sexuality" (260). In Jackson's story, of course, no one intervenes to prevent the stoning. Similarly, Tessie Hutchinson's name suggests both Thomas Hardy's Tess of the D'Urbervilles and the spritual rebel Anne Hutchinson—both victims of male authority (261). The men Jackson describes seek to extirpate "a principle of rebellion that is specifically female and ... based in sexuality" (261), as other works by Jackson suggest (261–62). Although "Tessie fails to be a heroine, ... the way she does so testifies to the success with which the male-dominated order has imposed itself upon her. It is crucial to note that her most grievous failure lies in betraying another woman" (her daughter), and in other ways Jackson also emphasizes how patriarchy turns women against one another (262). Precedents for such betrayal and for such persecution existed in the Salem witch trials, about which Jackson also wrote (263). Although men, theoretically, have the same chances as women of being selected as victims, the chief social result of the lottery "involves women's turning over the control of their fertility to men. Jackson depicts a society in which authority is male, potential resistance female" (264). **FEM, HIST, NHIST**

Jac 11. Oppenheimer, Judy. *Private Demons: The Life of Shirley Jackson.* New York: Putnam's, 1988. Pp. 127–31.

As Jackson began to conceive of "The Lottery," she remembered a book her husband had recently brought home. It "discussed tribal units in which each member was willing to stand up for the others. How, she wondered, would such a rite work today," in the village in which she lived? (127). The story was written "in less than two hours" (128), and when asked by the editors of *The New Yorker* magazine to explain its meaning, she had no simple answers (128). She finally agreed that it might be termed "an allegory which made its point by an ironic juxtaposition of ancient superstition and modern setting" (128). The response of readers to the tale was immediate and volcanic: Jackson had "struck a nerve in mid-twentieth century America the way few writers have ever succeeded in doing, at any time. She had told people a painful truth about themselves, and the people were fighting mad" (129). Some correspondents claimed "that they did not understand the story; but their emotional reaction, raw and defensive, showed that they understood only too well" (129). Many friends were convinced that Jackson's husband, who had a strong interest in anthropology, had influenced the work, and indeed he did provide the rhyme "Lottery in June, corn be heavy soon" (130). The husband and some friends claimed that Jackson herself never understood the story, although Jackson did tell one friend that the tale "was based on anti-Semitism and grew out of her encounters with one particularly prejudiced shopkeeper" in the village where she lived (130). To another friend, she identified particular characters with particular citizens of her town (130–31), but she also told a former teacher that the story had been inspired by his course in folklore (131). However, the story is typical of Jackson in its strong focus on human evil (131). At one point Jackson explained the tale by saying, "'I suppose I hoped, by setting a particularly brutal rite in the present and in my own village, to shock the readers with a graphic dramatization of the pointless violence and general inhumanity of their lives'" (131). **HIST, THEM, READ-R**

Jac 12. Parks, John Gordon. "The Possibility of Evil: The Fiction of Shirley Jackson." Ph.D. Dissertation, University of New Mexico, 1973. Pp. 61–66.

The story offers unusual insight into how fiction is sometimes received by readers; even Jackson's parents disapproved of the work (61). "The violence is shocking to the reader precisely because of the ordinary, matter-of-fact way that it is carried out. It is not shocking to the [fictional] community, and it is not a symbolic act or ritual to them. All of that has been long forgotten. It really has no significance beyond itself" (63). The story shocks us because we "do not like to admit a demonic side to our natures. The story suggests that basically we are beasts, ... that we can slip back to barbarism hardly batting an eye" (63). The work is "not just concerned with what we do, but with who we are" (64). The community is the protagonist in this story, which depicts "a universe ... where life and death are decided by chance and not by human volition" (65). **THEM**

Jac 13. Stark, Jack. "Shirley Jackson's 'The Lottery.'" *Censored Books: Critical Viewpoints.* Ed. Nicholas J. Karolides, Lee Burress, and John M. Kean. Metuchen, NJ: Scarecrow, 1993. Pp. 358–62.

Most persons who seek to censor the story are probably troubled by its alleged violence, although no actual violence is described (358). Instead, Jackson "concentrates on violence's social and psychological roots. That emphasis, along with the understated prose style and the profusion of homey details, distances the impending violence," which Jackson obviously condemns (358). The story can be successfully taught to students, who inevitably are caught up in rituals of their own, and it can be used to show how "an activity leading to a triumph of antisocial forces over civilized restraint" can be "carried out very meticulously according to 'laws'" (359). Because tradition, ritual, and law lead the villagers to consider their actions inevitable, they can deny personal responsibility (359), but the story can also be used by teachers to explore the theme of the relations between generations (360). Because Tessie Hutchinson arrives late and speaks inappropriately even before being selected as the victim, she demonstrates even then "that she is incompletely socialized and thus does not fully accept the lottery ritual's legitimacy. Unfortunately, for the village, the lottery destroys its only apparent opponent, albeit a very minor one" (360). Jackson's story is not completely pessimistic, however, for she does not depict human lives either as completely determined or as completely governed by chance. Because the lottery is still a choice by the community, Jackson suggests that "meaningful moral decisions are still possible" (361). Tessie is not a victim either of predetermined fate or of random chance but of a social institution that can be changed (361). Since the story was written in the immediate aftermath of World War II and the holocaust, it raised (and can still raise) important questions concerning "the power of mass psychology, the possibility that blind adherence to tradition will forestall judgment, and the ease with which responsibility can be denied" (361–62). Paradoxically, if the story does fall victim to contemporary censorship its fate may well be the result of the very forces it describes (362). An editor's note points out that although the story was frequently published in high school anthologies in the 1950s and 1960s, the release of two films associated with it in the 1970s raised controversy, and by the 1980s it "had disappeared from all anthologies" (362). **THEM, FORM**

Jac 14. Yarmove, Jay A. "Jackson's 'The Lottery.'" *The Explicator* 52 (1994): 242–45.

Written in the aftermath of the holocaust, Jackson's story disrupts the reader's complacent sense that "it can't happen here"; by making the lottery take place on June 27, she chooses a date mid-way between the summer solstice (June 21) and the American Independence Day (July 4). The first date "has a long, heathen, orgiastic tradition behind it" while the other symbolizes such values as democracy, freedom, and justice (242). "June 27 bisects the two weeks between these dichotomous dates and may well embody the contrast between superstitious paganism and rational democracy, a dynamic that plays a central role in 'The Lottery,' especially in light of the story's locale" (243). That setting, probably a small New England village, is meaningful not only because such villages were associated with "participatory democracy" but also because they also had associations with witch trials and religious persecution, such as the persecution of the significantly named Anne Hutchinson (243). Tessie Hutchinson's name may allude to this incident, and perhaps she is also ironically associated with the title character of Thomas Hardy's *Tess of the D'Urbervilles*, an innocent victim (243–44). Jackson's character is neither innocent (like Tess) nor a martyr who adheres to larger values (like Anne Hutchinson); instead, she is "a hypocrite who has been hoisted with her own petard" (244). **THEM**

R.C.E.

"THE BEAST IN THE JUNGLE"

Jam 1. Aswell, Mary Louise. *The World Within: Fiction Illuminating Neuroses of Our Time.* New York: McGraw-Hill, 1947. Pp. 160–61.

"The Beast in the Jungle" is an excellent study of neurosis (160). The hero's Beast is "the symbol of nameless dread, nameless because it has no conscious substance in reality" (161). The hero is so anxious about what may happen in his life that he "loses the present" (161). **PSY**

Jam 2. Dauner, Louise. "Henry James and the Garden of Death." *University of Kansas City Review* 19 (1952): 137–43.

For James the garden is frequently "the ambivalent symbol for a kind of life-and-death struggle" (140). In "The Beast in the Jungle" May's tomb, which John Marcher sees as a "garden of death," also becomes a kind of Garden of Eden (or Dr. Rappaccini's garden) as it brings "both pain and wisdom" (140–41). Like Dr. Rappaccini, who sacrifices his daughter through his pride, Marcher sacrifices May through his "self-complacency and utter selfishness" (141). **THEM**

Jam 3. Gargano, James W. "Imagery as Action in 'The Beast in the Jungle.'" *Arizona Quarterly* 42 (1986): 351–67.

James uses "interrelated images and symbols" to create drama in a story in which nothing happens (351). In addition to the frequently noted references to the calendar, James's imagery of "links or connections, light, and burial" creates mystery, "quickens or retards narrative pace, provides ironic reversals, and creates climactic tensions" (352). It also shows the stages "of Marcher's fascinating psychological disintegration" (352). James's seasonal imagery draws attention to the deadness of Marcher's life: He cannot cross the barrier of April, the time of the key scene, when the reader learns that Marcher "will never discover in May Bartram the quickening force of the month for which she is named" (355). In the first section images of linkage raise the possibility that through May he might be able to bridge the gap between himself and life (355). Light imagery shows the faultiness of Marcher's memory and perceptions and the "clarity" of May's (356–57). In the second section images of linkage reveal that Marcher's "connection with May" is only to exploit her (358), and burial images focus on the secret knowledge about Marcher that May is hiding (359). A pattern of "sibyl-seeress-sphinx images" (353) emerges in the second section to convey May's "almost prophetesslike acuteness" while the "skillful blurring of the time scheme" emphasizes Marcher's wasting of his life (359). In the fourth section images of light and linkage help bring May and Marcher's relationship to a climax as May, whose "'light might at any instant go out,'" tries once more to bridge "'the distance between them'" (362). At their last meeting May is "a tender sibyl who speaks in riddles and mysteries," conveying only that she knows "he has met his fate" and that he should not try to learn what it was (364). In the final section all the images come together in the "psychological climax" of the story: at the cemetery where all his possibilities for life are buried, the autumn light reminiscent of the meeting at Weatherend enables Marcher to see in the grief of the mourner the bond he had missed with May and the answers that the sphinxlike May had hinted (365–67). All these have "given birth to half-formed alarms and insights" in the shape of a beast "in Marcher's subconscious" (367). The beast remains "[c]oncealed as long as Marcher is not ready to see him," finally springing to life from "those primal energies Marcher had repressed" to become "only the active climactic image in a book of images remarkable for their intellectual content, emotional depth, and narrative accumulation of suspense and movement" (367). **FORM, PSY, THEM**

Jam 4. Hansot, Elisabeth. "Imagination and Time in 'The Beast in the Jungle.'" In *Twentieth Century Interpretations of 'The Turn of the Screw' and Other Tales: A Collection of Critical Essays*. Ed. Jane P. Tompkins. Englewood Cliffs, NJ: Prentice-Hall, 1970. Reprinted in *Modern Critical Views: Henry James*. Ed. Harold Bloom. New York: Chelsea House, 1987. Pp. 131–37.

Instead of experiencing life, John Marcher watches it "as a spectacle" (131). He manages to remain detached from life by maintaining "a curiously passive attitude ... toward his own past and future" as if he has no control over events and can see no causal relationship among them (131–32). Marcher also "declines to live in ordinary time—the time in which people fall in love, get married, assume responsibilities, acquire possessions" and so on (133). When he first deals with May, he seems to choose freely a relationship of the imagination, waiting for the future, but as he grows older, he seems less able to do anything besides live in the mind and await his fate (133–36). May, on the other hand, lives in the present, perhaps interested most in Marcher's immediate needs (136). As she had for the treasures at Weatherend, she becomes "witness and keeper" over Marcher's destiny (136). Although he thinks of himself as above "ordinary time" and as unselfish in his treatment of May,

in fact his "studied consideration ... is really a mask for the purest egotism" (137). His fate is to realize too late that "he had lived, been measured, and found wanting—by ordinary time" (137). **THEM**

Jam 5. Kerner, David. "A Note on 'The Beast in the Jungle.'" *University of Kansas City Review* 17 (1950): 109–18.

   The opening of the story raises three questions. How was Marcher
able to confide in May in Sorrento? If he did, why did he let her go afterwards? How could he have forgotten his confession? (110). On considering these questions, one might think that if Marcher had been able
to confide in her he probably would not have allowed her to get away
or at least would not have forgotten "his one experience of perfect sympathy" (110). Those who have read other James stories might thus wonder whether May might be a hallucination or a ghost (110). It seems
very likely that a man who is so susceptible to self-deception could have
created May in his mind just as he created his beast (111–12). The
opening scene shows May as a real person, but she may also be a
dream, the representation of ideal love, or "the projection of Marcher's
realizable nature by which he can judge his failure to live" (116). May
Bartram is also a "ficelle," "a dramatic catalyst," a character James invented "in order to expose the essential character" (116). But none of
these possible explanations of May's function in the story is important
because the story "is a parable, and parables are not concerned with
questions of verisimilitude," but in fact illustrate "a law of human conduct" (117). James wanted his story "to terrify the reader out of wasting
his humanity" (117). **PSY, FORM, THEM**

Jam 6. Knights, L.C. "Henry James and the Trapped Spectator."
The Southern Review 4 (1939): 600–15.

   James presents "The Beast in the Jungle" through the eyes of John
Marcher, but James's "unobtrusive irony" allows the reader also to
know James's view (612). James enters only occasionally, but when he
does, he provides "an angle on Marcher's attitude towards himself, on
his egotism, his calculated unselfishness, and on his exalted view of his
own refinements" while seeming to convey only Marcher's thoughts
(613). James moves quickly and smoothly between the "subjective and
objectively critical" points of view, sometimes even presenting them
simultaneously (613). With this method "the reader is made to share
Marcher's horror" while also receiving "a detached and penetrating
analysis of the ravages of an obsession" (613). **FORM, READ-R**

Jam 7. Lindholdt, Paul J. "Pragmatism and 'The Beast in the Jungle.'" *Studies in Short Fiction* 25 (1988): 275–84.

Likely sources for John Marcher and May Bartram in "The Beast in the Jungle" were Henry James's brother William and their cousin Minny Temple (275). Henry found "a paradigm for the character of John Marcher" in William's *The Varieties of Religious Experience* in the case studies of what he called "sick souls," including one later known to be autobiographical (276). Like these sick souls, Marcher believes himself to be at the mercy of universal forces he cannot control, is obsessed with "his spiritual welfare," and has a distorted image of his self-worth (278). In particular, the autobiographical case study of William's emotional breakdown provided Henry with "a moment of self-realization" like John Marcher's at the end of the story (279). In both the real and fictional accounts, "the personal epiphany comes with a rush produced by the sight of a stranger's face" (280). By living the safe life of one afraid to take risks, John Marcher also appears to embody the opposite of what William advocates in his philosophy of pragmatism (277). A source for May Bartram can be found in Minny Temple, with whom both Henry and William seem to have been in love (282–83). A puzzling reference to May as a sphinx seems to echo the "epithet of 'Pyramid'" given to Minny and William's image of "'"a sculptured Egyptian cat,"'" which could have applied to her (284). Although Minny died young, her character was much like May's, and had she lived until the story was written, she would have been about the age of May at the end of the story (284). **HIST**

Jam 8. O'Faolain, Sean. *The Short Story*. New York: Devin-Adair, 1951. P. 210.

This story "wastes" far too many words to tell what a writer like Oscar Wilde could have written much more concisely (210). **FORM**

Jam 9. Przybylowicz, Donna. "The 'Lost Stuff of Consciousness': The Priority of Futurity and the Deferral of Desire in 'The Beast in the Jungle.'" In *Desire and Repression: The Dialectic of Self and Others in the Late Works of Henry James*. Tuscaloosa, AL: University of Alabama Press, 1986. Reprinted in *Daisy Miller, The Turn of the Screw and Other Tales*. Modern Critical Interpretations. Ed. Harold Bloom. New York: Chelsea, 1987. Pp. 93–116.

Unlike most Jamesian characters who look toward the past, John Marcher wastes his life "fixated ... on the ontological magnetism of the future" (93). As Heidegger suggests, being aware that the future holds death for everyone should make one live fully in the present, but for most of his life Marcher does not recognize his own mortality (98). By "enter[ing] imaginatively" into Marcher's watching for his beast, May joins him in waiting passively for the future, so that both have unlived lives (99–103). May serves as a "mirror" in which he could see "his suppressed love and passion that she quietly reflects," but he will not "read ... the double meanings in both her words and gestures" (100). Even when he realizes her death is near, "his passivity continues to immobilize him" (103). The objects around them are evocative: "The fireless chimney-piece points to their lack of passion, the French clock to their wasted lifetime together, and the rosy Dresden figurines to their petrified, static relationship" (104). The green of May's scarf and the "redemptive, fertile qualities" implied by her name contrast sharply with her "dazzling, wintry whiteness," but even then Marcher will not understand (104–5). His "suppressed libidinal impulses and love for May" have been "transformed into an amorphous energy" spent watching for the beast (105). Like many Jamesian characters, Marcher "encase[s] the female within the bounds of [his] imagination so that she does not become threatening" (106). His "fear of women and sexuality causes him to lead a chaste life that involves no fleshly union" (108). After May's death Marcher finally realizes all he had missed when he sees the grief of the mourner at the cemetery, but now knowing that the future holds only death and that happiness is not possible in the present without May, "he turns to the past for comfort" (110–11). Marcher is "the central consciousness" in the story, but "the narrator's critical, moral, and controlling voice is still felt" as the reader is able to know "May's tacit point of view" and understand the ironic contrast between Marcher's view of himself as unselfish and his "active exploitation of" May (112). In most of the story "the slow and repetitious rhythm reinforces the aura of the futility and emptiness of Marcher's life" and suggests that the scenes "represent iterative occurrences" (113). In the final section, however, "historical time approximates narrative time," and the language suggests "the unmeditative functioning of the mind" (113). After May's death Marcher seeks in "the past an explanation of his empty present," but the past offers him no more than he had found in his "fixation on the future" (114). **THEM, FORM, FEM, PSY**

Jam 10. Rogers, Robert. "The Beast in Henry James." *American Imago* 13 (1956): 426–53.

The sense John Marcher has of "missing" something in his life reflects James's own despair on thinking he had failed to live fully (427). According to Dr. Saul Rosenzweig, James felt he could not "compete with his father and his gifted older brother" and consequently suffered "'a profound repression of aggressiveness'" and ultimately "sexual repression" (427). The impact of his repression is felt in stories like "The Beast in the Jungle" where the female becomes a mother surrogate (427). May Bartram offers Marcher "motherly care and indulgence," but he cannot marry her because "one cannot marry one's mother" (432–33). James's beast metaphor is probably associated with his father and brother and is "mysterious, vulgar, hideous" (445). It "suggests the male penis crouching—ready to spring—in a dark jungle of pubic hair" (445). James "identified himself with his father in an unsatisfactory way, became helplessly fixated on his mother in such a manner as to inhibit normal sexual activity, and thus had to face the beast figure of an unsatisfied sexual drive" (451). His diverted energy was spent trying to capture his mother in his stories "since he could not possess her in reality" (451). **PSY, HIST**

Jam 11. Sedgwick, Eve Kosofsky. "The Beast in the Closet: Henry James and the Writing of Homosexual Panic." In *Sex, Politics, and Science in the Nineteenth-Century Novel*. Ed. Ruth Bernard Yeazell. Baltimore and London: Johns Hopkins University Press, 1986. Pp. 161–82, 184–86. Reprinted in *Henry James: A Collection of Critical Essays*. Ed. Ruth Bernard Yeazell. Englewood Cliffs, NJ: Prentice Hall, 1994. Pp. 154–70.

Although John Marcher's story seems to address "'universal'" heterosexual experience, close examination suggests that it reveals "male homosexual panic," like that which might have been reflected in James's relationship with Constance Fenimore Woolson (155–56). Homosexual panic is what a "nonhomosexual-identified" male might feel over homoerotic desires (156). Marcher's secret destiny is apparently devoid of "content" ("'nothing ... was to have happened'" to him), but in fact his "unspeakable fate" can be seen as "the perfectly specific absence of a prescribed heterosexual desire," or perhaps latent homosexuality (161). Direct mention of homosexuality has been avoided "in Christian tradition" through *preterition*, a rhetorical device which avoids naming ("the 'detestable and abominable sin, amongst Christians not to be named'"; "'the Love that dare not speak its name'") (161–62). Surprisingly, James uses language reminiscent of these indirections to refer to "Marcher's 'secret'": "'the thing [May] knew, which grew to be at last, with the consecration of the years, never mentioned between them save as the real truth about him'" or "'dreadful things ... I couldn't name'" or "'more monstrous than all the monstrosities we've named'" (162–63). James also includes other words that are more suggestive of "a homosexual meaning: 'The rest of the world of course thought him *queer*, but she, she only, knew how, and above all why, queer' ... She took his *gaiety* from him.... She traced his unhappy *perversion* ...'" (162). Because of his fear of the possibility that his secret may involve "something homosexual," Marcher lives in the "closet" of his secret that he shares with May, allowing her to help him "'pass for a man like another'" (164). Ironically, though she is aware "that he is imprisoned by homosexual panic" and would help him escape, her complicity "*consolidates and fortifies* [his] closet" and confines her as well (165). With this reading the ending of the story does not reveal Marcher as "the finally self-knowing man who is capable of heterosexual love" (168). Nor does he acknowledge "the possibility of *desire for* the man" at May's grave (169). Instead he "*identif[ies] with* the man in that man's (baffled) desire for some other female, dead object" and remains "the irredeemably self-ignorant man who embodies and enforces heterosexual compulsion" (168–69). **PSY, MULTI**

Jam 12. Smith, F.E. "The Beast in the Jungle: The Limits of Method." *Perspective* 1 (1947): 33–40.

James's choice of method restricts what he can do in "The Beast in the Jungle" (33). Because of the kind of man John Marcher is, James cannot show him as a traditional hero performing heroic deeds or thinking heroic thoughts (33). In fact, since Marcher is not very perceptive, James must "rely not on the greatness of thought but on the smallness of it, on the intricacies, the delicacies, and the nuances of it" (33–34). And he must "maintain the reader's suspense" through all the subtleties (34). The story traces the relationship between Marcher and May Bartram, as he watches for his beast and she struggles not to "[damage] his ego" by telling him that the beast does not exist (34–35). James tells his story through six important scenes "separated ... by long analysis of [Marcher's] thoughts and motives" (35). Within the scenes, brief passages of dialogue are also interspersed with detailed thoughts in a method that is "too foreign to ordinary experience to be completely convincing" (36). Although the "precision of the thought" revealed by this method helps to characterize Marcher, it slows the story too much (36–37). James's abstract method foregoes references to physical setting or physical action but allows the reader to see the paradox and irony of John Marcher's situation, in particular the underlying irony associated with the image of the title (37–38). However, the method "is too specialized, too barren of action, too empty of emotion," and the characters "have more of the nature of propositions than of human beings" (40). **FORM, READ-R**

Jam 13. Stone, Edward. "James's 'Jungle': The Seasons." *University of Kansas City Review* 21 (1954): 142–44.

References to the calendar in "The Beast in the Jungle" are evocative, and the names are "allusive" (142). "Marcher" suggests the cold of March; "May," the warmth of spring (142). In April, the two characters have their final meeting, where Marcher's chill seems about to be transformed by May but finally overcomes her (143). The story begins on a cheerful autumn day in October, moves into spring, and then ends on a "'grey afternoon'" of another autumn, the light that May could have brought into his life now gone (142–44). Marcher now realizes "May was what he had missed," but he tries once more "to seek in her embrace" the warmth she had offered (144). **FORM**

Jam 14. Tate, Allen. "Three Commentaries: Poe, James, and Joyce." *The Sewanee Review* 58 (1950): 1–15.

James creates an "excessive foreground" in the story, using what he called an "Indirect Approach" to reveal the "objective situation through the trial-and-error of a Central Intelligence" (7). In only two scenes of the story does James make his characters "visible," in Part IV, when May moves toward John as if to offer her body to him, and in the final scene at the grave (7–9). The former is more successful, because in the latter James introduces without sufficient preparation the stranger, "a *ficelle*, a character not in the action but brought in to elicit some essential quality from the involved characters" (9). Although the story has flaws, it is still "one of the great stories in the language" (9). **FORM**

Jam 15. Van Leer, David. "The Beast of the Closet: Homosociality and the Pathology of Manhood." *Critical Inquiry* 15 (1989): 587–605.

Although Eve Kosofsky Sedgwick has made an outstanding contribution to scholarship on homosexuality in literature, she writes as a feminist-Marxist critic and therefore often makes assumptions that harm the cause she tries to support and perpetuates the very stereotypes she tries to destroy (587–88). For example, in her discussion of James's "The Beast in the Jungle," Sedgwick identifies John Marcher's problem as "homosexual panic" and "implies that greater self-knowledge would help Marcher overcome" it (593). However, Marcher's acknowledgment of his homosexuality seems unlikely to have dispelled his panic because the story is set in a time when homosexuals were put in jail, a fact which Sedgwick acknowledges with her discussion of the trials of Oscar Wilde (593). Also a problem is Sedgwick's stereotypical characterization of May as the kind of woman who is attracted to men suffering from homosexual panic (594–95). Even discussing the idea of Marcher's closet perpetuates the stereotype of "the closet queen" (598). **MULTI, NHIST**

A.C.L.

"A WHITE HERON"

Jew 1. Ammons, Elizabeth. "The Shape of Violence in Jewett's 'A White Heron.'" *Colby Library Quarterly* 22 (1986): 6–16.

While numerous critics have seen "A White Heron" as a discussion of opposing values (such as male versus female or commercialism versus nature), the story is an argument against forced heterosexuality (6). The story's rural setting, Sylvia's newly acquired world—comprising her grandmother, the cow, and nature's plants and creatures—is obviously female and clearly conducive to the growth of Sylvia's spirit, which had been stunted in the masculine world of the city, her previous home (7). As the story opens, Sylvia and the cow are meandering away from the setting sun towards the east, the direction of the rising moon, a common female symbol (7). This self-sufficient female world represents the separate feminine sphere in nineteenth-century American culture that was disappearing as more and more women entered into the male domains of commerce, arts, medicine, and education. While the tradition of separate spheres for man and women was indeed limiting to women, the practice did encourage female bonding (8). Jewett in "A White Heron" favors the separatism that allows for close female relationships and the growth of the female values of harmony and nurture (9). "A White Heron" is an argument against the institution of heterosexuality (9) which, as Adrienne Rich has argued, is essential to sustain a patriarchy. Sylvia, at age nine and on the brink of puberty, refuses to leave the feminine world of childhood and enter as a maturing female into the heterosexual and patriarchal world as represented by the hunter, a world in which the female offers her body in return for "money, social approval, and the affection of a man" (10). "A White Heron" incorporates elements of a classic fairy tale (10): a young girl is isolated or secluded until puberty when a young man arrives to rescue her. However, Jewett rewrites the traditional ending (11). While Jewett hints that perhaps a non-threatening heterosexual world is possible (as suggested by the pair of herons and by the symbolic old pine tree, which is seen as male), she then discounts the possibility as unrealistic (12) and portrays the actual heterosexual world, represented by the hunter, as oppressive (13). Jewett suggests, through her images and symbols, that a heterosexual world is against nature—the hunter kills and destroys—and that a matrisexual world, based on the bonds formed by females, including the primary ones between mother and child and those between females and nature, is natural and should not be relinquished (14). Sylvia, in declining to disclose the whereabouts of the heron's nest, refuses to renounce her first relationships and enter into the heterosexual patriarchal world (16). **FEM, MULTI, NHIST**

Jew 2. Atkinson, Michael. "The Necessary Extravagance of Sarah Orne Jewett: Voices of Authority in 'A White Heron.'" *Studies in Short Fiction* 19 (1982): 71–74.

"A White Heron" is, like many classical stories, a tale of innocence (71), but unlike the others, Jewett's is not a tale of innocence lost but innocence retained (72), innocence that is essential to the development of Sylvia's identity or self (72). Through manipulating the narrator's voice, Jewett shows nature empathizing with and supporting the girl (73)—the old pine tree assists her in her climb and the same narrator's voice presents Sylvia as one of nature's creatures: she and the white heron watch the dawn together. The narrator's intrusive voice, which directs Sylvia's gaze to the heron, confirms the natural wisdom of the tree (73). Thus both humankind and nature encourage Sylvia's bond with nature (73). Her decision not to reveal the location of the nest, which would result in the loss of her innocence, is supported by the narrator, whose point of view is more comprehensive than that of any other character or force in the story (74). **THEM, FORM**

Jew 3. Brenzo, Richard. "Free Heron or Dead Sparrow: Sylvia's Choice in Sarah Orne Jewett's 'A White Heron.'" *Colby Library Quarterly* 14 (1978): 36–41.

Narrating a story from the point of view of a child or a young adolescent as he or she becomes an integral part of society is common in American literature. Sylvia must battle with her awakening sexuality as she chooses between accommodating a young male hunter and remaining faithful to herself (36). At first, the hunter instills fear in Sylvia partly because of her innocence concerning sex, partly because he reminds her of the boy in the city who chased her, and partly because he kills the birds that she loves (37). Soon, however, she is charmed by the hunter and accepts a gift of a jackknife, an instrument of violence (38). She can please him by identifying the location of the heron's nest, but in the process betraying nature as well as herself, or she can reject the hunter and, by implication, society and heterosexual love (40). Armed with self-knowledge gained from ascending an ancient pine tree, she refuses to reveal the heron's location even for the offered ten dollars, thus rejecting an action that would be akin to prostitution (40). The conclusion of the story is somewhat ambiguous. Although Sylvia maintains her identity as she denies the young hunter and overcomes her "servile and unhealthy" (40) desire for him, a tone of sadness prevails. Must she reject male relationships in order to preserve her autonomy? The story suggests yes, for to enter into a relationship would mean for Sylvia "to allow herself to be caught, raped, killed, stuffed, and put on display in a man's house" (41). **THEM, FORM**

Jew 4. Griffith, Kelley, Jr. "Sylvia as Hero in Sarah Orne Jewett's 'A White Heron.'" *Colby Library Quarterly* 21 (1985): 22–27.

Analyzing "A White Heron" in light of Joseph Campbell's discussion of the hero as put forth in *The Hero with a Thousand Faces* shows that Sylvia goes through the same three phases that a hero does (22). The first stage, the "departure," contains the initial challenge or "call to adventure" (22). In "A White Heron" the challenge is issued by a stranger who eventually offers Sylvia ten dollars to reveal the whereabouts of a white heron's nest (23). During the second stage, the "initiation," the hero must cross a boundary, entering into a strange or unfamiliar world, and overcome a series of obstacles. In her early morning adventure, Sylvia, searching for the heron's nest, climbs an old pine tree, a difficult task, that enables her to see beyond her known world (23). The third stage, "the return," consists of the hero's returning home and either presenting the "boon" he or she has won or withholding it. Sylvia's journey back is fraught with indecision. Should she bestow the "boon," the location of the heron's nest, or not (24)? Sylvia chooses silence. "A White Heron" is more than a retelling of the story of the mythical hero, as is suggested by the final paragraph, which introduces a note of doubt concerning Sylvia's choice (25). Sylvia's silence not only represents the selection of nature over commercialism but also represents a woman choosing a career over marriage, a decision that Jewett herself made (26). And finally, on a more universal level, Sylvia's choice represents a search for knowledge and then a refusal to debase that knowledge (27). **ARCH, THEM**

Jew 5. Held, George. "Heart to Heart with Nature: Ways of Looking at 'A White Heron.'" *Colby Library Quarterly* 18 (1982): 55–65. Reprinted in *Critical Essays on Sarah Orne Jewett.* Ed. Gwen L. Nagel. Boston: G.K. Hall, 1984. Pp. 58–68.

Details of Jewett's own life are useful in understanding "A White Heron." Jewett's close relationship with her father and his death in 1878 and her subsequent close friendship with Annie Fields contributed to her dedication to a writing career and to her resolve not to marry (58–59), experiences which are fictionalized in "A White Heron" in Sylvia's decision to protect the white heron and in her rejection of the ornithologist (67). Sylvia's closeness to nature is also based on Jewett's own life (60). She herself, as Annie Fields remarked, was "one accustomed to tender communings with woods and streams" (60). While the story has autobiographical overtones, other readings are possible. The ornithologist also symbolizes the conflict between commercialism and the rural way of life, a conflict that results in the destruction of nature. He, as a hunter of trophies, is contrasted to the rural hunter of food (61–62). The heron, an appropriate symbol for this clash, was hunted around the turn of the century almost to extinction to supply the needs of the millinery industry (62). The threat to nature posed by commercialism is suggested by the hunter's offer of ten dollars for information concerning the location of the nest (63). Not only would the exchange result in the death of the heron, but the offer so distracts Sylvia that she loses her sensitivity to nature's creatures (63). The hunter's attempted bribe of Sylvia can be read as Satan's tempting of Eve in the Garden of Eden (63); in this case, however, innocence ultimately triumphs. Sylvia's strength and source of happiness result from her harmony with nature, but the hunter would have her betray one of nature's creatures. She is, like the white heron, threatened by the hunter (66). By refusing to reveal the nest's location, Sylvia not only rejects the commercialism represented by the hunter but also rejects female subservience and traditional gender roles (67). **HIST, THEM, FEM**

Jew 6. Heller, Terry. "The Rhetoric of Communion in Jewett's 'A White Heron.'" *Colby Library Quarterly* 26 (1990): 182–94.

The very rhetorical devices for which Jewett has been criticized are the ones that transform "A White Heron" into a "great story" (190). Jewett, writing in the tradition of realistic fiction, consciously violates some of its conventions (182). Rhetorical devices similar to her "odd shifts between past and present tense, apostrophes to objects in the story, and direct addresses by the narrator to the reader and to Sylvia" were often found in the romantic fiction of the day but were eschewed by serious writers of realistic fiction (182). Jewett as well had avoided these strategies in earlier stories, but she intentionally incorporated them in "A White Heron" (182). Elizabeth Ammons valuably suggests that the rhetorical devices, while jarring to the reader, are integral parts of the story (183). But while Ammons contends that these devices underline Jewett's rewriting of a masculine plot (184–85), Jewett seems to be employing these devices to establish a "rhetoric of communion" among the reader, the narrator, and nature (189). The first tense shift occurs as Sylvia, leading the cow home, is startled by the whistle of the ornithologist (186). The shift highlights the presence of the narrator in contrast to the usually invisible narrator of realistic fiction. Jewett's numerous tense shifts, direct addresses, sentence fragments, and other unusual rhetorical devices contribute in various ways to the story: the narrator becomes a visible creator of the story (186), a common view is being established between the reader and the narrator (187), the reader and the narrator become "self-conscious co-creators of the narration" (187), and nature is given a consciousness that can be entered into by the reader (190). Jewett, through her language, is insisting that the preferred life is one that establishes a communion between the natural and the human worlds (192) and that one without the other leads to incompleteness, as illustrated by the ornithologist (191). The hunter, blinded by "the excesses of his culture's ideology of masculinity" (192), cannot accept nature but must possess it. Sylvia, while she requires the solitude of nature as she develops her identity, will also be incomplete (as the last paragraph of the story suggests) if she ultimately rejects the human world (192). **FORM, READ-R**

Jew 7. Kelchner, Heidi. "Unstable Narrative Voice in Sarah Orne Jewett's 'A White Heron.'" *Colby Quarterly* 28 (1992): 85–92.

The shifting narrative voice problematizes discussions of the story's themes (85). The story is as much about questions concerning the narrator and narration as about female identity or commercialism (85). Because Jewett is seen as a local colorist or regionalist and as one of the American realists, one expects to find an objective narrator, one who maintains a distance from the narration (86). The first part of the story seems to maintain that illusion of separation, but the close reader will find instances in which the distance is bridged (86). For example, Jewett's habit of recording thoughts without employing quotation marks conflates the narrator with the character, usually Sylvia. Thus Sylvia's thoughts become the narrator's (87). Consequently, a tension is established between the illusion of narrative distance and the "shared consciousness" between narrator and character (88). The narrator is no longer invisible but in effect becomes another character (88). An examination of the effect the shift in tenses has on the position of the narrator suggests that a past tense implies both knowledge of events and a distant narrator while present tense suggests a narrator who is not in control (89). In the second part of the story, more frequent disturbances occur in the illusion of the distant and objective narrator (89): the voice of the narrator merges often with Sylvia's and the narrator intrudes with didactic statements (90). Thus Jewett is calling into question the position of the narrator and the concept of narration itself. Questions about theme cannot be discussed because without a stable and consistent narrator, interpretation is problematical (92). "A White Heron" explores the meaning of "'narrative,' narrator,' and 'reader'" (92). **DECON, THEM**

Jew 8. Moreno, Karen K. "'A White Heron': Sylvia's Lonely Journey." *Connecticut Review* 13 (1991): 81–85.

The story's events symbolize Sylvia's journey as she matures physically, psychologically, and spiritually (81). Ideas garnered from Jungian psychology suggest how various details of the story emphasize Sylvia's maturation. For example, the physical journey is suggested by Sylvia's age, nine, the brink of puberty; the psychological journey during which she must integrate all parts of her personality is suggested by the darkness of the woods she is about to enter, and the spiritual journey is indicated by the setting of the story, which begins in the evening and concludes with dawn (81). Thus like mythical heroes Sylvia must first enter into darkness before reaching a spiritual state (81). But Sylvia's journey can support a distinctly feminist reading as well (82). Sylvia achieves her identity in a world dominated by women, maternal symbols, and nature and away from men and the city, the domain of men (82). Her identity, closely linked to nature, is threatened by the intrusion of a male hunter from the city (82) who, while first seen as a threat, becomes attractive to Sylvia (82). She undertakes her early morning excursion to the top of the old pine tree to locate the heron's nest in order to please the young man, but during the climb she recognizes her affinity with nature (83). She resists the temptation posed by the hunter, allowing her own identity to exist, an identity dependent upon and allied with nature but threatened by the male world (84). **ARCH, FEM**

Jew 9. Orr, Elaine. "Reading Negotiation and Negotiated Reading: A Practice with/in 'A White Heron' and 'The Revolt of Mother.'" *CEA Critic* 53 (1991): 49–65.

Women, because of their subordinate position in a patriarchal society, must rely on negotiation to fulfill their needs. Literature written by women often reveals the practice of negotiation (49)—a process which, because it considers all views and does not maintain an either-or position, occupies the highest moral position (50). Negotiation in Jewett's "A White Heron" and in Mary Wilkins Freeman's "The Revolt of Mother" creates a new way of thinking which benefits all characters (51). Jewett's story opens with the hunter establishing a framework in which an exchange is set up: ten dollars for the location of the heron's nest, an exchange that would lead to the heron's death (52). Lacking empathy, the hunter is an adversary, capturing and killing what he loves (53). Sylvia's position, arrived at through her climb to the top of the pine tree, enables her to understand and to consider the needs of all (54). She appreciates the heron's difference and also recognizes its similarity to herself (54). The hunter's position is a business transaction while Sylvia's recognizes "the common right to life" (55). Her position is not an exchange but one that "affirms mutual desires and needs" (55). While this position is centered in women's emphasis on relationships, compromise, and negotiation (56), it does not exclude men but rather takes into consideration all voices (61). Freeman's "The Revolt of Mother" supports conclusions similar to the ones presented for "A White Heron." **THEM, FEM**

Jew 10. Smith, Gayle L. "The Language of Transcendence in Sarah
Orne Jewett's 'A White Heron.'" *Colby Library Quarterly* 19
(1983): 37–44. Reprinted in *Critical Essays on Sarah Orne Jewett.*
Ed. Gwen L. Nagel. Boston: G.K. Hall, 1984.

Jewett's language helps establish the connection between humans
and the natural world, both animate and inanimate, in "A White
Heron" (37). Jewett subtly, through her choice of language, establishes
her vision of reality in which the human and non-human worlds are
closely linked, an idea radical in her time but similar to Emerson's view
of nature (39). Sylvia is linked throughout the story with nature: she
and the cow are described as companions, and she is also identified
with the "wretched geranium" in the city (39). Not only is Sylvia shown
to be part of nature but so is the hunter, a finding that suggests that
Sylvia is not an anomaly: both characters are described as "creatures"
(40). Just as Sylvia and the hunter are linked with nature, so aspects of
nature are given human characteristics; the cow engages in a game of
hide-and-seek (39), the pine tree actively helps Sylvia in her journey to
its top (41), and the heron watches, like Sylvia, the sea and the dawn
(41). The direct address made by the narrator to nature is not disturbing
or jarring since nature has a sensibility just as humanity does (44). Not
only is the relationship between nature and humanity established by
Jewett's language but so, too, is the close connection between the past
and present. This link is made by a shifting between past and present
tense, a device other critics have faulted but which seems essential to
Jewett's vision of reality (42). **THEM, FORM**

B.W.

"ARABY"

Joy 1. Atherton, J.S. "Araby." In *James Joyce's* Dubliners: *Critical Essays*. Ed. Clive Hart. London: Faber and Faber, 1969. Pp. 39–47.

Although ironic, the tone of the story is also more compassionate and tender than that of other stories in the collection (40). Like much of Joyce's work, the story is partly autobiographical (40–42). Every detail of the story contributes to its total impact (44). "It is frequently said that Joyce had no interest in politics or social matters. This is not true, and one of the features of the stories is their precise presentation of social differences" (45). Typically, the story concludes with a sense of stasis, "but it differs from the rest in that the stasis is accepted, not with weary resignation but with anger that darkness and negation must be the conclusion. The very fact of the anger suggests that the boy's search for escape will not stop here, although years may have to pass before it can be successful" (47). **THEM, HIST**

Joy 2. Beck, Warren. *Joyce's* Dubliners: *Substance, Vision, and Art*. Durham, NC: Duke University Press, 1969. Pp. 96–109.

The story explores "everyman's puberty rite, imperious desire blunting itself upon limitations, and fragmenting into an opposite despair" (97). Although some critics have suggested that Mangan's sister's rope of hair symbolizes a noose, Joyce associates it with "pure enchantment" (100). Joyce shows how love encourages selective idealization (101) and suggests that "disenchantment" is "the typical fate of the romantic" (104). Such disillusionment "breeds melancholy, weakens self-possession, and may induce ambivalence," so that the boy at the end feels fragmented (104). "There was in Joyce himself that recurrent bitterness which ... indirectly punishes the self for overexpectation by derogating the world" (106). Any past love, remembered, causes sadness when we realize its impermanence, but this boy's quest is never even momentarily fulfilled (107). Although the boy had earlier faced frustrations imposed by reality (the lateness of his uncle's return and the slowness of the train), at the end he is devastated by a disappointment typical of life in general—the gap between the ideal and the real.

He has not yet achieved the wisdom of stoic self-containment (109).
THEM, HIST

Joy 3. Booth, Wayne C. "Pluralism and Its Rivals." *Now Don't Try to Reason with Me: Essays and Ironies for a Credulous Age.* Chicago: University of Chicago Press, 1970. Pp. 131–49.

Recent demonstrations at the University of Chicago have raised important questions about competing claims to truth (131–34). "Araby" offers an opportunity to examine how a single object can be approached from different perspectives (134). Many common-sense details of the story can be (and must be) accepted by any sensible interpreter (135–37); however, in other respects our readings of the story "are permanently doomed to partiality" (138). An Aristotelian critic, for instance, might focus on the story as an imitation of an action, stressing its successes of narrative manner, diction, and tone, and its sophisticated but sympathetic treatment of the main character (139–40). Although the story provides no catharsis (such a critic might say), Joyce demonstrates his artistic control of all the parts of the work and thus creates a pleasing artistic whole (140–41). In contrast, a critic influenced by Plato might emphasize the story's ability to corrupt its audience by encouraging us to sympathize with the immature, emotional boy and by satirizing decent citizens and worthy social institutions (141). Intelligent readers may laugh at the boy, but the less intelligent may be seduced into sharing his petty emotions (142). A Platonic critic might see the story as exemplifying a disturbing trend in modern fiction—a trend that mocks heroic aspirations, that stresses the absurdity of life, and that endorses emotional reactions (142). An unsophisticated Freudian critic might emphasize the boy's desires for sexual freedom; the imagery of the girl's petticoat; the boy's masturbatory incantations; and the disappointing penetration of the dark, dome-shaped hall at the end of the work (142–43). An even cruder Nietzschean reading might emphasize how the story shows a conflict between Apollonian and Dionysian impulses and how the story functions, like music, as a pure esthetic object (143–44). By the same token, a Marxist might see the story as "a portrait of decadent middle-class values, drawn by an aesthete who, despite his clever indictment of the bourgeois boy and his absurdly class-ridden quest, never never managed to shake off his allegiance to the romantic individualism of the artist" (144–45). A different kind of economist might see the story as a work written to sell (145). A literary historian might emphasize the work's innovations in narration and point-of-view (145). A cultural historian might see the tale as an indictment of romanticism, while a rhetorical critic might emphasize the story's impact on its audience (145). A sociologist might emphasize how the work indicates the development, at the time Joyce was writing, of a readership capable of appreciating nuance and unsentimental story-telling (145). In short, every possible viewpoint will have something to say about "Araby," thus demonstrating the pluralist argument that "every reality, every subject, can be and will be validly grasped in more than one way depending on the purposes and intellectual systems of the viewers" (146). This "does not mean that *every* view is valid, or that there are not differences of validity or usefulness among different views" (146–47). The ability to adopt and explore different perspectives is difficult but valuable (147). Pluralism also stresses the need to distinguish between slipshod or valuable work done even *within* a single perspective (148). The relative success of an interpretation can be judged "on the basis of *adequacy to the possibilities of the particular system*, when held up against *the potentialities offered to that system by the particular piece of reality examined*" (148). "A man is lucky if he learns to use even one intellectual mode well. He is luckier if he can master more than one. He is luckiest of all, I suppose, if he can invent a new road to truth that proves fruitful to other men, or can elaborate or extend an already existing one" (148). It is important to understand that "systems answering different questions for different purposes using different methods cannot be placed in direct opposition" (149). Realizing this fact can prevent many useless, dogmatic disputes. **ARIS, PLAT, PSY, MARX, HIST, PLUR**

Joy 4. Brooks, Cleanth, and Robert Penn Warren. *Understanding Fiction*. New York: Crofts, 1943. Pp. 420–24.

Numerous naturalistic details emphasize the boy's alienation from his disappointing world; by bringing the girl a gift from the romantic bazaar, he hopes to share his emotions (420–21). The clerk and her admirers symbolize both the intimacy he desires and his own exclusion from it (421). The pervasive religious imagery suggests "that romantic love and religious love are mixed up in his mind" (422). Joyce's detached irony prevents sentimentality; the narrator reminisces from a more mature perspective. Nevertheless, the "sense of isolation and disillusion which, in the boy's experience, may seem to spring from a trivial situation, becomes not less, but more aggravated and fundamental in the adult's experience" (423). The story deals symbolically with the fundamental human sensations of alienation and disappointment (423). **THEM, FORM**

Joy 5. Brugaletta, John J., and Mary H. Hayden. "The Motivation for Anguish in Joyce's 'Araby.'" *Studies in Short Fiction* 15 (1978): 11–17.

Because Mangan's sister is older than the boy, it seems unlikely that she would behave as bashfully as she seems to during their encounter (12–13). It therefore seems likely that he only imagines their conversation (14). Because he accepts this vision as reality, his anguish when his illusion is punctured at the end is all the more comprehensible (17). **THEM**

Joy 6. Collins, Ben L. "'Araby' and the 'Extended Simile.'" In *Twentieth Century Interpretations of* Dubliners: *A Collection of Critical Essays*. Ed. Peter K. Garrett. Englewood Cliffs, NJ: Prentice-Hall, 1968. Pp. 93–99.

At first the boy is "unaware of the real and all-embracing lack in his world and life—the void in which all attempts at beauty, love, faith, and belonging will be frustrated" (93). The apple tree and rusted bicycle pump suggest parallels with the fall from the garden of Eden caused by the serpent (94). Mangan's sister "represents Church (in that she includes Christ, Mary, the priesthood), Ireland, and the betrayer Judas" (95). Her apparent holiness is bogus; instead she is "earthly and material" (97). **THEM**

Joy 7. Gifford, Don. *Joyce Annotated: Notes for* Dubliners *and* A Portrait of the Artist as a Young Man. 2d ed. Berkeley: University of California Press, 1982. Pp. 40–48.

"Araby was a poetic name for Arabia and suggestive of the heady and sensuous romanticism of popular tales and poems about the Middle East" (40). Joyce himself resided for two years at North Richmond street (42); the Christian Brothers school emphasized practical education (43). The brown houses symbolize paralysis, while the Walter Scott novel features a youth transformed from insignificance to great importance (43). "Mangan" was the name of one of Joyce's favorite poets; a romantic who knew no Arabic, Mangan nonetheless often claimed that his poems were translations (44). Both the florin the boy receives and the shilling he gives were sizeable sums at the time (47–48). The reference to two men counting money at the bazaar may allude to the money-counters in the temple mentioned in the Bible's Matthew 21 (48). **HIST**

Joy 8. Leonard, Garry M. *Reading* Dubliners *Again: A Lacanian Perspective*. Syracuse: Syracuse University Press, 1993. Pp. 73–94.

Mangan's sister is a far more important character than critics have usually acknowledged, for what the boy "takes to be his identity has been constructed relative to another (Mangan's sister) and is destined to be taken apart" through his interaction with the shop girl at the bazaar (74). In Lacanian terms, the boy moves from being "the subject controlling the gaze to [being] the object controlled by it" (75). Because the boy sees Mangan's sister as a "representation of femininity," she "does not exist for him except as the representation of lack" who seems to confirm "the fullness and authenticity of his masculine subjectivity" but who in fact merely reflects back to him "a division that already exists within him" as a representative of masculinity (76). He looks at her and tries to control her (and thus establish his own identity) through his gaze, but he tries not to notice that she is looking back and is manipulating his gaze (78–79). Later he is forced to confront the controlling gaze of a woman when he encounters the shop-girl (79). In his concluding observation he tries to recapture control of the gaze by telling how he now saw *himself* (80). "At the conclusion of the story, he sees himself in order not to see that he is being seen and that his 'self' is nothing but what he imagines the Other sees" (81). "For the masculine subject, a woman becomes a symptom that helps ward off any discovery of how tenuous his subjectivity really is" (82). Desire results from a sense of lacking fullness of being; such fullness can never be achieved, but the continual quest to achieve it gives a person his or her sense of identity (83). The result of each quest will seem fraudulent or disappointing, but the person will never admit that it is his or her identity that is actually deficient (84). "The male subject *must* go on a quest so that the inevitable failure to complete himself ... will seem to be the failure of the quest and not of the quest(ion) of his own subjectivity" (86). Masculine and feminine positions are not inherently biological but are "effects of one's position in the Symbolic Order" (90); thus the boy at the end, subjected to the gaze of the shop girl, becomes passive and self-effacing (89). Even in deriding his vanity at the end, the boy only offers another interpretation of his identity—an identity no more stable or real than the one it replaces, since no identity can finally be stable or real (93). "The necessity of the boy's humiliation, which he presents to himself as 'knowledge,' is certainly a painful realization, but it is one that protects him from realizing the greater pain of psychic and symbolic castration" (94). **PSY, THEM**

Joy 9. Maglaner, Marvin, and Richard M. Kain. *Joyce: The Man, the Work, the Reputation.* New York: New York University Press, 1956. Pp. 77–79.

The story explores such characteristic themes of *Dubliners* as exile, disappointment, and the contrast between illusion and reality (77–78). The first name of Mangan's sister is not mentioned, perhaps to make her seem a more ideal and spiritual focus; she symbolizes an alternative to dreary Dublin (78). The story's epiphany shows that reality never meets one's expectations (79). "In some ways, the Araby bazaar suggests the church and is its symbol. The narrator's quivering eagerness to reach it, his willingness to overcome material obstacles for the joy of attaining his destination, has religious fervor. But the worldly, the trivial, the gross await him at journey's end" (79). In this as in other stories, Joyce relies more on implied symbolism than on mere plot to convey his meanings (79). **THEM**

Joy 10. Mellard, James M. *Four Modes: A Rhetoric of Modern Fiction.* New York: Macmillan, 1973. Pp. 335–37.

The story employs the lyric mode, filtering experience through the narrator's romantic, idealizing mind; imagery, metaphor, and symbol are more important here than plot (335). The boy's reactions to the girl are at once sensuous and spiritual (336); he sees her as both virgin and temptress (337). The bazaar shatters his romantic illusions, providing an epiphany or moment of insight (337). **FORM, THEM**

Joy 11. Stone, Harry. "'Araby' and the Writings of James Joyce." In *Dubliners: Text, Criticism, and Notes.* Ed. Robert Scholes and A. Walton Litz. New York: Viking, 1969. Pp. 344–67. Reprinted and abridged from *Antioch Review* 24 (1965): 375–410.

The story focuses on a recurrent concern of Joyce's life and fiction—the effort to free oneself from a constricting society (345). The boy's school is the same as Joyce's; their families are similar; the real Araby fair that Joyce experienced similarly "conveyed an ill-assorted blend of psuedo-Eastern romanticism and blatant commercialism" (346). The story parallels a similar tale of disillusionment by Yeats (346–47) and draws on other literary sources (347–51). Like other works by Joyce, this story demonstrates how "men, in their yearning to worship, contrive (perhaps even desire) their own betrayal and insure their own disillusionment" (353). Mangan's sister is reminiscent both of Mary Magdalene and of the Blessed Virgin Mary (354); she is perceived in a way that "combines hints of commercialism and sensuality with connotations of sexuality and betrayal" (354). The story seems to satirize the Irish church; to recall a famous political and sexual scandal; and (through the image of the florin) to allude to Ireland's subjugation by the British (356–60). The boy feels that he has betrayed himself in much the same way as his country has betrayed itself (360). Ultimately the boy "is no worse than the rest of Ireland—its dead priests (part of a dying church), its [materialistic] Mrs. Mercers, its faithless drunken surrogate fathers—and for that matter, no worse than Ireland's rulers. Ireland and Ireland's church, once appropriately imaged as a romantic lady or a sorrowful madonna, has now become cuckquean and harlot—she is sold and sells for silver" (363). Figuratively, the boy's trip is a journey into bondage to the flesh rather than a pilgrimage to the Holy Land (364). The three-fold denial expressed by the salesgirl near the end recalls Peter's denial of Christ (365). At the end the boy perceives his own ambivalence and ambiguities (366–67). **HIST, THEM**

R.C.E.

"THE DEAD"

Joy 12. Anspaugh, Kelly. "'Three Mortal Hour[i]s': Female Gothic in Joyce's 'The Dead.'" *Studies in Short Fiction* 31 (1994): 1–12.

The story's Gothic elements include the Christmas season, the dark house, the references to death and ghosts, and even the theme of live burial suggested by the final epiphany (1–2). Ironically, The Gothic elements help "contribute to a theme of regeneration and rebirth" (3). Since Gothic fiction was a genre pioneered by women and was first received (and has been read by later critics) as subversive of male power, the story's Gothic elements may support a feminist reading of "The Dead" (4). Numerous women in the story challenge Gabriel's conventional sexism, beginning with the self-assertive servant, Lily (5). Like the "Lass of Aughrim" who is the subject of the later ballad, Lily seems to have been victimized by a man, but unlike the Lass, she protests rather than pleading (5). Lily, Miss Ivors, and Gretta all challenge Gabriel's masculinity (6), and Joyce tends to emphasize trios of women (7). Even Michael Furey, because his situation resembles that of the Lass, is feminized (7) and functions almost as a Gothic ghost (10). At the end, "Gabriel is now at the mercy both of the feminine and of the dead. Indeed, he has died to his *male* self and, carried back in time, is put in the place of the female" (10). By opening himself to emotion, he becomes feminized and is reborn as a more fully human person (10–11). Joyce's story, like other Gothic fiction, subverts monolithic patriarchy (11). **THEM, HIST, FEM**

Joy 13. Brunsdale, Mitzi M. *James Joyce: A Study of the Short Fiction.* New York: Twayne, 1993. Pp. 36–47.

Although the story shows a Dubliner paralyzed by his environment, it suggests that an old self must die before a new one can be born (36). The musical allusions give the story a mythic dimension (37). Gabriel's insecurity makes him egotistically dismiss others, especially women (38), who symbolize his native land (39). The banal art and music at the party make him begin to realize his self-betrayal as an Irishman and as an artist (39), although his ensuing speech is still "pompously hypocritical" (39). Mary Jane's playing illustrates how excessive embellishment can be imposed on native art (41–42), while Aunt Julia's singing suggests the power of true art, which only Freddy (ironically) appreciates (42). Meanwhile, Julia's dismissal from the church choir symbolizes how the Church misuses Irish women (42–43). In his speech and throughout the story, Gabriel is a failed Irish bard, since those ancient poets spoke from the heart (like Michael Furey [43–45]). By the end of the story, Gretta's becomes the most powerful voice in a tale previously dominated by Gabriel's egotism (46); by heeding her words, Gabriel begins to awaken to his own potential as a bard—a poet deeply connected to other human beings (47). In this way and others, Joyce's story is relevant to his own life and draws on the resources of ancient Celtic culture (47). **THEM, HIST**

Joy 14. Chambers, Ross. "Gabriel Conroy Sings for His Supper, or Love Refused ('The Dead')." In *James Joyce's Dubliners: Modern Critical Interpretations*. Ed. Harold Bloom. New York: Chelsea House, 1988. Pp. 97–119. Reprinted from Chambers, *Story and Situation: Narrative Seduction and the Power of Fiction* (Minneapolis: University of Minnesota Press, 1984).

Gabriel symbolizes the artist as parasite (99): from one perspective he seems "warm and well intentioned; from another, forced, mendacious, and hypocritical" (100). The party teeters between disorder and harmony (101), just as the story alternates different kinds of meaningless "noise" with different types and moments of significant communication (116). The art "for which D'Arcy [the singer] is the model, the art of verbal noise and snowy disorder," anticipates Joyce's own "modernist, 'writerly' texts" such as *Ulysses* and *Finnegans Wake* (117), as Joyce both implicates us in and distances us from Gabriel's experiences (118). **THEM, READ-R**

Joy 15. Ellmann, Richard. "The Backgrounds of 'The Dead.'" In *Critical Essays on James Joyce*. Ed. Bernard Benstock. Boston: G.K. Hall, 1985. Pp. 90–101. Reprinted from Ellmann's *James Joyce* (New York: Oxford University Press, 1959).

The story is based on a dying young man's real courtship of Nora Barnacle, Joyce's eventual wife (90). Joyce felt a little jealous of his dead rival, and the story reflects his persistent theme that the dead interact with the living (91). The tale began to take shape in Rome, which (like Dublin) was full of reminders of the dead (91); while there, Joyce was haunted by thoughts of Dublin and began to appreciate the unusual hospitality of the Irish (92). The story's party is similar to ones the young Joyce attended at his aunts' house; indeed, many characters in the story are based on real persons (93). In particular, Gabriel mirrors not only Joyce himself but also Joyce's father and (especially in his nervous insecurity) Joyce's friend Constantine Curran (93–94). In Gretta's description of Michael Furey (whose name suggests passion), Joyce pays tribute to Nora's own "artless integrity" (95); the story's final reference to the "west" suggests "the primitive, untutored, impulsive country from which Gabriel had felt himself alienated before" (96). The final tone is one of concession and self-sacrifice, emphasizing that Ireland is stronger than Gabriel (96). "The dead lover who comes between the lovers, the sense of the husband's failure, the acceptance of mediocrity, the resolve to be at all events sympathetic" all come from George Moore's book *Vain Fortune*, while the final image of falling snow may have come from a passage in Homer's *Iliad* (97) and suggests the links between all humans, living and dead (98). Gabriel is depicted with some sympathy (98), and the story shows Joyce's new appreciation for the land he had sought to escape (100). **HIST, THEM**

Joy 16. Levenson, Michael. "Living History in 'The Dead.'" In *James Joyce: The Dead.* Ed. Daniel R. Schwarz. Boston: Bedford Books, 1994. Pp. 163–77.

Although Joyce's story was written at a moment in Ireland's colonial history when the need to define the relation between politics and literature was especially significant (163), Gabriel tries ineffectually to keep them apart (164). Joyce himself felt this conflict between the claims of nationalist politics and pure art—positions respectively represented in the story by Miss Ivors and by Gabriel (165). Joyce considered either attitude, by itself, to be flawed; the story brings them into dialogue and conflict so that a synthesis of the two might result (165). Joyce himself was initially sympathetic to a focus on pure art; the early stories in *Dubliners* therefore emphasize the aesthetic deadness of Irish life. By the time he came to write "The Dead," however, he was more sympathetic to Ireland and more interested in Irish politics (166–69). He opposed British colonial rule, but (partly out of professional self-interest) he was skeptical of arguments in favor of abandoning the English language and using Gaelic instead (169–70). These tensions are embodied in Gabriel: "Implicated as a citizen of his country and yet estranged from such a fundamental source of national identity as a separate language, Gabriel bears internally the stresses and conflicts of an unresolved Irish nationality. He is no more autonomous or coherent than the country that contains him. Such entanglement of personal identity within the matrix of social discourses is an abiding concern of 'The Dead,' much as it is a working assumption of current New Historicist inquiry. The task of securing an integral selfhood merges with the task of formulating a context ... in which a self might live" (170-71). The story shows its characters caught up in a *process* of history (171); the annual dance provides little sense of stability but instead is associated with a cultural decay that reflects the larger instability of Irish colonial culture (172–

73). Gabriel's attempts to achieve an independent, stable self are repeatedly undermined, partly because his nation is a colony (174). "As Joyce's writing shows in many diverse ways, the significance of a life depends on the frame that surrounds it" (175). Joyce himself sought to escape the same pressures to which Gabriel is subject; by dealing with them in a work of his own creation, he seeks to contain them (176). Although the story's final vision suggests that it can be read as a rejection of politics in favor of a universal vision of mankind, it is nonetheless significant that the snow falls all over a unified Ireland (177). The final vision, then, encapsulates the tension that is at the heart of the whole story. **NHIST, DIALOG, HIST**

Joy 17. Loomis, C.C., Jr. "Structure and Sympathy in 'The Dead.'" In *Twentieth Century Interpretations of Dubliners: A Collection of Critical Essays*. Ed. Peter K. Garrett. Englewood Cliffs, NJ: Prentice-Hall, 1968. Pp. 110–14. Reprinted from *PMLA* 75 (1960): 149–51.

The final epiphany or moment of revelation embodies Joyce's "fundamental belief that true, objective perception will lead to true, objective sympathy" (110). The final glimpse of snow seems "paradoxically warm" as "Gabriel at long last feels the deeply unifying bond of common mortality" (110). It is a moment of intuitive, emotional perception for Gabriel and reader alike (110), but to make its impact most effective, Joyce must prevent us from identifying or sympathizing with Gabriel too soon (111). Only by perceiving Gabriel's earlier flaws do we appreciate and share his new vision (111). The story evolves in five sections, moving from a slow pace and general focus to a faster pace and more narrow focus (111). Joyce maintains authorial objectivity while still letting us see the party through Gabriel's condescending, defensive eyes (112). Only at the end does Gretta emerge into full focus (112); in the hotel room, both we and Gabriel suddenly perceive her complexity (113). Although previously the pace has quickened and the focus has narrowed, in Gabriel's final vision of the snow Joyce abruptly reverses both movements (113). Now Gabriel's vision broadens "from Gretta, to his aunts, to himself, to Ireland, to 'the universe'" (114). We have moved from the general (the party) to the particular (the couple) and then a final, universal vision in which "intellectual perception and emotional intuition, form and content, blend" (114). **READ-R, FORM**

Joy 18. Lytle, Andrew. "A Reading of Joyce's 'The Dead.'" *Sewanee Review* 77 (1969): 193–216.

The guests are dead in a Christian sense; they neglect the real meaning of Christmas (193). Ireland is dominated by England as Israel was by Rome at the the time of Christ's birth (194), but Christ has already come to offer salvation (194). The snow symbolizes dead life (frozen water) waiting to be renewed by the sun/Son (194). Gabriel, like the other characters, represents the divine Word buried in flesh (196). His pride is gradually undermined by loss and guilt (198), and Gretta's pure heart helps revive his capacity to love (198). The Christmas feasting celebrates only worldly appetite, and the Morkan house suggests a morgue (201). Later, through pity for Gretta, Gabriel leaves behind the dead carnal world; "pity transforms lust into love" (213). Through humility, understanding, and charity toward Michael Furey, Gabriel overcomes his own pride and alienation (214). Both his ego and the material world dissolve (214), while the snowflakes hitting the window symbolize that the ghost of Furey "is returning to the substantial world to renew the promise of life eternal" (215). Michael "suffered and died for one human being as God the Son suffered and died for all" (215). The falling snow becomes a symbol of salvation (216). **FORM, THEM**

Joy 19. Norris, Margot. "Not the Girl She Was at All: Women in 'The Dead.'" In *James Joyce: The Dead*. Ed. Daniel R. Schwarz. Boston: Bedford, 1994. Pp. 190–205.

The story critiques patriarchy by counterpointing an overt "male" narration that is "challenged and disrupted by a 'silent' or discounted female countertext that does not, in the end, succeed in making itself heard" (192). Female characters in the text often express protests that are "voiced, then silenced; sounded but rejected; there, but negated" (193); examples include Lily, Molly Ivors, and Gretta (193–95), who challenge Gabriel's "complacencies in order of increasing intimacy as servant, colleague, and wife" (195). The narrative voice itself is patriarchal and tends to discount women even while seeming to treat them sympathetically (197–200). Readers can choose to respond to the patriarchal narrative as various women in the story respond to the patriarchy they confront—either with passivity, with resignation, or with protest (204). The latter response (the response of Molly Ivors) is "disruptive, challenging, critical, and activist" and subverts the "intellectual graciousness that Gabriel praises so warmly" but that helps retard genuine political progress (204). **FEM, DIALOG, READ-R**

Joy 20. Rabinowitz, Peter J. "'A Symbol of Something': Interpretive Vertigo in 'The Dead.'" In *James Joyce: The Dead*. Ed. Daniel R. Schwarz. Boston: Bedford Books, 1994. Pp. 137–47.

Although the story is fundamentally ambiguous, producing a sense of instability in its readers, neither formalist nor psychoanalytic criticism can fully explain this effect (137). Instead it seems worth emphasizing that reading is a process that actively alters the text being read, that it involves not only choosing from a range of possible responses but also practicing a variety of common procedures (138–39).

Reading practices are influenced by one's culture, and the culture of Joyce criticism has encouraged practices that heighten one's sense of the ambiguity of this story (141–42). Critics have often tended to assume, for instance, that any link between any two aspects of the story is a meaningful link and that the etymologies of words are usually meaningful in Joyce's writings (142–44). These assumptions tend to multiply greatly the number of potential meanings, yet critics have also assumed that the story has a larger meaning that is coherent (144). Readers are thus pulled in two directions—toward multiplicity and toward coherence—and thus experience a sense of vertigo when responding to the story (144). Critics have interpreted the final paragraphs, for instance, in many different ways (146). Realizing the variety of ways in which the story has been (and can be) interpreted should help make us less naive and more self-conscious as readers and thus open up the possibility of new ways of seeing the text (146–47). **READ-R**

Joy 21. Riquelme, John Paul. "For Whom the Snow Taps: Style and Repetition in 'The Dead.'" In *James Joyce: The Dead*. Ed. Daniel R. Schwarz. Boston: Bedford, 1994. Pp. 219–33.

The story's ending can be (and has been) read either as indicating Gabriel's growth and new insight or as indicating his stagnancy and imperception, but a deconstructive reading blurs the differences between these apparent alternatives and undermines the hope of any single interpretation; the story's tensions cannot be resolved (220). No single reading can do justice to the instability of the text, for Joyce's language encourages us to see from multiple perspectives all at once (220–21). The final scene epitomizes the essential ambiguity of the work (223), allowing us to see the story as one in which Gabriel is both destroyed and renewed (227). Although Joyce repeats certain words and motifs over and over again, each repetition highlights a different meaning or connotation; snow, for instance, is mentioned repeatedly, but it has multiple significances in this story (228). Again and again (especially in his dealings with women), Gabriel's desires do not coincide with reality (229–30); his efforts to make reality conform to his interpretations are continually defeated, just as the story continually defeats our attempts to impose a single reading on it (231–33). **DECON**

Joy 22. Schwarz, Daniel R. "Gabriel Conroy's Psyche: Character as Concept in Joyce's 'The Dead.'" In *James Joyce: The Dead*. Ed. Daniel R. Schwarz. Boston: Bedford Books, 1994. Pp. 102–24.

Gabriel represents the kind of conventional, passionless neurotic Joyce feared becoming (103–4). Gabriel and Joyce regard themselves with "alternating sympathy and irony" (104), revealing an inner emptiness and self-consciousness typical of modern life (105). Although

Gabriel seeks control, his pretensions (especially class distinctions) are stripped away (106). Although a man of words, he cannot really communicate, and in his self-doubt he allows himself to be defined by others (107–8). He feels uncomfortable with self-confident women (110); his hell consists of his "obsessions, fixations, memories, insecurities, and dimly acknowledged needs" (118). By emphasizing Gabriel's sexual awkwardness, Joyce satirizes the impact of the Church (118–19) and also symbolizes the paralysis both of modern man and of Ireland (121). Yet Gabriel has "the potential for growth and transformation" (121), and the ending suggests what he "needs and lacks: song, lyricism, metaphoricity, escape from time into non-rational, passionate states of being, a loosening of the bonds of self-consciousness" (122). The snow symbolizes the natural world outside the self (123). **PSY, HIST, FEM, THEM**

Joy 23. Tate, Allen. "'The Dead.'" In *Dubliners: Text, Criticism, and Notes.* Ed. Robert Scholes and A. Walton Litz. New York: Viking, 1969. Pp. 404–9. Reprinted from Caroline Gordon and Allen Tate, *The House of Fiction* (New York: Scribners, 1950), 279–82.

The story demonstrates Joyce's great talent for transforming objective details into symbols (404). A distanced perspective on Gabriel helps enhance the abruptness of his final recognition of his egotism (405). From the start he exhibits an "inadequate response to people and even his lack of respect for them" (405). Throughout, Joyce effectively *shows* rather than didactically stating his meaning; everything is dramatized and made active (405). We see through Gabriel's limited perspective; the encounter with Miss Ivors dramatizes an aspect of Gabriel's life that Joyce would otherwise have had to report (406). A narcissist, Gabriel lacks the reader's growing and increasingly ironic awareness of the reversal Gabriel will face (407). Joyce's skill at using details is exemplified by the wall and tree he mentions in describing Michael Furey: these small items make the picture seem real and convincing (408). Just as Gabriel experiences a reversal, so the snow reverses its meaning, changing from a symbol of coldness to a symbol of Gabriel's "expanded consciousness" of his links with other human beings (409). **FORM**

Joy 24. Walzl, Florence L. "Gabriel and Michael: The Conclusion of 'The Dead.'" In *Dubliners: Text, Criticism, and Notes.* Ed. Robert Scholes and A. Walton Litz. New York: Viking, 1969. Pp. 423–44. Reprinted from *James Joyce Quarterly* 4 (1966): 17–31.

Although critics have disagreed about the conclusion, especially about the snow symbolism, the story's ambiguity seems intentional (423). When the story is read in the larger context of *Dubliners*, the ending seems to typify the theme of paralysis emphasized elsewhere in the volume, but when the story is read in isolation it seems to suggest spiritual growth and transformation (423–24). Earlier stories in the volume, designed for publication in 1906, emphasize Ireland's paralysis, provinciality, and conformism by tracing a "progression in which children are depicted as disillusioned, youths as frustrated or trapped, men and women as passive and non-productive, and social groups as completely static" (426). In these stories, Joyce "devises plots in which characters are immobilized by weakness or circumstance, symbolizes the resulting psychological situations by imagery of traps and cages, and employs settings with constricted spaces" (427). Movements east often symbolize attempts by youths to escape Dublin, while public groups are often shown as stagnant (427). Imperception is another pattern: the "youths are painfully aware of their disappointments; the more mature suffer but lack insight; characters in the final stories seem totally insensitive" (427–28). Often the reader is granted insights denied to the characters (428). When *Dubliners* was finally published in 1914, "The Dead"—a longer, more sympathetic depiction of Ireland—was added as the last story (428). In the oscillating plot, Gabriel moves back and forth between confidence and feelings of inferiority (429); the story's emphasis on growing perception reverses the earlier pattern of *Dubliners* (430). In some ways the story is the logical conclusion to the earlier works; in other respects it is a departure from them (430). By using ambiguous imagery, Joyce manages to make the story fit the larger book while also marking a new development (430). "Paradoxical images of arrest and movement, darkness and light, cold and warmth, [and] blindness and sight" are used in the story's conclusion "to recall both the central paralysis-death theme of *Dubliners* as a collection and the rebirth-life theme of 'The Dead' as a narrative" (431). For example, in some respects the movement east (toward Europe) is associated in "The Dead" with freedom, but by the end "the east suggests the old, traditional, and effete; the west, the new, primitive, and vital" (431). Eastern Ireland (especially Dublin) seems deadening; western Ireland (associated with Gretta and with Michael Furey) seems more vital (432). Joyce thus "builds an ambivalent symbolism of motion and direction that in some contexts equates the east with dawn and life and the west with sunset and death, but in other contexts associates the east with the old and sterile and the west with the new and vital" (432–33). Similar ambiguity exists in the imagery of dark/cold and light/warmth and in the related snow imagery (433). Also complex is the mirror imagery, which successively suggests "illusion, human reality, and intuitive vision" (434). "Gabriel's final epiphany involves a vision in which snow is both falling and melting. The inherent flexibility of snow as a symbol allows Joyce to shift symbolic suggestions rapidly in these contexts" (434). Gretta associates Michael Furey with rain (symbolizing life), while Gabriel associates him with snow (suggesting the death of his illusions about his own life [440]). The final statement about moving westward can suggest either life or death, while the final image of snow falling into the ocean can suggest an absorption into the "great waters of life" that reflects the transformation of Gabriel, "whose cold conceit has disappeared with his warming humanitarianism" (442). **FORM, THEM, HIST**

R.C.E.

"THE ROCKING-HORSE WINNER"

Law 1. Burroughs, William D. "No Defense for 'The Rocking-Horse Winner.'" *College English* 24 (1963): 323.

W.R. Martin cannot protect the story from the criticism levelled by F.R. Leavis and Graham Hough. In this story Lawrence repeats his usual themes, and the beginning and concluding tones conflict (323). "The plot is skillful, but lacks imagination. Lawrence starts his characters at the top, letting them degenerate to poor souls in the denouement. This arrangement could be tragic if Lawrence had bothered to show some cause-effect for the parents' insistence on social supremacy at Paul's expense; however, the plot is merely the reversal of the fairy-tale climb from rags to riches. It is, although having tragic possibilities, not tragic, but only pathetic" (323). The work relies too much on simple emotional reactions in favor of Paul and against the parents (323). The story is too propagandistic in endorsing basic instincts, and the combination of fantasy and didacticism is indefensible (323). The plot, diction, imagery, and symbolism are effective, but the characters are flat and lifeless (323). **FORM**

Law 2. Davies, Rosemary Reeves. "Lawrence, Lady Cynthia Asquith, and 'The Rocking-Horse Winner.'" *Studies in Short Fiction* 20 (1983): 121–26.

The story "was probably suggested by the tragic illness of [Lawrence's close friend] Lady Cynthia's eldest son John and by the Asquith marriage," with its "destructive materialism" (121). Both Paul and the real boy are similarly wild, self-absorbed, and isolated; Paul's rocking may even suggest the autism from which the real boy probably suffered, and which caused an estrangement from his mother (126). Although Lawrence admired Lady Cynthia, he felt that defects in her character had damaged her relations with her son (126). **HIST**

Law 3. Davis, Robert Gorham. "Observations on 'The Rocking-Horse Winner.'" In *D.H. Lawrence: The Rocking-Horse Winner.* Ed. Dominick P. Consolo. Columbus, OH: Charles E. Merrill, 1969.

Pp. 41–42. Reprinted from *Instructor's Manual for Ten Modern Masters: An Anthology of the Short Story.* 2d ed. New York: Harcourt, Brace, and World, 1959.

"This story begins like a fairy tale, and maintains an appropriately simple, rapidly flowing style throughout. Notice the short paragraphs, the short sentences, the repetitions and recurrences, the exclamations and questions. Most of the story is in dialogue, and here too the speeches are very brief, with the characters repeating each other's phrases, or answering each other's queries. The thematic words are 'luck' and 'money'" (41). Realistic writing blends with a focus on magic, while the central theme is the inability to love (41). Increasing tension and intensity parallel a "pattern of successive revelation" (42). By focusing on gambling, Lawrence achieves plausibility while also using the frantic rocking to symbolize going nowhere (42). **FORM, THEM**

Law 4. Goldberg, Michael. "Lawrence's 'The Rocking-Horse Winner': A Dickensian Fable." *Modern Fiction Studies* 15 (1969): 525–36.

Like Dickens' novel *Dombey and Son*, Lawrence's story is a social fable that attacks the parental neglect and inhumanity caused by materialism (525). Previous critics, stressing psychological explanations, have ignored Lawrence's debt to earlier fiction (525). Lawrence's story resembles Dickens' novel in many ways: both feature a young protagonist named Paul; loveless, materialistic parents; strange voices; elements of fairy-tale and allegory; and the child's mysterious death (526). Both works focus on the destruction caused by failures of love, stifled sexuality, and rampant materialism (530). Both work through contrasts (532) and involve precocious children (533) corrupted by pressures from adults (534). Both children die from a physical illness caused by psychic damage and social strains (534–35). Lawrence's tale is less concerned with sexual than social aberrations, especially economic pressures (535). Paul's rocking suggests not masturbation but the futility and paralysis of his family's life and of his larger society (536). **HIST, THEM, FORM**

Law 5. Gordon, Caroline, and Allen Tate. *The House of Fiction.* 2d ed. New York: Scribner's, 1960. Pp. 227–30.

The story is effectively structured by objective "blocks" of described action; only rarely does the narrator intrude to explain the boy's thoughts (227). The "Complication" involves the sensitive Paul; the "Resolution" involves his discovery of his luck; the "Enveloping Action" (i.e., the social situation) is embodied by the mother (228–29). "At a key moment, midway of the story, the direct presentation is suspended and a panoramic view, belonging to the Enveloping Action, flows in and tightens the main current of the story so that it hurls itself

faster towards its goal. This panorama—the occasion on which the boy
puts five thousand pounds at his mother's disposal—is presented in
brilliant detail, muted only by 'distance'" (228). Lawrence's realistic details are admirable and help the story succeed as drama (229). Repetition of the word "religious" in connection with Bassett helps prepare us
"by indirection for the revelation of the boy's being in the grip of a supernatural power" (229). When the mother discovers Paul rocking, the
scene is described using a technique often employed by Henry James:
we see each character from the perspective of the other, so that the "two
viewpoints fuse to make a rounded whole" (229). Lawrence effectively
uses objective symbolism, implying rather than stating his message
(230). "This story has extraordinary Total Unity. Carefully chosen cadences [as in the first sentence] play their part in the dramatic effect"
(230). Even the exotic names of the horses on which Paul bets show
Lawrence's effective use of single words (230). **FORM, ARIS**

Law 6. Harris, Janice Hubbard. *The Short Fiction of D.H. Lawrence.*
New Brunswick, NJ: Rutgers University Press, 1984. Pp. 224–27.

Lawrence implies that mothers shape their sons to compensate for the
deficiencies of their husbands (225). "The money ethic, the devouring of
sons by mothers, and the preference for masturbation are parallel in
cause and result. All develop and respect only the kind of knowledge
that will increase one's capacity to control" (226). In all three cases,
something is manipulated; the fundamental desire is not for mutual exchange but for dominance; ultimately, too, all three efforts prove self-
defeating (227). **THEM**

Law 7. Holland, Norman N. *The Dynamics of Literary Response.*
New York: Oxford University Press, 1968. Pp. 255–58.

In this story, the common human "fantasy of return to the original
mother-child unit is flawed or defeated or absent" (255). If Paul eventually falls, blinded, from his horse (as did St. Paul), then perhaps the
story can be seen as one in which "Lawrence sets off a slavish, money-
grubbing religion of children and slaves against an ampler, matriarchal
paganism" (256); or perhaps it can be seen "as a tragedy of sublimation,
of accepting more and more complex and devious substitutes for one's
real desires" (257); or perhaps it can be seen as involving "the boy's
trying to achieve a real relationship or union with the Great Mother by
a devious Christian money-grubbing and money-charity" (257). In any
case, Paul's deep hunger goes unsatisfied, and the story's few references
to mouths suggest not feeding but mere facial expressions (257–58). The
story deals with failing to unite with a mother (except perhaps by
death) and therefore lacks psychological resonance (258). **PSY, ARCH,
THEM**

Law 8. Junkins, Donald. "'The Rocking-Horse Winner': A Modern Myth." *Studies in Short Fiction* 2 (1964): 87–89.

Attacks on the story have failed to perceive how it "dramatizes modern man's unsuccessful attempt to act out and emerge from his oedipal conflict with the woman-mother" (88). "The story is couched in the symbols of the ancient myths. The mother is the poor, unsatisfied fairy princess who yearns for happiness; Paul is the gallant knight on horseback who rides to her rescue. But Paul's stallion, the traditional symbol of the self, or potency or masculinity, is only a wooden rocking horse. As such it denotes Paul's impotency, his pre-pubertal innocence, his unrealized manhood" (88). **PSY, ARCH**

Law 9. Koban, Charles. "Allegory and the Death of the Heart in 'The Rocking-Horse Winner.'" *Studies in Short Fiction* 15 (1978): 391–96.

Lawrence believed that a marriage should grow out of a total spiritual and physical fusion between a man and woman, but in this story the mystical energy such love would provide "has been transformed into an ugly passion, greed" (393). In this sense "the story can be read as the climax in the chronicle of the death of love in Hester, the death of her heart, and ... as such it ought to be read primarily as an allegory of the death of the child in her, the death of innocence and love. Mystically and allegorically speaking, Paul's death is her death" (393). The relation between mother and son provides the "central human interest" in this work (393), and in a sense her spirit almost possesses him (394). Because the story has the style of a parable, it encourages us to read it allegorically (395). **THEM**

Law 10. Lamson, Roy, Hallett Smith, Hugh Maclean, and Wallace W. Douglas. *The Critical Reader.* Rev. ed. New York: Norton, 1962. Pp. 542–47.

The story simultaneously "arouses and satisfies the reader's interest in a melodramatic suspense, in 'psychology,' and in a theme" (542). The parents are described in vague terms; the mother is not even named until the very end (543). This vagueness may reflect Paul's own perspective, but if the story were told from Paul's point of view, it would lack suspense and the ending would seem too sentimental. The distanced perspective helps create a sense of tragedy (544). "As mediators between the reader's natural skepticism and the fantasy element in the plot stand Uncle Oscar and Bassett," who are both "men of practical common sense" (544). Although subtly introduced, Oscar is fully described and plays the important role of voicing our own skepticism (544). Yet characters are less important here than symbols, and the sense of fear is very vivid (545). The desire for luck, symbolically contrasted with love, cheats the boy, yet Lawrence keeps control of the suspense, revelations, and irony until the end (545–46). Oscar's final comment may even imply "that Paul was luckier than he knew" (546). The humor earlier associated with Oscar counterpoints the mother's desperation (546). "What we have is a building up of Paul's confidence and strength ... at the same time [as] the antagonist is growing in strength too" (546). Paul's fever contrasts with his mother's coldness, just as his love contrasts with her focus on luck (547). Lawrence has effectively "woven together character and symbol, theme and plot tension. These elements do not exist separately" but "must be seen in relationship to each other" (547). **THEM, PSY, READ-R, FORM**

Law 11. Lawrence, Robert G. "Further Notes on D.H. Lawrence's Rocking Horse." *College English* 24 (1963): 324.

The horse alludes to the wooden Trojan horse, a traditional symbol of deception. Although Paul hopes to use his horse to evade difficulties, he is deceived (324). Paul's relatively advanced age may make his obsession with the horse seem regressive, symbolizing a movement away from maturity (324). **THEM, PSY**

Law 12. Marks, W.S., III. "The Psychology of the Uncanny in Lawrence's 'Rocking-Horse Winner.'" *Modern Fiction Studies* 11 (1965): 381–92.

The story may have been influenced by Lawrence's reading of Freud, who linked obsessive action (such as gambling) with masturbation, secrecy, guilt, and fear (381–83). Paul is fixated "at a narcissistic stage of development" (383) and indulges in a fantasy of rescuing his mother (384). His rocking is a neurotic form of "*repetition compulsion*" (384) caused by his Oedipal attraction (385) for a mother who is sexually frustrated by her husband's failures (386). The name of Paul's mother suggests Hester Prynne (in Hawthorne's *Scarlet Letter*), whom Lawrence saw as an American version of Eve, the temptress (387). Lawrence's theme "is that matriarchy is the devil—man's just punishment for failing to assert his phallic divinity" (389). In the story as in Freud's case histories, the line between fantasy and reality is blurred (390), as Lawrence seeks to create revulsion for the breakdown of the "phallic" family unit (391). The natural result of that breakdown is an introverted, over-intellectual, narcissistic child like Paul (391), who symbolizes the tragedy of the conflicts and distortions common in modern life (392). **PSY, THEM**

Law 13. Martin, W.R. "Fancy or Imagination? 'The Rocking-Horse Winner.'" *College English* 24 (1962): 64–65.

The paragraph describing the mother's discovery of her son's rocking can be analyzed closely to defend the story against criticisms levelled by F.R. Leavis and Graham Hough (64). The real race-horses, with their vivid names, suggest a vitality that contrasts with the lifeless, mechanical, artificial, and anonymous horse Paul rides (65). The frantic rocking parallels the frantic whispering of the house, and both suggest the "futility of the parents" (65). The story effectively implies its meanings through symbols ("objective correlatives") and focuses on a typical Lawrentian theme: "the nature and nemesis of unlived lives" (65). **FORM, THEM**

Law 14. San Juan, E., Jr. "Theme Versus Imitation: D.H. Lawrence's 'The Rocking-Horse Winner.'" In *From Fiction to Film: D.H. Lawrence's "The Rocking-Horse Winner."* Ed. Gerald R. Barrett and Thomas L. Erskine. Encino, CA: Dickenson, 1974. Pp. 70–74. Reprinted from *D.H. Lawrence Review* 3 (1970): 136–40.

"The organizing principle of Lawrence's story inheres in the system of actions, the plot, which represents the change in Paul's fortune ('fortune here refers to a relative condition of acting in a morally determinate way')" (71). Paul is not corrupted but preserves his "integrity, his naiveté and innocence" to the end, when he rejoices (72). The second half of the work focuses on the mother; earlier she caused his actions, and now she causes his illness (72). At the end we feel "awe and wonder at Paul, pity for the mother, and horror at the whole situation" (73). The story uses its plot to imitate an action and to synthesize incidents, character, thought, and diction and thus move us in a specific emotional direction (73). "The profundity and relevance of our response of course depend on our accurate grasp of the story as an artistic whole, a configuration of various meaningful elements" (74). **ARIS, THEM, FORM**

Law 15. Snodgrass, W.D. "A Rocking Horse: The Symbol, the Pattern, the Way to Live." In *D.H. Lawrence: A Collection of Critical Essays*. Ed. Mark Spilka. Englewood Cliffs, N.J.: Prentice-Hall, 1963. Pp. 117–26. Reprinted from the *Hudson Review* 11 (1958): 191–200.

The mother's dissatisfaction is partly sexual in origin (117); Lawrence believed that a woman would put up with almost any material deprivation if she felt truly loved and in love (118). She, her husband, and their son all deny their emotional needs and withdraw, instead committing themselves to external values: luck and money (118). Because externals are beyond personal control (118), pursuing them leads to destruction; money becomes "a symbolic substitute for love and affection" (118). As in a fairy tale, Paul pridefully pursues forbidden power (119); like the other characters, he seeks external goods rather than self-under-

standing (120). He thus symbolizes modern man, who pursues possessions (including colonies) rather than knowledge of self (121).
Lawrence's essay "Pornography and Obscenity" claimed that by sup-
pressing sexual impulses, conventional Christian idealism encouraged
self-absorbed masturbation rather than the full contact with others represented by mutual sexual relations (122–23). Paul's obsession with his
rocking-horse symbolizes this kind of self-destructive isolation and
withdrawal (125). **PSY, THEM, HIST**

Law 16. Thornton, Weldon. *D.H. Lawrence: A Study of the Short Fiction.* New York: Twayne, 1993. Pp. 72–77.

The story effectively combines supernatural, psychological, and social
emphases (72), using realistic dialogue to make the other aspects more
believable (73). Although the mother does love her son (74), the children
sense their parents' financial needs (75), and Paul tries to transform his
love for her into luck (76). The parents' confusion "about the relative
importance of love and money" destroys their family and suggests the
modern world's lack of values (77). **THEM**

Law 17. Turner, Frederick W., III. "Prancing in to a Purpose:
Myths, Horses, and True Selfhood in Lawrence's 'The Rocking-
Horse Winner.'" In *D.H. Lawrence: The Rocking-Horse Winner.* Ed.
Dominick P. Consolo. Columbus, OH: Charles E. Merrill, 1969.
Pp. 95–106.

The story contrasts egocentricity with a more generous notion of self
and shows a movement from focus on the self to selflessness (97). Paul
achieves a kind of transcendence and rebirth through his death, as the
word "winner" in the title suggests (97). The story, which reflects elements of at least sixteen motifs often found in folk tales, is especially
similar to two kinds of tales (98). It parallels the story of Bellerophon
and his horse Pegasus; like Bellerophon, Paul is transported by his
horse into a superior world of freedom (100–1). Paul becomes more
fully human by committing himself to values that transcend his
personal ego (101). Both Bellerophon and Paul are exiles from their
homes, but Paul's final ride is not motivated by pride and therefore he
(unlike Bellerophon) does not end in defeat (103). He seeks the money
not for himself but for others whom he pities (103). His last ride is
selfless (104), and his death is an example of admirably heroic self-
sacrifice (105). His death should help inspire Lawrence's readers to seek
their own liberation from the materialistic egotism that makes us
resemble Paul's parents (105). **ARCH, THEM**

Law 18. Widmer, Kingsley. *The Art of Perversity: D.H. Lawrence's Shorter Fictions.* Seattle: University of Washington Press, 1962. Pp. 92–95.

Often in Lawrence's writing, the feminine mind best reveals important social phenomena (92), and the mother's bourgeois preoccupation with money here is the focus of a "mockingly simple" children's story that ironically uses many fairy-tale techniques (93). Paul resembles the autobiographical Paul in Lawrence's novel *Sons and Lovers* (93), while his rocking-horse provides a "masturbatory toy counterfeit of passion" in a passionless middle-class environment centered on money rather than love (94). Although both the uncle and mother are conventionally good and decent, both exploit Paul's "magic" to profit financially (95). The story is effective because of its emphasis on dramatic dialogue, its terse descriptions, its "allegorical neatness," its lack of authorial editorializing, and its ironic theme of destructive luck (95), but its "detachment and precision" should not be used to censure the quite different styles of some of Lawrence's other stories. **FORM, THEM, HIST**

R.C.E.

"TO BUILD A FIRE"

Lon 1. Adams, George R. "Why the Man Dies in 'To Build a Fire.'" In *The Critical Response to Jack London*. Ed. Susan M. Nuernberg. Westport, CT: Greenwood, 1995. Pp. 27–35.

In revising the original story he had written for boys, London added both the dog and the man's death—a fact that suggests that the two may be thematically linked (27). The story is ambiguous, and standard readings cannot account for all of its ambiguity (27–28). Is the man's fate dictated by his limitations as a human, or is it determined merely by bad luck? (28). London's addition of the dog suggests that his own thinking had changed during the time since the original story was published. "In what amounts to a capsule history of the relationship between the 'superior' and 'inferior' species," the dog is described first as a "native husky," then as slinking, then as a tool for discovering traps, then as a "toil slave" kept in line by whips and commands, then finally as a potential victim of death in order to keep the man alive (30). London also ironically suggests that "humans will finally produce a dog so dependent and so objectified that it can no longer survive in its environment and hence will no longer be available to serve or save humans in that environment" (31). The traveller is an exploiter of anything he deems "inferior," including the environment and the native population (31–32). Eskimos are nowhere mentioned, for instance, and trees are randomly burned, because "anyone or anything defined as inferior does not register in any significant way on the man's consciousness; we are not surprised then when without reflection he intends to slaughter the dog" (32). Whereas earlier versions of the story had given the man a name, by the final version he becomes an anonymous symbol of "the arrogance and failings of a species, the assumption that since it is a superior species [mankind] has the right to consume everything on the planet" (33). The man's willingness to kill the dog symbolizes his general willingness to exploit the Yukon (33). The man's rejection of companionship suggests an ideology of individualism that conflicted with London's developing socialism (33), although early socialism had not yet developed into "a denunciation of the human consumption of the planet" (34). With poetic justice, the man is killed by nature, including the snow falling from the tree and abandonment by the dog (34). This "proto-environmentalist" story suggests that the man dies not because of bad luck or bad genes (neither of which is subject to moral judgment) but because of a bad ideology—a bad attitude toward the planet (34). **HIST, THEM, MARX**

Lon 2. Bowen, James K. "Jack London's 'To Build a Fire': Epistemology and the White Wilderness." *Western American Literature* 5 (1971): 287–89.

The story does not simplistically contrast rationality (represented by the man) and instinct (represented by the dog); in fact, London emphasizes the limits of the man's use of reason by showing that "he does not possess the ability to connect isolated phenomena, an essential act for valid inference" (287). Mentally deficient and forgetful, the man is no match for "the keenly instinctual dog" (288). However, London does not therefore endorse an abandonment of rationality for emotion. Instead, in the old-timer from Sulphur Creek, he offers a model who combines masculine reason and feminine intuition (288–89). London is not advocating "any kind of animalistic return for man to a presymbolic state of existence in order to survive; on the contrary, he seems to strongly imply that animals survive through instinct; men of limited mental capacity fail; and that human beings who exercise good judgment, tempered with emotional insights, are the human beings who win out over a hostile environment" (289). **THEM**

Lon 3. Clasby, Nancy. "Jack London's 'To Build a Fire': A Mythic Reading." *Jack London Newsletter* 20.1 (1987): 48–51.

D.H. Lawrence argued that "the excessively dualistic quality of the American male psyche required that the emotional, instinctive aspects of the self, which is perceived as 'feminine,' be projected onto a dark, devalued alter-ego" while the "primary *persona* remains detached" (48). In London's tale the two halves of this duality are represented by the man and the dog, and "by using the dog, London represents the instinctual side of the divided psyche in a uniquely degraded way" (48). The man seeks "to dominate and control" nature and rejects the intuitive wisdom of the old man, who, like the prophet Tiresias, blends "the feminine, instinctive aspects of the psyche with the rational, masculine side" (49). When the freezing traveller tries and fails to grasp and kill the dog, he demonstrates his loss of control of the instinctive side of the self and of his dominance over nature, and the process of freezing to death is described "as involving a gradual isolation from the self" (50). "All the humble, yet life-giving aspects of the maternal earth are focused in the subhuman figure of the dog" (50), yet although "the dog wins our sympathy," its "wolf-like qualities are emphasized" (50). "The dog is presented here as being a party to a relationship of mutual use, rather than of shared life. Its needs are for food and fire, and it will turn to anyone who provides them. Both figures, the man and the dog, are degraded archetypes of the masculine and the feminine aspects of the pscyhe which they respectively represent. The image of the man's thwarted but murderous embrace of the dog recapitulates the meaning of London's savage portrait of a distorted sensibility" (51). **PSY, ARCH, THEM**

Lon 4. Hedrick, Joan D. *Solitary Comrade: Jack London and His Work.* Chapel Hill: University of North Carolina Press, 1982. Pp. 48–55.

London's Alaskan stories emphasize an aloneness rooted in man's awareness of death and implying "the need for human solidarity" (48). The death in this story could have been avoided if the protagonist had possessed the imagination to realize the need "to rely on others for mutual support and protection" (49). Whereas other stories by London imply the solace of companionship, this tale does not provide even that comfort (54). **THEM, HIST**

Lon 5. Labor, Earle, and King Hendricks. "Jack London's Twice-Told Tale." In *The Critical Response to Jack London.* Ed. Susan M. Nuernberg. Westport, CT: Greenwood Press, 1995. Pp. 9–16. Reprinted from *Studies in Short Fiction* 4 (1967): 334–41.

The story combines "vivid narrative, graphic description of physical action, tension (*e.g.*, human intelligence *vs.* animal intuition, man's intrepidity *vs.* cosmic force, vitality *vs.* death), a poetic modulation of imagery to enhance mood and theme, and—above all—a profound sense of irony" (9). An earlier version of the story, written for a boys' magazine, had featured a named protagonist (Tom Vincent) who discovered the hard way that man cannot travel alone but whose survival implied London's initial confidence in the human ability to overcome great odds (10). The boys' story had featured an attractive hero, a clear message, and a helpful moral or lesson (11). The later version is much longer (7235 *vs.* 2700 words), and London uses the extra length to enhance atmosphere and mood (11). Symbolism of "heat (sun-fire-life) and cold (darkness-depression-death)" immediately creates a sense of impending doom (12). "Unlike Tom Vincent, the protagonist of this 'To Build a Fire' is nameless. He is the naturalistic version of Everyman: a puny, insignificant mortal confronting the cold mockery of Nature as Antagonist" (12). He is "practical, complacent, insensitive, and vain" (12) and thus cuts "a frail and pitiable figure when pitted against the awful majesty of cosmic force" (13). By adding the dog and using it as a foil in the later version, London helps avoid the need for authorial commentary; the man's cold relationship with the animal parallels the surrounding outer cold (13). London effectively alternates between the viewpoint of the dog (associated with instinctive wisdom) and that of the man (associated with a foolish dependence on mere reason [13]). Many important themes fuse in the final paragraph (14). **FORM, HIST, THEM**

Lon 6. Labor, Earle, and Jeanne Campbell Reesman. *Jack London: Revised Edition.* New York: Twayne, 1994. Pp. 34–37.

The story's success depends less on plot than on "mood and atmosphere, which is conveyed through repetitive imagery of cold and gloom and whiteness" (34). Yet the tale also fits many of Aristotle's criteria for tragedy: "It is a representation of an action that is serious, whole, complete, and of a certain magnitude. The action is rigorously unified, taking place between daybreak and nightfall. The protagonist, neither an especially good man nor an especially bad man, falls into misfortune because of a tragic flaw, notably hubris, an overweening confidence in the efficacy of his own rational faculties and a corresponding blindness to the dark, nonrational powers of nature, chance, and fate" (34–35). The narrator, like a chorus, provides explanation and moral commentary; the antagonist is the setting; the dog is a foil whose humility and reliance on instinct highlight the man's pride and rationality (35). As in tragedy, too, the catastrophe seems inevitable (35). "Being human and therefore fallible," the man makes a mistake; and, as Aristotle recommends, recognition (or the achievement of new knowledge) coincides with reversal of fortune when the snow snuffs out his fire (36). By "resigning himself to his fate, the man achieves a certain heroic stature; and his tragic action inspires both pity and fear" (36), for we realize that we share his weakness (37). **ARIS**

Lon 7. May, Charles E. "'To Build a Fire': Physical Fiction and Metaphysical Critics." In *The Critical Response to Jack London.* Ed. Susan M. Nuernberg. Westport, CT: Greenwood, 1995. Pp. 22–26. Reprinted from *Studies in Short Fiction* 15 (1978): 19–24.

Critics trying to prove the value of the story have asserted its generic success, its use of mythic themes (e.g., rebirth), and its parallels with classical tragedy (22). The man's death, however, seems to lack any larger meaning in the story itself (23–24); nothing is really at stake because he is presented simply as a physical body who dies from mere physical coldness (24). Indeed, "London, like his protagonist, is without imagination in this story, because he too is concerned here only with the things of life and not with their significance" (25). The major change in the protagonist involves simply a steady loss of sensation (25); his only discovery is that the self is mere body (26). Imagination is demonstrated by London's critics rather than by London or the main character (26). **THEM**

Lon 8. McLintock, James I. *White Logic: Jack London's Short Stories.* Grand Rapids, MI: Wolf House Books, 1975. Pp. 116–18; 158–59.

Human isolation is emphasized by the fact that the old man and dog are the only other living beings mentioned besides the traveller (116). Although earlier stories by London had implied the value of reason, this tale suggests a loss of such faith (117). Although the man does possess reason and is not therefore a mere fool, reason cannot protect him (118). Indeed, neither imagination nor reason can "sustain life. The romantic and the realistic impulses both lead nowhere" (118). The death of the fire symbolizes the man's lack of imagination (158–59). **THEM**

Lon 9. Mellard, James M. *Four Modes: A Rhetoric of Modern Fiction.* New York: Macmillan, 1973. Pp. 260–64.

The opening combines pictorial and popular modes, emphasizing the landscape in a way that calls attention to the myth-making skill of the story-teller (260–61). London tries to treat the protagonist "as just as much an object as the hostile universe itself," exploiting the dramatic mode to "tell a tragic story objectively through act, gesture, and event" (261). The story combines ritual (obsessive, repetitive action) and myth (explanation), emphasizing the former in a way that moves toward tragic drama (261). Because fire-making is a rite associated with life (261), the story describes three repetitions of it, the last unsuccessful (262). The tale has the rising-and-falling pattern of fortune associated with tragedy and ends with a tragic reversal (263). Other tragic elements include man's alienation from nature, the protagonist's hubris or pride (263), and his stoic acceptance of death (264). Although the story suggests the myth of Prometheus (stealer of fire who was punished by the gods), London's objective tone provides no clear interpretation of the story's meaning (264). **ARCH, FORM**

Lon 10. Mitchell, Lee Clark. "'Keeping His Head': Repetition and Responsibility in London's 'To Build a Fire.'" *Journal of Modern Literature* 13 (1986): 76–96.

London's flat, naturalistic style, speed of composition, and somewhat childish plots have caused critics to neglect his technical skill (76). Yet although naturalism contradicts the assumptions of realism, a naturalistic style is not for that reason incompetent (76). The final paragraph of the story, for instance, shows London deliberately rejecting subordinate clauses and intentionally using inverted syntax (77). Similar skill is shown in London's use there of alliteration (and other forms of repetition), cumulative prepositional phrases, and similar-sounding transitional words (77). "Phonemic and syntactic repetitions, in other words, reveal not an interdependent world larger than the sum of its grammatical parts, but the very absence of an organizing grammar to the text"

(78). Likewise, the plot is also based on repetitions of a few simple, similar events (78). "Just as verbal repetition disrupts a normal grammatical progression by breaking phrases into autonomous units, so the recurrence of things themselves has a curiously disruptive narrative effect. By disconnecting things from each other, repetition instills a certain static quality to the story's motion," eventually calling into question "the very notion of plot as onward narrative progress" (78). "The repetition of things and events creates an environment that seems to resist human intention—one in which desires fail over and over to be able to shape results" (80). Both reader and protagonist seem stalled and must repeat the same experiences (81). The flatness of the style parallels the flatness of the landscape (81–82); the repeated simple sentences describe an environment and experiences that seem unchanging (82). Each repetition of a word robs it of any special significance (85). The few violations of this repetitive pattern help absolve the traveller from blame for his fate: "Only retrospectively can ignorance be seen to have led to disaster, and questions of responsibility are excluded by the stress on unanticipated events" (86). The story thus itself undercuts the narrator's efforts to assign blame (87). "Knowledge appears in some radical sense not to matter in this kind of world, and by denying the possibility of prospective choice, the text exposes the inappropriateness of retrospective regret" (87). As the man succumbs to the cold he is described in terms of his body parts rather than in terms of a whole self (88–89). Conflicting points of view contribute to the story's effectivenes: "The man's increasingly panicked consciousness is set against a narrative omniscience that alternates between fierce moralizing and cold impersonality" (89). By criticizing the traveller, the narrator paradoxically causes us to sympathize with the man (90). Both the man and the narrator take the idea of an independent self for granted, although the narrative subtly calls such an idea into question (92). London's stylistic repetitions reflect his philosophical determinism—a determinism that subverts the notion of an independent self possessing free will (96). The flat, mechanical style fits London's mechanistic view of the universe. **THEM, FORM, DECON**

Lon 11. Peterson, Clell. "The Theme of Jack London's 'To Build a Fire.'" In *The Critical Response to Jack London*. Ed. Susan M. Nuernberg. Westport, CT: Greenwood Press, 1995. Pp. 3–8. Reprinted from *American Book Collector* 17 (November 1966): 15–18.

Like his protagonist, London was a relative newcomer to Alaska, but in this story, "writing within that narrow range of experience, he recreated a moment of truth about the Yukon more clearly and credibly than anywhere else in his fiction," implying a deeper, richer significance than the story's surface details might suggest (3). The opening sentence effectively uses alternating iambic and anapestic rhythms to mimic the traveller's movement into an unfamiliar, mysterious, but meaningful world (4). Like an Everyman on a pilgrimage, the traveller journeys into the unknown, facing not only risk but also the possibility of new knowledge (4). A Jungian psychologist might see a parallel with the process of rebirth, which involves disintegration and death followed by reintegration and enriched, renewed life (4). Because the traveller, ignorant of life, is in that sense already dead, his actual death forces him to face "the inadequacy of his conception of the nature of things"; the extreme cold he endures "is a metaphor for a whole range of experiences beyond the man's awareness" (4). Yet London's character achieves no full illumination and is not transformed by his experience (4–5). The white landscape symbolizes everything the man does not comprehend; the lack of sunlight suggests the limits of human reason and common sense (5). Although the traveller is no fool and is in fact perceptive and resourceful, "his thought is always practical and immediate, never looking beneath the surface of things" (5). London seems to suggest that by relying too much on reason, modern man permits "his primal instincts to atrophy" (6). "Modern man reasons his way with false confidence, unaware that he may at any moment break through the shell of his comfortable, rational world into a universe of terrifying dimensions." Yet "the moment of illumination London seems to prepare for us never comes. The man dies with only a glimmer of insight" (6). Earlier versions of the story seemed to celebrate "human strength and endurance in opposition to nature" (7), while the present version seems to imply "that the instinct to cling to life at any cost, like an instinctive awareness of cold or other danger, has decayed in civilization" (7). Nonetheless, the story does achieve a tragic tone since the man confronts his limitations and responds with a kind of dignity (7). He shows himself capable of the sort of "tragic vision that both ennobles and conceals his fall from nature" (8). **HIST, ARCH, THEM**

R.C.E.

"BARTLEBY THE SCRIVENER"

Mel 1. Abrams, Fred. "Don Quijote and Melville's 'Bartleby the Scrivener.'" *Studies in Short Fiction* 18 (1981): 323–24.

A character in *Don Quijote* who responds to Sancho Panzo with repetition of "I prefer not to" is "a provocative prefiguration of" Bartleby (323–24). **HIST**

Mel 2. Anderson, Walter E. "Form and Meaning in 'Bartleby the Scrivener.'" *Studies in Short Fiction* 18 (1981): 383–93.

A "Christian-moral reading" of "Bartleby" is the best approach, and "Christ's commandment that we be our brother's keeper ... is a central issue" (383). But most critics do not understand what Melville was trying to do (383). They believe the narrator-lawyer fails Bartleby in some way, although they disagree on how much he does so (383). The assessments of Bartleby also vary, from depictions of him as a kind of "monster" (a view which results if "truly free will were to exist") to views of him as "Christ reincarnate" (385). However, a more "balanced" approach considers "both the lawyer's humanism and his limitations" and notes that Bartleby "represents the most provoking test of brotherhood one is ever likely to encounter" (386). The lawyer's charity does have limits, but he does much more for Bartleby than most people would do because total obedience of the commandment to love one another is impossible (386). As Jonathan Edwards defined it, one follows the commandment as completely as possible, while keeping in mind one's "'*own safety and interest*'" (387). Melville shows the lawyer to be "a flexible, tolerant, kind-hearted man," although "'*safe*' rather than rash" (388). His sense of humor allows him to excuse others' weaknesses, and he feels sympathy for Bartleby (388–89). But as he is tested by Bartleby's "preferring" not to work, he balances his obligation to Bartleby as his fellow man against his own self-interest by using "prudence and common sense" (390). Most people would do the same, Melville wants the reader to acknowledge (393). Few could behave more charitably than the lawyer, and only those who could can judge him a failure (393). The lawyer's "'Ah, Bartleby! Ah, humanity!'" at the end of the story reveals that he understands the difficulty human beings have in following the commandment to love one another (393). **THEM, HIST, READ-R**

Mel 3. Arvin, Newton. *Herman Melville.* New York: William Sloane, 1950. Pp. 242–44.

"Bartleby" conveys "a whole group of meanings, no one of which exhausts its connotativeness" (242). The story evokes the struggle between the artist and the business world, in particular between Melville himself and Wall Street lawyers like his own brother (242). The story can also be read as "a wonderfully intuitive study in what would now be called schizophrenia," an element of which can be seen in Melville's own detachment (243). Most important, however, is the story's examination of "the bitter metaphysical pathos of the human situation itself; the cosmic irony of the truth that men are at once immitigably interdependent and immitigably forlorn" (243). Bartleby's death is "an act of suicide" as he fails to recognize his dependence and "accept[s] his forlornness" (244). **PLUR, HIST, THEM, PSY**

Mel 4. Barnett, Louise K. "Bartleby as Alienated Worker." *Studies in Short Fiction* 11.4 (1974): 379–85.

In "Bartleby the Scrivener" Melville created a character who exemplifies Karl Marx's description of "the worker's alienation in a capitalistic society" (379). The lawyer takes pride in the efficient layout of his office, but the walls and screen he describes contribute to the unpleasant atmosphere in which Bartleby must work (380). Bartleby's tasks are mechanical, and "although the narrator describe[s] himself as an 'easy-going' man," he expects his employees to work quickly (380). He does, however, tolerate their quirks when they do not interfere with profits and when they are balanced with apparent submissiveness (381). Despite their hope of less demeaning work, Turkey and Nippers show signs of the "malaise" Marx saw in workers: drinking and nervousness (381–82). The narrator, on the other hand, regards his employees as his property, another factor Marx notes in the worker's plight (382). As long as he can get any work out of Bartleby, the lawyer tolerates him, but when Bartleby's strangeness begins to infringe on business, the lawyer moves (382). In response to the narrator's later suggestion that he take another job, Bartleby says he is not particular, but will not agree to any of the proposed jobs, thus revealing "the worker's dilemma": none of the options available to him would improve his life (383). And the invitation to go home with the narrator seems a temporary, self-interested gesture (383). The lawyer's concern for Bartleby at the Tombs is patronizing, and the lawyer's final "acknowledgment of the common humanity of all men" at the end of the story ironically underscores the "considerations of class and position" that governed his relationship with Bartleby (384). The epilogue further exposes the narrator's failure

to take responsibility for Bartleby as a fellow human being (384).
MARX, HIST

Mel 5. Chase, Richard. *Herman Melville: A Critical Study.* New York: Macmillan, 1949. Pp. 143–49.

Although the four years following the publication of *Pierre* were difficult, Melville's stories during that time (including "Bartleby the Scrivener") show him "seeking out new kinds of wisdom" (142–43). In "Bartleby" Melville examines a victim of "schizophrenia" whose "gradual recession is ... emphasized by a sort of counterpoint of mania and depression" in two other characters (143, 145). The story is a "starkly simple" one "told with great economy of metaphor and symbol," not building to the "apocalyptic crescendo" of *Moby-Dick* and *Pierre*, but proceeding instead "toward a gradually encroaching silence" (144). Written as Melville was examining his role as a writer, the story is "a parable of the artist" in "a capitalist society" that "expects him to write on demand" (146). Bartleby represents the writer who resists, while Nippers and Turkey represent those who "have sold out to the commercial interests and suffer from the occupational diseases of the compromised artist" (146–47). Melville's own relationship with his father might have shaped the "strained and complex relationship between Bartleby and the lawyer" (147). One can see the parallels between Bartleby, who might have worked in a Dead Letter Office, and Melville, a "practitioner in the moribund profession of letters," but parallels between Melville and the lawyer are also apparent (147). Each has lost "a lucrative position," and before *Pierre*, Melville had been successful, a "man of action, aggression, and authority" like the lawyer (148). The story can also be read as another in which Melville explores his "central theme: the relationship between the father and the son and their failure or success in achieving the atonement, in redeeming each other" (148).
HIST, FORM, PSY

Mel 6. Felheim, Marvin. "Meaning and Structure in 'Bartleby.'" *College English* 23 (1962): 369–70, 375–76.

Little attention has been given to the structure of "Bartleby" beyond Marx's identification of the story's "'three consecutive movements'": the first focusing on Bartleby's withdrawal, the second, on the lawyer's efforts "'to enforce the scrivener's conformity,'" and the third, on "'society's punishment'" of Bartleby (370). However, since the story is not Bartleby's but instead is the lawyer's and on another level the reader's, the focus of Marx's divisions seems inaccurate (370–71). The first part of the story "introduces" the characters: the nameless lawyer, a "prudent" man; his employees, referred to only by nicknames, Turkey, Nippers, and Ginger Nut; and then Bartleby, the only named character (371). The second part of the story deals with "the lawyer-scrivener relationship" in which Bartleby gives the lawyer three problems: his preferring not to work, his living in the law offices, and his refusing to copy (375). The lawyer's response to the first problem is "selfish acceptance"; to the second, "pity"; and to the third, Christian "charity" (375). In the third section of the story, society intrudes, "forc[ing] the lawyer to desert his chambers, his principles, and Bartleby" (376). But when society is unable to deal with Bartleby, he dies (376). The final paragraph adds a postscript emphasizing "the central point, that society must be responsible" (376). Everything represented by the dead letters is wasted, and the "choral comment" is the only appropriate response (376). **FORM, READ-R, THEM**

Mel 7. Forst, Graham Nicol. "Up Wall Street Towards Broadway: The Narrator's Pilgrimage in Melville's 'Bartleby the Scrivener.'" *Studies in Short Fiction* 24 (1987): 263–70.

Critics disagree on whether the lawyer develops during the course of "Bartleby the Scrivener" and, if he does, about how he changes (263). The fact that he tells the story, however, suggests that Bartleby has influenced him (264). If, as some critics suggest, Bartleby is "a Christ-figure," then the lawyer becomes a kind of Nicodemus, the "literalist" who when told he must be "'born again'" doubts that one can enter the second time into his mother's womb" (264). Although Nicodemus seemed to miss Jesus's message, he is seen later performing "the great redeeming love-labour of the embalming and entombment of the Christ," an act which suggests that Nicodemus has been transformed (264–65). The lawyer's growth is clearly presented in several stages, including his anguish when he learns that Bartleby is living in the law office, his attempts to aid Bartleby, his realization that we must love one another, and "his acknowledgment that Bartleby has arisen from the Tombs, to live ... 'with kings and counselors'" (266–68). Most important in showing how thoroughly the lawyer has changed, however, is the epilogue (269). This shows that he needs, like the Ancient Mariner, to tell his story and feels a need to learn more about Bartleby (269). The compassion and anguish the lawyer reveals in his account of the dead letter office proves that his encounter with Bartleby has transformed him (269). He now knows that he had in fact failed Bartleby (270). **FORM, THEM**

Mel 8. Humphreys, A.R. *Melville*. New York: Barnes & Noble, 1962. P. 95.

One of Melville's best tales, "Bartleby" offers comedy, but the "presiding impression is of the simple intensity of Bartleby's courteous, dignified, uncommunicating withdrawal, which obtains a moral ascendancy over the reader as over the narrator" (95). **READ-R, THEM**

Mel 9. Mitchell, Thomas R. "Dead Letters and Dead Men: Narrative Purpose in 'Bartleby the Scrivener.'" *Studies in Short Fiction* 27 (1990): 329–38.

Most critics sympathize with Bartleby and condemn the narrator, but the fact that the narrator tells Bartleby's story suggests that he is not as "'safe'" a man as he says he is (329–31). The narrator conveys the account of Bartleby so that Bartleby will not himself be a "Dead Letter" like those where the epilogue suggests Bartleby might have worked (331). Like Bartleby, the narrator has withdrawn into the safe world where "'the easiest way of life is the best,'" but in stating this fact, he is mocking himself for the tendency (333). Although he had accommodated the quirks of Nippers and Turkey, Bartleby's behavior jolts him out of his "complacent isolation" as he recognizes "'the bond of common humanity'" they share (334–35). He ultimately "fails to liberate Bartleby from his deadly solitude, [but] he succeeds in liberating himself" (337). Telling the story becomes a final step in the process as well as a way of preventing Bartleby from becoming a "Dead Letter" (337). **THEM, FORM**

Mel 10. Mumford, Lewis. *Herman Melville*. New York: Harcourt, Brace and Co., 1929. Pp. 236–39.

"Bartleby the Scrivener," one of Melville's better short stories, reveals something about Melville in 1853 (238). Urged by people around him to seek another profession or write what others wanted to read instead of what he wanted to write, Melville responded with Bartleby's "stereotyped and monotonous answer: I would prefer not to" (238). **HIST**

Mel 11. Murphy, Michael. "'Bartleby the Scrivener': A Simple Reading." *Arizona Quarterly* 41 (1985): 143–51.

"Bartleby the Scrivener" has only one character, the nameless lawyer, almost an Everyman (143). All the other characters, only partially named, are "facets of his personality or stages in his career" (143–44). Ginger Nut and Nippers represent the stages the lawyer struggled through to reach a life of security and comfort; Turkey is the old age of near poverty he might have if he does not continue to work; and Bartleby is the previously hidden part of himself that now rises in protest against doing meaningless work (145). The lawyer had lived with the "manageable dissatisfaction" of Ginger Nut, Nippers, and Turkey, but after taking the "dubious" job of Master in Chancery, he begins to hear and try to ignore the insistent objections of Bartleby (146). Through Bartleby he can see his "barren" life, especially in the law office where Bartleby lives, but he finally manages to put Bartleby away so that he no longer has to hear him (147–51). **FORM, THEM**

Mel 12. Newman, Lea Bertani Vozar. *A Reader's Guide to the Short Stories of Herman Melville*. Boston: G.K. Hall, 1986. Pp. 19–78.

"Bartleby" was first published anonymously in *Putnam's Magazine* in 1853 and in *The Piazza Tales* in 1856 (19–20). Scholars have offered as possible models for the lawyer various people such as Melville's brothers, uncle and father-in-law, who had often helped Melville "'on their own terms,'" and as models for Bartleby, two friends of Melville, one an agoraphobic and the other an invalid who had worked as a law copyist (21–23). Critics have found possible sources for the story in an 1853 novel and contemporary newspaper articles on dead-letter offices, the murder of Samuel Adams by John C. Colt, and the trial of a forger (three people alluded to in the story [24–25]). Cited as influences are writers as diverse as Hawthorne, Poe, Thoreau, Dickens, Shakespeare, and Cervantes (26–32). Several studies relate the story to Melville's other works, in particular *Pierre*, the critical rejection of which might have shaped the portrait of Bartleby, who refuses to "'copy'" the writings of others (35). The similarities between Bartleby and Pierre (both are writers with eyestrain who cannot communicate and die in the tombs), recurring images in both works, and similar themes (especially the criticism of society) are the focus of several articles (37–39). Numerous parallels to *Moby-Dick* (especially in imagery and characters) have also been noted (39–40). The closest links "stylistically and thematically" are between "Bartleby" and Melville's other stories, with their enclosed settings, "'distrusted'" narrators, and characters who must deal with failure (41–42). "Cock-A-Doodle-Doo," the narrator of which "must choose between 'the expediency of the world or defiant individualism,'" has been called a "'companionpiece'" to "Bartleby" (42–43). Parallels are also apparent in the lawyers of "The Paradise of Bachelors," "the three-way (narrator/title character/reader) perspective" of "Benito Cereno," and the isolation of Hunilla in "The Encantados" (43–46). Much early attention to "Bartleby" focused on autobiographical elements (49). Connecting the stages of Bartleby's withdrawal to periods in Melville's career, Marx called the story Melville's "most explicit and mercilessly self-critical statement of his own dilemma" (50). Psychological critics see the story as an examination of such things as schizophrenia, the "war between father and son," autism, and anorexia nervosa (50–54). The story is also called a critique of society's rejection of the artist, its business practices and ethics, and northern wage-slavery (54–55). Marxist readings offer Bartleby as a worker oppressed by his capitalist employer (55). The story has been examined from legal and feminist perspectives, from religious perspectives (Christian, Hindu, Buddhist), and philosophical perspectives (necessitarian and existentialist), but the Christian and existential are the most numerous (56–60). Several critics draw parallels between Bartleby and Christ; in existential terms Bartleby becomes the "Modern Exile" (59). Formalist critics examine

Melville's artistry: the story's "triadic" structure, his "skillful handling of point of view," the richness of the imagery and symbolism (61–64). Deconstructionist Rowe sees Bartleby as "a decentering force that disrupts the narrator's stable world" (64), and reader-response critic Norman focuses on the reader's discomfort in identifying with the lawyer yet also having "to question him as a representative of democratic and Christian values" (65). The most persistent concern among critics has been the issue of "whether the narrator learns from his experience," with many taking each side in varying degrees (65–66). Acclaim for the story is, however, "almost unanimous," as many credit Melville with anticipating and influencing modernist writers like Dostoevsky, Kafka, and Camus (66–67). The story has prompted "four handbooks and over three hundred published commentaries" yet remains richly ambiguous and for many of Melville's readers "second only to *Moby-Dick*" (67). **HIST, FORM, THEM, PLUR**

Mel 13. Parker, Herschel. "The 'Sequel' in 'Bartleby.'" In *Bartleby the Inscrutable: A Collection of Commentary on Herman Melville's Tale "Bartleby the Scrivener."* Ed. M. Thomas Inge. Hamden, CT: Archon, 1979. Pp. 159–65.

Melville might have gotten the idea for the conclusion to "Bartleby" from one of the many articles on Dead Letter Offices published in 1851 and 1852, in particular one which has a tone similar to Melville's (159–60). Although Melville's contemporaries probably shared "the narrator's perplexity" with Bartleby and thought the "sequel" a fitting explanation of "his extraordinary peculiarities," today's readers are more likely to note the faults the narrator reveals about himself (161). The story itself demonstrates "two kinds of melancholy" (162). The first is genuine, an "overpowering stinging melancholy," when the lawyer learns that Bartleby has been living in the law offices, but this feeling is short-lived (162). The second is "a comfortable, self-indulgent variety" that brings a kind of pleasure (163). The latter is what the lawyer feels in the "sequel" of the story when he offers a possible explanation for Bartleby's behavior (163). Although the narrator believes his "'Ah Bartleby! Ah humanity!'" to be an honest expression of grief, the reader understands his blindness and knows his grief to be a final "cheap purchase of a 'delicious self-approval'" (164). **HIST, THEM, READ-R**

Mel 14. Perry, Dennis R. "'Ah, Humanity'": Compulsion Neuroses in Melville's 'Bartleby.'" *Studies in Short Fiction* 24 (1987): 407–15.

Rather than singling out Bartleby's behavior as being aberrant, one should look at the "compulsion neuroses" of all the characters, comparing them to one another (407). By doing so, one can see that "the tale's structure is based on a continuum of the ego defenses each character erects" in order "to reduce the anxiety produced by the sterile activity of the law office" (407–8). The lawyer represents one extreme, where the "id seems nearly totally suppressed" (409). Nippers and Turkey represent a "split in the ego": sometimes the id is in control and sometimes the ego dominates (411). Bartleby represents the other extreme, as his id gradually takes over (413–14). At one point in his dealings with Bartleby, the lawyer's id assumes control, and he retreats to his womb-like rockaway in order to find "the state of the 'ideal ego,' wherein the id and ego are in harmony" (410–11). The impact of the story comes from knowing "that Bartleby is not an isolated case, a freak who alone cannot handle modern life" (415). The "'normal' characters" are "fight[ing] the same neurotic battles" (415). **PSY, FORM**

Mel 15. Pribek, Thomas. "The 'Safe' Man of Wall Street: Characterizing Melville's Lawyer." *Studies in Short Fiction* 23 (1986): 191–95.

Most critics agree that the narrator's description of himself as "'safe'" is ironic, but he may be more aware of the implications of the word than has been assumed (191–92). Among the connotations of "safe" is to be "thoroughly dependable in [political] office—dependable in the sense that he can be relied on not to disturb the vested interests to whom he owes his position, whether elective or appointive" (192). "Safe" may also mean turning one's back on crime; in the case of the lawyer this could apply to his "perhaps wilful inability to see that Wall Street merely *uses* people" (193). The word may also imply that the lawyer is one who "'play[s] it safe'" or "take[s] the easiest course of action" (194). Because a lawyer is one who is aware of the subtleties of language, the narrator is very likely to understand the implications of his label, and if so, his calling himself safe may indicate that his experience with Bartleby has made him more aware of his own faults (194–95). **HIST, THEM**

Mel 16. Schaffer, Carl. "Unadmitted Impediments, Unmarriageable Minds: Melville's 'Bartleby' and 'I and My Chimney.'" *Studies in Short Fiction* 24 (1987): 93–101.

Like other Melville bachelors, the narrator in "Bartleby the Scrivener" is a man who has failed to confront life, but Bartleby becomes the means of jolting him "out of complacency" and showing him "the limitations of a life without commitment" (93–94). His encounter with Bartleby helps him to grow to "a deeper understanding of the pathos of the human condition" (101). **HIST, THEM**

A.C.L.

"WHERE ARE YOU GOING, WHERE HAVE YOU BEEN?"

Oat 1. Coulthard, A.R. "Joyce Carol Oates's 'Where Are You Going, Where Have You Been?' As Pure Realism." *Studies in Short Fiction* 26 (1989): 505–10.

Although some critics argue that Arnold Friend represents Satan or that he is a fantasy created by Connie, the story is realistic and not allegorical (505). Oates based her story on the real-life Charles Schmid and his murder of Alleen Rowe. Unlike Schmid's other two teenage victims, Alleen Rowe was fifteen, had just washed her hair and was home alone (506). In addition Schmid, although older, frequented teenage hangouts, was short though physically fit, dyed his hair, wore make-up, stuffed his boots, drove a gold car, and listened to rock music—all details that Oates incorporated into her story. Because Oates fictionalized Schmid and his actions in a realistic and naturalistic story, allegorical interpretations are unconvincing (506). Connie, a vapid teenager with uncaring and perhaps irresponsible parents, romanticizes love and sex, but she does not have sexual fears that she projects onto an imagined Arnold Friend (507). Instead Friend is real, and Connie's trance-like state at the conclusion of the story is a natural reaction for one about to be murdered (508). Friend is a psychopathic killer and should not be interpreted as a devil figure or as a creation of Connie's mind (508). His seemingly supernatural powers can be explained: his knowledge about Connie could easily have been acquired in her small home town or even gathered through his own observations (509). Some of his statements are clever guesses (he mentions the type of food at the picnic, corn, and the activities of the guests, sitting and drinking) and other comments are wrong (he describes one guest as a fat lady, a statement that startles Connie, although she fills in a name and wonders why the woman is at the picnic [509]). Reading the story as an allegory lessens its impact (510). **HIST**

Oat 2. Easterly, Joan. "The Shadow of a Satyr in Oates's 'Where Are You Going, Where Have You Been?'" *Studies in Short Fiction* 27 (1990): 537–43.

Although a commonly accepted view sees Arnold Friend as the personification of the devil (537), instead he represents a satyr (537). Oates was interested in Greek mythology, and Friend's appearance suggests that of a satyr or the Greek god Pan: his wig-like hair hides animal ears and horns, and his feet do not fit properly into the boots not because the boots are stuffed so that Friend will appear taller but because his feet are really hooves (538). In addition Friend's sexual interest in Connie is more appropriate to a satyr than to Satan, and Friend's domain, the sunny open landscape, does not suggest Satan's Hell (539). Perhaps the most compelling reason to accept Friend as a satyr is the prominent position that music plays in the story; in myths, music often accompanies seduction (539). Friend's familiarity with the rock music that Connie loves reduces her resistance (539). If Friend is a satyr, then Connie is a nymph, the frequent companion to a satyr (541). Connie's sexual inexperience, lack of identity, and lack of a strong value system provide no means for her to resist him; she thus plays the nymph to his satyr (541). The fear that she experiences at the conclusion of the tale also supports the reading of Friend as a satyr. In the classical myths, satyrs were threatening because of their excessive and uncontrolled sexual habits; women were more often raped by them than seduced (541). But in Oates's story, an even more violent ending is implied: Connie will not see her family again (542). **HIST, ARCH**

Oat 3. Gillis, Christina Marsden. "'Where Are You Going, Where Have You Been?': Seduction, Space, and a Fictional Mode." *Studies in Short Fiction* 18 (1981): 65–70.

Oates symbolically employs space in her story of initiation, a variation of the sentimental narrative, to suggest seduction (65). Oates, similar to the writers of eighteenth-century seduction narratives, uses domestic interior space to suggest the inner space associated with the private self (66). The teenage protagonist Connie, at the outset of the story, has a definite sense of the home or interior space that is inhabited by her parents and sister as opposed to the outside world that is filled with the experiences of the night: boys, sexual excitement, and music (67). The title itself indicates the predicament that Connie faces: she is in transition between the future, the excitement of the outside world, and the past, the safety of home (67). Unfortunately the passage becomes a nightmare when Arnold Friend appears at her home (68). Connie at first refuses to leave the interior space of the home, seeking its refuge and protection (68). But she, unable to remain in the world of innocence, crosses the threshold represented by the kitchen door and enters into the world of experience (69). For her, however, as for some of the protagonists of the eighteenth-century narratives, the end of innocence is also the destruction of the self (70). **THEM, HIST**

Oat 4. Healey, James. "Pop Music and Joyce Carol Oates' 'Where Are You Going, Where Have You Been?'" *Notes on Modern American Literature* (Spring/Summer 1983): item 5.

Connections exist between popular music and Oates's story, beginning with her dedication to Bob Dylan, who, in "A Hard Rain's A-Gonna Fall," stresses the negative undercurrent of being a teenager. The song's lyric "Oh, where have you been, my blue eyed son?" provides Oates with her title. Connie, the protagonist, with a name that is suggestive of several popular singers of the decade, internalizes the messages about romantic love found in the music. But Arnold Friend, with a voice and speaking style reminiscent of those of a disc jockey, represents the brutal physical desire that is also a theme in some of the songs. Connie, if she survives her encounter with Friend, will have lost her innocence and romantic view of love. **HIST, THEM**

Oat 5. Hurley, C. Harold. "Cracking the Secret Code in Oates's 'Where Are You Going, Where Have You Been?'" *Studies in Short Fiction* 24 (1987): 62–66.

An alternative interpretation of the numbers—33, 19, 17—found written on Arnold Friend's car differs from the one offered by Mark Robson, who bases his reading on passages in Genesis and Judges (62). Robson's reading is strained and not consistent with the story or with the character of Arnold Friend (64). More plausible is an understanding of the numbers as an indication of "Arnold's sexual deviancy" (64). Adding the numbers provides the total of 69, a sexual expression, which is more likely to be written on Friend's car than a biblical reference (65–66). **THEM**

Oat 6. Hurley, D.F. "Impure Realism: Joyce Carol Oates's 'Where Are You Going, Where Have You Been?'" *Studies in Short Fiction* 28 (1991): 371–75.

A.R. Coulthard's contention that Oates's story should be read as realistic and not as allegoric or symbolic is flawed (371). Although Oates based her story on the case of Charles Schmid, she did alter a number of details (372). For example, Connie, Oates's protagonist, unlike Alleen Rowe, one of Schmid's victims, is not an only child of a divorced mother (372). Oates altered the details to suit her purposes, but the details themselves are suspect since many of them were divulged by the murderers or by informants (372). Adding another level of interpretation to a story that already has several interpretations is not only acceptable but also strengthens it (374). The story can be read, for example, as a dream allegory (372). References to dreams or to sleep abound (373), and the language itself suggests a sleep-like state (374). **HIST, THEM**

Oat 7. Petry, Alice Hall. "Who Is Ellie? Oates' 'Where Are You Going, Where Have You Been?'" *Studies in Short Fiction* 25 (1988): 155–57.

Ellie Oscar, Arnold Friend's companion, has been overlooked in critical discussions. He resembles Elvis Presley: the hair curling on the forehead, the sideburns, the open and upturned collar, and the unbuttoned shirt (155–56). In addition, just as Elvis combined vulnerability and aggressiveness in his behavior, so does Ellie (156). He is at once, in Oates's words, "embarrassed" and "fierce" and has the "face of a forty-year-old baby." He appears passive but when he speaks he utters a threat (156). Ellie's similarity to Elvis suggests that the rock music to which Connie listens is implicated in her very probable rape and murder (157). The music, with its empty promises of romantic love, has led Connie into an unrealistic understanding of the world (157). **HIST, THEM**

Oat 8. Quirk, Tom. "A Source for 'Where Are You Going, Where Have You Been?'" *Studies in Short Fiction* 18 (1981): 413–19.

A very probable source for Oates' short story exists in the news magazine accounts of Charles Howard Schmid, convicted of three murders (414). Oates's fictionalizing of actual people and events does not detract from the impact of the story but rather heightens it, for the evil she depicts exists (413). Schmid, short and muscular, frequented teenage hangouts, although expelled from high school, and did so until his arrest at twenty-three for the murders of three teenage girls ranging in age from thirteen to seventeen (414). Like Arnold, he stuffed his boots to appear taller and wore make-up and dyed his hair to appear younger (414). Also like Arnold, he bragged of his expertise in love-making and drove a gold-colored car (415). Arnold's last name may be based on one of Schmid's aliases, Angel. Both of the names, Friend and Angel, are ironic given the characters (416). The crime of rape and murder implied in Oates's story is also based on Schmid's actions. Certain details are the same: fifteen was the age of one of Schmid's victims who had also, like Connie, just washed her hair and who enjoyed rock music. Schmid had two accomplices, one woman and one man, the man having been rejected by the first victim (416). Schmid and his cohorts persuaded the girl, who was alone at home, to go for a ride with them. In Oates's story Arnold himself was casually snubbed by Connie, and the role of Ellie, Arnold's companion, is reduced (417). The effect of these changes identifies evil with a specific character and thereby heightens it (417). Not only did Oates borrow the details of the events and characters from the accounts of Schmid and his crimes, but she also based her themes on suggestions made in the news magazines (417), reports which suggested that the American Dream was fraudulent (418). The American Dream, as represented in rock music, promised romance, innocence, and no responsibility (419). **HIST, THEM**

Oat 9. Rubin, Larry. "Oates's 'Where Are You Going, Where Have You Been?'" In *Joyce Carol Oates, "Where Are You Going, Where Have You Been?"* Ed. Elaine Showalter. New Brunswick, NJ: Rutgers University Press, 1994. Pp. 109–12.

Connie's encounter with Arnold Friend on a Sunday afternoon occurs in a dream and is a result not only of her interest in sex but also of her fear of it (109). Language in the text suggests sleep or implies that Connie is in a dreamlike state (110–11). Arnold Friend, a projection of her desires and fears, has a voice that resembles the disc jockey's on the radio program to which Connie is listening, and his car radio is tuned to the same station as hers (111). Her inability to react when threatened also suggests a dream, as does her "noble sacrifice" for her family (112). The danger to Connie, however, is real. Her emphasis on sex alone will lead to "the potential destruction of Connie as a *person*, on a humanistic level" (111). Connie's subconscious recognizes the potential threat that sexual fulfillment can be, resulting in the nightmare quality of the dream (112). **PSY, THEM**

Oat 10. Schulz, Gretchen, and R.J.R. Rockwood. "In Fairyland, Without a Map: Connie's Exploration Inward in Joyce Carol Oates' 'Where Are You Going, Where Have You Been?'" *Literature and Psychology* 30 (1980): 155–67.

Although Oates borrowed details from the life of three-time murderer Charles Schmid (155), she is actually indebted to fairy tales for the power of her short story (157). The story represents Connie's view of the world, and Arnold Friend, the Schmid figure, exists in her mind (156). Connie, a confused adolescent who creates the Arnold who matches her view of reality, is at "the boundary between childhood and adulthood, hesitant and yet anxious to enter the new world of experience which is opening before her" (156). Unfortunately Connie does not have the needed help that would enable her to make this passage successfully, assistance that has been provided to children of the past through folk lore and fairy tales, which supply symbolic maps of and for the passage (157). Connie has received her messages from movies and songs, insufficient guides with their romantic and idealized themes (157). As in *The Pied Piper of Hamlin*, parents and adults are to blame for Connie's generation's lack of preparedness; they failed in their responsibilities, and Arnold, closely identified with music, is the modern Pied Piper (158). Bruno Bettelheim's *The Uses of Enchantment: The Meaning and Importance of Fairy Tales* can be used to analyze the story in terms of its similarities to several fairy tales: *The Spirit in the Bottle* (158–59), *Snow White* (160), *Cinderella* (161), *Rapunzel* (162), *Little Red Riding Hood* (162), and *The Three Little Pigs* (163). In these tales Arnold is both the prince and the wolf, representing Connie's ambivalence toward her sexuality

(164). Connie, without the lessons taught by the fairy tales, is not prepared to complete safely the passage from childhood to adulthood. Instead she fails to integrate the various parts of her personality into a coherent whole and regresses more into her childhood (164). She will not be able to survive the transition (165). **THEM, ARCH, PSY**

Oat 11. Tierce, Mike, and John Michael Crafton. "Connie's Tambourine Man: A New Reading of Arnold Friend." *Studies in Short Fiction* 22 (1985): 219–24.

An alternative interpretation to the commonly held one of Arnold Friend as the Devil and of Connie as being raped and murdered (219) suggests that just as Satan has been seen by authors such as Blake and Shelley as embodying positive traits, so too can Friend (219). In fact Connie's fear is more a product of her imagination than a rational reaction to Friend himself (220). Friend can be viewed more as a savior than as a devil (220). For example, Connie utters "Christ" when he arrives, and he makes the sign of an "X" or cross (220). Supporting this interpretation is the fact that Oates dedicates the story to Bob Dylan, popular enough in the sixties to be considered a "messiah" (220). Similarities in physical attributes exist between Dylan and Friend (221). Most important in this reading is Friend's association with music (221). Because Connie centers her life around music, Friend can be viewed as a creation of her imagination, a music-induced fantasy, occurring as a reaction to her erotic longings (222). Her leaving the house at the conclusion of the story can be interpreted as her moving beyond the limitations of her childhood into new territory, frightening because it is unknown but not necessarily destructive. **THEM**

Oat 12. Urbanski, Marie Mitchell Olesen. "Existential Allegory: Joyce Carol Oates's 'Where Are You Going, Where Have You Been?'" *Studies in Short Fiction* 15 (1978): 200–3.

Although many critics find Oates's fiction to be realistic, "Where Are You Going, Where Have You Been?" is a religious allegory with a "contemporary existential theme—that of a young person coming to grips with externally determined fate" (200). Connie, the teenage protagonist, initially feels powerful, her confidence derived from her beauty and sexuality, and she rejects her family's influence, as illustrated by her refusal to attend a family picnic (200). But she does not have the control she imagines. Like Eve, Connie is seduced by Satan (in the form of Arnold Friend), although instead of employing an apple, Friend uses music (201). Religious imagery and language are used throughout the story. For example the local restaurant, a hangout for teens, is described as a "sacred building," and Connie encounters Arnold on a Sunday (201). As Connie capitulates to Arnold, realizing her lack of control over her fate (202), she moves from a belief in free will to an acceptance of an "externally determined fate" (203). **THEM**

Oat 13. Wegs, Joyce M. "'Don't You Know Who I Am?' The Grotesque in Oates's 'Where Are You Going, Where Have You Been?'" In *Joyce Carol Oates, "Where Are You Going, Where Have You Been?"* Ed. Elaine Showalter. New Brunswick, NJ: Rutgers University Press, 1994. Pp. 99–107.

Adding elements of the grotesque to the story allows Oates to suggest the complexity of Connie as she discovers the negative side of her romantic illusions (99). Oates, employing components of popular culture in her setting, points out the negative effects of the messages promoted by the music, movies, and magazines (100). Her use of religious imagery to refer to a drive-in restaurant and to rock music permits her to make a critical comment concerning the values of contemporary culture (100). Connie's distorted value system can be traced to her parents, who "have disqualified themselves as moral guides" (100). Connie's mother, like Connie, prizes appearance, and her father is uninvolved in family issues (101). Thus, Connie has no moral basis that can protect her from Arnold Friend, who represents in a distorted fashion the ideal presented in popular songs (102). Friend is not just a murderer but also represents the devil (102). Connie, who has accepted the values of popular culture for her religion (103), mistakenly sees Friend as a savior (103). Friend, whose name suggests "fiend," appears to know all about Connie, cannot cross a threshold without being invited, places his sign on her (103), and wears boots to hide his cloven feet (114). But Friend also represents Connie's sexual desires and fears (104); her terror paralyzes her to the point that she is unable to call for help (105). Connie cannot direct or control her actions, but the blame lies with her parents and a culture that give her no moral guidance (106). **THEM**

Oat 14. Weinberger, G.J. "Who Is Arnold Friend? The Other Self in Joyce Carol Oates's 'Where are You Going, Where Have You Been?'" *American Imago: A Psychoanalytic Journal for Culture, Science, and the Arts* 45 (1988): 205–15.

Oates's story, like many other familiar works (such as Melville's "Bartleby the Scrivener") is based on the *Doppelgänger* motif (205). However, unlike the other stories, Oates's creates a double that is of the opposite sex and is perceived as threatening (205). Connie's life, as the story opens, is that of a typical middle-class teenager: she has a mother who nags and a father who reads the paper. While Connie has some limits (for instance, her 11 p.m. curfew), no one asks her the questions of the title (205–6). Connie, at the brink of adulthood, creates in Arnold Friend "her vision of the evil and often irrational world of adulthood"

(207). He does not exist outside her imagination: her friend Eddy does not notice him (207). While adulthood is threatening, refusal to enter into it would result in a life like that of Connie's twenty-four-year-old sister June or like that of Arnold's friend Ellie, a forty-year-old whose face resembles a baby's (208). The stage is set for Connie's vision. She refuses to attend a family picnic, asserting her independence (208), and then she spends the morning alone listening to rock music, placing herself into a trance-like state (210). Arnold represents adulthood—including potential violence, unknown sexuality, and the misogynist attitude of society (212)—but he is also her projected self. He is of her height and knows a great deal about her and her family and friends (215). He even expresses her previously voiced hostility towards her family (211). He cannot enter her house because she needs to leave childhood voluntarily (210). Although hesitant, Connie abandons the house of her childhood and steps into the adult world (215). **THEM**

B.W.

"A GOOD MAN IS HARD TO FIND"

O'CFl 1. Asals, Frederick. *Flannery O'Connor: The Imagination of Extremity.* Athens: University of Georgia Press, 1982. Pp. 142–54.

The story's mixture of comedy, violence, theology, and seemingly random death makes it highly representative of O'Connor's fiction; it plays on some of our deepest fears (142–43), and tension between the brutal killings and the beauty of grace is at the work's center (143). Exactly at mid-point, the car wrecks—symbolizing "a world radically off balance" (143). The story's first half seems as "random and purposeless" as the contentious, empty, superficial family itself (144), but a more important "inner journey" toward death begins after the wreck (145). "The characters are now so motionless that small gestures acquire a disproportionate expressiveness" (145), and the Misfit's talk with the grandmother is a "mutual unmasking" of false selves that has more coherence than the story's first half (145). The Misfit gradually reveals himself to be an "anguished and angry child" (146). Although the grandmother initially stands over the squatting Misfit, she finally sinks "down to his level of anguish and uncertainty," and "as he discloses his deepest torment, she responds with her deepest self" (147). The detached narrative tone unifies the story, making the first half satirical and later keeping the horror both bearable and non-sentimental (148–49). The final image is ambivalent: "a beatific corpse in a puddle of blood" (152). When the Misfit shoots the grandmother, in a sense he acts out Bailey's earlier suppressed anger (153). **FORM, THEM**

O'CFl 2. Bellamy, Michael O. "Everything Off Balance: Protestant Election in Flannery O'Connor's 'A Good Man Is Hard to Find.'" *Flannery O'Connor Bulletin* 8 (1979): 116–24.

The grandmother's sudden conversion makes sense from a point of view of evangelical Protestantism, while the Misfit, like O'Connor, is "a Bible Belt Fundamentalist in spite of himself" (116). The story exposes the tension between O'Connor's "avowed Catholicism and her tendency to view religious experience in the context of Protestant Election" (117). In their spiritual pilgrimage, the family is headed nowhere until the Misfit (a kind of Anti-Christ who cannot suffer the presence of children) enters (117). Like many fundamentalists, the Misfit is a literalist who "has inordinate respect for the written word" (118). He delivers a kind of sermon whose "reduction of life to two antithetical alternatives is the Protestant insistence on man's total depravity without God's saving grace" (119). By emphasizing the sudden salvation of the previously hypocritical grandmother, O'Connor stresses the Protestant view that faith, rather than good works, leads to redemption (121). The grandmother's sudden transformation shows that grace is not won but is instead bestowed as an unmerited gift. The transformation is effectively dramatic but seems to defy Catholic, humanistic views of justice (124). **THEM**

O'CFl 3. Brinkmeyer, Robert H., Jr. *The Art and Vision of Flannery O'Connor.* Baton Rouge: Louisiana State University Press, 1989. Pp. 185–88.

By the second section, readers find themselves abandoning their earlier satiric superiority. "By guiding the reader into this closer relationship with the family, the narrator seeks to cloud the reader's eyes with sentimentality (that which excuses human weakness because weakness is human) and so divert the reader's attention from the stunning climax—the clobbering—that is to come" (186). O'Connor's shift from an ethical to a religious and theological point of view jolts us by challenging our sentimental compassion (187). Just as the Misfit jolts the grandmother, so the narrator jolts the reader, opening us to a larger theological vision (187–88). **READ-R, DIALOG**

O'CFl 4. Browning, Preston M., Jr. *Flannery O'Connor.* Carbondale and Edwardsville: Southern Illinois University Press, 1974. Pp. 54–59.

The Grandmother exploits her self-conscious goodness and gentility (55). Her "inauthenticity" is measured against the "Misfit's honesty and spirituality, perverse though they be" (57). While his name ironically connects him "to the world of popular psychology and textbook sociology in which he is merely a deviant from society's norms, The Misfit himself sees his problem religiously and metaphysically" (57). Like Dostoevsky's "tortured agnostics," he reasons that everything is permissible (58). He pierces platitudes, raising radical questions of good and evil (58). "In his terrifyingly perverted lucidity, The Misfit implies that, if evil is defined as mere maladjustment, the concept of good then becomes meaningless. By insisting that he himself is *not* a good man, The Misfit evinces a rudimentary awareness of goodness as a possibility, even if not for him" (58). **THEM**

O'CFl 5. Bryant, Hallman B. "Reading the Map in 'A Good Man Is Hard to Find.'" In *"A Good Man Is Hard to Find": Flannery O'Connor*. Ed. Frederick Asals. New Brunswick, NJ: Rutgers University Press, 1993. Pp. 73–82. Reprinted from *Studies in Short Fiction* 18 (1981): 301–7.

O'Connor's references to actual and fictional towns not only serve as foreshadowing and help emphasize theme but also make it possible to determine almost exactly how far the family travels (73). Her reference to the fictional town of Timothy is probably intended to allude to the Biblical epistles to Timothy, which deal "essentially with three topics: the opposition of false doctrine; the organization of the church and establishment of ecclesiastic regulations; and exhortations which indicate how to be a good citizen and Christian"—topics which are all relevant to O'Connor's story (75–76). I Timothy 3:4–5, for instance, counsels that a father "must manage his own family well and see that his children obey him with proper respect" (76). O'Connor probably also alludes to the Tower of Babel when naming Red Sammy's restaurant, and towers were also traditionally associated with the Virgin Mary, were considered places of sanctuary, and could also be associated with forthcoming disaster (79). The distances described suggest that the family finally travels approximately 130 miles (80). **THEM, HIST**

O'CFl 6. Di Renzo, Anthony. *American Gargoyles: Flannery O'Connor and the Medieval Grotesque*. Carbondale and Edwardsville: Southern Illinois University Press, 1993. Pp. 134–60.

The story violates generic conventions (134) to depict "the complexity of people we would normally consider stereotypes" (135). O'Connor highlights the act of reading (137), then produces a "verbal comic strip" of "small, self-enclosed scenes" with "abrupt juxtapositions" (137). She combines beauty with its apparent opposites (139), blending lyricism and satire (140) and refusing "to separate what repels her from what delights her" (141). Some critics judge her cartoon characters falsely by realistic standards (142). She mixes "tenderness and compassion" with "caricature and satire to ward off cheap pity and sentimentality" (142), achieving a complex tone (143). The grandmother's "clownish beauty makes her more sympathetic" (145). By mixing genres (145), O'Connor explores both the trivial and the ennobling (146). She does not glorify her characters (146), and exclusively secular or religious approaches to her fiction can't capture its complexity (148): the family is "doomed by goofiness" (148). The story explores the dialogue between skepticism and faith (149), and because "The Misfit is as much a cartoon as the grandmother" (153), he is not heroic (154). He shoots her "because he cannot abide the touch of her ordinary humanity; but it is that ordinary humanity, vulgar and self-indulgent, that the story values above hero-

ism" (155). The previously comic family elicits more complicated responses as death nears (155); the story's power and humor "derive from
its fascinating interplay of disparities" (157). "Like the Misfit, we are left
unsettled and thoughtful," even though "O'Connor insists on the
grandmother's silliness right up to the very end" (158). Her gesture
challenges his egotism (158); when he "finally does encounter goodness,
it takes the form of the banal and the mundane" (159). Sainthood can
only be presented indirectly (160). **THEM, FORM, HIST**

O'CFl 7. Doxey, William S. "A Dissenting Opinion of Flannery
O'Connor's 'A Good Man Is Hard to Find.'" In *"A Good Man Is
Hard to Find": Flannery O'Connor.* Ed. Frederick Asals. New
Brunswick, NJ: Rutgers University Press, 1993. Pp. 95–102.
Reprinted from *Studies in Short Fiction* 10 (1973): 199–204.

Although the story has some merit, it is flawed by a structural failure:
the sudden shift in point-of-view from the grandmother to the Misfit
(95–96). Although at first the grandmother seems the main character,
the Misfit has the final words (97). The shift occurs because of O'Connor's Catholic doctrine of grace ("is it kosher to confront fundamentalist
Protestant characters with Catholic theology?" [99]), so that the work
"might best be considered an 'inside' story understandable only to confirmed initiates" (99–100). Once "one sees that the awareness of grace
requires a face-to-face encounter with evil in all its malicious splendor,
then he can understand the necessity for the Misfit (who represents this
evil) to be strongly characterized" and can understand—if not approve—the confusing shift in point-of-view (100). **FORM**

O'CFl 8. Driskell, Leon V., and Joan T. Brittain. *The Eternal Cross-
roads: The Art of Flannery O'Connor.* Lexington: The University
Press of Kentucky, 1971. Pp. 67–72.

This is the first story in a collection that moves "from denial toward
acceptance or from awareness of sin toward awareness of salvation,"
which is implied in the final story, "The Displaced Person" (67). In "A
Good Man," the Tower restaurant suggests the Tower of Babel, a symbol of materialism and pride (67). Both the Grandmother's and Red
Sammy see the world's problems "in purely material terms" (67). Even
the children accept material values, and their innate greed helps cause
the accident (68). The Grandmother is "superficially genteel" and her
ethics are narrow (69). For her, religion is "an easily acquired part of her
respectability," whereas the Misfit takes it far more seriously (70). When
the Grandmother touches him with grace and compassion, he is startled
because "that is not the truth he seeks" (71). Her death is a good one,
partly because it prevents "resumption of her conflict between truth
and survival" (71). O'Connor's "concern is less to provide comfort and

'uplift,' ... than to actualize evil" (71). The Misfit is less concerned with "legalistic justice than with divine justice" (72). Perhaps he rejects her gesture because he sees that it results from a "humanist proclivity to pity which blurs moral distinctions" (72), or perhaps he thinks she reaches out only because he wears her son's shirt, in which case she "is still concerned only with the external" (72). **THEM**

O'CFl 9. Feeley, Sister Kathleen. *Flannery O'Connor: Voice of the Peacock.* New Brunswick, NJ: Rutgers University Press, 1972. Pp. 69–76.

Each character displays a different attitude toward reality: Bailey feels burdened by it; the grandmother tries to rearrange it, then retreats into nostalgic fantasy; the mother is passive toward it; while the Misfit, children, and monkey respond with objective honesty. Indeed, the story "seems to imply that the children instinctively see the visible world truly, and are therefore open to invisible reality" (71). Yet both the grandmother and the Misfit are alienated from spirituality, one by romantic fantasy and the other by agnostic "realism." As the grandmother's confrontation with the Misfit becomes more intense, her false, plebeian gentility (symbolized by her hat) is stripped away (72); in reaching out to the Misfit, she overcomes her alienation, returns to reality, and is transformed from a mere "lady" to a true "good woman" (73). Although the "blankness of the sky suggests the Misfit's spiritually unlighted, unnourished world" (74), O'Connor depicts him more sympathetically than she does Bailey or Red Sammy, partly because he has a "clear conception of the significance of the Redemption" (74). Yet his pride in his self-sufficiency and reason "blocks his apprehension of spiritual reality" (74). He is a misfit "because he belongs neither with the complacent nor with the believers" (75). "Faith implies an acceptance of mystery, which, for the Misfit, is impossible, because he has to know 'why'" (75). The grandmother "does not discern life's mystery; the Misfit does not accept it. Their conflict brings both face to face with religious reality. The gradmother embraces it, and the Misfit's response is deliberately ambiguous" (76). **THEM**

O'CFl 10. Gentry, Marshall Bruce. *Flannery O'Connor's Religion of the Grotesque.* Jackson and London: University Press of Mississippi, 1986. Pp. 31–39.

The narrator is initially vicious and mean and tends to blame the grandmother for the family's fate (32). The grandmother is not solely responsible for events (particularly the deaths), although her final gesture toward the Misfit is partly manipulative (34–35). The story's apparently unsteady "point of view is in fact at the heart of the story"; "O'Connor was a more skillful technician" than she or her critics admitted (37). The apparent inconsistency results from the narrator's diminishing meanness, which by the second half is aimed primarily at Bailey, whom the narrator resembles and had earlier favored (37). By the conclusion, we "witness the redemption of the narrator's consciousness more clearly than we are able to witness the grandmother's" (37). This shift causes a loss of narrative control, just as the grandmother and Misfit also lose control of events (37). "The narrator becomes silent only after having been transformed from a figure with much of Bailey's repressed anger and The Misfit's destructiveness into a redeemed consciousness" (38). **FORM, DIALOG**

O'CFl 11. Giannone, Richard. *Flannery O'Connor and the Mystery of Love*. Urbana and Chicago: University of Illinois Press, 1989. Pp. 46–53.

Because some readers blame the grandmother and neglect her "subtle spiritual change," the "action of grace can go unnoticed" (46), outshone by the Misfit's Freudian psychopathology (47). Although the grandmother seems an unworthy moral focus (47), the story's "events deepen into felt love the evident shallowness of [her] moral claims" (47). The Misfit flaunts the evil she conceals (48). "Guilt without responsibility and suffering without meaning define [his] despair" (49). Mark 10 is relevant to the Misfit's view of Jesus (50). The Misfit misunderstands faith; thinks seeing is believing; and thereby forgets the fallibility Christ's disciples displayed (50). He avoids facing his vulnerability; killing makes him feel free and powerful (50–51). He suffers from lack of pleasure and wills his own dejection (51), but the grandmother finally finds pleasure through love (52) and thus escapes anger and vengeance (52–53). **THEM, PSY**

O'CFl 12. Hendin, Josephine. *The World of Flannery O'Connor*. Bloomington: Indiana University Press, 1970. Pp. 148–51.

The story conveys little "sense of human death, human life or directly felt passion," emphasizing "consuming meaninglessness" instead (148). By claiming that the Misfit is one of her "babies," the grandmother not only reminds us that her closest descendents are dead because of her manipulative behavior but also attempts to dominate the Misfit by treating him as a child (149). She tries to "buy off the Misfit's revenge with a gesture" (150). The grandmother and Misfit function as Christ figures who finally crucify one another. "The most powerful crucifixion for O'Connor is the one you live out daily for a lifetime, the constant agony involved in human contact, human needs, and human striving.... For O'Connor it is the horror she sees at the core of family life" (150). The fact that the accident results from the random jump of the cat suggests the meaninglessness of the whole subsequent experience (150–51). **THEM**

O'CFl 13. Martin, Carter W. *The True Country: Themes in the Fiction of Flannery O'Connor.* Nashville: Vanderbilt University Press, 1968. Pp. 163–67.

This obviously Gothic story (163) emphasizes "the pathos of common vulgarity and quiet desperation in an almost infernal domestic situation" (164). The countryside implies horror in the first half (165). In general, "... grotesque inversions in which a distinctly dissimilar character replaces a child, parent, or close relative [as the Misfit replaces Bailey] are frequent in O'Connor's fiction and constitute one element of the Gothic quality" (166). **THEM**

O'CFl 14. May, John R. *The Pruning Word: The Parables of Flannery O'Connor.* Notre Dame and London: University of Notre Dame Press, 1976. Pp. 60–64.

The story is intelligible even without O'Connor's explanations (61). Martha Stephens' criticisms are misguided (61). The story assumes the sudden possibility of meaning intruding into everyday life (61). Elements in the first half prefigure the final tragedy (62). "For the first time in O'Connor's fiction, but hardly the last, a self-consciously demonic character opens up the possibilities of existence for the protagonist" (62). The grandmother is the mother of the Misfit's sin "inasmuch as she helped to make the world that created his need" (63). Her confession "reveals a sure basis of human goodness, the admission of our involvement in the sins of the world" (64). **THEM, FORM**

O'CFl 15. Montgomery, Marion. *Why Flannery O'Connor Stayed Home.* La Salle, IL: Sherwood Sugden, 1981. Pp. 249–60.

The Misfit, like Milton's Satan, is "an agent of good though he intends no good"; his nickname makes him seem legendary (249). He pays closer attention to the grandmother than anyone else in the story (251). His philosophy of meanness carries to a logical extreme the family's earlier "petty acts of rudeness" (253). The bespectacled John Wesley looks and acts like the Misfit (both are into everything), while the grandmother is a kind of Eve and the Misfit a kind of Cain (Eve's son); "she comes to see that Eden [symbolized by the mansion] cannot be regained, and also that she is responsible for its loss, as we all share that responsibility in the mystery of Original Sin" (255–56). The conversation between the Misfit and grandmother is like a distorted confessional (257); the Misfit rejects her loving gesture "as if fearing exorcism" (258). **THEM**

O'CFl 16. O'Connor, Flannery. In *Mystery and Manners: Occasional Prose.* Ed. Robert and Sally Fitzgerald. New York: Noonday, 1969. Pp. 107–14.

The story "calls up a good deal of the South's mythic background" and should elicit from readers "a degree of pity and terror, even though its way of being serious is a comic one" (108). The story takes for granted certain basic Christian ideas to which many modern readers take exception (109). "The heroine of this story, the Grandmother, is in the most significant position life offers the Christian. She is facing death" (110). She is not evil; rather, she lacks understanding, even though her heart is basically in the right place (110). "It is true that the old lady is a hypocritical old soul; her wits are no match for the Misfit's, nor is her capacity for grace equal to his; yet I think the unprejudiced reader will feel that the Grandmother has a special kind of triumph in this story which instinctively we do not allow to someone altogether bad" (111). The story's effect depends on an act that is both appropriate and unexpected, one not easily explained, one both simple and mysterious (111): the Grandmother suddenly realizes, "even in her limited way, that she is responsible for the man before her and joined to him by ties of kinship which have their roots deep in the [religious] mystery she has been prattling about so far. At this point, she does the right thing, she makes the right gesture" (111–12). Although this gesture puzzles many readers, without it there would be no story (112). "Our age not only does not have a very sharp eye for the almost imperceptible intrusions of grace, it no longer has much feeling for the nature of the violences which precede and follow them" (112). "... I have found that violence is strangely capable of returning my characters to reality and preparing them to accept their moment of grace. Their heads are so hard that almost nothing else will do the work" (112). Paradoxically, the grandmother's unexpected loving gesture may gnaw at the Misfit and eventually "turn him into the prophet he was meant to become" (113). In this work the reader "should be on the lookout for such things as the action of grace in the Grandmother's soul, and not for the dead bodies" (113). Confronting violence often forces us to reveal the most essential parts of our personalities—the parts we take into eternity when we die (114). **THEM, ARIS, READ-R**

O'CFl 17. Orvell, Miles. *Invisible Parade: The Fiction of Flannery O'Connor*. Philadelphia: Temple University Press, 1972. Pp. 130–33.

The family members are "nicely individualized," both physically and morally (130). Only the grandmother (despite her flaws) shows care and reaches out. Her early genteel graciousness ironically foreshadows her later act of grace (131). The plantation house not only symbolizes a past "imagined innocence and order" but also contrasts with "the depicted shabbiness of present-day life" (131). The house suggests the heavenly mansion or spiritual home" and implies "a return, through death, to an earlier state of innocence and purity, to a place far off the main road, away from the sterility of the city, where one was a child, and to which one can return again only as a child" (132). In the Misfit, O'Connor "mixes just the right amount of classic American drifter and morbid sophisticate to lend credibility and authority to an essentially enigmatic figure" (132). He sees redemption as fixed at one point in the past, but just as he confesses his "privation from grace, ... the grandmother is given *her* moment of grace" (133). Although the Misfit rejects the adoption she offers, his last words suggest his dissatisfaction with his earlier attitudes and thus raise the possibility that his thinking may evolve. **THEM, FORM**

O'CFl 18. Schenck, Mary Jane. "Deconstructed Meaning in ['A Good Man Is Hard to Find']." In *"A Good Man Is Hard to Find": Flannery O'Connor.* Ed. Frederick Asals. New Brunswick, NJ: Rutgers University Press, 1993. Pp. 165–73. Reprinted from *Ambiguities in Literature and Film*, ed. Hans P. Braendlin (Tallahassee: Florida State University Press, 1988), 125–35.

In O'Connor's stories, "ironic doubling" between and within characters "leads to a complete disintegration of the self at the moment when the character must confront the absence of grounding behind the linguistic self" (167). The grandmother structures her reality by relying on texts (e.g., newspapers) and fictions (her stories); as the family travels, "she provides a continual gloss on the physical world they are passing," explaining "relationships between events or her own actions which have no logic other than that which she lends them" (167–68). "The scene with The Misfit is the apogee of the grandmother's use of 'fictions' to explain and control reality, attempts that are thwarted by her encounter with a character who understands there is no reality behind her words" (169). Bailey and the wife are linguistically impoverished, and "even the grandmother soon starts to lose her voice, the only mechanism that stands between her and reality" (169). When the Misfit rejects her explanations, her sense of self is demolished (170). The Misfit understands both the limits and the power of language, and his "strange alterations between polite talk and cold-blooded murder and his last statement demonstrate the radical shifting back and forth between selves that cancel each other figuratively as he has literally cancelled the shifting consciousness of the grandmother" (171). O'Connor's story depicts characters who "either are confronted by the natural worlds whose laws mock their interpretations, or they are confronted by a character who understands that language is mere convention. If the conventions are not shared, the encounter will lead to devastating physical or emotional violence" (172). "By the end, when the language of the doubled selves has been unmasked, the characters behind it are totally deconstructed and no longer exist" (172). **DECON, THEM**

O'CFl 19. Stephens, Martha. *The Question of Flannery O'Connor.* Baton Rouge: Louisiana State University Press, 1973. Pp. 17–36.

The story's failure results from the drastic shift in tone that occurs when the Misfit enters, and this problem of tone is typical of O'Connor's fiction (18). Until the Misfit's entry the story had provided "easy enjoyment of the domestic comedy of this very ordinary family excursion" (19), in which the "comedy issues, as it often does in O'Connor, from the author's dry, deadpan, seemingly unamused reporting of the characters' hilarious actions and appearance" (20). Yet the grandmother is not totally ridiculous; we respond to her with some warmth, partly because she demonstrates a vitality the other characters lack (23). When the Misfit enters, however, the story "breaks in two" (27); by the end we hear "the mean tonal snarl the story has wound itself into" (29). But although we pity the family, the story presents them with contempt; they seem "in death just as ordinary and ridiculous as before" (30). The story seems to insist that we see the Misfit as morally superior to his victims (33); that we consider the grandmother better in her death than in her life; and that we consider ordinary human pain and pleasure unimportant (34). The fact that O'Connor had to explain and justify the story in external statements proves the failure of the story itself (35). O'Connor's "formidable [Christian] doctrine" implies that receiving grace "is rather an expensive process" (35). **FORM**

O'CFl 20. Tate, J.O. "A Good Source Is Not So Hard to Find." *Flannery O'Connor Bulletin* 9 (1980): 98–103.

A 1952 newspaper article on an Atlanta thief calling himself "The Misfit" probably gave O'Connor the name of her character, though the latter "is out of place in a grander way than the original" (98). Aptly enough, the Misfit's clothes don't fit well, and through him O'Connor mocks pop-psychology excuses for aberrant behavior (98). Ironically, the real Atlanta "Misfit" was eventually confined to the state mental hospital in O'Connor's home town (99). During that same year, however, a more notorious criminal was active who bore several resemblances to O'Connor's character: "First, he had inspired a certain amount of terror through several states. Second, he had, or claimed to have, a certain *politesse*. Third, he wore spectacles. Fourth, he had two accomplices, in more than one account" (99). Quotations from newspaper articles suggest many striking parallels with O'Connor's story (100–1). **HIST, THEM**

O'CFl 21. Walters, Dorothy. *Flannery O'Connor.* Boston: Twayne, 1973. Pp. 70–73.

Like many O'Connor stories, this one emphasizes tensions within a family (70), and just as the grandmother attempts to manipulate her family, so she attempts to control the Misfit through talk (71). The Misfit's comments about allegiance to Jesus seem to express O'Connor's disdain for "all who refuse either to affirm or deny, choosing instead to drift aimlessly in the ambiguous realms of the trimmer" (71). However, even though the grandmother transcends her earlier pride at the end of the story, her death seems excessive (72). "In O'Connor's view, there seems to be no place in the divine scheme for human imperfection. The common frailties of humanity are unacceptable, and the imperfect specimen deserves to be damned for his failings or blasted to salvation by a final insurgence of grace that is produced in an extreme moment" (72). The familiar-looking Misfit may symbolize fallen humanity, weighed down by guilt whose origin it cannot recall (72). Although the ending can even seem nihilistic, the story is highly effective, especially in the sudden shift from comedy to tragedy (73).

R.C.E.

"EVERYTHING THAT RISES MUST CONVERGE"

O'CFl 22. Brinkmeyer, Robert H., Jr. *The Art and Vision of Flannery O'Connor*. Baton Rouge: Louisiana State University Press, 1989. Pp. 68–73.

Both "Julian and the narrator share a monologism that binds them closely together: Both are cynical authority figures who seek to impose their views on those blind souls who do not see what they do. In their efforts to show people up, both Julian and the narrator distort and demean; they manipulate to teach a lesson, simplifying the complexity of human experience to validate their own—but no one else's—integrity" (72). Here as elsewhere, "O'Connor uses the fundamentalist narrator to critique severely that fundamentalist part of herself, and at the same time she uses her fundamentalism to critique her Catholic self. Such a dynamic is taut and tension filled, and its presence in large part explains the great power of much of O'Connor's fiction" (73). **DIALOG, THEM**

O'CFl 23. Browning, Preston M., Jr. *Flannery O'Connor*. Carbondale and Edwardsville: Southern Illinois University Press, 1974. Pp. 100–8.

The story is almost a clinical analysis of Julian's denial and projection (100). Like other O'Connor characters, Julian is an older child whose impotence leads them to reject the values of their region and parents (100–1). Nevertheless, what Julian "thinks he detests, he also loves and longs for. What he believes he is free of he is, in fact, fearfully dependent upon" (101). Julian's mother *is* exasperating, but he is "more pitifully confused" (102). Her existence and values threaten his idealized self-image (104). Like other stories by O'Connor, this one "focuses upon the existential dilemmas of the self—its anxiety before the truth of its condition, the contemptible dodges it employs to deceive itself, and the inescapable surge of guilt as the shock of awareness is delivered" (106). The story suggests that "redemption is never easy and always involves suffering" (107). Julian can achieve a healthy ego only by overcoming his need to belittle others (108). **PSY, THEM**

O'CFl 24. Crocker, Michael W., and Robert C. Evans. "Faulkner's 'Barn Burning' and O'Connor's 'Everything That Rises Must Converge.'" *College Language Association Journal* 36 (1993): 371–83.

O'Connor greatly respected Faulkner, and her writings and those of her critics contain many previously ungathered references to him (371–78). O'Connor was probably familiar with "Barn Burning" and may have been influenced by it when she came to write "Everything That Rises." The endings of the stories, in particular, reveal numerous intriguing comparisons and contrasts. Both are stories of abrupt initiation; both feature large white houses; both focus on conflicts between parents and children; both end in violence; in both, the sons are shown running alone in darkness after a parent's death for which the sons are partly responsible; and both sons call out to their dying parents (379–81). However, the many differences between Sarty and Julian are also important: Sarty is younger but more mature than Julian, and he is motivated by a sense of justice that contains little of Julian's pettiness (381–82). Ultimately, Sarty wakes up to a new dawn and experiences a sense of freedom, whereas Julian, burdened with guilt, is left running into the darkness (382–83). **HIST, FORM, THEM**

O'CFl 25. Desmond, John F. "The Lessons of History: Flannery O'Connor's 'Everything That Rises Must Converge.'" *Flannery O'Connor Bulletin* 1 (1972): 39–45.

O'Connor borrows her title from Pierre Teilhard de Chardin, the French anthropologist and theologian, who argued that evolution works through love toward final convergence with God and who "warned strongly against isolation or refusal of reconciliation in any form, racial or individual" (39). In the world around her, O'Connor saw "not only prideful refusals of redemptive grace on the part of man, but the more fundamental refusal to admit any *need* for redemption" (40). The story depicts a clash "whose racial manifestations are the terms of deeper spiritual conflict" (40). Mrs. Chestny is more adaptable than her son (41), whose "moral adolescence" has provided him with "no mature spiritual identity" (45). **HIST, THEM**

O'CFl 26. Feeley, Sister Kathleen. *Flannery O'Connor: Voice of the Peacock.* New Brunswick, NJ: Rutgers University Press, 1972. Pp. 101–5.

This story is "O'Connor's only attempt to deal directly with the Southern racial problem" (101). It reveals "the obsolescence of the 'old manners' and the failure of the new ones, which are based, not on charity, but on justice—a virtue of the mind" (103). "Eventually, the mother's 'culture of the heart' fails because it is unreal: Julian's 'culture of the mind' fails because it does not touch his whole being. But the mother accepts her moment of grace when she holds to good manners (the next best thing to Christian charity, in Flannery O'Connor's view) in a moment of psychic confrontation with the new egalitarian culture. Julian moves toward participating in the real world when, at the story's end, he moves toward a new relationship with his mother" (105). If a person knows that he is "a creature fallen from grace but redeemed by Christ" (105), he can go anywhere. The "convergence of heart and mind" (represented by the mother and Julian) "would inaugurate the 'new manners' on which Flannery O'Connor relied to save the South" (105). **THEM**

O'Cfl 27. Fowler, Doreen Ferlaino. "Mrs. Chestny's Saving Graces." *Flannery O'Connor Bulletin* 6 (1977): 99–106.

Although previous critics have attacked the mother, "O'Connor's treatment of Julian is merciless, [while] her treatment of Julian's mother is merciful" (99). Although Julian fancies himself a persecuted martyr, it is his mother who has suffered hardship and displayed self-sacrifice (101). Julian, like his famous namesake, is an apostate who has renounced an old tradition; his treatment of his mother amounts to torture (101). His mother's death is like that of a "triumphant martyr, her past suffering rewarded by a final vision of glory" (102). Child imagery also makes her sympathetic, for she "errs as does a child, not out of wickedness, but out of a lack of understanding"; whereas Julian is deliberately cruel, his mother never commits a "willfully malicious act" (103). In her relations with Carver and Julian, she is both loving and, finally, loved. "Though prejudiced, Julian's mother is nonetheless loving and warm-hearted; though condescending, she has mastered the martyr's art of patient selflessness; though narrow-minded, she demonstrates unswerving faithfulness; and though petty, she is as innocent as a little girl" (104). **THEM**

O'Cfl 28. Giannone, Richard. *Flannery O'Connor and the Mystery of Love.* Urbana: University of Illinois Press, 1989. Pp. 160–66.

Julian's mother renders her son "helpless" by helping him so much, thus depriving him of "self-awareness" (161). She "preempts affection by putting Julian's feelings on a level of guilt congenial to her sacrifices," so that her "self-denying love erects a wall of virtue that Julian cannot scale" (162). Rather than acknowledging the personal guilt he feels for accepting his mother's help, Julian pretends to feel guilt as a white person for the sufferings of blacks (163). Similarly, Carver's mother at first expresses her hostility toward whites by mistreating Carver (164). The very ending of the story shows that Julian takes love as seriously as his mother; both, indeed, are witnesses to love (165). Paradoxically, by dying Julian's mother "weans her adult child into mature life. A frightened, lost son must find his way up a new road" (166). **THEM**

O'Cfl 29. Hopkins, Mary Frances. "Julian's Mother." *Flannery O'Connor Bulletin* 7 (1978): 114–15.

Chestny is the *maiden* name (not the married name) of Julian's mother (114). O'Connor was always careful in naming her characters, and in this case she wishes to stress the woman's role as a mother and, to a lesser extent, as a daughter (115). **THEM**

O'Cfl 30. Jauss, David. "Flannery O'Connor's Inverted Saint's Legend." *Studies in Short Fiction* 25 (1988): 76–78.

Julian's name ironically alludes to the legendary saint associated with hospitality (76). As a young man, saint Julian was cruel and inadvertently killed his parents; after repenting, he became famously unselfish and spent much time assisting travelers (77). In the end he rose to heaven, whereas the final fate of O'Connor's Julian is not as obviously hopeful (77). **HIST, THEM**

O'Cfl 31. Maida, Patricia Dinneen. "'Convergence' in Flannery O'Connor's 'Everything That Rises Must Converge.'" *Studies in Short Fiction* 7 (1970): 549–55.

Julian's cynicism isolates him, especially in the microcosm of the bus, and he misuses his intelligence (550). "Because Julian, unlike anyone else in the story, is distinguished by name, the story focuses on him and his development" (551). "In his immediate situation he is his own worst enemy and the cause of his own failure; but ultimately, he is less than a man—and, in this sense, his position is tragic. However, he does receive a revelation that may 'redeem' him; that is, make him the man he could be" (553–54). His revelation is not something he seeks; rather, it comes through a kind of violent grace," and the story's stylistic "combination of realism and the grotesque with simplicity and starkness effects a unique intensity" (554). **THEM, FORM**

O'Cfl 32. McDermott, John V. "Julian's Journey into Hell: Flannery O'Connor's Allegory of Pride." *Mississippi Quarterly* 28 (1975): 171–79.

At the end of the story Julian enters a kind of hell as he tries to escape the ugly realization of his own pride (171). Since the story functions as a parable, nearly every event is symbolic (171); O'Connor's "allegory ... reveals how man, through excessive pride, may lose all touch with reality and, in the process, destroy himself" (172). Julian's "terror at the end is caused by the shock of his realization that he does not truly know himself" (173). Even when he calls out to his mother at the end, she understands that he is not motivated by love for her but by fear and despair (175). The aggressive black woman merely embodies Julian's own malicious motives (175), and although she physically assaults Julian's mother, it is Julian's reaction to the attack that finally kills his mother's spirit (176). O'Connor is not interested in forced and legal integration of groups but rather in "a true integration of the spirit, an integration, freely given, by which man allies himself to his fellow man out of love" (178). Ironically, the attempts by various people on the bus to preserve their identities only isolate them, and the final image of the story is one of isolation (178). **THEM**

O'CFl 33. Montgomery, Marion. "On Flannery O'Connor's 'Everything That Rises Must Converge.'" *Critique* 13 (1971): 15–29.

Typically, O'Connor focuses on a character's clichéd response, pushing it until its inadequacy, especially as an explanation of evil, becomes apparent (18). This story is told from Julian's point-of-view, although occasionally the author intrudes (18). As we watch Julian watch his mother, we become aware that his "distortions are those that a self-elected superior intellect is capable of making through self-deception"; he considers himself more mature than his mother because more modern (19). Ironically, though, he dislikes the bus as much as she—not because it is integrated but because it brings him into contact with other people (20). As a kind of childish, less impressive version of the Misfit (in "A Good Man Is Hard to Find"), he "is more nearly naughty than malevolent" (20–21). In contrast, "there is a more fundamental rightness about Julian's mother than her inherited manners and social clichés reveal" (23–24). Her "gesture of love with the penny has removed from it any concern for the worldly value of her gift. It is a bright coin, given with an affection misunderstood by both Julian and Carver's mother" (24). Typically, Julian can only see the black woman as a representative of her race rather than as a symbol of the whole flawed human race (25). Although he tries to reform his mother's spririt, he finally breaks his own, and the "convergence of the story ..., at its most fundamental level, is not that of one person with another but of Julian with the world of guilt and sorrow" (26). Although Julian realizes by the end the pain that comes from rejecting love, he has at least arrived at the possibility of a new beginning (27). Ultimately, the story can be understood in terms of the words (by the theologian Pierre Teilhard de Chardin) from which O'Connor borrowed its title: "Remain true to yourself, but move ever upward toward greater consciousness and greater love! At the summit you will find yourself united with all those who, from every direction, have made the same ascent. *For everything that rises must converge*" (27–28). **FORM, THEM**

O'CFl 34. Niland, Kurt R., and Robert C. Evans. *"A Memoir of Mary Ann* and 'Everything That Rises Must Converge.'" *Flannery O'Connor Bulletin* 22 (1993–94): 53–73.

The story's references to Julian as a saint are especially ironic because in the period during and preceding the tale's composition, O'Connor was involved in work on a project describing the life of a small, fatally cancer-stricken girl whom she seems literally to have regarded as saintly. "Whether consciously or not, O'Connor seems to have been influenced by her strong admiration for the heroic, fun-loving, and compassionate child when she came to write her story about a prematurely embittered young man" (54–55). "Despite his greater age, [Julian] seems both emotionally and spiritually less mature" than Mary Ann (66), who died from a horrible facial cancer at age twelve, whereas in various ways Julian's mother embodies "some of the best qualities of Mary Ann, as well as of the [nuns] responsible for the little girl's care" (67). Especially notable are the many parallels between Mary Ann and Carver, the affectionate, rambunctious son of the bitter black woman (69–70), while the description of the death of Julian's child-like mother in some ways resembles the actual death of Mary Ann (70). **HIST, THEM**

O'CFl 35. Orvell, Miles. *Invisible Parade: The Fiction of Flannery O'Connor.* Philadelphia: Temple University Press, 1972. Pp. 6–10.

Although the story "uses black characters effectively in the dramatic development of the situation" (7), O'Connor's "concern was less with uncovering the tensions in race relations, less with the Southerner's adjustments in the modern world, than with uncovering the self-deceptions and evasions that keep us from recognizing our identities" in a larger moral and religious context (10). **FORM, THEM**

O'CFl 36. Petry, Alice Hall. "Julian and O'Connor's 'Everything That Rises Must Converge.'" *Studies in American Fiction* 15.1 (1987): 101–8.

O'Connor's Julian significantly resembles Julian the Apostate, the famous Roman emperor who renounced Chrsitianity and tried to re-impose the pagan gods on his empire (101). He was born into a privileged family, treated relatives violently, became socially withdrawn, lived in tumultuous times, and was simultaneously harsh and immature (101–3). He was given to fantasizing, was obsessed with learning, used his reading to help destroy the faith of others, and emphasized the importance of rationality and calculation (104–5). At the same time, he was reactionary and sentimental and eventually felt defeated by Christ (106). O'Connor's work "is more a story about the individual acceptance of Christianity in the increasingly secularized United States of the twentieth century than a story of racial tolerance" (107). Julian's rejection of his mother is analogous to the Apostate's rejection of Christianity (107). **HIST, THEM**

O'CFl 37. Walters, Dorothy. *Flannery O'Connor*. Boston: Twayne, 1973. Pp. 127–30.

O'Connor "is impartial in her stern evaluation and judgment; to her, the biased Southerner clinging to outmoded perception, the enthusiastic liberal eager to demonstrate his goodwill, and the sullen black resentful of white overtures are all examples of pride, absurdity, and vice. The work is a warning and an admonition to all involved—there is no major villain to be singled out and set against the others. The villain is lack of compassion, failure of sympathy, and, as such, it resides in the souls of all, black and white, young and old" (130). **THEM**

R.C.E.

"GUESTS OF THE NATION"

O'CFr 1. Averill, Deborah M. *The Irish Short Story from George Moore to Frank O'Connor*. Washington, DC: University Press of America, 1982. Pp. 249–53.

O'Connor depicts the Irish soldiers with some sympathy, refusing to judge them (251). "The story embodies almost perfectly the concept of 'organic form' that O'Connor presents in *The Lonely Voice*. Each detail of plot, character, and setting converges towards the climactic moment when the characters are changed permanently" (251). O'Connor effectively uses foreshadowing and irony and balances types of characters (251). "The setting is an unusual, almost metaphorical place.... Most of the action takes place at dusk or in the dark, when everything takes on a greater sense of mystery and obscurity" (252). Bonaparte, as narrator, contributes most to the unity of the work, and O'Connor's use of a first-person narrator is unusual in his stories about adults (252). The story begins with comedy and ends with tragedy, and the "experience of terror reaffirms the human values of compassion, tolerance, and courage" (253). **FORM, THEM**

O'CFr 2. Briden, Earl F. "'Guests of the Nation': A Final Irony." *Studies in Short Fiction* 13 (1976): 79–81.

"Name symbolism in general intensifies the ironies of the story" (79): Bonaparte "is a tragic parody of Napoleonic greatness," while Noble "is incapable of the exalted character that his quasi-allegoric name promises" (79). By collapsing into prayer, he "ignobly disburdens himself of the profoundly human responsibility his complicity demands" (79). Hawkins and Belcher are "complementary halves of a composite national type of the political Englishman": the radical and the conservative skeptic (79–80). Ironically, Hawkins learns "the dreadful lesson that in fact the human community ... may be subordinated to such bloodless doctrinaire principles as those he espouses" (80). Belcher, who never expected much from life, loses the little happiness he had found, all in the name of a "duty" he doesn't comprehend (80). Donovan, meanwhile, may have been named to suggest "the historic Jeremiah O'Donovan (1831–1915), a notorious Irish nationalist," while Feeney's name may have been suggested by the "Fenians," or Irish National Brother-hood, whom O'Donovan had helped organize (80). Perhaps the story suggests "that history may well fashion its legends of patriotic heroism from the stuff of such cold-blooded dullards as Donovan" (81). **FORM, THEM, HIST**

O'CFr 3. Crider, J.R. "Jupiter Pluvius in 'Guests of the Nation.'" *Studies in Short Fiction* 23 (1987): 407–11.

Previous critics have praised the story for its attack on political dog-matism and its restrained tone (408–9). Hints of the story's themes occur in its last sentence and in the last sentence of the first section (408). Al-though some critics have seen the old woman's statement about Jupiter Pluvius as merely superstitious and have treated her as an eccentric and humorous foil to Hawkins, O'Connor uses her to convey real meaning (408). Jupiter (Zeus) "for centuries symbolized in Western literature the moral values that the Irish soldiers will violate" (409), including hospi-tality and protection of strangers. The Irish soldiers are caught "between military duty and the ancient *sancta* of the moral law" the al-lusion implies (410). By killing their "'guests,' they violate obligations and decencies that stem from the depths of human nature and im-memorial custom" (410). The old woman's values transcend "the ideo-logical rivalries that divide" the English and Irish soldiers (411). **THEM, HIST**

O'CFr 4. Evans, Robert C. "'Guests of the Nation': A Close Read-ing." In *Frank O'Connor: New Essays*. Ed. Robert C. Evans and Richard Harp. West Cornwall, CT: Locust Hill Press (forth-coming 1997).

Extensive examination of the minute details of the story's phrasing, imagery, dialogue, structure, and themes reveals how carefully crafted a work it is. Although O'Connor is not often given credit for such subtle craftsmanship, in this story practically every detail contributes in some way to the impact of the finished work. Each aspect of the story is wo-ven into an artfully fashioned whole in which circular patterns, recur-rent phrases, and ironic undertones are particularly important. O'Con-nor skillfully blends comedy with tragedy, thereby enhancing the effec-tiveness of each tone. The characters are carefully distinguished from one another, and symbolism is used to great effect. The story is complex in tone, theme, technique, and moral perspective and reveals O'Con-nor's artistry at its best. **FORM**

O'CFr 5. Gordon, Caroline, and Allen Tate. *The House of Fiction: An Anthology of the Short Story with Commentary*. New York: Scrib-ner's, 1950. Pp. 441–44.

O'Connor's focus is almost always "the soul of the Irish people" (441). Although his work contains much vitality, he is generally a less careful craftsman than Joyce; often his stories "seem to fall apart in the middle, or present an indecisive Resolution" (442). "Guests of the Nation," however, is "as carefully wrought and as powerful" as anything by Joyce (442). Here O'Connor uses first-person narrative and colloquial diction to achieve unity of tone and a "seemingly inevitable climax" (442). "The Complication ... of the action is the growth of brotherly affection" among the men; the "Resolution is the spiritual desolation" that follows the killings (442). "The strong dramatic structure is largely the effect of this interweaving of Complication and Resolution, an interweaving so deft that one seems to grow naturally out of the other" (442). Belcher's character reveals itself gradually and dramatically, and his death carries great moral significance (443). "The Enveloping Action [the war] shares in the swift progression that distinguishes every incident of the story" (443). By the final paragraph, the "narrator seems more heroic than he has seemed heretofore. The author has doubled his stature, so to speak, by ascribing to him the sufferings of more than one man, and hence of all humanity" (443). The final sentence reveals "a remarkable compression of dramatic power, together with a pure and elevated, though idiomatic diction" (444). **FORM, ARIS**

O'CFr 6. Kavanaugh, Patrick. "Coloured Balloons: A Study of Frank O'Connor." *Journal of Irish Literature* 6.1 (January 1977): 40–49. Pp. 43–44.

The English soldiers, clichéd and sentimental, are designed to evoke "maudlin pity"; certainly they evoke it in O'Connor, "who weeps over their deaths and in this ... lacks the courage and integrity of the great artist" (44). O'Connor takes sides, and the "whole thing makes us sick and unbelieving" (44). The final scene (over-written but under-detailed) is too literary. The house is only vaguely described, and an "authentic note is seldom struck" (44). **THEM, FORM**

O'CFr 7. Lieberman, Michael. "Unforeseen Duty in Frank O'Connor's 'Guests of the Nation.'" *Studies in Short Fiction* 24 (1988): 438–41.

"Duty" is a significant word in this story narrated by the character "nicknamed Bonaparte," whose final line O'Connor derived from Gogol's story "The Overcoat" (438). Another word O'Connor emphasizes is "unforeseen," and in fact both it and "duty" appear more in the revision than in the original (439). The first two uses of "unforeseen" call attention to themselves because they are used as dialect to mean unthinking or inconsiderate (440). Later the meaning switches to "not anticipated in advance" (440). In the revision, O'Connor removed earlier hints of Bonaparte's cowardice (441). The original version "is a disillusioned young man's story," whereas the revision is in "the voice of someone older who recognizes the inevitable" (441). **THEM, FORM**

O'CFr 8. Prosky, Murray. "The Pattern of Diminishing Certitude in the Stories of Frank O'Connor." *Colby Library Quarterly* 9 (1971): 311–21. Pp. 311–14.

The story sets up a contrast between "instinctive" behavior and "abstract and mechanical" conduct (312). The tragedy results from sacrificing the former to the latter, although for the rigid, obstinate Donovan the choice is no problem (313). Ironically, Bonaparte's "transition to maturity coincides with his perception of human frailty, that men are like lost children" (314). **THEM**

O'CFr 9. Renner, Stanley. "The Theme of Hidden Powers: Fate vs. Human Responsibility in 'Guests of the Nation.'" *Studies in Short Fiction* 27 (1990): 371–77.

Whereas the card-playing emphasizes chance (371), Noble represents the Christian view that "the universe is controlled by a benevolent providence," while the old lady "introduces the notion of a vengeful deity who pays people off for violations of the divine order" (372). But besides exploring chance, providence, and punishment, the story also suggests that human institutions (such as capitalism and "duty") can bear responsibility for events (372). Indeed, the story's "keenest irony" is that Bonaparte and Noble commit avoidable brutality "as if compelled by a power beyond their control" (373), and Bonaparte "seems less concerned with the brutality ... than about the injury to his own feelings" (373). He drifts along, as if helpless, but does nothing (373). "Belcher's meliorating humanity, coupled with Hawkins's indignation against the remediable evils built into the established structures of society, seem to form the [story's] moral center ... against which the actions of the Irishmen are judged" (374). Like his namesake Napoleon, Bonaparte seems to see himself as a man of destiny: both "tend to shift the responsibility for their actions to destiny but suffer the consequences of such a view of life" (375). "The story also criticizes Noble's resort to the consolation of religion for his evasion of moral responsibility in this world through his fixation on the next" (375). Ironically, Bonaparte and Noble embrace "opposite forms of the same cop-out" (376). **THEM**

O'CFr 10. Robinson, Patricia. "O'Connor's 'Guests of the Nation.'" *The Explicator* 45.1 (1986): 58.

"Feeney's name recalls the Fenian brotherhood, an anti-British secret association that attempted several insurrections in the late 1800's and early 1900's. After the abortive Easter Rebellion, all the Fenian members involved were ruthlessly executed by the British. The Irish then retaliated with fanatical and merciless acts of revenge. Feeney's appearance in the story initiates a similar act of revenge without mercy" (58). Although an intelligence officer, his appearance helps destroy moral intelligence. After he appears, Bonaparte and Noble can no longer allow the prisoners to escape without seeming traitors. **HIST, THEM**

O'CFr 11. Storey, Michael L. "The Guests of Frank O'Connor and Albert Camus." *Comparative Literature Studies* 23 (1986): 250–62.

Despite numerous similarities, O'Connor's story and Camus' "The Guest" remain fundamentally different. Both "are set on or near bleak and isolated terrain" (250); both emphasize loneliness; and both show "the development of a relationship between captor and captive from formal hostility to intimacy, resulting in a moral dilemma" in which the captor must choose brotherhood or duty (251). Both main characters are reluctant and later regretful; both hope their prisoners will escape; each finally feels alone and insignificant (252). Minor characters are also similar (255–56). Although neither story assigns blame, both major characters exercise free will. "Deprived of moral outrage or scorn, the reader is left with the natural pathos of the situation" (256). No evidence suggests that Camus knew O'Connor's work; the similarities probably resulted from similar personal experiences (257–59). Yet while O'Connor's story "is predominantly a realistic, social commentary on the inhumanity of war," Camus' is "essentially a metaphysical parable about the human condition" (260); it "more quickly transcends its time, place, and characters and puts us in mind almost immediately of universal human existence" (261). O'Connor uses first-person narration to make his story concrete, immediate, and realistic; Camus uses third-person to make his parable seem more remote (261). **FORM, THEM, HIST**

O'CFr 12. Thompson, Richard J. "A Kingdom of Commoners: The Moral Art of Frank O'Connor." *Eire-Ireland* 13.4 (1978): 65–80.

"Guests" is one of the most typical, most successful, and most influential stories of the almost two hundred O'Connor wrote. It illustrates his great achievement: a powerfully "natural, congenial narrative voice" (69). At first the men exist in an unfallen world and engage in egalitarian rituals (such as card-playing); later, when the Irishmen learn that they may have to kill the Englishmen, O'Connor nicely hints that their sleep is disturbed. The story records a transforming event in Bonaparte's life. Although in describing the killings O'Connor risks sentimentality, he manages to avoid it, showing instead how Bonaparte also becomes a victim by losing his innocence. **FORM, THEM**

O'CFr 13. Tomory, William M. *Frank O'Connor.* Boston: Twayne, 1980. Pp. 29–31, 80–81.

The story's "starkness and lucidity" defy commentary and make it "quite simply one of the most eloquent commentaries on the inhumanity of war" (30). "In less than 5,200 words, O'Connor vividly individualizes six characters" (30). "The plot is fluid [but] inevitable in its relentless logicality," and although "the theme receives no overt statement from character or narrator," the events and reactions "speak plainly enough" (31). Although the final line "approaches a thematic statement," its "colloquially rendered sentiment is natural enough" (31). In later revising the story, O'Connor altered 108 lines but took the "ruthless pruning of Cockney dialect and Irish brogue" too far (31). The work's various versions illustrate "the primal technical struggle and achievement for O'Connor: the shaping of the narratorial voice" (31). Phrasing in the revision is less colorful, more neutral (80), but passages that sound "literary" or "written" also give way to a simpler tone suggesting normal speech (81). Pruning the dialect prevents the characters from sounding like caricatures, but perhaps O'Connor went too far (81).
FORM, THEM

R.C.E.

"I STAND HERE IRONING"

Ols 1. Bauer, Helen Pike. "'A child of anxious, not proud, love': Mother and Daughter in Tillie Olsen's 'I Stand Here Ironing.'" *Mother Puzzles: Daughters and Mothers in Contemporary American Literature.* Ed. Mickey Pearlman. New York: Greenwood Press, 1989. 35–39.

An examination of the relationship between the narrator of "I Stand Here Ironing" and her daughter Emily suggests that the mother's monologue, occasioned by the school counselor's request for a meeting to discuss Emily, is her attempt to understand her daughter and to explain her daughter's behavior. While she reflects on the nineteen years of Emily's life, years filled with "displacement and deprivation" (35), she examines her own life as well and the choices that she made, accepting responsibility for the difficulties that Emily faced as a child (36). But her reflection is not overburdened with guilt. As a young mother whose husband abandoned her and eight-month-old Emily, she managed as best as she could (36). Since "time is the first casualty of poverty" (36), the narrator, during Emily's infancy and childhood, suffered from time constraints and restrictions. She breast fed Emily according to a time schedule set by authorities rather than responding to Emily's and her own natural requirements (36). Her need to work reduced the time she had for Emily, time that was later available for her other children. In addition, the narrator's poverty contributed to her powerlessness (36): "The story is filled with expressions of compulsion and lack of choice" (36). Emily also faced the same difficult conditions as her mother, and she, out of necessity, helped with the younger children, often to the detriment of her school work. But both Emily and her mother, unlike the absent father, did not give up (37). The mother possesses "strength of character" (37) and intelligence, qualities that Emily shares and that have enabled both of them to survive. In addition, Emily's talent for comedy encourages a feeling of hope for her future (38). Still, the world that Olsen depicts is one of "poverty, monotonous labor, estrangement, and sickness" (38). But opposed to that harsh world are the mother's love and desires for Emily, which do not include a hope of marriage and children for Emily but a wish that she be a secure individual with a strong identity (39). **THEM**

Ols 2. Fisher, Elizabeth. "The Passion of Tillie Olsen." Review of *Tell Me a Riddle*, by Tillie Olsen. *The Nation*, April 10, 1972: 472, 474.

This review of *Tell Me a Riddle*, a collection of four stories, discusses Olsen's "masterpiece" (472), the title story, and then briefly mentions the others in the collection. "I Stand Here Ironing" is a tale that every parent will recognize, a tale of "wanting to do the best for her daughter ... [but of being] often forced to do the worst" (474). Even though the story presents a picture of poverty and abandonment, it incorporates a note of hope because the characters endure. **THEM, FORM**

Ols 3. Frye, Joanne S. "'I Stand Here Ironing': Motherhood as Experience and Metaphor." *Studies in Short Fiction* 18 (1981): 287–92.

Depiction or representation of motherhood in literature except as a metaphor for the creative process or as an obstacle in a male development pattern is rarely found (287). Olsen presents a realistic portrayal of motherhood in "I Stand Here Ironing" and simultaneously uses motherhood to explore the concept of selfhood (287). The story, ostensibly a reflection on the daughter's life, is also an examination of the mother's own (287). As the mother traces her daughter's development, she considers the options she had in satisfying her and her daughter's needs (288), and she does so without unnecessarily blaming herself (290). But the story moves beyond the narrator and her daughter and "becomes a mediation on human existence, on the interplay among external contingencies, individual needs, and individual responsibilities" (288). The story argues for the necessary separateness of all individuals (288). The mother is not to be defined solely in her role as mother nor is Emily to be considered solely her mother's creation (289). Emily is ultimately responsible for her actions and for the establishment of a viable selfhood (289). However, societal pressures exert a force on individuals. In the case of the narrator and her daughter, the depression and the ensuing poverty, war and the absence of fathers and husbands, and inadequate child care had an influence (290). Still the narrator accepts responsibility for her actions even though her options were limited by circumstances, just as Emily must (290). Emily makes choices, asserting herself as an individual (291). The mother and her daughter's story provide a comment on the establishment of a selfhood, suggesting that each individual must be responsible for creating a trustworthy life out of limited choices (291–92). **FEM, THEM**

Ols 4. Frye, Joanne S. *Tillie Olsen: A Study of the Short Fiction.* New York: Twayne, 1995. Pp. 19–36, 143–49.

Although the story seems (and is) autobiographical, it is also well crafted and deals with themes that are more than merely personal (20–21), including the ways larger circumstances inhibit and restrict individual lives (22). It is perhaps the first significant work of literature to emphasize a mother's perspective and voice, and it explores the problem of "how to communicate inchoate life comprehensions, how to shape human circumstances into narrative forms that evoke the complexity of people's lives and elude the available cultural constructions of those lives" (23). The narrative depends on an audience willing to listen (25), and the whole tale achieves a dialogical structure, highlighting not only a "projected dialogue with the external voice [of the counselor] but also the sense of the mother's internal dialogue" (26). Moreover, "the story asserts from the outset that narrative construction of past experience is necessarily tentative and arbitrarily shaped by present circumstance" (26). An important narrative pattern centers around constant interruptions, and "each interruption operates ... to create a shift of emphasis or an alternative interpretation, reminding us that the narrative is only an interpretation of events, never a total rendering of them. In this way the story never becomes 'fixed'" (28). The work therefore implies that "the narrative is a hypothesis, one possible answer, not an actual transcribing of life events" (29). In this non-linear organization, "two thematic concerns—the mother's anguish about societal harms and the daughter's increasingly independent existence—emerge as far more crucial guides for narrative selection than any concern with plot or narrative chronology" (30). "Resisting both the impositions of traditional coherence and the simple renderings of a monological voice, the narrative becomes an internal dialogue capable of rendering vividly the interactions between human hopes and possibilities and the constraints set by circumstances" (31). Such a dialogical structure "enables the mother to look back at the controlling power of what could not be helped, and yet to discover what can still be changed" (31). Emphasis on eye imagery is "a part of the story's other metaphorical patterns that invoke change, process, flexibility, and resistance to fixity: growth, nourishment, and interaction rather than rigidity, hunger, and separation" (34). The story emphasizes experiences not often treated in literature and makes those experiences available to various interpretations (35). In an interview about the story, Olsen stresses its rhythm, its "'back and forth movement as the iron itself moves'" (143). She notes that because the story was written in the aftermath of the dropping of the first atom bomb, it emphasizes "'how precious young life, *all* life, is'" (144). Olsen questions conventional critical focus on the mother's "guilt," arguing that one "'is guilty only for what one oneself is responsible for. But if the situation is that it's the terrible schools; the poor child care; the competitive putdown world; if it's exhaustion; if you can't be there when needed and there's nobody else to care, then the anguish, anger, even powerlessness is a *reality* reaction. And to a situation common with others. About which something *can* be done'" (146). For these reasons, to stress the mother's "guilt" is to deny society's responsibilities. At the time she wrote the story, Olsen "'did not realize ... that this was the first time the direct voice of the mother herself appeared in literature'" (147). **FORM, FEM, DIAL, MARX, THEM**

Ols 5. Kamel, Rose. "Literary Foremothers and Writers' Silences: Tillie Olsen's Autobiographical Fiction." *MELUS: Society for the Study of the Multi-Ethnic Literature of the United States* 12 (1985): 55–72.

The life experiences of Olsen—her lack of a college education, her marriage to a laborer, her raising of her four daughters, her low-paying jobs, and her postponement of writing until the demands of a family lessened—are translated into her fiction (55–56). Her stories explore the difficulty of life in the working class and the frustration of a woman who is shunted into a domestic life with no creative outlet (56–57). In Olsen's fiction one finds "The tyranny of class struggle eroding the bodies and minds of workers and the children of workers; household drudgery and child care undermining a woman writer's creativity" (58). "I Stand Here Ironing," published when Olsen was fifty (59), shows that the years when the narrator's daughter Emily was young were years of hardship caused by low paying jobs and abandonment by the narrator's husband (60). But the loneliness and emptiness of that period continue even after her economic condition improves with her second marriage (60). The reason is that "Her entire adult life has been interrupted by child care" (60). The narrator's language indicates her loss, an atrophying of an inherent talent (60). Her daughter Emily also suffers from the lack of opportunity to express herself, even though she has won through her acting "some attention and affection and to a limited extent a control of life's randomness" (61). She, resembling the dress that her mother is ironing, is flattened and oppressed by circumstances (61). Examination of Olsen's "O Yes" and "Tell Me a Riddle" supports the claim that Olsen is a writer who has broken the silence imposed by her working class background and gender, thus empowering others to do the same (71). **MARX, HIST, FEM, THEM**

Ols 6. Kloss, Robert J. "Balancing the Hurts and Needs: Olsen's 'I Stand Here Ironing.'" *Journal of Evolutionary Psychology* (March 1994): 78–86.

The research of Nancy Chodorow and other psychologists helps explain the effect the narrator's actions have upon the development of her daughter Emily. Because of the twelve separations Emily undergoes,

she learns that the world is not to be trusted (79). She suffers the desertion of her father and the absences of her mother (sometimes due to a job or to the birth of a sibling). Her own illness occasions her being placed in a convalescent home (79). All of these actual or emotional abandonments result in Emily exhibiting the symptoms of separation anxiety disorder, including sleeping and eating problems and depression (80). Emily's eating disorders, manifested in her not eating in her early childhood years and then eating ravenously later, can be linked to the traumatic separations (82). Her lack of physical growth can be the result of "emotional deprivation" but can also indicate a desire to avoid adulthood and the responsibilities that accompany it, responsibilities that Emily faced at too early an age (82). Her nightmares, another symptom of separation anxiety disorder, begin with the birth of her sister Susan, but her mother, either because of exhaustion or because of hostility towards Emily occasioned by her physical resemblance to her father, rarely comforts her (83). The mother's behavior—nursing Emily according to a book's schedule, not smiling at her (80), leaving her alone at five so that she and her new husband can go out at night (81), and not comforting her (83)—contribute to Emily's fear of separation. But these events also result in Emily's not having a clear sense of her own identity (84). Lacking the contact that normally occurs with smiling, nursing, and holding, Emily does not receive the mirroring that is necessary to establish herself as an individual and thus validate her existence (84). The importance of Emily's discovering her talent as a comedian lies in the fact that she realizes that she is somebody (84). Even so, the ending does not bode well for Emily; after all, she sees the world as being destroyed by a nuclear bomb (85). **PSY, THEM**

Ols 7. O'Connor, William Van. "The Short Stories of Tillie Olsen." *Studies in Short Fiction* 1 (1963): 21–25.

Placing "I Stand Here Ironing" in the context of other stories by Olsen reveals that often "Olsen writes about anguish" (21). The daughter in "I Stand Here Ironing" is without hope and the mother cannot alleviate her daughter's despair (22). Characteristics of Olsen's stories include the following: the universal is presented rather than particular details about specific environments and individuals (24), chronology is ordered by the character's thoughts, and the character is revealed through his or her thoughts and actions rather than through exposition (24–25). **THEM, FORM**

Ols 8. Orr, Elaine Neil. *Tillie Olsen and a Feminist Spiritual Vision.* Jackson: University of Mississippi Press, 1987. Pp. 77–85.

This "is a story, in religious terms, that cries for redemption (of the mother's and child's loss) and for reconciliation, for coming back together in terms of original promises" (77). "In the representation of a

life in story, in interpreting history, Olsen seems to suggest that we actually redeem individual and communal loss" (79). The story's tension
derives from its twin focus on past loss and the possibility of future
transformation (79). The work is constructed through the mother's
"sifting moral consciousness" (79): everything is seen from her perspective and told in her voice (80). Contrasting images of the material and
the human help organize the work (80), and many passages link Emily
with machines (81). The three separations of the mother and daughter
provide the main plot developments (81) and are linked to the mother's
loss of time (82). "The story, then, concentrates on the time the mother
and daughter did not have; that is, it calls to attention the mother's absence and the daughter's alienation" (83). Because the work "presents
struggle rather than resolution, cutting off in ambiguity rather than triumph," it implies "Olsen's historic perspective and her sense of reality
as evolving through human relationships" (84–85). Readers come to
share in the mother's loss, hope, values, struggle, and transcendence
(85). **THEM, FORM, READ-R**

B.W.

"THE CASK OF AMONTILLADO"

Poe 1. Bonaparte, Marie. *The Life and Works of Edgar Allan Poe: A Psycho-Analytic Interpretation.* Foreword by Sigmund Freud. Trans. John Rodker. London: Imago, 1949. Pp. 505–10.

"The Cask of Amontillado" reveals Poe's "deep-rooted, infantile Oedipal rivalry with the father," the recurrence of which may have been prompted by rivalry with Rufus Wilmot Griswold (later Poe's literary executor) over poet Frances Osgood (505–6). Like Poe's father, who whipped him, Fortunato is "'a man to be respected and even feared'" (506). Fortunato also has some of the characteristics, including a cough, of other father-figures in Poe's life (506–7). The carnival setting of the story could suggest "the theatrical ambience into which Poe was born," and the cavern into which Montresor lures Fortunato and where he kills him evokes "the interior of the woman's body" that both father and son desire (507–8). With Fortunato's death "the father's penis is finally captive and the phantasy wish to return to the womb, as to a once-experienced beatitude, is converted into a horrible phantasy of anguish and death" (509). **PSY, HIST**

Poe 2. Gargano, James W. "The Question of Poe's Narrators." *College English* 25 (1963): 177–81. Reprinted in *Critics on Poe: Readings in Literary Criticism.* Ed. David B. Kesterson. Coral Gables, FL: University of Miami Press, 1973. Pp. 56–62.

Those who dismiss Edgar Allan Poe's work for its "'cheap' or embarrassing Gothic style" often do so because they assume the narrators of his stories are Poe himself and accept the narrators' "shrieks and groans" as Poe's effusions (56). Careful study, however, shows that Poe has constructed his stories to expose "his narrators' limited comprehension of their own problems and states of mind" (57). Controlling the stories is "an ironical and comprehensive intelligence critically and artistically ordering events" in order to reveal the weaknesses of the narrators (57). The control Poe has over his narrators can be demonstrated in such stories as "Ligeia," "The Tell-Tale Heart," "William Wilson," and "The Cask of Amontillado" (57–59). With carefully controlled

irony, Poe shows Montresor, the narrator of "The Cask," to be "a deluded rationalist who cannot glimpse the moral implications of his
planned folly" (59). He is a "compulsive and pursued man" who thinks
he has achieved the perfect revenge against Fortunato, but has instead
condemned himself to a life obsessed by guilt (59). He exposes his guilt
when he "unconsciously" calls Fortunato "'noble'" and "confesses that
his own 'heart grew sick'" at Fortunato's approaching death (60). Although Montresor hastens to blame "'the dampness of the catacombs'"
for his sick feeling, Poe makes clear that for his narrator the crime has
become "the obsession of his life" (60). **FORM, THEM**

Poe 3. Harris, Kathryn M. "Ironic Revenge in Poe's 'The Cask of
Amontillado.'" *Studies in Short Fiction* 6 (1969): 333–35. Reprinted
in *Critics on Poe: Readings in Literary Criticism*. Ed. David B.
Kesterson. Coral Gables, FL.: University of Miami Press, 1973.
Pp. 121–24.

Montresor's trowel is both an ironic "symbol of brotherhood and instrument of death," thus unifying the story and offering a motive for
the murder of Fortunato (121). When Montresor ironically produces a
trowel in response to Fortunato's query of whether he is a mason, Montresor draws attention to an important distinction between the two men:
Fortunato is a freemason; Montresor is a Catholic (121). Several references in the story further link Montresor to religion, especially Catholicism: the confessional beginning, the image on his coat of arms alluding
to the church's triumph over evil cited in Genesis, the pre-Lenten carnival setting of the story in catacombs reminiscent of the early church,
and references to wine, an element of the Eucharist (122). Montresor
refers to "'masonry'" and "'mason-work'" again several times, most
significantly and suggestively (noting the preposition) in "'Against the
new masonry I re-erected the rampart of old bones,'" and ends his tale
with "'*In pace requiescat*,'" the close of the requiem mass (122), thus suggesting that his motive has been to conduct his own personal inquisi-
tion against Fortunato (123). **FORM, THEM, HIST**

Poe 4. Hoffman, Daniel. *Poe Poe Poe Poe Poe Poe Poe*. New York:
Avon, 1978. Pp. 214–21.

Poe handles the death wish of his characters by various means. In
"The Cask of Amontillado," as in several other stories, he "doubles his
character and then arranges for one self to *murder the other by burying
him alive*" (214), a "horrifying" fate (215). A strong Montresor, whose
name is "synonymous" with Fortunato's (218), walls in a weaker Fortunato, dressed in a costume that underscores the latter's foolishness
(220). The phallic sexual imagery evoked by Fortunato's foolscap makes
"man's lustful nature ... absurd and comical" (220). When Montresor
kills Fortunato, he "has symbolically slain his own father and rival for

his mother's affection," as Mme. Bonaparte suggests (219), but also "forever interred his own passion, his own fertility, his own vitality" (221). Although Montresor's act could allow him "to experience the transcendent bliss" of his revenge, he is in fact burdened by guilt (221). This "dreadful aggression against the self" occurs in "the family vault," a place suitably suggestive of "the mother's womb" and "undoubted source of Montresor's/Fortunato's being" (221). **PSY, THEM**

Poe 5. Pribek, Thomas. "The Serpent and the Heel." *Poe Studies* 20.1 (1987): 22–23.

Although Montresor leads Fortunato into the catacombs to get revenge, he "loses his mastery of the situation and becomes a follower" (22). He is the murderer, but in response to Fortunato's screams, "Montresor is 'thrust ... violently back'" (23). Montresor's new position reveals that he "has an Achilles heel" and his revenge is not as complete as he suggests (23). **THEM**

Poe 6. Rea, J. "Poe's 'The Cask of Amontillado.'" *Studies in Short Fiction* 4 (1966): 57–69.

Most critics believe Montresor when he says he killed Fortunato to avenge Fortunato's "thousand injuries" against him (57). But Montresor's words conceal another motive, perversity, which Poe believed is the urge to do what one knows one should not do, including the urge "to hurt or to kill or to bury alive someone because he has been good to us" (58–59). Despite the exaggerated reference to Fortunato's "injuries," Fortunato's goodness is evident through Montresor's words and actions (59). Montresor refers to Fortunato as a friend and greets him as such, acknowledges that Fortunato is "'respected, admired, beloved,'" admits his "good nature," and finally calls him "'noble'" (59). The perversity of Montresor's behavior is like that seen in "The Black Cat," "The Tell-Tale Heart," and "The Imp of the Perverse," in each of which a narrator kills someone who has been good to him and then tries to offer a "reasonable excuse" for the murder (60–61). In "The Cask" Montresor's failure to tell Fortunato that he is killing him for revenge betrays the fact that revenge is not his real motive (61). Perversity requires not "analytical power" but *"ingenuity,"* which Poe considered a synonym for *"stupidity"* (61). Montresor tries to use perversity to lure Fortunato into the catacombs, but Fortunato goes with him not out of perversity, which his intellect allows him to control, but out of courtesy, which also often "makes one do what he should not" (62). Perversity also causes each narrator to act against his own best interest and confess (65). The more the narrator dwells on the impulse, the more quickly he confesses, but the longer one waits to confess, the fuller his confession is (65). Thus, in contrast to the others', Montresor's confession, delayed fifty years, is "long and detailed" (66). Like the other narrators, however, Montresor's "delight" in the telling is proof that he is acting out of perversity and not conscience (66–67). Although aware that the tendency to perversity exists in everyone, Poe admitted to loving those who loved him and was therefore not controlled by perversity himself (67). He might have learned about the theory of perversity from a number of sources including Pascal, and Poe in turn influenced Baudelaire's theory (67–68). Poe's own theory was developed in a number of stories that prepared him to write "The Cask of Amontillado" (68). **THEM, HIST**

Poe 7. Reynolds, David S. "Poe's Art of Transformation: 'The Cask of Amontillado' in Its Cultural Context." In *New Essays on Poe's Major Tales.* Ed. Kenneth Silverman. Cambridge: Cambridge University Press, 1993. Pp. 93–112.

Borrowing from popular literature and culture, Poe created in "The Cask of Amontillado" a tale that is both "derivative and freshly individualistic" (93). His own rivalry with author Thomas Dunn English and newspaper editor Hiram Fuller could have prompted Poe's creation of the revenge tale (93), and sensational stories of live burial could have provided plot details (94). One such story describes a murder in which a man is slowly walled in while his enemy watches (94). In another story two men are accidentally trapped in a wine vault, and in another a man takes his victim into catacombs containing the unlikely combination of a wine cellar and skeletons (95). The man later suffers guilt, as some critics believe Montresor did (95). Like "The Black Cat," "The Cask" was also influenced by "dark temperance" stories that show the horrible consequences of drinking (96–97). Already drunk when Montresor finds him, Fortunato is lured to his death by the promise of wine and made drunker along the way (97). Even when he is facing death, Montresor's words still focus on the Amontillado (98). References to masonry in the story reflect contemporary attitudes against a "private all-male order widely thought to be involved in a heinous crime" and add to the story's "black humor and mysterious aura" (98). Montresor's trowel could allude to a brick-and-stone mason probably murdered to prevent his exposing the order (99). Also an influence was anti-Catholic sentiment, present in the story through the linkage of criminal images to Catholic ones: the setting at carnival, a pre-Lenten Catholic festival; the heel crushing the serpent, suggestive of "the Church militant triumphing over the forces of evil"; and "'*In pace requiescat,*'" which closes the requiem mass (100–1). Though influenced by many sources, Poe's story surpasses them (101). Its construction is so tight that even the omissions are highly suggestive (102). Poe's characters, although not thoroughly sketched, "come alive" because of their "psychological realism," especially Montresor's motives and the reverse psychology with which he manipulates Fortunato and his own servants (103–4). The carnival image is central to the plot, allowing Fortunato's costume to underscore "his obtuseness" and Montresor's to offer a disguise (105). The carnival atmosphere also provides an ironic contrast to the grim murder (105). Poe's puns and double meanings add resonance not present in tales from which he borrows, enabling him to "entertain us with skeletons in the cellar" while having us "contemplate ghosts in the soul" (106–9). **HIST, FORM, PSY**

Poe 8. Robertson, Patricia. "Poe's 'The Cask of Amontillado'—Again." *Arkansas Philological Association* 14.1 (1988): 39–46.

The central images of the foot and the serpent on Montresor's coat of arms in "The Cask of Amontillado" may be interpreted in three ways in relation to the two main characters. First, the images could both symbolize Montresor as he "struggles" with his psyche "and fails" (39). Second, Fortunato could be the foot that crushes Montresor while Montresor as the snake gets his revenge (39). Third, Montresor could be the foot getting revenge on Fortunato, and Fortunato the serpent which ultimately triumphs (39–40). The motto associated with the coat of arms (translated "'no one attacks me with impunity'") could apply ironically to all three interpretations "since it could fit either what is represented by the foot or what is symbolized by the snake or both" (41). The mention of the coat of arms at the "high point" of the story conveys its importance (41). In the first interpretation Montresor is the foot that crushes Fortunato to get revenge, and the serpent is a Jungian or Gnostic symbol of Montresor's unconscious, his "own internal evil, his anger, his unforgiving spirit [that] eats away at him" (42). This reading, however, "ignores the very real presence of Fortunato in the story" (42). The second reading implies that Montresor will be punished for killing Fortunato, but the story offers no evidence that Fortunato's "'thousand injuries'" of Montresor were "powerful and aggressive," as the foot suggests (42). The third reading of the images seems the most accurate (43–44). Although Montresor uses serpent-like craftiness to lure Fortunato into the catacombs, the force he exerts to secure and kill Fortunato is more appropriately represented by the foot (44). Montresor's language in describing the coat of arms suggests he identifies with the "'huge human foot d'or,'" and the verb "'crushes'" conveys "the power, the force, the superiority" he sees in the foot (44–45). The clause describing the action of the serpent ("'whose fangs are imbedded in the heel'") suggests Montresor includes it almost as "an afterthought," but the image also implies that Montresor will finally be "overcome" by the evil he "believes he has mastered" (45). **PSY, ARCH, FORM**

Poe 9. Stepp, Walter. "The Ironic Double in Poe's 'The Cask of Amontillado.'" *Studies in Short Fiction* 13 (1976): 447–53. Reprinted in *The Tales of Poe*. Modern Critical Interpretations. Ed. Harold Bloom. New York: Chelsea, 1987. Pp. 55–61.

Montresor clearly sees himself as the foot when he describes his family crest to Fortunato: "'A huge human foot d'or ... that crushes a serpent rampant whose fangs are embedded in the heel'" (56). Poe, on the other hand, appears to see Montresor as the serpent (56). Montresor has the "cunning" and "subtlety" of the snake, whereas the "large, powerful, and very clumsy" Fortunato seems more likely the foot that "has blindly stepped on a snake" (56). More importantly, however, the crest points to their "mutual destruction" (56). Similar in some ways to "William Wilson," "The Cask of Amontillado" is a *doppelgänger* story, but unlike Wilson, Montresor never acknowledges his double (56–57). He creates an elaborate "'facade-system' to deny" Fortunato but "ends by creating a perfect double-in-reverse," an "ironic double" (57). Montresor tries to show how different Fortunato is from himself, but instead reveals a bond between them, a kind of kinship; for example, at one point he slips and calls Fortunato "'noble,'" and later, although blaming the catacombs instead of Fortunato's stunned silence, admits his own "'heart grew sick'" (58). Montresor's failure to identify himself as an "avenger" to Fortunato, one of the requirements for successful revenge, also suggests the "common substance" of the two men (57). Most significant in establishing their relationship, however, is the "diabolical doubling" of Montresor's "'mocking echoes'" as he taunts Fortunato in a kind of "'murderous identification'" (58–59). While the double in "William Wilson" obviously "represents conscience," the connection of Fortunato to Montresor is not so direct because Montresor is trying so hard "to portray himself as a man—nay, *the man*—without conscience" (60). The reader is comforted by the justice implied by Wilson's recognition that he murdered his conscience and thus himself, but "The Cask" forces a more complex response (60). Although one might argue that Montresor will finally be punished with damnation or at least with "the suffering that must lie at the heart of 'the compulsion neurotic,'" Montresor has managed to preserve the "armor" of his "powerful lie" for fifty years (61). Poe creates the "slow horror of the story" through "the reader's ambivalent wish-belief that Montresor did indeed triumph, that he did indeed sin with impunity: that he *did* slay his conscience" (61). Thus the reader "who so well know[s] the nature of [Montresor's] soul" may also be another "ironic double" (61). **THEM, READ-R**

Poe 10. Stewart, Kate. "The Supreme Madness: Revenge and the Bells in 'The Cask of Amontillado.'" *The University of Mississippi Studies in English* 5 (1984–1985): 51–57.

"The Cask of Amontillado" contains elements of Elizabethan revenge tragedy, including the protagonist's descent into insanity, here signaled by the ringing of the bells on Fortunato's costume (51). Like Elizabethan revenge tragedy, the story involves "revenging an insult to a family member" and includes the visit of ghosts of family members, in the story represented by the bones in the catacombs (51–52). Montresor becomes "the prototypical hero" who plots his revenge so long that he slips into insanity (52–53). Although the bells on Fortunato's costume reduce him to a "dupe," their jingling reveals Montresor's mental collapse (54). Montresor mentions the bells as he and Fortunato enter the catacombs and seems constantly aware of them, referring to them three more times (54). The space inside the crypt as Montresor walls Fortunato in suggests "the play-within-the-play motif of revenge tragedy," and the rattling of the chain becomes a kind of imitation of the bells (55). The last sound Montresor hears is the ringing of the bells, and he is haunted by this sound for fifty years (56). **HIST, THEM, FORM**

Poe 11. Thompson, G.R. *Poe's Fiction: Romantic Irony in the Gothic Tales.* Madison: University of Wisconsin Press, 1973. Pp. 13–14.

Several of Poe's stories, including "The Cask of Amontillado," have a framework in which Poe uses dramatic irony to reveal "a confessional element" (13). In the opening of "The Cask" Montresor "seems calmly or gleefully" to recount a vengeful murder he had committed fifty years before (13). One realizes, however, that the "'you'" to whom he is telling the tale "is probably his death-bed confessor" (13–14). Although Montresor implies he has gotten his revenge by escaping punishment (one of his requirements for success), he has not (14). Poe succeeds in creating "the double effect of feeling the coldly calculated murder at the same time that we see the larger point that Montresor, rather than having successfully taken his revenge 'with impunity,' as he says ..., has instead suffered a fifty-years' ravage of conscience" (14). **FORM, THEM**

Poe 12. White, Patrick. "'The Cask of Amontillado': A Case for the Defense." *Studies in Short Fiction* 26 (1989): 550–55.

Most readers see Montresor's revenge as "outside the normal range of behavior" (550), but Poe allows for another reading: that Montresor acts out of "allegiance" to his family at a time in history when family was a "political unit" (551). He feels no guilt about the murder of Fortunato because the revenge is "fully sanctioned" by his family coat of arms and motto (553). Montresor must act as the representative of his family and become the serpent retaliating against the gold foot of the enemy (552–53). The death Montresor inflicts is slow and cruel, but he "can relish" it like a soldier who kills to serve his country and believes his act is justified (553). The person Montresor addresses as one who knows "'the nature of my soul'" is any member of humanity who has felt justified for retaliating for "a grievance against [his or her] tribal unit" (554). **HIST, THEM**

A.C.L.

"THE FALL OF THE HOUSE OF USHER"

Poe 13. Abel, Darrel. "A Key to The House of Usher." *University of Toronto Quarterly* 18 (January 1949): 176–85. Reprinted in *Interpretations of American Literature.* Eds. Charles Feidelson, Jr., and Paul Brodtkorb, Jr. New York: Oxford University Press, 1959. Pp. 51–62.

The setting of "The Fall of the House of Usher" is both "descriptive and symbolic" (51). On the descriptive level the setting first creates a mood of "remoteness, decadence, horrible gloom" that prepares Anthropos [the narrator] for "the horrible ideas which grow in his mind during the action," and then provides "details which reinforce, but do not produce, those ideas" (51–52). Although the story has little action, Poe creates horror through the symbolism (53). The "'peculiar sensibility of temperament'" for which Roderick Usher's family had been known becomes "introverted" with Usher and, instead of bringing him closer to life, propels him toward death, as the "central action and symbolism of the tale dramatize" (54–55). Some of the symbols of the story have "a historical function; they symbolize what has been and is" (55). Other symbols are "prophetic," suggesting "what is becoming and what will be" (55). But all reflect "the opposition of Life-Reason to Death-Madness," especially "ascendant evil encroaching upon decadent good" (55–56). The tarn and Roderick's abstract painting symbolize "absolute evil triumphant" (56). The House of Usher, with its dead trees, "'rank sedges,'" and "'eyelike windows,'" "displays all the qualities ... of Life-Reason, corrupted and threatened by Death-Madness," as do Roderick and his song of the "Haunted Palace" (56–57). The tarn and Roderick's abstract painting, though, lack "any hint or reminiscence of Life-Reason" (58). The tarn, "dead water" symbolizing "Death-in-Life," is in effect connected to the house by the fissure (58–59). Much of the horror of the story "depends on the artfully inconspicuous iteration and reiteration" of the symbols that show the encroachment of Death-Madness on Life-Reason (60). Although not as symbolically suggestive as details of the setting, some events, like the collapse of the house into the tarn, also have symbolic import (60–61). Throughout the story Anthropos "tries to find rational explanations for the horrors which agitate him," but by the end he simply reacts to the cumulative effects of what he has seen and "flees 'aghast'" (62). **FORM, THEM, HIST**

Poe 14. Bonaparte, Marie. *The Life and Works of Edgar Allan Poe: A Psycho-Analytic Interpretation.* Foreword by Sigmund Freud. Trans. John Rodker. London: Imago, 1949. Pp. 237–50.

   In "The Fall of the House of Usher," probably written after Poe knew his wife Virginia was dying, both Roderick Usher and the narrator are Poe (237), and the House of Usher becomes a kind of mother figure for all three (238–39). Afflicted with "an acute form of anxiety-hysteria," Usher feels bound to his home while he fears its influence (241). His condition is worsened by observing the deterioration of Lady Madeline, whose malady seems like Virginia's, and Usher searches for a means "to assuage his anguish," as Poe had done (242). The "'sentience'" of the house evokes "the dead mother who still survived in the unconscious memory of her son" (243), and Lady Madeline, as the twin of Usher, represents Virginia, who was the sister and mother figure for whom Poe felt a "repressed incestuous attachment" (244–45). As Lady Madeline dies, her "double," the house, breaks apart and Usher dies with her (249). But "the narrator-friend, Usher's double, escapes from ... the dead and avenging mother" in order "to tell the story" (249). "Usher–Poe," however, is punished for his many sins, including "having betrayed his mother in loving Madeline–Virginia," treating his sister badly, and having incestuous desire for his mother, as is suggested by the reenactment of the Oedipus myth in the *Mad Trist* (249). Although the return of Lady Madeline as "the emissary of justice" brings punishment, it also fulfills the kind of wish Poe himself had for "'life-in-death'": "brother with sister and mother with son" asleep together forever (250). **PSY, HIST**

Poe 15. Davidson, Edward H. *Poe: A Critical Study.* Cambridge: Harvard University Press, 1957. Pp. 181–98.

   Despite his protestations against allegory, Poe was an allegorist, although not one who attempted to convey a moral in any traditional sense (181–82). Instead, adapting the ideas of nineteenth-century popular psychology (195), he used allegory to project his own vision of reality (182). In Poe's universe, everything is "tripartite: body, mind, and soul" (194). Man reflects the universe, and "the universe is a macrocosmic extension of man" (194). In a healthy person all three parts are balanced and harmonious, but any part could dominate or be repressed (195). These ideas underlie Poe's work as a whole, but are especially notable in "The Fall of the House of Usher," which studies "the self in disintegration" (196). Here one can see both "the tripartite division and identity of the self" and "an attempted demonstration of the theory that spirit is extended through and animating all matter" (196). The parts of the House of Usher (outside as body, tarn as mind) reflect the inhabitants, "Usher [who] represents the mind or intellectual aspect," and "Madeline ... the sensual or physical side" that Roderick rejects (196–97). Although he tries to get rid of her, she returns, and both of them, "body and mind ... die together" in her embrace (197–98). Then the house that mirrors them collapses into the tarn (198). Poe presents this tale of disintegration from the outside using a "pictoral" method as if to emphasize that "the material world is an outward demonstration of some inner and cosmic drama" and can display it more powerfully (198). **THEM, HIST, PSY**

Poe 16. Hill, John S. "The Dual Hallucination in 'The Fall of the House of Usher.'" *Southwest Review* 48 (1963): 396–402. Reprinted in *Twentieth Century Interpretations of Poe's Tales: A Collection of Critical Essays*. Ed. William L. Howarth. Englewood Cliffs, NJ: Prentice-Hall, 1971. Pp. 55–62.

Although most readers believe "Madeline Usher escapes from her tomb and throws herself upon her brother," she could not possibly have done so (55). The vault in which she is placed has little oxygen; the copper floor will not admit air; and the coffin and vault are sealed too tight to allow a weakened Madeline to escape (56). Because the narrator's description suggests she looked alive at the time of her entombment and because he believes she has escaped from the vault, readers tend to believe she has (56). But she is in fact a hallucination (56). Already unbalanced because of in-breeding and the gloomy influence of the house, Usher "cross[es] the line into madness" with Madeline's death and believes he sees her (57–58). Her appearance is a hallucination resulting from his madness, as is made clear by the text that shows she could not possibly have survived (58–59). Moreover, neither Roderick nor the narrator would be likely to have put Madeline in the vault if there had been even a small possibility that she was alive (59). With his keen sense of hearing and his interest in torture, evident from his "'favorite'" book, *Directorium Inquisitorium*, an insane Roderick Usher could easily believe he had committed an act as terrible as burying his sister alive and then think he hears her returning from the vault (60–61). But Poe wanted to explore more than Roderick's insanity; he wanted to show the narrator's as well (61). The atmosphere of the house had affected the narrator from the beginning, and by the time Roderick has descended into madness, the narrator has too, as Roderick recognizes when he twice addresses his friend as "'MADMAN!'" (62). Although the narrator believes he sees Madeline returned from the vault, like Roderick he is hallucinating in his madness (62). In "Usher" Poe examines insanity through two characters (62). **THEM, PSY**

Poe 17. Hoeveler, Diane Long. "The Hidden God and the Abjected Woman in 'The Fall of the House of Usher.'" *Studies in Short Fiction* 29 (1992): 385–95.

The book that is Roderick Usher's "'chiefest delight,'" the *Vigiliae Mortuorum secundum Chorus Ecclesiae Maguntinae*, seems to be a clue to the "deep structure and meaning" of "The Fall of the House of Usher" (385–86). This book, "the orthodox prayer service for the burial of the dead from the cathedral in Mainz, Germany," becomes a "trope" for the cathedral, which itself tropes "the triumph of Christianity" (386–87). But the cathedral was constructed on the remains of a pagan shrine to the god Mogon and his consort/sister Mogontia, a fact that Poe probably knew through the word "Maguntinae," a derivation of "Mogon" in the book's title (387–88). Mogon and Mogontia were a fertility god and goddess who were "later ... appropriated by adherents of the Roman god" and goddess who in turn were replaced by Jesus and Mary (387–89). As we read the story, we are "reinscribing the traces of past discourses" from those earlier times "on our present reading" (387). In meditating on this "cultural residue" from the past, Roderick attempts to understand or "mak[e] real" his relationship to his sister (387). By including the reference to the book, Poe implies his criticism of the religious impulses that created these gods and goddesses and suggests that he finds religion "a panacea" for people like Roderick who are "afraid of life and its challenges" (389). Poe may even hint "something even more sinister—that religions function to institutionalize female power and status" and that "women ... use religion ... to subject and sexually oppress men" (389). Although this stance denies the restrictions "patriarchal religions" have placed on women, men "convince themselves that religion actually elevates the power of women," and thereby "attack religion while absolving themselves of its hegemony over women" (390). With the image of Mogon "buried" in the story, Roderick becomes an "Abject Hero" as he "abjects [or 'casts'] out of himself his loathing of his own body, his distrust of his emotions, his 'femininity[,]' and thereby creates Madeline, his "'twin sister,'" his "fragmented self, the idealized double or alter-ego" (390–91). According to Kristeva, woman's "body can only remind man of his own mortality, his own origins in the womb as unclean" (391). Roderick is also reacting to "the incest taboo" as Poe attacks the "religious (and psychoanalytic) fantasy of an idyllic dual relationship of male and female—mother-son, father-daughter, brother-sister" and "makes such an ideology out to be a pernicious historical lie" (392). Roderick's library, with its rare "masculine" books from "times before women read, ... wrote and actually became competitors within the literary marketplace" signifies "his complete divorce from the (female) body" (392–93). Although Roderick has planned well his abjection of Madeline, her return "represents the moment in the text when the signifier goes out of control" (393). Her "haunting" may be "analogous to the haunting of the buried god Mogon on Apollo and of Apollo on Christ and of Christ on Roderick" and "analogous to the act of reading ... as we consume the ideas, the ideologies of the others who have gone before us in our own constructions of meaning" (393). In examining Poe's clue, "we participate in the fantasy that we are excavating the hidden god Mogon, and in doing so we give him meaning, a reified ideological construction that suits our purposes as postmodern critics" (394). However, "we cannot pretend that such an act has a significance beyond the one that we ascribe to it" (394). **FEM, PSY, DECON, POSTM**

Poe 18. Kaplan, Louise J. "The Perverse Strategy in 'The Fall of the House of Usher.'" In *New Essays on Poe's Major Tales*. Ed. Kenneth Silverman. Cambridge: Cambridge University Press, 1993. Pp. 45–64.

Students who "reduce 'The Fall of the House of Usher' to Poe's personal traumas or his inclinations to sexual aberration and violence" have failed to see the functioning of his "perverse strategy": "mechanisms of mystification, concealment, and illusion" to create ambiguities Poe invites the reader to resolve (46–47). Poe used his concealing techniques "to preserve the borders of the moral order" while still "render[ing] a picture of moral disintegration" (48–49). "The Fall of the House of Usher" is a moral allegory that shows what Richard Wilbur in "The House of Poe" calls "'civil war in the palaces of men's minds,'" here "between Desire and Authority" (52). Using a perverse strategy that is "analogous to fetishism," Poe "substitute[s] pleasurable emotions for painful ones" and "replaces what might otherwise be a feeling of overwhelming dread with playful shudders, thrills, excitements" (53). Poe uses "the ambiguity and illusory quality of Roderick's works of art ... to distract and conceal" (54). As we try to understand "the enigmas suggested by Roderick's art" and books, our attention is diverted from the horrible fate of Lady Madeline (54). After seeing the reality of Usher's decaying house, the narrator tries to transform it into something less painful by looking at its reflection in the tarn (55). Thus distanced from the reality, he finds the frightening experience "'thrilling'" (55). Similarly, Poe communicates the "thrilling tale" about "the torments of [Usher's] soul," without the reader experiencing the actual "mental sufferings—anxiety, depression, madness"—that Usher feels (55). Like the narrator, Poe uses Art, Roderick's "poetry, painting, music," to "conceal yet reveal" his collapse (56). The narrator (and many critics) sees "The Haunted Palace" as evidence of the deterioration of Usher's mind, but a closer look suggests it might be "a tribute to [the] innocence and free imagination" of childhood (58). The incestuous overtones of the relationship of Madeline and Roderick are apparent throughout the story, and "The Haunted Palace" may also be "an expression of his desire to restore the spirituality of his love for Madeline" (62). But "a spiritual merger" with Madeline would be "a more insidious violation of the moral order" than a physical union (62). Madeline's fall on Roderick at the end of the story may suggest either their physical or spiritual merger, but either way it "represents a destruction of the symbolic order and a violation of social morality" (63). As a result "Heaven cries out, venting its full wrath on the House of Usher, which cracks apart along its fissure, collapses like a house of cards—and is no more" (64). **THEM, READ-R**

Poe 19. Kendall, Lyle H., Jr. "The Vampire Motif in 'The Fall of the House of Usher.'" *College English* 24 (1963): 450–53. Reprinted in *Twentieth Century Interpretations of "The Fall of the House of Usher": A Collection of Critical Essays.* Ed. Thomas Woodson. Englewood Cliffs, NJ: Prentice Hall, 1969. Pp. 99–104.

In their symbolic, psychological, and cultural examinations of "The Fall of the House of Usher," most critics overlook the fact that the story "is a Gothic tale, like Ligeia" and must be interpreted in light of its "vampirism, the hereditary Usher curse" (99). A number of literary works on vampirism appeared in the years preceding "Usher" and could have been sources for Poe (99–100). Many occurrences in the story contribute to a reading of vampirism: Madeline's behavior, "fraught with darkly suggestive significance"; Roderick's symptoms that seem like pernicious anemia (appropriate for the vampire's victim), for example, his "'ghastly pallor,'" "nervous agitation," "weakness," and extremes of behavior, for which there is no cure; the narrator's "'astonishment,'" "'dread,'" and "'stupor'" on meeting Madeline, a typical response to meeting a vampire; the old books Usher and the narrator consult after Usher declares Madeline dead; the "whirlwind (traditionally signalizing a spiritual presence)" that flies through the narrator's room as Madeline is escaping; the "'heavy and horrible beating of her heart'" ("traditionally characteristic of preternatural creatures"); and finally her falling on her brother after her return (100–4). **HIST, THEM**

Poe 20. Lawrence, D.H. "Edgar Allan Poe." *The Symbolic Meaning: The Uncollected Versions of Studies in Classic American Literature.* Ed. Armin Arnold. Fontwell, Arundel, Sussex: Centaur Press, 1962. Pp. 116–30. Reprinted in *Critical Essays on Edgar Allan Poe.* Ed. Eric W. Carlson. Boston: G.K. Hall, 1987. Pp. 91–101.

After Cooper's Leatherstocking, "the last instance of the integral, progressive, soul of the white man in America" (91), Poe represents "the end of a great era" when "nothing remains but the seething reduction back to the elements" (91). "The Fall of the House of Usher" is one of

Poe's two stories in which "love is still recognisable as the driving force" (92). Although love can bring "new life" (92), it can also be "frictional, destructive" (93), as it is in the incestuous relationship of Roderick and Madeline Usher. The love they share is one in which they are "absorbed away from themselves, into a unification in death" (99). After Madeline emerges from being buried alive by Roderick, she falls onto her brother, taking him to his death (100). Although the tale is "lurid and melodramatic," it shows "a symbolic truth" about the "last stages" of a love in which two people "can recognise none of the sacred mystery of *otherness*, but must unite into unspeakable identification, oneness in death" (100). **THEM, HIST**

Poe 21. Obuchowski, Peter. "Unity of Effect in Poe's 'The Fall of the House of Usher.'" *Studies in Short Fiction* 12 (1975): 407–12.

Critics often focus their attention on themes in "The Fall of the House of Usher," but the better approach suggested by Poe's own criticism is to examine the story's unity of effect (407). Poe creates the effects he seeks "through the careful selection of details and actions to present in the narrator (and ... the reader) the terror in one's losing his mind" (407). Although most critics see the story as Usher's, he is in fact a static character, whereas the only character who changes is the narrator, as Poe traces his disintegration and shows his movement from sanity to madness (407–9). In the beginning of the story the "isolation and atmosphere" of the House of Usher create in the narrator a "vague and undefined" fear that he cannot explain rationally, although he tries (407). As he looks into the tarn, he admits "'that the consciousness of the rapid increase of my superstition ... served mainly to accelerate the increase itself'" (408). When isolated from the rest of the world with Usher, the narrator is affected by his friend's madness (409). Usher's painting, music, poem (which reveals that he is aware of his madness), and books on magic and the occult prepare the narrator's mind to accept Usher's strange decision to hide Madeline's body (409–10). As Usher's condition deteriorates, the narrator's does as well (410). He seeks rational explanations for such events as the storm and struggles to maintain his sanity, but Madeline's return from the vault during the reading of the *Mad Trist* is more than he can endure (411). He loses his sanity and runs from the house (411). Through the narrator's consciousness Poe allows us to experience the narrator's fear as he goes mad (412). We do not know whether Madeline returned from the vault or whether the house actually collapsed, but Poe has created "real terror" in the narrator's descent into madness (412). **FORM, THEM, READ-R**

Poe 22. Quinn, Patrick F. "A Misreading of Poe's 'The Fall of the House of Usher.'" In *Ruined Eden of the Present: Hawthorne, Melville, and Poe*. Eds. G.R. Thompson and Virgil L. Lokke. West

Lafayette, IN: Purdue University Press, 1981. Pp. 153–59.
Reprinted in *Critical Essays on Edgar Allan Poe*. Ed. Eric W. Carlson. Boston: G.K. Hall, 1987. Pp. 303–12.

G.R. Thompson, not the narrator, is unreliable in telling what happens in "The Fall of the House of Usher" (153). Nothing in the text supports Thompson's argument that Usher's house looks like a skull to the narrator, that the many references to the skull-like facade make it a central image, or that the narrator and Usher are "psychological doubles" linked also to the skull-like house (154). Likewise, Thompson's conjecture that the story examines the "progressive deterioration" of the narrator's mind is also unconvincing (155–56). The narrator does not succumb to Usher's "obsessions with ... fear," but instead tries to "distract Usher from them" until late in the story when he acknowledges that he is being affected by Usher's terror (156). However, the narrator is not overcome by fear but instead resists its influence (157). When Usher opens a window, the narrator himself notices "an 'unnatural light' glowing about the house" (157), but tries to convince Usher that the glow is "only hallucinatory" (157). Although Usher cannot overcome his terror, the narrator retains his self-control well enough to flee from the house (157). Thompson speculates that the narrator is too unreliable to raise doubts about what finally happens to the house and offers an elaborate theory that lightning ignites the remains of gunpowder stored in the crypt and blows up the house (158). But the theory does not seem plausible because the little gunpowder that would remain in the crypt would be insufficient to destroy so large a house (158). Even if enough gunpowder existed, however, it seems unlikely to be ignited in the manner Thompson describes (158), especially since the text says "'nor was there any flashing forth of the 'lightning'" (159). Although Thompson suggests Poe's story "ironically 'mocks the ability of the human mind ever to know anything with certainty,'" Poe certainly would have understood that such a point could not have been made unless the narrator's mind was sound (159). **FORM, THEM**

Poe 23. Thompson, G.R. *Poe's Fiction: Romantic Irony in the Gothic Tales*. Madison: University of Wisconsin Press, 1973. Pp. 3–18, 87–98.

Critics often dismiss Poe's work as "'merely' a Gothic art" (3) and denigrate the excesses of his style (4), not realizing that Poe uses exaggerated effects to burlesque the Gothic as he employs it (17). In "The Fall of the House of Usher," Poe follows the American Gothic tradition, offering psychological instead of supernatural explanations for the mysteries the narrator describes (76–77). Poe conveys the narrator's state of mind "so subtly," however, that the reader tends to believe the narrator's perceptions (77) and fails to realize that the narrator is simply a psychological double of Usher (77). The image of the skull that the narrator sees as he approaches the house of Usher is "the central image of the tale," here and throughout the story evoking death: the death of Usher, his house, and his mind as well as the death of the narrator, all of which are linked in a pattern of doubling and redoubling (89–90). The deterioration of Usher's mind and the fear that promotes it are apparent to both the narrator and the reader (90). But the terror that acts on Usher also affects the narrator from the beginning (90–91). Although the narrator tries to explain rationally the atmosphere surrounding the house of Usher, his reactions suggest "horrible and supernatural" qualities that the reader attributes to the house, not the narrator's "subjective impressions" of it (91). Throughout the story Usher's terror increases the narrator's so that by the time Usher says Madeline has emerged from the grave, the narrator "sees" her too (93). When Usher dies, "'a victim to *the terrors he had anticipated*'" [Thompson's italics], the narrator flees in fear (93) and is therefore unreliable as a witness to what actually happens to the house (94). Because the narrator's perceptions have been shaped by his terror, the reader cannot know whether the house collapses, but if it does, even that occurrence can be rationally explained: "'a highly combustible substance'" stored in the dungeon could have caused an explosion (94). To those not convinced that the narrator's fear can explain the apparently supernatural elements in the story, "the recurrent dream imagery" and the dreamlike organization of the opening can suggest another psychological reading: that the events, especially Madeline's return from the grave, occur in a dream (94). As he does in other stories, Poe "destroys the Gothic illusion" he has created, in "Usher," by including the "purposefully ludicrous" tale of the "Mad Trist" that "call[s] attention to the real psychological situation of the two protagonists engaged in their own mad tryst" (95). Adding to the dreamlike quality and the irony of the tale are the parallels between the images of Usher (said to look much like Poe), the house, and the narrator (95–96). Acknowledging a psychological reading of the story does not refute other readings but in fact "incorporates them into its overall pattern, while wrapping a layer of dramatic irony about the whole" (96). With this technique "the delusiveness of the experience is rendered in and through the consciousness of the narrator so that we participate in his Gothic horror while we are at the same time detached observers of it" (96). As the house of Usher collapses, "both the self and the universe" are destroyed (96). But since we cannot know whether the events of the story actually happened or were creations of the narrator's disturbed mind, "this redoubled nothingness" finally leaves us with "nothing" (97). **HIST, PSY, READ-R**

Poe 24. Walker, I.M. "The 'Legitimate' Sources of Terror." *Modern Language Review* 61 (1966): 585–92. Reprinted in *Twentieth Century Interpretations of Poe's Tales: A Collection of Critical Essays*. Ed.

William L. Howarth. Englewood Cliffs, NJ: Prentice-Hall, 1971. Pp. 47–54.

In the Preface to *Tales of the Grotesque and Arabesque* Poe corrected the critics who thought his stories contained "'Germanism,'" or supernatural elements, by saying that in his works the "'terror'" comes "'only from its legitimate sources'" (47). Even today, however, in "The Fall of the House of Usher" critics fail to see that the function of the tarn and the return of Madeline, which at first seem "characteristically 'German' elements," can be interpreted rationally (47). Although the tarn is part of the Gothic setting of the story, it also "contributes actively to Usher's destruction" (48). The "'rank miasma of the tarn'" creates the kind of "'noxious'" atmosphere surrounding the House of Usher that, according to medical opinion of Poe's day, could cause physical and mental illnesses like those from which Usher suffers (49–52). Although the narrator seems "detached and rational," he too is affected by the atmosphere surrounding the house and Usher's psychological state (52–53). His account of Madeline's escape from the tomb is convincing, but examination of the details raises questions about its accuracy (53). It seems unlikely that Usher could have heard Madeline trying to get out of her coffin or that in her weakened state she could have survived in a tightly closed vault or could have had the strength to break out of a coffin that is screwed shut or open an iron door that is bolted (53). What seems more likely is that both Usher and the narrator are deluded (54). Although the reader tends to believe the narrator's account, Poe probably meant Madeline's resurrection to be real only in "the deranged minds of the two protagonists in the tale" (54). It is unlikely that he would have been as proud of the story as one of his letters indicates if it had contained "such a 'German' contrivance as a physical resurrection eight days after death" (54). **HIST, PSY**

A.C.L.

"FLOWERING JUDAS"

Por 1. Gwin, Minrose. "Mentioning the Tamales: Food and Drink in Katherine Anne Porter's *Flowering Judas and Other Stories*." *Mississippi Quarterly: The Journal of Southern Culture* 28 (1984–1985): 49–57.

Porter uses realistic details to suggest the inner workings of her characters, resulting in a combination of "the exterior and the interior, the realistic and the mysterious" in her fiction (49). The details, while suggesting concreteness, mask the ambiguities found in Porter's writing (50). Food imagery in the stories supplies not only specificity but also a sense of the mystery of life (51). For example, "Flowering Judas" presents Braggioni, a revolutionary, as an image of gluttony, and the story concludes with Laura's dream, in which she imagines eating the flowers of the Judas tree. Afterwards Eugenio, also in the dream, accuses her of being a cannibal (52). The ending suggests that Laura realizes that she, and not Braggioni, is the glutton because she does not commit herself to living but lives vicariously through others (52). In Porter's fiction, food, essential to life, is made a symbol for and serves as a comment upon life (52). Porter "makes the very physical acts of an imperfect humankind—eating and drinking—suggestive of a mysterious life rhythm which is, at once, both physical and beyond the physical" (57). **THEM, FORM**

Por 2. Johnson, E. Shirley. "Love Attitudes in the Fiction of Katherine Anne Porter." *Philological Papers* 13 (1961): 82–93.

Romantic love in Porter's fiction is the delusion of "only men and young girls" (83). Several of Porter's works—including "Virgin Violetta," "Old Mortality," "Maria Concepcion," and "Flowering Judas"—suggest that a sense of duty and not love cements relationships, including marriage (87–91). In "Flowering Judas" Laura, disillusioned, bitterly rejects love and commits herself to a life of duty without hope or dreams (92–93). **THEM**

Por 3. Lavers, Norman. "'Flowering Judas' and the Failure of Amour Courtois." *Studies in Short Fiction* 28 (1991): 77–82.

Although some critics interpret "Flowering Judas" as a religious allegory, the story is instead patterned after the tradition of Courtly Love
practiced in the Middle Ages, a tradition in which a married woman of
the nobility was courted by a young man who had no hope of success
(78). While a physical union was not possible, a "kind of spiritual
union" was, the relationship leading the suitor to a higher plane, to "the
contemplation of spiritual beauty" (79). In "Flowering Judas," Laura is
the courtly lady and her courtly lovers are the young typographer, the
captain, and the revolutionary Braggioni (79). In true courtly fashion
she denies each and remains chaste (79). Braggioni and Laura represent
two sides of a person, body and spirit. Without both, one is incomplete,
as Laura comments about herself (80). Descriptions of Braggioni center
on the physical and those of Laura suggest the "ethereal" (80). Her rejection not only of Braggioni but also of the other suitors and the children that she teaches implies a rejection of the physical (80). Although it
is Laura's obligation "in the Courtly Love tradition to connect the
fleshly, through her love, to the spiritual" (80), she fails. However,
Braggioni's wife, with her willingness to wash her husband's feet and
forgive him his indiscretions, does what Laura cannot (81). Additional
hints in the story should suggest to the reader the Courtly Love tradition. For example, Laura's name is the same as that of Petrarch's mistress (81). Just as Petrarch wrote poems to his mistress, Braggioni writes
songs for Laura, and Braggioni's Tuscan background suggests Petrarch's own (81). But Laura cannot provide the compassion that a lover
would expect from his mistress in the Courtly Love tradition (81). Her
denial of the body results in a weakening of the spirit (81). Laura's cry
of "No" at the conclusion of the story represents her negation of her
earlier position of asceticism (81). Her dream vision allows her to see
where her asceticism leads, and she rejects that "barren death" (82).
HIST, THEM

Por 4. Redden, Dorothy S. "'Flowering Judas': Two Voices." *Studies in Short Fiction* 6 (1969): 194–204.

The tensions inherent in Laura are caused by "her way of living and
her feeling of what life should be" (194). Laura is ruled by fear: fear of
life with its components of love and sex and paradoxically fear also of
death (195). In contrast, the revolutionary Braggioni, with his sensuality, embraces life (196). Laura, repulsed by him, cannot escape him because, in a sense, the alternative is death (196). Her life is denial, but she
senses that another possibility exists, a life in which religious faith and
human contact are possible (197). Eugenio, the political prisoner who
commits suicide, symbolizes for Laura the possibilities of the alternative
to her present life (197). Thus, if Braggioni represents Laura's fear of
life, then Eugenio represents her desire for life (197). In her dream she
follows Eugenio, who offers her the flowers of the Judas tree to assist

her journey (199). But she cannot reject her old assumptions; she cannot rid herself of her fear of life (199). Believing that she is unworthy of the flowers which are suggestive of communion, she denies herself once more, whereupon Eugenio calls her a murderer (200). Her shout of "No" signals her rejection once more of life and suggests that she "will remain in her private limbo indefinitely" (200). **THEM**

Por 5. Unrue, Darlene Harbour. "Revolution and the Female Principle in 'Flowering Judas.'" In *Katherine Anne Porter, "Flowering Judas."* Ed. Virginia Spencer Carr. New Brunswick, NJ: Rutgers University Press, 1993. Pp. 137–52.

The issue of betrayal as it relates to Laura and the revolution is an important aspect of the story (137). Porter's notes from her stay in Mexico suggest that Laura is a mixture of Mary Doherty, a friend of Porter's, and Porter herself (139). Laura, like Doherty, arrives in Mexico to contribute to the revolution and, like Porter, becomes disillusioned (139). The betrayals in the story are many. Laura abandons her Catholicism in order to support the church-oppposed revolution (139). Then she herself feels betrayed because the revolution does not meet her expectations (139). One of the causes for disillusionment is Braggioni, a revolutionary leader based on the labor organizer Yudico (140). Braggioni, ironically described in religious terms, uses the revolution to support his desire for power (141). Mrs. Braggioni, often considered a positive figure because she forgives her husband his infidelities and washes his feet, also has betrayed her beliefs (142). Although active in the feminist movement, she subordinates herself to Braggioni, considering herself his possession (she is referred to only as Mrs. Braggioni). She is "not dedicated to an ideal but to a man" (143). Just as Braggioni and his wife have betrayed their values, so has Laura. She has failed the revolution because she does not acknowledge the faults of its leaders, and she betrays the revolutionary Eugenio because she provides the drugs for his suicide (143). However, Laura's most serious offense is that she has "withheld love" (144), substituting a commitment to revolution for passionate, personal relationships. As her dream of eating the flowers of the Judas tree suggests, Laura has denied life (145). The many references to flowers underline Laura's betrayal of herself and of the female principle (146). Laura's life-denying actions reflect incidents in Porter's life: her approaching middle age, her childlessness, and her unsuccessful relationships (147). Flowers, representing the female life force, are opposed by machines and technology, often seen by Porter as "life-negating" (148). Laura is caught in the middle. Technology should be beneficial to the peasants but instead it is used by the capitalists as another tool of oppression (150). Laura's rejection of it (she does not like machine-made lace) is an affirmation of life (150). **HIST, THEM**

Por 6. Walsh, Thomas F. "Braggioni's Jockey Club in Porter's 'Flowering Judas.'" *Studies in Short Fiction* 20 (1983): 136–38.

Braggioni, a man of contradictions, is a revolutionist who is an elitist and a leader who treats his followers with callousness and disdain (136). The primary source for him is Samuel Yudico, an important official in Casa del Obero Mundial (CROM), a major labor union in Mexico (137). In 1915 CROM had its headquarters in a sixteenth-century mansion that had housed the prestigious and elitist Jockey Club for fifteen years. Although the union felt it gained respectability with its new location, "Porter's allusions to Jockey Club suggest that the Braggionis of the Revolution do not represent change, only frightening continuity" (137). At the time of Porter's arrival in Mexico in 1920, CROM was no longer headquartered in the mansion, but in Sanborn's, an exclusive restaurant, which Porter had frequented (137). Her references in the story to Braggioni's cologne, Jockey Club, clearly indicate her disapproval of the revolutionary leaders who "had grown fat at the expense of their followers" (137–38). "Flowering Judas" chronicles Laura's disillusion with the revolution and also Porter's own skepticism (138). **HIST**

Por 7. Walsh, Thomas F. "Braggioni's Songs in 'Flowering Judas.'" *College Literature* 12 (1985): 147–52.

The two songs, "La Nortena" and "A la Orilla de un Palmar," that Braggioni sings to Laura are significant (147). Porter was familiar with Mexican ballads; she had written an essay on the subject and also counted Mexican musicians as friends (147). Although she claimed that "La Nortena" was written for her, it was not (147–48). Porter, out of jealousy, fabricated the tale in response to a song being written in honor of an American reporter, Alma Reed, who was engaged to a Mexican radical (148). In "Flowering Judas," Braggioni sings "La Nortena," a song about a beloved woman, to Laura, who is incapable of becoming involved emotionally (148). She resists Braggioni's advances, a stance supported by the reader, but she also resists all commitment (149). Laura's fears and resistance stem from her fear of pregnancy, as symbolized by Braggioni's physical attributes; the description of the corpulent Braggioni resembles that of a pregnant woman (149). The second song ("A la Orilla de un Palmar") features a woman, orphaned and alone and thus available for sexual conquest (150). Braggioni seems to identify Laura with the woman in the song (150). As Walsh contends, Laura is torn between her revolutionary ideals (as represented by the first song) and her sexual fears (as suggested by the second and illustrated graphically by Braggioni's obese body [151]). **HIST, THEM**

Por 8. Walsh, Thomas F. "The Making of 'Flowering Judas.'" *Journal of Modern Literature* 12 (1985): 109–30.

The recollections of Mary Louis Doherty (Porter's friend and compatriot in Mexico) and other records help determine the extent of autobiographical elements in "Flowering Judas" (109). Even though Porter has commented on the autobiographical details of the story, "her reputation for fictionalizing her life" creates the necessity of considering other sources (109). From 1942 on, Porter gave varying versions of the genesis of the story. Beginning with a brief comment, she added details over the next thirty years. She identified Laura of the story as Mary Doherty, a Catholic and teacher of children, but in later versions Porter herself assumed some of Laura's actions, asserting that it was she who carried messages to prisoners and political dissidents (110). The political background of Mexico during the period encompassing Porter's stay (which began in September 1920) is discussed (111). The political leaders of the government and of the opposition are described, as are the details of Porter's contact with them and her participation in various meetings (111–13). Also discussed are Mary Doherty, her friendship with Porter (which lasted over fifty years), and her involvement with Mexican politics (113). It was Porter and not Doherty who became disillusioned with the revolutionists, and the "uneasiness" that is felt by Laura is Porter's (114) and was occasioned by her name being placed in May of 1921 on a deportation list (115–16). Records show that Doherty, also on the list, responded with humor (116). "Flowering Judas" depicts the fear of death that Porter experienced at that time (117). Sources are also suggested for Braggioni (117), for "a certain Roumanian Jew agitator" (115), and for the "Polish agitator" (118). Porter wanted to create a fictional record of her impression of and her involvement in the political turmoil of Mexico (119). Intending to write a novel, she accomplished her goal with "Flowering Judas," of which she said in 1930, "It's by far the best thing I ever did" (119). Her presentation of the political side of the story is seen in the portrait of Braggioni, who is a combination of several political figures (120), chief of whom are Samuel Yudico, a labor leader whom Porter disliked because of his chauvinistic attitude toward women (121), and Luis Morones, also a labor leader, who acquired a reputation for corrupt politics and had a preference for elegance (122). Additional details, such as Braggioni's interest in dynamite and his Mayan and Italian heritage, were borrowed from others (123). Braggioni, a composite of several revolutionists whom Porter had met, symbolizes her disillusionment with the radical movement (124). Laura, the protagonist, is also a composite, but in Laura one finds a measure of Porter herself—perhaps more than Porter would care to admit (124). The character has similarities to her friend Mary Doherty, who was serenaded by Yudico (124), was Catholic, dressed conservatively (125), had grey eyes (125), taught Indian children in Xochimilco (126), and whose horse bolted from a former Zapatista (126). But Mary did not experience the disillusionment so apparent in Laura (126), nor did she request Porter's presence during Yudico's visit as Porter claimed (126). Porter may have been transferring her own sexual anxiety onto Mary and into Laura (127). In other fiction Porter's alter ego is named Miranda, but here Porter, shying away from unpleasant or difficult aspects of her own nature, used the name Laura and then suggested that Doherty was the model for the character (127). Porter had a history of being "detach[ed] from people" (127); she herself commented that "love is not for me" (127). Thus, Laura's rejection of involvement becomes a criticism of Porter herself (127). Even though Porter at first identified Doherty as supplying the pills that resulted in a political prisoner's death, something Doherty denies, Porter in a later interview admitted that she herself did (128). Porter also recalls carrying messages that resulted in the deaths of five men, an event that explains Laura's sense of guilt (128). Rejecting love and fearing death, Laura withdraws from life (128–29). Porter, in 1931, wrote her father about her own struggle against suicide (129). Although Laura rejects involvement in life, she, like Porter, rejects suicide in spite of Eugenio's invitation (129). "Flowering Judas," based on Porter's experiences in Mexico, allowed her to examine her own shortcomings under the guise of examining Doherty's (130). **HIST**

Por 9. Walter, James. "Revolution and Time: Laura in 'Flowering Judas.'" *Renascence: Essays on Value in Literature* 38 (1985): 26–38.

Laura, resisting life with all its ambiguities and change, rejects the one thing, love, that could offer her meaning (26). She seeks a timeless state where the vagaries of life would disappear (26), a state that ironically is already inhabited by the political prisoners who "confuse night and day" (27). Laura twice attempts to remove herself from the restrictions of time and cannot—first when she is listening to Braggioni's singing and then also when she counts herself to sleep at the conclusion of the story (27). Although critics have offered allegorical and religious readings of "Flowering Judas," Porter's own comments about Katherine Mansfield should be applied to Porter herself: the fiction presents "a moment of experience, real experience, in the life of some human being ... states no belief, gives no motives, airs no theories, but simply presents to the reader a situation, a place, and a character, and there it is" (28). Porter creates a rich realism with details. Even though the story is set in Laura's apartment, revolutionary Mexico is depicted (28). The story's meaning is enhanced through Porter's use of details (30). For example, the lace is both part of the clothing on the statue of the saint and is also valued by Laura. The lace symbolizes soul, and Laura, while displaying a little, keeps the rest in storage (31). Laura, detached and aloof, resists the love offered to her by her suitors and by the children she teaches (32). Although dissatisfied with her life, she is unwilling to accept the change that embracing life will bring (33). Unable to give of herself, she is the cannibal that Eugenio calls her (34). In fact, all except Braggioni's wife can be so labeled (34). At the conclusion of the story,

Laura's dream depicts not only her need for human contact but also her fear of death. However, she fears not just a physical death but also a death of "inner experience" (36). When shown that her detachment from life leads to death, she cries "No," a response that does not signal change on her part but one that instead expresses "horror" (36–37). Perhaps there is salvation for Laura after her confrontation with her "spiritual death" in her dream (37). Evidence suggests that the love and attention of the young typographer is "as though it were founded on a law of nature, which in the end it might well prove to be" (37). Laura might discover life while following the "law of nature" rather than searching for it in social constructs such as those found in revolutionary Mexico. Porter found her own answers in the "redemptive power of art" and created fiction that celebrated the individual (37–38). **FORM**

Por 10. Warren, Robert Penn. "Katherine Anne Porter (Irony with a Center)." *The Kenyon Review* 4 (1942): 29–42.

Porter can be grouped with those writers such as James Joyce and Ernest Hemingway who have done serious work in the short story (29). She has not sacrificed her artistic sensibility to appeal to a larger audience or to produce a larger output (30–31). Her style is praiseworthy for its concrete details and precise images (32), and the details of passages in "Flowering Judas" mirror and enhance the point of the story (33). The contradictions inherent in a revolutionary who revels in luxury, is obese, and is cruel to his followers provide the sense of moral ambiguity that is at the story's core, ambiguity that is carried by the irony found in the story (34–35). Many of Porter's stories explore guilt (41) with its accompanying interplay of tensions, conflicts, demands, and obligations (42). **FORM, THEM**

Por 11. Warren, Robert Penn. "Uncorrupted Consciousness: The Stories of Katherine Anne Porter." *The Yale Review* 55 (1965): 280–90.

Even though Porter's fiction is rich in detail, its appeal is due to its universality (280–81). Porter's characters are caught in the tension of finding a truth that they can live by and one that they can accept as their own (283). The successful characters are ones that establish a clear "moral attitude" that governs their lives and provides direction (283). Laura in "Flowering Judas" is still searching for her truth. Already disillusioned with the Catholicism of her youth, Laura now questions the commitment of the revolutionaries in Mexico (284). Even though Porter's characters might exist in confusion, Porter retains a strong control over the structure of her fiction (285). The "most powerful tension in her work is between emotional involvements ... and the detachment, the will to shape and assess experience" (285). Porter accepts the existence of evil in the world but believes in the "sanctity of ... the individual soul" (286). The problem that Porter explores in her fiction is the difficulty faced by the individual trying to establish the balance between "ethical responsibility and the sanctity of the individual soul" (286). Laura is caught in the dilemma of deciding how much to involve herself: too much and she loses herself, not enough and she does not experience life (288). Porter is skilled in relating nuances of feeling and emotion as they correspond to a character's changing attitudes (289). In confronting the serious questions of life, she responds with a "celebration of life" (290). **FORM, THEM**

B.W.

"THE JILTING OF GRANNY WEATHERALL"

Por 12. Barnes, Daniel R., and Madeline T. Barnes. "The Secret Sin of Granny Weatherall." *Renascence* 21 (1969): 162–65.

There is a reason for Granny Weatherall's concern for her soul as she nears death (162). The jilting that took place so many years before almost exposed her unintended pregnancy, a result of premarital sex. John, her future husband, saved her from the shame that would have accompanied such a disclosure, but she still suffers from the guilt (165). Evidence for this reading can be found in a close examination of the stream-of-consciousness technique that Porter employs. Numerous references to babies or births and ambiguous hints about a problem and about something lost are juxtaposed with Granny's thoughts about George, the man who did not show up on their wedding day (163). Hapsy, a somewhat ambiguous presence in the story, is the result of Granny and George's union. Mirroring her mother, Hapsy also had an illegimate child, but unlike her mother, she did not marry (164). **FORM**

Por 13. Becker, Lawrence A. "'The Jilting of Granny Weatherall': The Discovery of Pattern." *English Journal* 55 (1966): 1164–69.

The jilting of Granny Weatherall is the central event of Granny's life and influences all her actions (1165). Because of the jilting, Granny tries to control the rest of her life in order to prevent "any occurrence which would result in surprise, waste, or disappointment" (1165). Thus, at sixty she prepares for her death and visits her children, although ironically her death does not occur until many years later (1166). Parallels exist between the jilting of Granny and her death, at which time another jilting occurs (1166). At the first jilting, she loses her faith (1167) because there is no sign that God is watching out for her. At the second jilting, Christ, often referred to as a bridegroom in Christian thought, does not provide a sign that she is saved (1167). Granny is thus alone at her death, abandoned because of her sin of not being able to forgive George, the man who jilted her (1168). Hapsy is Granny's last child and died at birth, presenting another storm that Granny has to weather and another part of God's plan for her that she refuses to accept (1168–69). **THEM**

Por 14. Estes, David C. "Granny Weatherall's Dying Moment: Katherine Anne Porter's Allusions to Emily Dickinson." *Studies in Short Fiction* 22 (1985): 437–42.

Critics have offered differing interpretations concerning the conclusion of "The Jilting of Granny Weatherall": some have suggested that her blowing out the light is an act of defiance, others that it is a sign of failure (437). Allusions within the story to three poems by Emily Dickinson provide important clues (438). The first Dickinson poem ("Because I could not stop for Death—") is used as a contrast to Granny's situation (438): Granny's ride in the "cart" is not the smooth ride of the carriage of the poem's narrator. Unlike the narrator, Granny does not believe that she is headed "toward Eternity," nor does she accept death as tranquilly (439). The second two poems more closely mirror her situation (439). In "I heard a Fly buzz—when I died—" the narrator, at the moment of death, is futilely awaiting the appearance of Christ (440). In Porter's story the references to a storm, the window in the bedroom, the color blue, and the absence of Christ are all suggestive of the poem (440). In the third poem ("I've seen a Dying Eye," told from the point of view of someone watching one dying), there is no discernible difference in the person at the moment of death, a situation similar to that in Porter's story (441). Both Porter and Dickinson suggest that religion fails to provide comfort and assurance and that essentially one is alone in the final moments of life (441). While Dickinson's "Because I could not stop for Death—" contains an acceptance of death and an affirmation of a belief in an afterlife, her other two poems despair of both, much as Granny herself does (442). And at the moment of her death, Granny, faced with the futility of life, blows out the light and thus, according to Estes, shows an act of "weakness" by denying life (442). **HIST, FORM**

Por 15. Goodman, Charlotte. "Despair in Dying Women: Katherine Anne Porter's 'The Jilting of Granny Weatherall' and Tillie Olsen's 'Tell Me a Riddle.'" *Connecticut Quarterly* (March 1979): 47–63.

Four stories—Thomas Mann's "Death in Venice," Tolstoy's "The Death of Ivan Ilych," Olsen's "Tell Me a Riddle," and Porter's "The Jilting of Granny Weatherall"—reveal interesting differences in how men and women approach death (49). The research of psychologist Erik Erikson suggests that the eighth and final stage of life should be a period of ego integrity (49), but for those who have doubts or regrets concerning the past, despair will be present as death nears (50), a situation that Goodman finds with Granny as well as with the protagonist of "Tell Me a Riddle" (50). Granny spends her dying moments occupied with thoughts about her much earlier jilting (50) and about her children in their youth (52). Throughout her lifetime, she, as a mother, wife, and neighbor, provided for the needs of others (51). But the roles of care-giver and nurturer were not fulfilling (57), and Granny is overcome with anger and bitterness at her death (53). Even though Tolstoy's and Mann's male protagonists experience despair in their dying moments, they despair over their unwise choices whereas the female protagonists consider themselves as victims, with little control over their own lives (59). Thus, their last thoughts concern men and the negative effects of their relationships with men (59). Another difference is that the men eventually accept death whereas the women do not and, therefore, do not find peace (61). Since the roles of men and women in Western society are so different, it is not surprising to find differences in their approaches to death (62). **FEM, PSY**

Por 16. Hoefel, Roseanne. "The Jilting of (Hetero)Sexist Criticism: Porter's Ellen Weatherall and Hapsy." *Studies in Short Fiction* 28 (1991): 9–20.

Past readings of "The Jilting of Granny Weatherall" have been tainted by heterosexual tenets. The chief of these is that a woman derives her identity from her relationship to men and from her role in the family (9). Readers thus have assumed that Granny is still affected by the jilting that occurred sixty years ago and that her life has since centered on her husband and children (9). These assumptions have led readers to assume that Hapsy is Granny's daughter. Instead, however, Hapsy is a close friend, but not necessarily a sexually intimate friend (9). Reading the story with a lesbian/feminist focus will not only add richness to it but also contribute to understanding the position of women in the culture (10). For instance, critics usually refer to the protagonist as Granny, thus emphasizing her position in the family, and not as Ellen, the name the protagonist herself uses (10). The appellation "Granny," combined with her surname, which establishes her relationship to a man, completely erases her identity (10). Ellen's relationships with men are not as satisfying as the one with Hapsy (11). George abandons her, she has outgrown her husband John, and the doctor is condescending (11–12). Critics suggest that after the jilting, Ellen was afraid to love again; however, Ellen loved not only her children but Hapsy as well (12). Fulfilling the role of a traditional wife in her marriage to John, Ellen, after his death, moves outside the confinements of the role, changing so much that she believes John would no longer recognize her, a metamorphosis resulting from her newly acquired independence (13). Ellen, however, does not forsake her religion and her family, with their many demands. Only in her relationship with Hapsy is she not "self-sacrificing," and that relationship provided the center she needed in her life (13). Lines in the text suggest that Hapsy is someone other than a daughter; perhaps she was a black servant (14), the common experience of childbirth establishing a bond (16). It is Hapsy's death or disappearance, not the jilting, that Ellen finds most painful (15). Losing Hapsy was difficult to accept, but her absence in an afterlife would be unbearable for Ellen, so she asks for a sign from God (17). When there is none, she blows out the light, thus ending her life, a "triumphant" action (18). Ellen, just as she asserted her right to choose Hapsy, chooses the time to die (18). **MULTI, FEM**

Por 17. Laman, Barbara. "Porter's 'The Jilting of Granny Weatherall.'" *Explicator* 48 (1990): 279–81.

At the conclusion of the story, Granny Weatherall expects a sign from God indicating that she will go to Heaven. Although most critics assume that a sign is not forthcoming, a sign does appear, but one that Granny does not recognize since it comes not from God but from Hapsy—Granny's favorite daughter, who died while giving birth (279). After being jilted and after the death of her husband, Granny created an independent life, but because she accepts the cultural assumptions concerning the importance of men, she "fails to realize the power of the feminine spirit" (280). She mistakenly looks to Christ for a sign (280) and misses that which comes to her through Hapsy (281). Granny visualizes Hapsy with a baby on her arm, an indication that the deceased daughter is waiting for her in an afterlife. The sign is there, but Granny, because of her Catholic beliefs, expects it to come from a male god (281). **FEM**

Por 18. Meyers, Robert. "Porter's 'The Jilting of Granny Weatherall.'" *Explicator* 44 (1986): 37.

In Porter's "The Jilting of Granny Weatherall" the protagonist, Ellen, almost faints when her intended groom does not appear for the wedding. A man supports her, but from the ambiguous pronoun reference, his identity is unclear. Possible candidates include the priest and her future husband, but her father seems the most likely possibility (37).

Por 19. Timson, Steven. "Katherine Anne Porter and the Essential Spirit: The Pursuit and Discovery of Truth in 'The Jilting of Granny Weatherall.'" *Kyushu American Literature* 27 (1986): 71–80.

While declaring Porter's style clear and direct, critics find much ambiguity concerning the themes of her stories (71). However, Edmund Wilson's discovery of an "essential spirit" in Porter's stories provides a starting point for analysis. In Porter this spirit is a search for truth; Porter's fiction focuses on the human condition, arguing that people need order and a sense of control over their lives, that they often distort the truth they search for, and that understanding is reached through self-awareness (71–72). Thus Granny is a woman who, after a bitter disappointment, attempts to find meaning in life and to control her life through order, only to discover that much resists ordering (72–73). At sixty she arranges her death (making farewell visits to her children and writing a will), and through her preparations she feels that she has wrested control over her death (73–74). But at sixty her death is not imminent; at eighty, when it is, she is not ready (74). The control she thought she had was an illusion. On her deathbed Granny waits for a sign from God but not, as critics have argued, a sign indicating the existence of an afterlife but rather a sign dispelling her fear that her life was futile (75). The lack of response is another rejection. The frequent references in the story to light symbolize Granny and her importance to the family. In their early years, her children, in order to reduce their fears, came to her as she lit the lamp; now as she nears death, the children have "become the keepers of the light" (75). At her dying moment Granny, in an apparent act of defiance, extinguishes the light, but ironically the act is also a surrendering to death (76). Although some critics view Granny's final act as an admission of failure, the conclusion is "about the discovery of a truth, however insignificant about ourselves" (77). Granny sought truth in her religion but found it in the self-awareness she achieved through her thoughts as she lay dying (78). When she blows out the light, she has reached an understanding of herself (79). **THEM**

Por 20. Wiesenfarth, Joseph. "Internal Opposition in Porter's 'Granny Weatherall.'" *Critique: Studies in Modern Fiction* 11 (1969): 47–55.

The story concerns order, a theme Porter used in some of her other fiction, specifically in "The Source," a short story about "women's need for order, the good that order effects, and the inconvenience it causes" (47). Granny's early experience of being jilted created the need for order in her life. She attempted to control her life to the extent that she thought that she could control her own death (49). However, the memory of George intrudes into her ordered world and disrupts her dying thoughts (50–51). The jilting is her first major disappointment; the second is Hapsy's absence; and the third is the absence of Christ at her deathbed (52). Overwhelmed by these abandonments, Granny blows out the light and dies (52). After being jilted, Granny mistakenly centered her life around order, forgetting that human attachment and contact are the essence of life (53). She never allowed herself to love again but "settled for ... order ... [and] in spite of showing great courage ... in spite of doing more than many another person might have done in similar circumstances, she has lived a less than truly satisfying life" (54). **THEM**

B.W.

"THE CHRYSANTHEMUMS"

Ste 1. Hughes, R.S. *Beyond the Red Pony: A Reader's Companion to Steinbeck's Complete Short Stories.* Metuchen, NJ: Scarecrow, 1987. Pp. 58–62.

"In Aristotelian terms, Elisa's discovery [of the abandoned flowers] constitutes a 'recognition scene' in which she acquires vital knowledge previously withheld from her. In addition, it brings about a 'reversal,' or change of fortune" in her feelings (59). The discovery is both surprising and also well prepared (59–60). Elisa is in some ways a Freudian "ego" attracted by the "id" the tinker symbolizes but repressed by the "super-ego" her husband represents (61). **ARIS, PSY, PLUR**

Ste 2. Hughes, R.S. *John Steinbeck: A Study of the Short Fiction.* Boston: Twayne, 1989. Pp. 21–27, 154–65.

The story was written February 1934, and Steinbeck himself considered it very subtly effective (21). Although most critics agree that its main theme is Elisa's frustration or repression, they suggest different sources, including a yearning for a better marriage, for spiritual or sexual satisfaction, for children, for a fulfilling woman's role, or for artistic appreciation (22). The story may have been based on Steinbeck's own first wife, who may have felt constricted; even her husband's sympathy may have seemed limiting (23). Steinbeck emphasizes Elisa's strength, energy, and obsession with household chores and perhaps implies that her marriage is unfulfilling and uneasy (23–24). Her static, stereotypical husband serves mainly as Eliza's foil: her reactions to him reveal her own complexity (24). Unlike the tinker, Henry never enters her garden, but the tinker's rambling, romantic life contrasts with her literally "fenced-in existence" (24–25). At first the chrysanthemum stalks suggest phalluses, and Elisa's enthusiastic cutting implies castration (25), while her later transplanting suggests sexual union (26). Although later still the blossoms suggest children and the flowering of creativity, Steinbeck wisely keeps the symbolism ambiguously suggestive (26). Imagery of the seasons, colors, and animals (especially dogs) is also effectively used; the dogs often mirror their owners (26–27). Steinbeck's objective, third-person viewpoint makes Elisa mysteriously ambiguous and highly memorable (27), while the story also suggests the limits imposed by traditional gender roles (27). **HIST, PSY, FORM, FEM**

Ste 3. Marcus, Mordecai. "The Lost Dream of Sex and Childbirth in 'The Chrysanthemums.'" *Modern Fiction Studies* 11 (1965): 54–58.

The story is almost perfect in form, style, rhythm, and suggestiveness, and Elisa is effectively ambiguous—both sexual and spiritual, feminine and masculine, passive and rebellious (54). The story provides evidence for Freud's ideas about bisexuality, penis-envy, and the individual yearning to feel "self-created" (55). At the beginning of the story, the plowed earth and Elisa's devotion to her flowers suggest her desire for children, and she is described in both feminine and masculine terms (55). Although at first she seems satisfied with her accomplishments and her husband's success, by the end of the story she realizes that she is unfulfilled (55). Despite the tinker's defects, he symbolizes the free life she desires; thus, although at first she keeps a masculine distance from him, increasingly she responds to him sexually (56). As he leaves, Elisa "feels the sexual and maternal triumph of having created her chrysanthemums [which function as substitute offspring] and sent them out into the world" (56). She alternates uncertainly between conventional and masculinized versions of femininity, trying to cope with her frustrated desire for children (57). Her attitudes toward her husband are ambivalent (partly because he fails to understand her complicated needs), and her response to the sight of the abandoned flowers is equally complex (57). Her desire to witness the fights suggests a need to see men punished, but she also wishes to punish herself for her failure as a woman (57). Finally she feels defeated and passive (58). The story appeals to a common human desire to repossess the world through sexual union and through having children (58). **PSY, THEM**

Ste 4. McMahan, Elizabeth E. "'The Chrysanthemums': Study of a Woman's Sexuality." *Modern Fiction Studies* 14 (1968): 453–58.

In explaining Elisa's frustrations, critics have overlooked her sexuality, which should not be confused with a desire for motherhood (453–54). Although her husband is thoughtful and successful, he and Elisa share little warmth or rapport, partly because he is prosaic and fails to appreciate her femininity (455). Bored with her life and marriage, Elisa desires romance and sexual satisfaction (455). The tinker seems more intuitive, eloquent, and adventurous than her husband, and although she resists his sales pitch, she is excited by his admiration for her flowers (456). She is embarrasssed when he fails to understand or respond to her "erotic mysticism" (457), and, feeling "shame after her display of passion before the stranger" (457–58), she "cleanses herself before returning to her husband, the man to whom she should lawfully reach out in desire" (457–58). She feels guilty and resolves to cope with her husband's insensitivity, but she despairs when she sees that the tinker has thrown away the flowers that symbolize her femininity (458). At first she feels a desire for revenge, then tries to settle for the small touch of romance suggested by the wine she and her husband will share (458). Finally, though, she feels defeated, as if any prospect "for romance has died" (458). **FEM, THEM**

Ste 5. Mellard, James M. *Four Modes: A Rhetoric of Modern Fiction.* New York: Macmillan, 1973. Pp. 272–77.

Objective description of dialogue, expression, and gesture make the story dramatic; the state of the couple's relationship must be inferred (273). Although both nature and Elisa are initially linked with activities of regeneration (274), Elisa herself needs regeneration (274). Her unemotional, highly structured dialogue with Henry already implies their flawed marriage (274). After encountering the tinker, she wants to be treated as an adult woman, but Henry "prefers instead to displace the more intimate relationship toward a safer, cooler one—dinner and a movie out" (277). The story ends with ironic disillusion, focusing on the abandoned flowers, the defeated Elisa, and an unchanged, dismal nature (277). **FORM, THEM**

Ste 6. Owens, Louis. *John Steinbeck's Re-vision of America.* Athens: University of Georgia Press, 1985. Pp. 108–13.

The story explores the sometimes unsuccessful "repression of powerful human impulses" in a "would-be Eden set in the fallen world of the valley" (109). Imagery links Elisa with a desire to achieve "deep fulfillment" (111) through "deep human contact and commitment, the most significant symbols of which are sex, childbearing, and sacrifice" (112). The imagery of blood and wine at the end of the story emphasizes the theme of "commitment through sacrifice" (112). Elisa, feeling isolated and sterile geographically, spiritually, and psychologically, yearns for a profound connection through which she can overcome her loneliness (112). The story is effective because it cannot be explained simply (113). **FORM, THEM**

Ste 7. Renner, Stanley. "The Real Woman Inside the Fence in 'The Chrysanthemums.'" *MFS: Modern Fiction Studies* 31 (1985): 305–17.

Feminist interpretations of the story fail "to square with its figurative design and structure, in which the female protagonist appears to be less a woman imprisoned by men than one who secures herself within a fortress of sexual reticence and self-withholding defensiveness" (306). Elisa's name suggests the Virgin Queen; she controls her enclosure and rebuffs not only her husband's efforts to enter but also his amorous advances (307). She rejects invitations to come out of her fenced-in enclosure (308–9). The flowers she grows symbolize her fruitlessness and infertility (309). Her cutting of the male stems symbolizes emasculation, just as Henry is linked with steers—castrated cattle (310). She fails to respond to his efforts to court her (311). The tinker succeeds in penetrating her barriers because she romanticizes him, and Steinbeck mocks her for doing so (313). By rejecting the imperfect reality of her husband in favor of a "patently falsified romantic fantasy, she defeats her own impulses toward a fuller life" (313). She shows a typically feminine resentment of "the direct genital nature of male sexuality" (314). The story criticizes her idealized rejection of reality (314). The calculating tinker exploits her romanticism, while she rejects her husband's prosaic sincerity (314) and his desire for a mutually fulfilling relationship (315). Elisa "invites her own exploitation" by the tinker (315). Steinbeck's letters suggest that he himself was sexually fenced out by his wife and felt bitter about her sexual reticence (315). The story expresses "traditional 'masculinist' complaints: against the sexual unresponsiveness of the female, against an ambivalent female sexuality that both invites and repels male admiration, against the woman's rejection of her biological role, against the sexual delicacy of the female who, repelled by sexual reality, holds out for indulgence of her emotional and spiritual yearnings, and ultimately against female control over the sexual relationship itself" (316). **THEM, HIST**

Ste 8. Sweet, Charles A., Jr. "Ms. Elisa Allen and Steinbeck's 'The Chrysanthemums.'" *Modern Fiction Studies* 20 (1974): 210–14.

Elisa is an incipient feminist who dresses and acts like a man and is dissatisfied with a woman's conventional role (211). When the tinker arouses her sexuality and causes her to behave in typically feminine ways, she begins to lose her earlier power (212). "Steinbeck seems to indicate that the sexuality inherent in woman prevents her from attaining equality" (212). The tinker exploits her financially and rejects her sexually; in the end her desire for equality has been broken, and she feels like an old woman (213). Elisa illustrates that defeats of feminist ideals of equality are rooted partly in the emotional nature of women (213). **FEM, THEM**

Ste 9. Timmerman, John H. *The Dramatic Landscape of Steinbeck's Short Stories.* Norman: University of Oklahoma Press, 1990. Pp. 169–77.

Steinbeck's obsession with the topic of the story may have made the composition of the work more difficult (169). Manuscript references show his preoccupation with the project and the various stages of the story's development (169–73). He softened the sexual suggestiveness of the work to make it more suitable for publication in *Harper's Magazine* (173). The final story shows how Elisa "has regimented her bursting creativity into rituals" (173) and also how she is pulled in two directions (174). In many details the tinker is her opposite, but even though she recognizes his deceitfulness, she is still attracted by the freedom he seems to represent (174). When she lets down her hair she symbolically shakes off her repressions (174), but when the tinker departs with the plant "she knows full well [it] is as doomed as her momentary dream" (175). Elisa symbolizes the repression both "of womanhood and of the artistic gift" (175). Although some critics have argued that Steinbeck presents Elisa unsympathetically, such a reading contradicts Steinbeck's sympathy for victims of repression (177). He depicts her as unfairly subjugated, not as egotistically self-assertive. "The personal disillusionment that Steinbeck felt at this point in his artistic career—the frequent rejections, the sense of loss of self worth, the overwhelming loneliness—is also the guiding motif in shaping Elisa's character" (177). **HIST, THEM**

Ste 10. Timmerman, John H. *John Steinbeck's Fiction: The Aesthetics of the Road Taken.* Norman: University of Oklahoma Press, 1986. Pp. 63–68.

Steinbeck deliberately tried to communicate different levels of meaning and evoke subtle emotion (63). Although the story can be read as focusing either on women's roles, rejection, or a realistic setting, it also explores the "artistic sensibility" (63). Elisa's world is literally closed-off (by fog and mountains), and whereas she is associated with energy, order, and beauty, the tinker seems slow, shabby, and philistine (64–65). The way Elisa works with flowers is analogous (for Steinbeck) to the way a writer works with a story, and because the tinker seems to appreciate both her creativity and her worth as a woman, she begins to feel romantically attracted (66). Her sight of the discarded flowers, however, dashes her dream of being valued both as an artist and as a strong woman (67). The story explores one of Steinbeck's favorite themes—freedom and constraint—and ends with Elisa retreating into her earlier repression (67). **HIST, THEM**

R.C.E.

"THE CELEBRATED JUMPING FROG
OF CALAVERAS COUNTY"

Twa 1. Branch, Edgar M. "'My Voice Is Still for Setchell': A Background Study of 'Jim Smiley and His Jumping Frog.'" *PMLA* 82 (1967): 591–612. Reprinted in David E.E. Sloane, ed., *Mark Twain's Humor: Critical Essays.* New York and London: Garland, 1993. Pp. 3–29.

Many of the tale's features can be related to some of the hundreds of newspaper articles Twain wrote in 1864 and 1865 and to "strong emotional currents in his life during the fall of 1865" (3). A friend named Ben Coon told a tale of a man named Coleman and his frog, which probably suggested the story's basic plot (4–5). Coon (in a later article by Twain) speaks in a tone like Smiley's (6), although Twain alone probably "conceived the full range of Smiley's love for betting and his paternalistic exploitation of talented animals" (7). The description of the nag may have been influenced by recent newspaper articles on horse-racing (8–10), while the sight of a three-legged dog at a freak show (and two famous fighting dogs from San Francisco [12]) may have helped suggest the similar creature in the story (10–11). Other aspects of Twain's tale may have been influenced by reality. Thus, in an 1864 editorial Twain praised the honesty of the Daniel Webster Mining Company (13); in 1865–66 he showed a fondness for the name Leonidas (14); he actually knew a man named Wheeler (15); and Artemus Ward was demonstrably on his mind as he conceived the story (16). Twain's tale, which may have been composed during 16–23 October 1865 (20), is a parable of his current state of mind (22). As individualists and humorists, Wheeler and Smiley possess traits Twain valued in himself, although he was then unsure whether to pursue the "new but risky direction" their examples suggested (24). The various social and political meanings critics have found in the tale were less important in shaping the story than were "past events experienced in San Francisco as well as in the mining camps, and certain tension-laden problems, closely connected with [Twain's] need to find himself, that were pressing for immediate resolution" (24–25). **HIST, THEM**

Twa 2. Covici, Pascal, Jr. *Mark Twain's Humor: The Image of a World*. Dallas: Southern Methodist University Press, 1962. Pp. 48–52.

The story relies on strategies of indirection, repetition, equality of emphasis, and attention to detail (49–50). Its humor derives mainly from Wheeler's "apparent failure to discriminate between the real and the fabulous, or between the important and the trivial" (50). Twain shows contempt for the narrator; both the narrator and Wheeler underplay the significance of Wheeler's narrative method, which is the real source of the story's interest (51). "A large part of the story's appeal lies in the reader's pleasure in discovering that he himself belongs to the poker-faced fraternity that sees through the characteristic [poker-faced] pose of the western storyteller" (51). **FORM, READ-R**

Twa 3. Gerlach, John. *Toward the End: Closure and Structure in the American Short Story*. University, AL: University of Alabama Press, 1985. Pp. 65–69.

Twain distinguished comic stories (which are brief and end with a clever point) from humorous stories (which can ramble and seem inconclusive and in which the comedy consists in the manner of narration). Anyone can tell a comic story, but humorous stories (such as this one) require more skill and art (61). The story achieves an effectively casual tone, and although the narrative seems driven by random thoughts, it reveals a "submerged sense of sequence" (62) that relies partly on events that seem increasingly insignificant (63). Twain writes with "controlled indirection," achieving "order beneath apparent disorder" (64); the work displays a "step-by-step progression ... from an account of the actual to fiction, from reliable testimony to an account probably intended to gull the listener, just as the frame narrator had been gulled. The true subject of the story is storytelling itself, the teasing way a story involves us, makes us part of its world" (64–65). We respond less to the sense of the words than to the rhythm and imagination they display (65). Delaying the ending is crucial to this kind of indirect tale; the art of the work lies in its apparent artlessness (65). **READ-R, FORM**

Twa 4. Krause, S.J. "The Art and Satire of Twain's 'Jumping Frog' Story." *American Quarterly* 16 (1964): 562–76.

The story's apparent simplicity is ironic, partly because it uses implied social symbolism. For instance, social satire is suggested by giving the names "Andrew Jackson" to the dog and "Dan'l Webster" to the frog. In addition, the story's complex form offers at least eight levels of interest or points of view: (1) the narrator's attitudes toward his friend from the East, toward Simon Wheeler, and toward the stranger; (2) Wheeler's attitudes toward the narrator, the Eastern friend, Easterners

at large, Jim Smiley, animals, and the stranger; (3) Wheeler as a representative of the West; (4) the attitudes of the stranger toward other
characters; (5) Clemens' attitudes toward the characters; (6) Smiley's attitudes; and the attitudes of (7) the bull-pup and (8) the frog. In addition, "Twain employs an order of increasing details and of ascending
absurdity and fantasy" (564). The movement from mare to pup to frog
also involves movement toward greater complexity, surprise, and personality. Wheeler's story involves satire of the East at large and of the
narrator in particular; the narrator "stands somewhat in the relation to
Wheeler that Smiley does to the stranger" (566), since both are mocked.
The characters are appropriately named: Wheeler is a "free-wheeling
yarn-spinner," while Smiley is an optimistic gambler and Westerner
(567). The names "Andrew Jackson" and "Dan'l Webster" suggest the
conflict between West and East, and between a frontier Republican and
a representative of Whig capitalism. The pup's pugnacity, confidence,
willpower, gambling spirit, and "self-made" qualities reflect aspects of
Andrew Jackson's reputation. The real Daniel Webster resembled
Twain's frog "in appearance, conservatism, education, jumping com-
placeny, cupidity, and worth" (573). The "story favors Jackson over
Webster, despite the satire on *both* men" (575). **FORM, HIST**

Twa 5. Lynn, Kenneth S. *Mark Twain and Southwestern Humor.*
Boston: Little, Brown, 1960. Pp. 145–47.

The original tale may have been told by slaves ("the slyness with
which the defeat of the champion is managed" suggests this), but by the
time Twain arrived out West it had become popular in the mining
camps and published in various newspapers (145). Twain added the
frame story (145); the tone of its narrator is similar to (but less formal
than) the familiar Self-controlled Gentlemen of Southwestern fiction
(146). By cunningly adopting the role of a Western simpleton, Wheeler
cons the sophisticated visitor, reversing the usual pattern of Southwestern plots (146). By calling the dog Andrew Jackson, Twain seemingly
ridicules a president he never admired, but his decision to name the
frog Daniel Webster suggests that Twain is not taking political sides: his
story "rejects the [political] past altogether, and turns toward the West
and the future," endorsing democracy by mocking notions of superiority (147). Although the story shows the triumph of the "underfrog," it
also shows that Twain hadn't yet resolved the problem of how to characterize his own narrative voice (147). **HIST, FORM, THEM**

Twa 6. Mellard, James M. *Four Modes: A Rhetoric of Modern Fiction.*
New York: Macmillan, 1973. Pp. 22–25.

Since the frame, narrators, plot, and characters are all conventional,
the story's strength depends on its clarity of form and the strength of
Twain's style (22–23), including his use of inventive similes and com-

parisons (23) and his use of recurrences signalled by repetitions, especially the repeated bettings and the reiterated introductions of new creatures (24). The abrupt ending effectively breaks these cycles (25). **FORM**

Twa 7. Michelson, Bruce. *Mark Twain on the Loose: A Comic Writer and the American Self.* Amherst: University of Massachusetts Press, 1995. Pp. 27–32.

Twain's works often subvert and play with literary conventions and readers' expectations, undermining even our most basic assumptions about what and how words mean (27). Therefore, any attempt to interpret a Twain sketch inevitably simplifies it, thus exposing the inadequacies of interpretation (27). This story is structured like a series of nesting dolls, with each narrative containing another (28); partly for this reason, the text cannot "be stabilized and fully understood" (29). The story calls each participant's "reality" into question (including the reader's) and thus creating a sense of absurd uncertainty (31). "If the narrator wonders what he is doing, in hearing and then retelling this evidently pointless tale, then the reader's situation is even odder, precisely because it is taken up voluntarily" (31). "Mark Twain's comic West is a world where the self that is founded on psychological consistency, logic, decipherable speech and behavior, on education even loosely based in values of a too-civilized world, is a self jammed full of quailshot, a self that cannot move" (32). Yet even to say this is to risk trying to make sense of a story that consistently subverts any such attempt (32). **DECON, READ-R**

Twa 8. Rodgers, Paul C., Jr. "Artemus Ward and Mark Twain's 'Jumping Frog.'" *Nineteenth Century Fiction* 28 (1973): 273–86.

Critics have offered various explanations of the relations between Wheeler's tale and the frame that surrounds it, mainly disagreeing about whether the frame narrator is a fool or is only pretending to be (273–76). When one recalls that the story was originally addressed by Twain to the humorist Artemus Ward, whose deadpan comic style Twain greatly admired, one realizes that both Wheeler and the frame narrator himself are using that style (277). Twain was closely involved with Ward at the time the story was written, and in fact Ward hoped to include it in a collection he was editing (277–82). Twain had several options for dealing with the frame narrator (282–84), but the one he chose was elaborate: to present to his favorite deadpan humorist (Ward) "the spectacle of a deadpan humorist solemnly recounting how a second deadpan humorist recalled how one deadpan gambler was outwitted by a second" (284). In subsequent criticism, however, Ward's original "function as Twain's audience was ignored" (285). **FORM, HIST**

Twa 9. Schmidt, Paul. "The Deadpan on Simon Wheeler." *Southwest Review* 41 (1956): 270–77.

In previous southwestern humour, the author identified with the frame narrator, using the frame to distance himself from the vernacular story-teller (271). By mocking the frame narrator, Twain innovates, mocking not only the conventions of local-color writing but also the presumed superiority of genteel culture (271). Simon Wheeler "deliberately assumes the role of an unconscious barbarian as a play upon his visitor's preconceptions and with the intention of turning the tables on him" (272). Wheeler is completely aware of what he is doing; he only plays stupid to mock the visitor's cultural prejudices (272). Among the prejudices the story mocks, for instance, are romantic and "humanitarian sympathy for the Noble Animal" (273), "romantic individualism, the doctrine that the individual is free *by nature*" (273), romantic ideas of "pastoral modesty" (274), and romantic illusions about education as a means to progress and about the nobleness of poverty (275). Twain prized the values of relaxed friendliness represented by Wheeler, whose language implies his familiarity with brotherhood achieved through common work (276). The genteel frame narrator, on the other hand, represents an egotistical, competitive individualism, and in turning away from Wheeler at the end, he turns away from brotherhood (277). **HIST, FORM, THEM**

Twa 10. Smith, Lawrence R. "Mark Twain's 'Jumping Frog': Toward an American Heroic Ideal." *Mark Twain Journal* 20.1 (1980): 15–18.

Critics have debated whether Simon Wheeler is implicitly and deliberately making fun of the narrator or is simply telling a pointless tale (15). The tale is highly meaningful, but Twain does not adopt a narrow ideological position (15). Rather, he uses the story to depict a conflict between "the false and the true" and to "define and explore just what is true and valuable about Simon Wheeler and the qualities he represents" (15). "What results from the whole tale is a synthesis of the best American traits: shrewdness, a spirit of enterprise and aspiration in Jim Smiley and his animals, and in the stranger the skeptical pragmatism necessary to keep the other characteristics within a useful and realistic framework" (16). Wheeler shows a trickster being tricked even as he himself tricks the pretentious narrator, particularly by exploiting the narrator's "ignorance of country life" (16). Apparently the narrator does not realize, for instance, that frogs have no chins, cannot scratch their heads with their legs, and cannot be picked up by the neck (17). "Like the unimposing Simon Wheeler, Jim and his animals prefer to look harmless, hiding their wit and power until the proper moment. They forego a desire for, or a trust in, show and appearance for the superior benefits of strategy" (17). Although Twain depicts Smiley and his animals attractively, the stranger, functioning as "a dispenser of reality therapy ...., necessitates a reevaluation, and perhaps a tempering of extravagant optimism" (18). Smiley's deception by the stranger challenges "the American ideal of the shrewd, aspiring common man, which Twain has presented as an amalgam of the images of Daniel Webster and Andrew Jackson" (18). That ideal only works "if it is combined with a healthy portion of the skepticism, realistic outlook, and pragmatism of the stranger" (18). All lessons are lost, though, on the uncomprehending narrator, who learns nothing from the tale (18). **THEM, HIST**

Twa 11. Wonham, Henry B. *Mark Twain and the Art of the Tall Tale.* New York: Oxford University Press, 1993. Pp. 67–68.

Twain wrote three different versions of the story. In the first a naive narrator listened reverently to Wheeler's inventive tale (67). In the second an urbane, ironic narrator condescended to Wheeler (67). Neither version involved any dramatic conflict of perspectives (67). The final version, however, achieves such conflict. "What Twain sought after two false starts was a plausible and realistic drama of performance through which to relate the fictional storyteller to his fictional listener" (68). In this unprecedented story, it is "the drama that unfolds between these two competing imaginations, and the contrast between their chosen media, that fuels the sketch with interest and ignites its satire" (68). **HIST, FORM**

R.C.E.

JOHN UPDIKE

"A&P"

Upd 1. Dessner, Lawrence Jay. "Irony and Innocence in John Updike's 'A&P.'" *Studies in Short Fiction* 25 (1988): 315–17.

Although Sammy generally underrates life's dangers (especially as they affect others), at the end he comically overrates them (315). In his evaluations of others, he shows little sympathy or empathy, instead displaying "the guileless narcissism of youth" (316). Ironically (but typically), he exaggerates the importance of losing his job (317). **THEM**

Upd 2. Detweiler, Robert. *John Updike.* New York: Twayne, 1972. Pp. 67–69.

Sammy's brash vernacular is an effective counterpoint to the romanticism and sentimentality of his final gesture, and Updike's alternation "between the past and historical present tenses" provides "a tight little dramatic episode that his fiction does not often exhibit" (68). "Since the tale builds upon an increasing tension of embarrassment, the play-by-play technique of the present tense description heightens the precise moments of strain and offers the reader, at the same time, a vicarious participation" (68). One of Updike's few comic tales, the story uses humor rooted in clever phrasing, irony, incongruous action, and tightly controlled pathos (68). The ironic comments made about the girls expose the limitations of those who make them, but in his final act Sammy "achieves a new integrity, one that divorces him from his unthinking conservative environment and leaves him ... with a loneliness that signals his birth into alienation" (68). Sammy is capable of this gallant act because he is as yet untainted by the need to compromise (68). "Bare beauty could brighten even the A & P; but since it is dangerously out of place there, it must be exorcised to safeguard" rigid conventional propriety (69). **FORM, THEM**

Upd 3. Emmett, Paul J. "A Slip That Shows Updike's 'A&P.'" *Notes on Contemporary Literature* 15.2 (1985): 9–11.

Although Updike is sometimes accused of superficiality, details in his work are often meaningful (9). At first, for instance, Sammy claims to be occupying the third check-out slot; when the girls are ready to check out, he seems to be speaking from the first (9–10). The claim that slot three is "unmanned" is not Updike's slip but is instead an unconscious reflection of Sammy's doubts about his own manhood, which he then attempts to display by quitting (10). "Indeed, self-doubt resulting in overcompensation, the imaginary journey from unmanned to hero, can be seen repeatedly beneath the dancing surface of Sammy's narration" (10). He wants to believe he is number one, and this need implies his immaturity and reveals him as an unreliable narrator (10–11). **THEM, FORM**

Upd 4. Goss, Marjorie Hill. "Widening Perceptions in Updike's 'A&P.'" *Notes on Contemporary Literature* 14.5 (1984): 8.

The story shows "how human perceptions may widen" by showing Sammy's "moral development"; noticing McMahon's reaction to the girls, Sammy sees "his own meatmarket outlook virtually parodied" and begins to think differently. As Lengel speaks to the girls, Sammy presumably ponders; his decision to quit indicates an abandonment of his earlier sexism. **THEM, FEM**

Upd 5. Greiner, Donald J. *The Other Updike: Poems/Short Stories/Prose/Play*. Athens: Ohio University Press, 1981. Pp. 117–19.

Although Sammy is recalling the incident, his tone is not nostalgic but brashly colloquial (117). His sense of heroism stimulated, he performs a "quixotic gesture," covering his "sentimental act" with "brash slang" (117). Although his act is "mildly moving," he learns that "no one welcomes or even tolerates idle idealism" (118). **THEM, FORM**

Upd 6. Hurley, C. Harold. "Updike's 'A&P': An 'Initial' Response." *Notes on Contemporary Fiction* 20.3 (1990): 12.

Many of Updike's first readers would have known that "A&P," besides being the name of a grocery store (and thus a symbol of middle-class culture) was a common abbreviation for college classes in anatomy and physiology. **HIST**

Upd 7. Luscher, Robert M. *John Updike: A Study of the Short Fiction*. New York: Twayne, 1993. Pp. 35–37.

Although the story's flowing, fast-paced narrative and cocky narrator are unusual for Updike, the hints of nostalgia, the conflict between "romance and realism," and the "bittersweet" final tone are not (35). Sammy's individualism makes him sympathetic, but by the end he is still somewhat immature (35). Although he tries to be a hero, his treatment of women is initially condescending; he is more impressed with Queenie's status and body than with her character (36). Still, he does begin to appreciate the girls as persons as the story progresses, and while "his defense of the girls may be motivated by a combination of lust, admiration for Queenie's social status, and sentimental romanticism," his defense of them "is not without principle and quickly assumes more serious overtones" (36). His resignation is the logical result of his growing distance from the conventional world of the A&P (36). Sammy rejects self-pity; instead, he uses the experience to prepare himself for future disappointments (37). **THEM, FORM**

Upd 8. McFarland, Ronald E. "Updike and the Critics: Reflections on 'A&P.'" *Studies in Short Fiction* 20 (1983): 95–100.

Although critical comment on Updike has often been patronizing (95), Sammy and his story have been praised, partly because both are accessible to students (96). Yet the story's ambiguity and irony also make it effective, and Updike uses references to brand-names creatively and meaningfully (97). Sammy is a less appealing protagonist than some critics have suggested: he lacks self-perspective, sensitivity, maturity, and compassion (99). Yet he achieves a kind of heroism by following through on his (initially egotistical) impulse; finally he is both "victor and victim" (99). Updike's refusal to simplify Sammy helps account for the story's popularity (99). **FORM, THEM**

Upd 9. Petry, Alice Hall. "The Dress Code in Updike's 'A&P.'" *Notes on Contemporary Literature* 16.1 (1986): 8–10.

Although the story illustrates Updike's uncanny ability to describe contemporary American life with remarkable accuracy, the details usually contribute to the meaning of his fiction (8). The fact that the girls are nearly naked makes them seem natural, in contrast with the artificiality of the store (9). When Sammy shrugs off his apron he implies "physical and emotional freedom" (9), and the details of Updike's description of the act suggest Sammy's purity (the white shirt) and sense of personal identity (emphasized by "my" [9]). Appropriately, his rejection of artificial confines is symbolized by his removal of clothing (9). The story emphasizes contrasts between naturalness and artificiality (10). **THEM, FORM**

Upd 10. Uphaus, Suzanne Henning. *John Updike*. New York: Ungar, 1980. Pp. 124–27.

The story "derives its impact from the narrative voice, comic contrast, and the ironic distance between the intentions of the protagonist and what he actually accomplishes" (124). Updike uses "present tense for dramatic impact" (124) and shows, as in much of his fiction, that "the heroic gesture is often meaningless and usually arises from selfish rather than unselfish impulses" (125–26). Sammy's blunt tone prevents the story from seeming too sentimental (126), although the work ends by emphasizing his sense of alienation (127). **FORM, THEM**

Upd 11. Wells, Walter. "John Updike's 'A&P': A Return Visit to Araby." *Studies in Short Fiction* 30 (1993): 127–33.

Updike's story was influenced by James Joyce's "Araby": even the titles sound alike, and both deal with a young man's romantic self-delusion and subsequent disillusionment (128). Although Sammy's tone is more graphic and explicit, both boys associate attractive girls with queens and with whiteness, and both become distracted (128–29). Both girls behave seductively, but in Updike's story materialism is even more strongly emphasized (especially since Updike ironically echoes a passage from Bunyan's *Pilgrim's Progress* [129–31]). As in Joyce's story, the boy offers the girl a gift—in Sammy's case, "an assertion of principle" (132). Both boys experience epiphanies of disappointment, and both stories suggest the irrelevance of chivalry in the modern world (132–33). However, whereas Joyce's narrator is older and wiser, Updike's Sammy has not yet achieved distance from his disillusionment (132–33). **THEM, HIST**

A.C.L. and **R.C.E.**

"EVERYDAY USE"

Wal 1. Baker, Houston A., Jr., and Charlotte Pierce-Baker. "Patches: Quilts and Community in Alice Walker's 'Everyday Use.'" *The Southern Review* 21 (1985): 706–20.

Quilts and quilting can be seen as attempts to make sense out of chaos, to make a whole out of pieces (706). Quilting, an effort to fashion out of fragments a usable, functional product (713), is often a community undertaking; patterns are handed down and skills are transferred from one generation to the next, thereby connecting the generations (713). Another link is provided by the stories told in the patterns or those associated with specific fabric pieces (713). In "Everyday Use," quilts serve as a metaphor for the creative process, represent the creations of unknown artists who worked with available materials, and indicate the importance of belonging to a community (713–14). The three women in Walker's story are survivors who have attempted to make whole lives out of scraps (714). Dee, the returning daughter, always concerned about style, now appreciates her heritage because it is currently fashionable to be black (716). Dee, accepting "institutional theories of aesthetics," does not value the handmade quilts until they are in vogue (716). She represents "that longing for the 'other' that characterizes inhabitants of oppressed, 'minority' cultures" (717). Even the mother, who is proud of her ability to kill a hog, is drawn to that "other," but she ultimately understands the difference between exploiting one's heritage and living it, as does Maggie, her other daughter (717). Maggie, scarred by a fire and eclipsed by Dee, is "the arisen goddess ... who bears the scarifications of experience and knows how to convert patches into robustly patterned and beautifully quilted wholes" (718). Maggie, taught to quilt by her grandmother and aunt, preserves tradition and functions as a link between generations (718). On the other hand, Dee, not understanding tradition or heritage, wants to appropriate the quilts for display; thus, she takes from the community but does not give anything in return (718). The mother, in insisting that Maggie have the quilts, recognizes Maggie's role as a bearer of their heritage (719). And Maggie, in receiving the quilts, smiles because she realizes that more than quilts have been conferred (719). The story shows that women's ability to quilt is tantamount to the ability to make a whole out of fragments, order out of chaos. In addition, while quilting is generally a women's skill, the quilt is a gift to the whole community, including its males (720). **THEM, MULTI**

Wal 2. Bauer, Margaret D. "Alice Walker: Another Southern Writer Criticizing Codes Not Put to 'Everyday Use.'" *Studies in Short Fiction* 29 (1992): 143–51.

The subtitle of Walker's collection of short stories *In Love and Trouble—Stories of Black Women*—is misleading because her fiction "achieves universal appeal" (143). Walker shares traits with major writers such as William Faulkner, Katherine Anne Porter, Eudora Welty, and Flannery O'Connor and, like them, should be seen as a Southern writer and not labeled as a black woman writer (143). Walker's story "The Child Who Favored Daughter," is comparable to Faulkner's *The Sound and the Fury*, since both criticize the Southern code which assigns oppressive roles to women and blacks (146); Walker's "The Diary of an African Nun" can be paralleled with Porter's "The Jilting of Granny Weatherall," since both fault Christianity with its emphasis on salvation rather than on a satisfying, fulfilling life (147–48); Walker's "The Welcome Table" is similar to Welty's "A Worn Path," because both contain strong women characters who are considered unstable by others (148); and Walker's "Entertaining God" resembles O'Connor's *Wise Blood*, since both explore "man's tendency to worship a false god" (149). "Everyday Use" is compared briefly to several O'Connor stories, including "Good Country People" (150). Daughters in these stories view arrogantly their home and family. In Walker's story Dee does not achieve self-awareness, but her mother, understanding her heritage, bestows handmade quilts on her other daughter, who not only appreciates the tradition but lives it (151). Walker, like the other writers, fights against the Southern traditions and codes that oppress and exploit the individual (151). **MULTI, THEM**

Wal 3. Byrne, Mary Ellen. "Welty's 'A Worn Path' and Walker's 'Everyday Use': Companion Pieces." *Teaching English in the Two-Year College* 16 (1989): 129–33.

Welty's "A Worn Path" and Walker's "Everyday Use" share points of comparison that can be explored in college classrooms (129). Both stories contain elderly black women as protagonists, are set in the rural South, and concern journeys. The journey of Welty's protagonist Phoenix Jackson to a town to obtain medicine for her grandson is a universal, mythic journey fraught with many obstacles (129–30), and, more important, it is a journey made out of love. The journey in Walker's story is that of the narrator's daughter Dee returning home to acquire everyday household items that have become fashionable. In contrast to

Phoenix's, her journey is undertaken for selfish reasons (130). The narrator in Walker's story and Phoenix in Welty's are both identified by their roles in the family or by their association with home (130). Both value the education they, being black, did not receive and are aware of the power of the white community (131). Phoenix, in her encounters with whites, acquires what she needs (131). The narrator of "Everyday Use," although encountering no whites, expresses her trepidation (131). Both stories are set in the rural South. However, in Welty's story Phoenix is seen as part of nature whereas the narrator in Walker's must subdue nature and control it (131). The differences between the two stories are most evident in their narrative strategies (132). Welty tells the story in third person, enabling the narrator to establish a distance from Phoenix (132). Thus the narrative voice, educated and sophisticated, can indulge in poetic language that would be inappropriate for Phoenix. Walker's narrator is a mother whose language is less educated. Her comparisons refer mostly to nature and animals, things within her ken (132). Both stories emphasize the importance of the family, of loving relationships, and of an acceptance of hard work. And both stories allude to the oppression of blacks (133). The main difference between the stories lies in the choice of the narrator. Welty's third-person narrator allows for a distance that promotes the mythologizing of Phoenix (133), whereas Walker's first person narrator helps present an intimate portrait of the mother (133). **FORM, THEM**

Wal 4. Callahan, John F. "Reconsideration: The Higher Ground of Alice Walker." *The New Republic*, September 14, 1974, pp. 21–22.

One of Walker's strengths as a writer is her concern with the wholeness of an individual, a wholeness which includes being responsible for one's actions (21). Another strength is her documentation and exploration of the pain of black women who have to confront not only racism but also the sexism of black men who turn against women as a counter to their own oppression (21). The characters in Walker's fiction who endure are the ones who receive and give love and are aware of the importance of their black heritage (21). The stories in the collection *In Love and Trouble*, set in the rural South, present the variety and the "complexity of pain and beauty ... in black Southern lives" (22). They are also concerned with tradition and black culture. The mother in "Everyday Use" recognizes Dee's sudden appreciation of the handmade quilts as fleeting and consequently presents them to Maggie, who has never veered from her heritage (21). In "To Hell with Dying," the old man wills to the narrator his steel guitar, symbolizing his spirit (22). Part of Walker's effectiveness as a writer comes in her ability to portray accurately both female and male sensibilities (22). **THEM, MULTI**

Wal 5. Christian, Barbara T. "Alice Walker: The Black Woman Artist as Wayward." In *"Everyday Use" by Alice Walker*. Ed. Barbara T. Christian. New Brunswick, NJ: Rutgers University Press, 1994. Pp. 123–47.

One recurring theme in Walker's novels, short fiction, essays, and poems is the importance of the creativity of the black woman to herself and to her community (123); a second is the importance of change even though it is often accompanied by pain (124). Walker merits praise for her courage in supporting unpopular positions, such as her appreciation for African-American heritage rather than African (125), her insistence that blacks assume more responsibility for their lives rather than accept victimization (127), and her acknowledgment of sexism in the black community (136). In "Everyday Use," the quilt represents both "idea and process" (128). As a process, the quilt symbolizes how Walker "creates out of seemingly disparate everyday materials patterns of clarity, imagination, and beauty" (128). As an idea, the quilt illustrates the artistry of black women who, with limited resources, were able both to express their creativity and to contribute to their community (129). The quilt, as an example of female heritage, establishes links between generations as knowledge of quilting and the stories that accompany the quilts are passed down. In "Everyday Use" Walker examines "the use and misuse" of one's heritage and questions the motives of those who, in the seventies, suddenly accepted their black roots (129). For Dee, the desired quilts have no meaning beyond the value acquired from being fashionable. By changing her name to Wangero, Dee denies her relationship to her grandmother Dee, the maker of the quilts (129). On the other hand, Maggie truly appreciates the quilts, partly because she herself can quilt and partly because the quilts are a reminder of her grandmother (130). **FEM, MULTI, THEM**

Wal 6. Kane, Patricia. "The Prodigal Daughter in Alice Walker's 'Everyday Use.'" *Notes on Contemporary Literature* 15 (1985): 7.

"Everyday Use" can be seen as a variation of the Biblical story of the prodigal son (7). Dee, the returning child, has suddenly acquired an appreciation for the things she once rejected (7), specifically two quilts that have been promised to her sister Maggie for her upcoming marriage (7). But Dee's appreciation is based on the current fashion rather than on an acceptance of her heritage. The mother, in rejecting Dee's claim and returning the quilts to Maggie, "bestows the riches of her domestic kingdom not on the prodigal but on the familiar daughter" (7). **THEM**

Wal 7. Kelly, Margot Anne. "Sisters' Choices: Quilting Aesthetics in Contemporary African-American Women's Fiction." In

"Everyday Use" by Alice Walker. Ed. Barbara T. Christian. New Brunswick, NJ: Rutgers University Press, 1994. Pp. 167–94.

Quilting is important in works by Alice Walker, Gloria Naylor, and Toni Morrison. The colors and designs of African fabrics have influenced quilts by African-Americans. These quilts have distinct differences from the standard–traditional quilts sewn by Anglo-Americans (169). Strips of fabric are utilized, thus leading to large and often abstract patterns (171); strong contrasting colors are used instead of harmonious ones placed on a neutral background (172). In addition, there is an element of improvisation as the quilter varies the pattern in sometimes startling ways (173). Such quilts contain stories that represent the history of a family; thus the quilts form a link between generations, especially generations of women (169). Quilting provides a motif that is prevalent in fiction by African-American writers; it offers "the promise of creating unity among disparate elements, of establishing connections in the midst of fragmentation" (176). **HIST, MULTI**

Wal 8. Korenman, Joan S. "African-American Women Writers, Black Nationalism, and the Matrilineal Heritage." *CLA Journal* 37 (December 1994): 143–61.

African-American women writers have sometimes reacted negatively to their marginalization by black males in the civil rights movement (143). Black nationalism has been seen as a "threat to the matrilineal heritage. The search for African roots is shown to ignore—and thus efface—the mothers, aunts, and grandmothers whose lives constitute a vigorous African-American legacy" (144). Various works by Alice Walker, Toni Cade Bambara and Gloria Naylor "depict conflicts between well educated black nationalist daughters and their 'politically incorrect' mothers" (144). The mothers, treated sympathetically by the authors, have never become estranged from their roots and their heritage. In "Everyday Use" Dee, the black nationalist daughter, returns home to acquire items that have become fashionable because of the black nationalist movement (145), items that are part of the narrator's and her other daughter's lives. Dee's lack of understanding of her heritage is epitomized by her changing her name (146). Ironically, Dee rejects her black ancestors when she, acquiring an African name, thinks she is identifying with her race (153). Her forebears have become as invisible to her as they were to their "white oppressors" (146). Walker is not rejecting black nationalism entirely but only its "tendency ... to glorify blacks' African roots at the expense of the African-American heritage" (147). The negative appraisal of black nationalism found in the three authors is a reaction to the times. The sixties and seventies witnessed the rise of the contemporary women's movement, and women resented their marginalization by black males in the civil rights movement (155), a rejection that not only erased their contribution and experience but also their mothers' and grandmothers' (155). Unlike many Anglo-Americans, black daughters respected and valued their mothers and grandmothers for their enduring strength (156): "Everyday Use" begins with the dedication "for your grandmama." This work and similar stories conclude with a positive image of the mother/daughter relationship (157). In "Everyday Use" the narrator and her younger daughter Maggie sit together and just enjoy each other's company (157). These stories celebrate women and their heritage and reject the aspects of black nationalism that denigrate their contribution (161). **FEM, MULTI, HIST**

B.W.

"TO HELL WITH DYING"

Wal 9. Hollister, Michael. "Tradition in Alice Walker's 'To Hell with Dying.'" *Studies in Short Fiction* 26 (1989): 90–94.

"To Hell with Dying," a story about love, depicts an old man, Mr. Sweet, who (often near death) requires "reviving" and a narrator who (from the time she is a young girl) does the "reviving" (90). Mr. Sweet receives the narrator's love and responds in kind: he "revives the endangered capacities of the soul" (90). Sweet, whose ambitions as a young black man were discouraged, has acquired the traditionally feminine qualities of gentleness and empathy (91). The narrator, who is able to pursue her dreams, becomes a doctoral student in the North; however, she has lost touch with her spiritual roots (91). But her capacity for feeling has not atrophied, as is evident in her quick return home when she learns of Mr. Sweet's need (91). Mr. Sweet follows in the tradition of redeemers, blind seers, and mystics (91–92). Walker views Christ as a "female spirit," and in "To Hell with Dying" she feminizes the redeemer figure, Mr. Sweet (92). However, instead of using the term *feminist*, Walker prefers *womanist*, which she sees as not excluding men; for example, gentleness is possible and desirable in both genders (92). Instead of emphasizing gender, the story promotes "universalist" values of love and generosity (92–93). Walker, following in the style reminiscent of an oral tradition that can also be found in Twain and Zora Neale Hurston, undercuts values that are promoted in the traditional culture—values such as ambition and competition—and substitutes other qualities—such as love and emotion (93). **THEM**

Wal 10. Michelson, Anne Z. "Winging Upward: Black Women: Sarah E. Wright, Toni Morrison, Alice Walker." In *Reaching Out: Sensitivity and Order in Recent American Fiction by Women.* Metuchen, NJ: The Scarecrow Press, 1979. Pp. 112–74.

Being black and female is essential to Wright, Morrison, and Walker as writers (112), and the struggle to survive in white America colors their fiction (113), as can be seen in Walker's novel *Meridian* and her short story collection *In Love and Trouble* (which includes "To Hell with Dying"). The collection illustrates Walker's concern for the fight of blacks, especially women, against oppression, her interest in their striving for dignity, and her admiration of the old who have endured against great odds (154). "To Hell with Dying" reveals the importance in the narrator's life of old Mr. Sweet, who taught her about "tradition, love, the past, joy of living, a sense of black people as complete, healthy, undiminished" (159). The effectiveness of Walker's stories lies in their "truthfulness to individualistic experience," which contributes to their universality (160). **MULTI, THEM, FEM**

Wal 11. Washington, J. Charles. "Positive Black Male Images in Alice Walker's Fiction." *Obsidian II: Black Literature in Review* 3.1 (1988): 23–48.

Critics who fault Walker for negative portrayals of black males neglect to emphasize that the negative images are balanced by many positive portraits of black males in her fiction (23–25). Walker wrote in *In Search of Our Mothers' Gardens*, a collection of essays, that she is "preoccupied with the spiritual survival, the survival whole of my people," thereby providing evidence that she is committed to understanding both black men and women (26). Thus her frequent focus on the oppression of black women should not be read as an anti-male bias (26). Instead, Walker's concern is with women taking control over their own lives and creating a stable identity (27). The act of self-definition does, in a patriarchal society, pit men against women, and the success of women does result in a diminution of men's power over them (27). Even though traditional gender roles oppress women, Walker is more concerned about the oppression that occurs when an individual does not take responsibility for his or her life (28). Although *The Color Purple* and *The Third Life of Grange Copeland* contain negative male characters, the men in Walker's collection of short stories, *In Love and Trouble*, can be read as positive (29)—that is, as exhibiting "the potential for growth, development, and change" (25). Thus the woman in "Really, Crime Does Not Pay" is more responsible for her own victimization than is her husband, who, although limited by his acceptance of the tenets of a patriarchal society, bases his actions on love (38). Similarly, in "To Hell with Dying," the goodness of Mr. Sweet is unquestioned. As critics have suggested, old men in Walker's fiction are generally positive. Walker agrees, suggesting that old people who have survived racism and other forms of oppression have much to teach the young (39). The story moves from Mr. Sweet's old age to his death and from the narrator's youth to her development as a young woman (41). As a young adult, she pursues doctoral work at a Northern university, but when summoned, she returns home immediately to revive Mr. Sweet, but this time his death is out of her control (41). He bequeaths to her his guitar, a symbol of unvanquished spirit, the last of many gifts to her (41). When she was a young girl, he contributed to her sense of self and to her understanding that she controls her own life (41). He fostered in her a "positive image of adults" (44) and now, through the gentle nature of his own death, he reduces her fear of death (44). His life provides an example for her. Though thwarted by racism in his early ambitions, he controlled his life, making choices from what was available, taking responsibility for his actions, and never losing his spirituality (45–46). Walker is drawing upon two traditions in her work: the classical Greek with its emphasis on the power of art to increase human potential (47) and the African tradition with its belief that "art is functional, collective and committing and committed" (48). Any criticism by Walker of black males is intended to alleviate problems and is made out of love (48). **FEM, MULTI, THEM**

B.W.

"A WORN PATH"

Wel 1. Byrne, Mary Ellen. "Welty's 'A Worn Path' and Walker's 'Everyday Use': Companion Pieces." *Teaching English in the Two-Year College* 16 (1989): 129–33.

Although "A Worn Path" and "Everyday Use" share similarities in theme, setting, and character, variances result from differences in the races of the authors (129). Both portray main characters who are elderly black women, both focus on family values, and both involve journeys (129). The journey in "A Worn Path," as Welty herself has pointed out, is fundamental to the story, introduces an allegorical level, and is done out of love (129). The journey in Walker's story, however, is undertaken by the daughter Dee for the selfish motive of acquiring family heirlooms (130). Both protagonists are associated with home. However, in "A Worn Path" the references to Phoenix as "Granny" and "Grandma" by white characters derogate her, but the frequent mention of her name by the narrator restores her status (130). Other similarities include the following: both protagonists recognize the value of an education although they did not receive one (130), both are marginalized by the white culture (131), and both stories have rural settings (131). However, in "A Worn Path" Phoenix is part of nature, whereas in "Everyday Use" the mother must exact a living from nature (131). Although the similarities are many, the foremost difference lies in the choice of the narrator (132). In Walker's story, the narrator is the mother, whose uneducated voice limits the perspective of the story (132). But in "A Worn Path," the story is related by a third-person narrator who is able to understand more than Phoenix, providing a distance that establishes a universal, mythical quality to the story (132). Through her choice of a third person narrator, Welty herself understands her own distance from black experience (133). **FORM, MULTI**

Wel 2. Donlan, Don. "'A Worn Path': Immortality of Stereotype." *English Journal* 62 (1973): 549–50.

Although Phoenix Jackson has been viewed by some readers as a stereotype, she can instead be seen as a symbol of immortality—an interpretation supported by many allusions to death within the story

(549). Phoenix undertakes her journey in winter, the season traditionally associated with death, and encounters dead birds and trees. Although she is surrounded by death, Phoenix is alive (549). In addition, frequent mention of her old age again suggests immortality (549). Finally, Phoenix's name recalls the mythical bird that renews itself (549). Additional allusions to the myth are present: the colors of gold and red mentioned in an early description of Phoenix, her manner of walking, her retrieval of the hunter's nickel as though it were an egg, and the frequent references to birds (550). Being aware of the symbolic level adds richness to an already effective story about human experience (550). **THEM, FORM**

Wel 3. Gardner, Joseph H. "Errands of Love: A Study in Black and White." *The Kentucky Review* 12 (Autumn 1993): 69–78.

Phoenix's blackness, a conscious choice by Welty, is essential to the narrative (69). Welty makes several assumptions concerning her protagonist, most related to her identification of Phoenix with the universal and mythic (70). Because her journey is described as "an errand of love," Phoenix illustrates the culture's assumption concerning the strong maternal love of black women (71). She also exemplifies the belief that blacks are closer to nature than whites, a belief that suggests the myth of Rousseau's Noble Savage (71). The assumed primitiveness of blacks allows for the justification of their exploitation, but it also can lead to the view that blacks are unsullied by civilization (71). Phoenix's lack of education is seen as positive, for it allows her to remain knowledgeable in folk wisdom and untarnished "by the rationalism of the European (i.e., white) Enlightenment" (73). Even though she desires medicine, a product of technology, she herself is part of "an animistic, magic realm" (73). As she journeys to town, she moves from the mythic and universal into an inferior domain where materialism and Santa Claus rule (73). When compared with Alice Walker's "Strong Horse Tea," Welty's story seems based on racial stereotypes. The differences between the landscapes and weather, the names of the protagonists, their relationship to animals, their physical appearance, their treatment by whites, and the different outcomes of their journeys, all point to Welty's acceptance of cultural assumptions about blacks (74–77). Walker, being black, has a more realistic view of black experience whereas Welty substitutes "mythic grandeur" for reality (78). **HIST, MULTI, ARCH**

Wel 4. Lewis, Thomas N. "Textual Variants in 'A Worn Path.'" *Eudora Welty Newsletter* 16 (1992): 11–13.

Although Welty made sixty-four changes between the story's first publication in *The Atlantic Monthly* and its inclusion in her short story collection *A Curtain of Green*, their effects are "slight" (12). **HIST**

Wel 5. Orr, Elaine. "'Unsettling Every Definition of Otherness': Another Reading of Eudora Welty's 'A Worn Path.'" *South Atlantic Review* 57 (1992): 57–72.

Although few critics have discussed the white attendant's labeling of Phoenix as a "charity case" at the conclusion of the story, the silence it engenders in Phoenix is crucial to understanding the story (57). The story is more than an account of Phoenix's journey; it is also "a complex analogy of fabulation—of invention, discovery, and subjective expansion" (57). The reader must solve the puzzle that is posed by Phoenix's character, discarding assumptions and entering into a new awareness (57). Some passages suggest an alternative reading of Phoenix, one that undercuts the stereotypes. The incident with the white hunter, for example, shows how Phoenix takes the man's assumptions and uses them to write her own version, redirecting his own assumptions against him and, in the process, acquiring what she wants, a nickel (58). Not accepting his version of herself—one that implies that she is simple-minded—she creates her own selfhood, her own subjectivity (58). The claim that Phoenix's acquisition of the medicine for her grandson signals closure for the story, or that the story is an example of love and selfishness, is a misreading and one that is mired in stereotypical assumptions about race and gender (59). Moreover the story itself does not support such a reading (59). Instead, the incident with the hunter helps explain the events of the conclusion (60). Phoenix, through her actions, challenges the assumptions of the attendant and nurse and of the reader as well (60). Indications that the story is not as straightforward as it appears lie in the selection of the name Phoenix for the protagonist and in the many contradictions that occur within the story (61). For example, although she is described as almost blind, she spots the nickel and identifies it as such (61). The title refers not to Phoenix's journey but to the reader's who, in reading the story, encounters obstacles to maintaining past beliefs (62). The first challenge comes in understanding the hunter, who, as tradition would have it, is the typical hero (62). But Phoenix undercuts his stature: her journey is more important than his (62). Another challenge comes with Phoenix's language, which is more sophisticated than critics and readers have assumed. She engages in word play and in a type of language called "doubletalk" in which the real meaning is hidden beneath the actual speech, a type of speech that marginalized groups, such as blacks and women, often employ with the dominant group (63). The inattentive reader can be likened to the hunter, one who misses the meaning because he or she is unwilling to discard past assumptions (64). Phoenix's encounter with the nurse in town is similar to her encounter with the hunter; both view Phoenix in terms of their own assumptions, marginalizing Phoenix (65). The hunter is blinded by his racism and sexism, and the nurse by her racism and classism (66). The nurse and the attendant expect Phoenix to behave humbly like "a charity case" and maternally like a grandmother (66). They attempt to define her, but through her silence, she resists their definition (67). When Phoenix does answer, she parodies their expectations, acting the role of the humble black woman (68). And the reader who has accepted the acquisition of the medicine as the reason for her journey is also being parodied (68). Emphasizing her control over her own selfhood, Phoenix manipulates the woman into giving her a nickel (69). Phoenix, like the mythic bird, creates herself (68). She questions the dominant culture's beliefs about women and blacks (69). Welty, in her story, undercuts the assumptions that keep marginal groups subordinate (70). **THEM, MULTI, READ-R**

Wel 6. Phillips, Robert L., Jr. "A Structural Approach to Myth in the Fiction of Eudora Welty." In *Eudora Welty: Critical Essays.* Ed. Peggy Whitman Prenshaw. Jackson: University Press of Mississippi, 1979. Pp. 56–67.

Although other critics argue that Welty begins with the myth and then grafts it on to a Mississippi setting, Welty starts with Mississippi and sees in it a mythic dimension (56). Welty discovers in her characters from Mississippi a universal quality (57) that has its roots in fantasy and myth (58). Welty typically uses myth in three different ways (58). In the first way, references and allusions are made to myths, but the characters themselves are unaware of the added dimension (59). "A Worn Path" falls into this category (60). The story began not with the Phoenix myth but with Welty's sighting one wintry day an old woman walking in the distance (60). To that image Welty added a narrative line and references to myths and legends (60). Allusions to Phoenix, the bird that renews itself, abound, but also, as other critics have pointed out, there are echoes of the myths of Aeneas, Persephone, Demeter, and Adonis among others (60). The protagonist, Phoenix, is not aware of the parallels, but the reader is, and this awareness adds another dimension to the story (60). Welty also utilizes myth so that reality itself seems to be questioned (61). In this second way, myths and legends figure predominantly in a story (61) which is set in "a symbolic, even allegorical, landscape full of mythical men and strange beasts" (63). Still, however, the characters are unaware of the added mythic dimension (64). But in the third way that Welty uses myth, the characters understand their part in the mythic tradition (64), recognizing their place in the history of myth (67). The reader, in order to understand Welty's fiction to the fullest, must be cognizant of the mythic level (67). **ARCH**

Wel 7. Porter, Katherine Anne. "Introduction." *A Curtain of Green and Other Stories* by Eudora Welty. 1941. New York: Harcourt, Brace and World, 1970. Pp. xi–xxiii.

Reminiscences about meeting the young Eudora Welty (xi) precede discussion of Welty's family and education and her beginnings as a writer (xii–xiv). Welty did not study creative writing in college but came by it naturally (xv). Welty shows a lack of interest in political systems (which often negate the individualistic impulse) and she also adheres to a strong moral code (xvi). Some of the stories contained in the volume "offer an extraordinary range of mood, pace, tone, and variety of material" (xix). "A Worn Path" contains a mixture of dream and reality (xxi). Even though Welty's writing style is straightforward, her themes are complex (xxiii). **HIST, FORM, THEM**

Wel 8. Robinson, David. "A Nickel and Dime Matter: Teaching Eudora Welty's 'A Worn Path.'" *Notes on Mississippi Writers* 19 (1987): 23–27.

The passage in which Phoenix encounters the white hunter, sees him drop a nickel, and distracts him in order that she might pick up the nickel is open to several interpretations (24). For example, either the hunter knows he dropped the nickel, or he realizes it only when he sees her pick it up, or he never knows (25). The most plausible reading is the last. The hunter stereotypes Phoenix and patronizes her, never realizing that his attitude enables Phoenix to profit (26). But because of the hunter's attitude, the reader excuses Phoenix's theft of the nickel. Welty is providing a comment on racism (26). **THEM**

Wel 9. Saunders, James Robert. "'A Worn Path': The Eternal Quest of Welty's Phoenix Jackson." *The Southern Literary Journal* 25 (1992): 62–73.

"A Worn Path" has occasioned various interpretations, having been seen, for instance, as a religious quest or as an examination of the deterioration of the protagonist Phoenix as she wrests with senility and oncoming death (62–63). Phoenix, however, shares a universal quality with Dilsey of Faulkner's *The Sound and the Fury* (65) and with Vyry in Margaret Walker's *Jubilee* (66). Contributing to her universality are several traits. The first is her oneness with nature, which is implied by the fact that the elements assist her in her journey: the thorny bush does "not harm the garments of an essential sister," and the dead trees salute her (67). Second is her overwhelming love: she "is the designated protector of another worthy innocent" (69). The third is her perseverance (71). **THEM**

Wel 10. Walter, James. "Love's Habit of Vision in Welty's Phoenix Jackson." *Journal of the Short Story in English* 7 (1986): 77–85.

Phoenix's love supplies the center of the story (77). Her love, based in Christianity, carries her forward as she patiently and persistently overcomes the obstacles she encounters along her journey (79–80). Her silence at the conclusion is a result of the attendant's questions, which force her to consider her own troubles; consequently she "withdraws into self-preoccupation" (82). But moments later she recovers and vows never to forget her grandson again (82). The reader is made to confront his or her own assumptions. Faced with a Phoenix who seems stereotypical, the reader misreads the story until the conclusion forces a reevaluation (83). **THEM, READ-R**

Wel 11. Welty, Eudora. "Is Phoenix Jackson's Grandson Really Dead?" *The Eye of the Story: Selected Essays and Reviews*. New York: Vintage Books, 1979. Pp. 159–62.

Eudora Welty discusses "A Worn Path" and specifically responds to the question she is most often asked: Is the grandson alive? Answering affirmatively, she points out that the narrative line and the story's aesthetics suggest his continuing existence (159–60). Welty continues her discussion of the story, pointing out that Phoenix's journey and her love for her grandson are the essential elements of the story (160) and identifying the catalyst as being her once viewing an old woman walking in the distance on a wintry day (161). She concludes by suggesting that the task of writing is similar to Phoenix's journey. In other words, writing is a struggle to arrive at meaning, a journey accomplished with the aid of "imagination ... dreams and bits of good luck" (162). **HIST, THEM**

B.W.

APPENDIX

APPLICATIONS:
DIVERSE RESPONSES TO KATE CHOPIN'S
"THE STORY OF AN HOUR"

with contributions by
Kathleen B. Durrer, Scott Johnson,
Barbara Larson, Jonathan Wright
and by
Lara Bridger, Randall Cobb, Mike Cunliffe, Foster Dickson,
Amanda Higgins, Mary Mechler, Dianne Russell,
and Geni Williams

One good way to grasp a literary theory is to see it in action—to witness how it might be applied to a particular work. Kate Chopin's brief tale "The Story of an Hour" provides excellent material for such a litmus test. Chopin's work, composed in 1894, typifies the style and concerns of an author famous mainly for her great novel *The Awakening*. Yet the present story is not only brief and clear but also compelling and complex, and it easily lends itself to a variety of critical approaches. In the text printed below, the passages numbered and highlighted in boldface are ones that actual students were asked to analyze as part of a final examination in a course in literary criticism. Some passages from the story are approached from single perspectives; others are approached from several varying points of view.

Excerpts from some of the student responses (keyed to the numbered passages) are printed following the story itself. These responses, of course, are meant to be suggestive rather than definitive; they are meant to show, for instance, not how *a* feminist critic *would* react to a particular passage but rather to suggest how *one* feminist reader *might* respond to a specific selection. For this reason, more than one response to each passage has been provided whenever possible. Critics adopting the same basic theoretical approach often reach divergent interpretations of identical data, and the diverse student responses reprinted here are intended to illustrate that fact.

"THE STORY OF AN HOUR"

by Kate Chopin

Knowing that Mrs. Mallard was afflicted with a heart trouble, great care was taken to break to her as gently as possible the news of her husband's death.

It was her sister Josephine who told her, in broken sentences; veiled hints that revealed in half concealing.[1] Her husband's friend Richards was there, too, near her. It was he who had been in the newspaper office when intelligence of the railroad disaster was received, with Brently Mallard's name leading the list of "killed." He had only taken the time to assure himself of its truth by a second telegram, and had hastened to forestall any less careful, less tender friend in bearing the sad message.

She did not hear the story as many women have heard the same, with a paralyzed inability to accept its significance. She wept at once, with sudden, wild abandonment, in her sister's arms. **When the storm of grief had spent itself**[2] she went away to her room alone. She would have no one follow her.

There stood, facing the open window, a comfortable, roomy armchair. **Into this she sank, pressed down by a physical exhaustion that haunted her body and seemed to reach into her soul.**[3]

She could see in the open square before her house the tops of trees that were all aquiver with the new spring life. The delicious breath of rain was in the air. **In the street below a peddler was crying his wares.**[4] The notes of a distant song which some one was singing reached her faintly, and countless sparrows were twittering in the eaves.

There were patches of blue sky showing here and there through the clouds that had met and piled one above the other in the west facing her window.

She sat with her head thrown back upon the cushion of the chair, quite motionless, except when a sob came up into her throat and shook her, as a child who has cried itself to sleep continues to sob in its dreams.

She was young, with a fair, calm face, whose lines bespoke repression and even a certain strength. But now there was a dull stare in her eyes, whose gaze was fixed away off yonder on one of those patches of blue sky. It was not a glance of reflection, but rather indicated a suspension of intelligent thought.

There was something coming to her and she was waiting for it, fearfully. What was it? She did not know; it was too subtle and elusive to name. But she felt it, creeping out of the sky, reaching toward her through the sounds, the scents, the color that filled the air.

Now her bosom rose and fell tumultuously. **She was beginning to recognize this thing that was approaching to possess her, and she was striving to beat it back with her will—as powerless as her two white slender hands would have been.**[5]

When she abandoned herself a little whispered word escaped her slightly parted lips. **She said it over and over under her breath: "free, free, free!"**[6] The vacant stare and the look of terror that had followed it went from her eyes. They stayed keen and bright. Her pulses beat fast, and the coursing blood warmed and relaxed every inch of her body.

She did not stop to ask if it were or were not a monstrous joy that held her. A clear and exalted perception enabled her to dismiss the suggestion as trivial. **She knew that she would weep again when she saw the kind, tender hands folded in death; the face that had never looked save with love upon her, fixed and gray and dead. But she saw beyond that bitter moment a long procession of years to come that would belong to her absolutely.**[7] And she opened and spread her arms out to them in welcome.

There would be no one to live for her during those coming years; she would live for herself. **There would be no powerful will bending hers in that blind persistence with which men and women believe they have a right to impose a private will upon a fellow-creature.**[8] A kind intention or a cruel intention made the act seem no less a crime as she looked upon it in that brief moment of illumination.

And yet she had loved him—sometimes. Often she had not. What did it matter! What could love, the unsolved mystery, count for in face of this possession of self-assertion which she suddenly recognized as the strongest impulse of her being!

"Free! Body and soul free!" she kept whispering.[9]

Josephine was kneeling before the closed door with her lips to the keyhole, imploring for admission. "Louise, open the door! I beg;

open the door—you will make yourself ill. What are you doing, Louise? For heaven's sake open the door."

"Go away. I am not making myself ill." No, she was drinking in a very elixir of life through that open window.

Her fancy was running riot along those days ahead of her. Spring days, and summer days, and all sorts of days that would be her own. She breathed a quick prayer that life might be long. It was only yesterday she had thought with a shudder that life might be long.[10]

She arose at length and opened the door to her sister's importunities. There was a feverish triumph in her eyes, and she carried herself unwittingly like a goddess of Victory. She clasped her sister's waist, and together they descended the stairs. Richards stood waiting for them at the bottom.

Some one was opening the front door with a latchkey. It was Brently Mallard who entered, a little travel-stained, composedly carrying his gripsack and umbrella. He had been far from the scene of accident, and did not even know there had been one. He stood amazed at Josephine's piercing cry; at Richards' quick motion to screen him from the view of his wife.

But Richards was too late.

When the doctors came they said she had died of heart disease—of joy that kills.[11]

---

1. *"It was her sister Josephine who told her, in broken sentences, veiled hints that revealed in half concealing."*

Barbara Larson: A FEMINIST critic might respond negatively to this sentence, not only because it implies the stereotype of the "weaker sex" but also because that stereotype is reinforced by another female character. This last problem might be particularly troubling to the feminist critic, since the reference to "sister" could have suggested a deeper, even more positive sense of sisterhood if the words that followed had not presented the character as weak and tentative. Her "broken sentences" reflect the unease with which she accepts the role of messenger. The word "veiled" implies a stereotyped feminine delivery, while the word "hints" suggests that the recipient of the message will be unable to accept the straight truth. Indeed, the phrase "revealed in half concealing" reiterates that inability. **Kathleen B. Durrer**: A FEMINIST critic might decry this presentation, ... since, despite the story's feminist theme and female author, Josephine represents the stereotype of women as weak, ineffectual, and emotional. Whether she is motivated by a desire to avoid the unpleasant or by a fear of Louise's reaction, Josephine is portrayed as weak. Had the story been written by a man, a feminist critic might argue that Josephine illustrates male writers' tendencies to portray women as characters who are unable to confront reality directly and who must therefore resort to "broken sentences" and "veiled hints" in ineffectual efforts to convey news that is best delivered quickly and concisely. **Amanda Higgins**: Even the diction seems to stutter, mirroring a common perception of women as being unable to communicate effectively and without hysteria. A **FEMINIST** critic might be especially disturbed by the fact that this stereotypical vision of women was penned by a woman, since Chopin would thus be providing further evidence that patriarchy has programmed even feminist writers to remain within certain acceptable limits in depicting female behavior. **Dianne Russell**: A **FEMINIST** critic might cringe when reading this sentence because it implies that Josephine is chosen over Richards to bear the tragic news simply because she is a woman. Because our patriarchal society teaches us that women are more emotionally supportive and nurturing than men, it comes as no surprise that Chopin depicts Josephine as knowing how to relate the news *gently* to Mrs. Mallard, using "broken sentences" and "veiled hints" to soften the shock.

2. *"When the storm of grief had spent itself ..."*

Kathleen B. Durrer: An **ARCHETYPAL** critic might respond to this phrase by highlighting the reference to "the storm." Storms have often been used to symbolize tremendous outpourings of emotion, the cleansings of the spirit that must occur after powerful disturbance before life can continue. Coupling this image with "grief" calls to mind the various rituals of grief that have existed throughout history. All societies have developed formal ways to acknowledge grief, thereby suggesting to an archetypal critic that this need is innate and universal. **Barbara Larson**: An **ARCHETYPAL** critic might respond to this phrase by arguing that it evokes a universal response from the audience. Since almost all humans have had repeated personal experiences with storms, almost any audience would react to the word "storm" by imagining a violent commotion or outburst of passion, and the word "grief" would similarly convey to anyone the common emotion resulting from a deep sorrow caused by a painful loss. In this phrase, Chopin thus draws on experiences and reactions to which almost all human beings can relate. **Dianne Russell**: An **ARCHETYPAL** critic might appreciate this passage not only because grief is an emotion that can seem uncontrollable and that afflicts people of all races, cultures, and genders, but also because a storm similarly stimulates feelings that all people can share. **Amanda Higgins**: By using an **ARCHETYPAL** image associated with powerful natural forces, Chopin implies that Mrs. Mallard grieves adequately and sincerely, not easily shrugging off her husband's death. **Lara Bridger**: An **ARCHETY-PAL** critic would appreciate Chopin's use of an archetypal image both to portray and to elict an emotional response. The "storm" image evokes both the fear of destruction and the promise of re-newal. A reverence for nature (a force beyond human power) is in-stinctual, and it informs Louise's intense emotion as she confronts the overwhelming power of her own nature. As Louise's shelter, or marriage, is destroyed by her husband's death, the "storm" of her inner turbulence indicates the destruction of old ideas. Ulti-mately, as the archetype also implies, a cleansing effect results. Louise's "storm of grief" washes away the emotional deadwood of her marriage and allows her to begin anew. **Mike Cunliffe**: An **ARCHETYPAL** critic might note that in Mrs. Mallard's case, the storm descends, unleashes its downpour, and then vanishes. Louise's storm is brief and singular; it spends itself totally, not to return. Moreover, Chopin's use of the storm image is archetypally appropriate in another way. The end of a storm generally brings sunshine and tranquility, just as Louise experiences calm after her thoughts turn from her husband to herself.

3. *"Into this she sank, pressed down by a physical exhaustion that haunted her body and seemed to reach into her soul."*

Kathleen B. Durrer: A Freudian **PSYCHOANALYTIC** critic might respond to this report by arguing that Mrs. Mallard's physical ex-haustion is evidence of the tremendous battle occurring in her un-conscious mind. Louise is experiencing a powerful conflict of the three zones of her mind—the id, the ego, and the superego. Pre-sumably she has led a sexually repressed life, as was not uncom-mon among women in traditional households of her time. Her re-action to her husband's death may imply that their marriage did not abound in sexual passion. A Freudian critic might focus on Louise's presumed sexual repression and argue that the news of

Brently's death touched off an internal battle in her unconscious mind. Upon learning the news, the id might immediately begin scheming to take control, to seize the freedom offered by Brently's death and begin a quest for pleasure. The superego, however, might be appalled by the thought of any pleasure being derived from the death of a husband and might fight to impose the proper social behavior expected of a grieving widow. The ego, of course, would attempt to mediate between these two extremes in order to prevent a complete mental breakdown from resulting. Although Louise is not aware of the battle raging within her unconscious, it physically exhausts her. **Barbara Larson**: A Freudian **PSYCHOANALYTIC** critic might note that almost every word in this sentence can suggest feminine sexuality, especially "sank," "pressed down," "her body," "reached into her soul," and "physical exhaustion." Here, however, the sexuality is passive and implies domination. **Lara Bridger**: A Freudian **PSYCHOANALYTIC** critic might contend that Louise's marriage has imposed such strict limitations on the expression of her deepest desires that a violent release of primal energy is now inevitable. **Geni Williams**: A Freudian **PSYCHOANALYTIC** critic might respond to this sentence by arguing that it almost seems as if Mrs. Mallard has been controlled by her superego for most of her life. She has had to strive for social perfection: to be the perfect wife, to be the perfect upper-class wife, and to be the perfect woman in general. Now that these pressures have subsided, it is almost as if the adrenaline has stopped pumping through her body and exhaustion has set in.

4. *"In the street below a peddler was crying his wares."*

Barbara Larson: A MARXIST critic might note how this sentence tacitly reflects the class power structure of Chopin's day. By placing the vendor in "the street below," Chopin reminds us of the social distance between the vendor who is below and the potential buyer who is above. By calling the vendor a "peddler," Chopin encourages us to view the seller as a wanderer, thus underscoring the "lower class" connotations of his profession. The mere presence of a figure "crying his wares" reminds the audience that the lower class does not have the means to visit distant stores and select expensive items of their choice; instead, they must accept whatever is available from the "peddler" on the street. A Marxist critic might see such phrasing as reflecting the author's own position of relative power in the socio-economic structure of her day.

Kathleen B. Durrer: A MARXIST critic might respond to this sentence by noting that it provides evidence of the class structure of Chopin's America. The fact that Louise looks down on the street might imply her social superiority and condescension toward the working class that provides for her day-to-day needs. Although the Mallards' social class is not explicitly stated, the story suggests that they are members of the upper class. Their financial status is implied in the description of their home, since Louise looks out on an open square from a comfortable, roomy chair in her second-floor bedroom. Her status is also implied by her complete lack of financial concerns as she contemplates her future. A Marxist might contrast the social condition of a street peddler in the late 1800s with the social condition of the Mallards and might assert that such inequity typifies the evils of capitalism. **Amanda Higgins:** A MARXIST critic might view such a sentence as an impediment to social progress because it uses the image of the peddler merely as an ornament, to create a mood, thereby underemphasizing the real hardship inherent in being a member of a lower socioeconomic class. **Lara Bridger:** A MARXIST critic might suggest that Louise, as a member of the upper class, is aware of, but unconcerned with, the peddler. She gazes out the window from her over-stuffed chair, rediscovering her identity, as the peddler diligently struggles to fuel an economy which affords Louise's self-indulgent contemplation. Conversely, the peddler is never afforded personal identity but is defined only as a member of the working class. **Dianne Russell:** A MARXIST critic might note how casually this sentence assumes that the existence of different social classes is the norm and will always be the norm. The existence of such a class system is made to seem as inevitable as the weather.

Kathleen B. Durrer: A DECONSTRUCTOR might respond to this sentence by emphasizing the contradictions inherent in its phrasing. Perhaps a deconstructor would focus, for instance, on the relationship between the words "peddler" and "crying." At first glance the relationship seems clear, because a peddler must sell items on the street; he must "cry" or orally advertise his goods. Therefore "crying" might be seen as a tool the peddler uses to accomplish his role in life. However, "crying" may also subtly suggest a public voice raised in protest or an inarticulate utterance of distress, rage, or pain. Therefore, instead of signifying a relationship of tool to job, "crying" and "peddler," taken together, may imply the pain or injustice of the peddler's lowly position in life.

Or perhaps a deconstructor would focus on Mrs. Mallard's elevated position and the peddler's lower position and argue that although the story appears to concern Mrs. Mallard's freedom from repression, she is still repressed by her social status. Therefore, her subordination to Mr. Mallard has only been replaced by her subordination to the dictates of upper-class society. The peddler, on the other hand, despite his lowly status, has more real freedom than Mrs. Mallard because society does not mandate his behavior to the degree that it mandates hers. **Barbara Larson:** A DECONSTRUCTOR might use this sentence to illustrate the inevitability of a multitude of interpretations being offered of any text, whatever meaning the author may have intended. Although this sentence does not seem particularly important to the story as a whole, by exploring various possible interpretations of it, a deconstructor could argue that it typifies the instability of all language. Perhaps the author included the sentence to remind the audience that while the main character is faced with a monumental event in her life, for others life goes on as usual. A reader, on the other hand, might view the introduction of the peddler as a distraction from grief or as an annoyance to one who is suffering. Another reader might see the peddler as more free than Louise, while another might see Louise as more free than the peddler. Still another reader might see Louise as a person who has just escaped one kind of oppression but who is herself implicated in the oppression of the peddler. A deconstructor would not fear such conflicting interpretations but would instead see them as evidence of the unstable meanings of any text. **Lara Bridger:** A DECONSTRUCTOR might emphasize the inconsistencies embedded in this sentence. Apparently the sentence implies that the peddler is "below" Louise, both literally and figuratively. He hawks his wares in the street while Louise relaxes in the safety of her home. However, while seemingly at a disadvantage, the peddler is a male and a participant in the economy, while Louise must depend on the financial support of her husband. The peddler's presence might suggest a similarity between these two oppressed persons, but their genders and different economic positions also create an unresolved friction. The peddler, as a male, participates in the oppression of Louise; Louise, as a member of the upper class, participates in the oppression of the peddler. A deconstructor would probably see this contradictory relationship as inevitable in a text which is, by its very nature, instrinsically unstable.

5. *"She was beginning to recognize this thing that was approaching her, and she was striving to beat it back with her will—as powerless as her two white slender hands would have been."*

Kathleen B. Durrer: LONGINUS might respond to this sentence by recognizing Kate Chopin's talent for using beautiful, powerful language to express Louise's feelings. Chopin's phrasing is concise yet manages to create a vivid image in the minds of her readers. Longinus advocated the use of "elevated language" to transport an audience, and he felt that to achieve the "sublime," a writer must use noble diction and dignified, elevated composition. A word such as "striving" and a phrase such as "white slender hands" add touches of sublimity here. **Barbara Larson:** Although the style of this sentence is not particularly elevated, LONGINUS would probably approve nonetheless because the phrasing does have the potential to capture the audience and sweep it dramatically along. By presenting the unseen invader so mysteriously, Chopin enthralls the audience and gives the passage a somewhat frenzied quality. By using such words as "approaching," "possess," "beat," "will," and "powerless," Chopin demonstrates her ability to use language to captivate her readers. Even the length of the sentence is worth noting, and the simile, full of adjectives, heightens the audience's response to the author's words. **Lara Bridger:** LONGINUS might consider this sentence a sublime illustration of Louise's sublime moment of inspiration. Louise's "possession" by a powerful force epitomizes Longinus's belief in the overwhelming power of beautiful truths. Louise, confronted with the truth of her nature, cannot resist possession by it.

Kathleen B. Durrer: A FEMINIST critic might object to this passage if it were analyzed as a single sentence, separated from the story as a whole, because this sentence portrays Louise as both mentally and physically weak (a typical stereotype of women at the turn of the century). Louise is presented as mentally weak because she lacks the needed will power to combat "this thing" that is approaching her. Louise is also presented as physically weak because her "two white slender hands" would probably be "powerless" to defend her from a physical assault. Both images reinforce the stereotype that women are unable to deal effectively with threats in their world. Women allegedly needed to be shielded from the harsh reality of the world and protected by males, who supposedly were both physically and mentally stronger. However, within the context of the story as a whole this passage might be applauded by a feminist critic because it serves to "set up" the reader for the shocking revelation that follows. The passage helps to convince the reader that Louise is the typical weak and submissive woman of her time. This image, however, is then shattered in the paragraphs that follow. The overall effect is a startling, perhaps shocking, yet insightful look into the feminine psyche and might thus be praised by feminist critics. **Barbara Larson**: A **FEMINIST** critic might object to this sentence not only because the character is portrayed as timid and as hesitant to welcome or even accept her new-found freedom, but also because the author's words seem to support the stereotype of the "weaker sex" to the detriment of women in general. Because the author in this case is herself a woman, a feminist might find such phrasing especially painful. By using the phrase "beginning to recognize," Chopin implies that a woman such as Mrs. Mallard could hardly conceive of a freedom such as she now faces. It is a "thing" unknown to her. The phrase "this thing that was approaching her" almost suggests that this future freedom seems a threatening monster of some sort, an impression reinforced by her "striving to beat it back." Emphasizing that both ("two") hands would not be enough to defend Mrs. Mallard, Chopin goes even further by describing the hands as "slender" and "white," implying that they have known little work or hardship and can provide no effective resistance. On the one hand, a feminist critic might be bothered by Chopin's perpetuation of the stereotype of a weak female; on the other hand, such a critic might argue that Chopin shows how such weakness inevitably results from the kind of sheltered life forced upon Mrs. Mallard and other women like her.

6. *"She said it over and over under her breath: 'free! free! free!'"*

Kathleen B. Durrer: A **READER-RESPONSE** critic might react to this sentence by acknowledging that different audiences might respond to it differently. For example, the majority of Chopin's contemporaries in 1894 would probably have considered her story rebellious and revolutionary in its questioning of traditional women's roles. However, another audience, consisting of women in the 1890s who were struggling for greater rights and freedom, might have viewed Louise's outburst as an inspirational rejection of a woman's traditional role. Even today, Chopin's words can elicit different reactions from different kinds of readers. Many women readers, for instance, can probably sympathize with Louise's desire for freedom. Many men, however, would probably be repelled by the idea of a woman rejoicing that her marriage has ended, especially by a tragic accident. However, the wide range of potential reader response need not be limited by differences in sex. A woman of the religious right, for example, might also react negatively to Louise's words, viewing them as degrading to the institution of marriage. Similarly, many other reactions can be imagined from many different kinds of readers. **Barbara Larson**: One kind of **READER-RESPONSE** critic might react to this sentence by noting how Chopin uses her powers of persuasion to encourage readers to respond as the author wishes. By using the phrase "She said it over and over," Chopin hints that the words have become a consoling mantra for the bereaved widow, thus implying a positive interpretation of them. The words "under her breath" might also encourage the reader to feel an intimacy with Louise and thus regard her sympathetically, since the reader is allowed to share a very personal moment. Likewise, by placing exclamation marks after each use of "free," Chopin may be encouraging the reader to share Louise's excitement about this new-found liberty. Of course, different kinds of readers may have differing reactions. One sort of reader, for instance, might be repulsed by the secret joy (expressed "under her breath") this woman feels at the death of her spouse. Reader-response critics, then, might try to show how Chopin *attempts* to shape her readers' responses, although these critics concede that no author can ever exercise absolute control over the text she creates. **Dianne Russell**: A **READER-RESPONSE** critic might suggest that different readers might respond in differing ways to this sentence. For instance, a man who has never been oppressed would be unlikely to respond to the sentence in the same way as a woman who had spent her life under the rule of a strict, domineering father and then under the control of a strict, domineering husband. Such a woman would fully understand Louise's feeling of emancipation.

7. *"She knew that she would weep again when she saw the kind, tender hands folded in death; the face that had never looked save with love upon her, fixed and gray and dead. But she saw beyond that bitter moment a long procession of years to come that would belong to her absolutely."*

Barbara Larson: A **DIALOGICAL** critic might note that although this passage relates Mrs. Mallard's thought processes to the reader, it also exemplifies a dialogue between the voice of her old life as a subservient wife and the voice of her new life as an independent woman. One voice (the widowed Mrs. Mallard) remembers her role as a recently married woman, while the other voice (the single Louise Mallard) recognizes that the time for sustained grieving is over. The words "tender hands" and "never looked save with love" are obviously provided by the woman who at least thought she was content with her married life. The phrase "fixed and gray and dead" is somewhat neutral and serves as a transition to the voice of the newly liberated Louise, who looks forward enthusiastically to a life without marital bonds. The words "that bitter moment" is a final concession to the voice of the old life before the new voice finally echoes far into the future by referring to "the long procession of years to come that would belong to her absolutely." By presenting this diversity, Chopin also perhaps implies a conflict (or dialogue) between at least one side of the character and the authority of the author herself, or perhaps Chopin inadvertently reveals a conflict or dialogue between competing perspectives within her own mind. Finally, a dialogical critic might also interpret this passage as epitomizing a dialogue between character and reader, in which the character is implicitly arguing her case for the right to feel liberated, conceding to the reader all of her husband's kindnesses before she gives way to complete ecstasy at the new life that fate had presented her. **Kathleen B. Durrer**: A DIALOGICAL critic might respond to this passage by first noting that it presents an intimate look into Louise's consciousness. Louise's thoughts are presented as they unfold. Dialogical critics often prefer works that allow their characters a kind of "freedom of speech" that permits a reader to respond to the character without direction from the author. Mikhail Bahktin, discussing Dostoevsky, argued that a writer could dramatize the internal conflicts and developmental stages of a single character by involving the character in dialogues with doubles, alter egos, or other beings. A dialogical critic might therefore note how the quoted passage (and indeed the majority of "The Story of an Hour") implies an internal dialogue within Louise as she reacts to the news of her husband's death. **Lara Bridger**: A DIALOGIC critic might suggest that the dialogue of voices in this passage indicates social conflict. Louise is torn between her duty to her husband and her desire to live for herself. Furthermore, responsibility to an institution which has repressed her is also compounded with her genuine feeling for her husband.

8. *"There would be no powerful will bending hers in that blind persistence with which men and women believe they have a right to impose a private will upon a fellow creature."*

Kathleen B. Durrer: A NEW HISTORICIST critic might respond to this sentence by noting that it not only provides evidence of the social structure which existed at the time Chopin's story was written but that it also contributes to a movement to change that structure. Up until the late 1800s, the dominant role of men in society went widely unchallenged. Men were "in power," and nowhere, perhaps, was their dominance more evident than in marriage. Women were usually expected to submit to their husbands' wishes even when they disagreed with them. This passage is especially intriguing because it not only illustrates the social structure that existed but because it also provides insight into the psychological stirrings that were emerging in the minds of many women who were subjected to such oppression. Even today, the new historicist might emphasize the applicability of this passage to the struggle of women to free themselves from subordinate relationships in a male-dominated work force. **Barbara Larson:** Because NEW HISTORICIST critics generally define reality in terms of power relations (including dominance and submission), this passage would offer an abundance of opportunities for close examination. In addition, the passage can be seen as an attempt to undermine the accepted male/female power positions of Chopin's time. The words "powerful will" are especially important because they suggest, through contrast, the subservient position Mrs. Mallard has heretofore occupied. Obviously her will has been previously bent. The words "blind persistence" remind the reader that often there is no examination of the appropriateness of one person's dominance of another; rather, the dominance is successfully perpetrated (and perpetuated) because it is traditional. Words such as "right" and "impose" again suggest the struggle for power that pervades so much writing (according to many new historicists). **Foster Dickson:** A NEW HISTORICIST might emphasize the stress on power in this passage, concentrating especially on the words "powerful" and "impose." Interestingly, although Mrs. Mallard obviously feels oppressed, her husband probably lacks any consciousness of oppressing her or any deliberate desire to do so. **Lara Bridger:** A NEW HISTORICIST might note how Louise's continued submission is ultimately maintained by the inevitable return of the establishment, embodied by her husband. Although the story seems at first to affirm Louise's escape, it finally reveals the victory of the status quo. **Dianne Russell**: A **NEW HISTORICIST** critic might suggest that this sentence depicts human beings as they typically behave—that is, trying to impose their wills on one another.

9. *"And yet she had loved him—sometimes. Often she had not. What did it matter! What could love, the unsolved mystery, count for in face of this possession of self-assertion which she suddenly recognized as the strongest impulse of her being!*

"'Free! Body and soul free!' she kept whispering."

Scott Johnson: A **STRUCTURALIST** critic might point out the paired opposites (or "dyads") implicit in this passage, such as dependence and freedom, indifference and love, and material and spiritual ("body and soul"). In fact, the story as a whole has a dualistic structure, based on a contrast in the location of the action— between upstairs and downstairs. When Mrs. Mallard is downstairs the first time, she hears of her husband's death and is struck with grief. The second time she is downstairs, she discovers that her husband is alive, and subsequently dies of a heart attack. When she is upstairs, on the other hand, she experiences almost an epiphany or revelation. Furthermore, the language in this part of the story abounds with connotations of life and vitality. The upstairs-downstairs dyad therefore symbolizes more basic contrasts: between exultation and grief, and between life and death. This contrast could also be seen—in terms of the Western culture of which the story is a part—as a reflection of the binary opposition of Heaven and Hell.

Jonathan Wright: A **THEMATIC** critic might suggest that this passage contributes to the story's central theme of "freedom," for within these lines, Mrs. Mallard, although having been initially reluctant to think of freedom following the news of her husband's death, now boldly embraces it. Indeed, when Mrs. Mallard thinks about how "she had loved him—sometimes" and confesses that "often she had not," she seems actually to exercise a freedom previously unknown to her. As the lines of "repression" on her face suggest, she may previously have quieted her thoughts of dissatisfaction with guilt, but now she seems guilt-free.

Scott Johnson: A **POSTMODERNIST** critic might highlight Mrs. Mallard's shifting attitudes and her willingness to accept new roles. Despite our culture's frequent treatment of love as undying (or at least as fairly resilient), this text shows Mrs. Mallard's love to be fluid and indeterminate. The contradictions implicit throughout this passage provide further evidence of the inevitable instability of Mrs. Mallard's convictions. For instance, the last two sentences of the first paragraph are phrased as questions, but they end with exclamation points rather than question marks. The exclamation points suggest a forceful declaration, but their interrogative phrasing exposes their actual tentativeness. Also, if Mrs. Mallard's "self-assertion" is truly "the strongest impulse of her being," why has she just "suddenly recognized" it as such? In fact, the description of her "self-assertion" as an "impulse" is enough to show that it is no more real, or lasting, than her love for her husband. It is also unclear, in the phrase "possession of self-assertion," whether Mrs. Mallard possesses the self-assertion or if she is possessed by it. If the former is true, then self-assertion is shown to be something which she has acquired, and can therefore lose, rather than an inherent part of "her being." If the latter is true, then how can she be said to be asserting herself at all, if she is allowing herself to be possessed by a mere "impulse"? **Jonathan Wright**: A **POST-MODERNIST** might note that this passage accurately reflects reality because it shows how individuals not only perceive and react to situations differently, but also because it demonstrates how they often vainly attempt to resolve the contradictions that invariably surface in life. A postmodernist might also suggest that because Louise Mallard's reaction to her husband's death is uniquely her own, she should be allowed to react according to her own feelings, without incurring harsh condemnation by an audience that can know her mind only in part. Although she initially tries to rationalize the fact that "often she had not" loved her husband, she eventually abandons such attempts when she decides that love is an "unsolved mystery." A postmodernist might argue that Louise is wise to recognize the futility of trying to resolve internal contradictions and self-doubt because life's problems are too complex to be resolved by simplistic rules or unambiguous explanations.

Scott Johnson: A **TRADITIONAL HISTORICAL CRITIC** might look at the influence the transcendentalist movement may have exerted on this passage. The diction of the passage, for instance, is extremely reminiscent of the language of Emerson. It also resembles the phrasing of Walt Whitman, who was himself strongly influenced by Emerson. The passage especially brings to mind Whitman's "Song of Myself" and Emerson's "Self-Reliance." Like Whitman, Mrs. Mallard is celebrating herself and her freedom. Also like Whitman, she expresses sentiments that seem deeply American. Futhermore, her focus on "self-assertion" is much like that of Emerson, who eschewed bland social conformity and strove for independence with a mystical fervor. Also, the many exclamation marks in this passage suggest an excitement and vitality that would have been appreciated by both Emerson and Whitman.

Jonathan Wright: A MULTICULTURALIST might wonder how Louise's views of "freedom" would be different if she were not a young, financially secure white woman. For instance, if Louise were an African-American woman whose parents and grandparents knew the harshness of slavery, she might not perceive her husband's death as "freedom." Furthermore, although an African-American woman at the end of the nineteenth century would probably have experienced financial difficulties even while enjoying the support of her husband, it would have been especially difficult for most black women to survive completely on their own at the turn of the century. Thus, if Louise were a poor black woman who viewed her husband's death as a bittersweet moment, a reader might well suspect the worst of Brently Mallard's character.

Scott Johnson: A MULTICULTURALIST critic might wonder how Mrs. Mallard's situation would be affected if, say, she were a lesbian or had latent lesbian tendencies. Such feelings might, to some extent, explain the power of her feeling of liberation at the death of a husband she may have felt compelled to marry. After all, Mrs. Mallard lived during a time when she would have been considered quite abnormal if she had attempted to live openly as a lesbian. She might feel more free after Brently Mallard's death, then, because her new role as a widow with lesbian feelings would be less constricting than her previous role as a married lesbian. As a widow, for example, she would not be chided for turning away the advances of men. Alternatively, a multiculturalist might also point out that a black woman reading this story probably would not be affected in the same ways as a white woman. An African-American woman from Chopin's period could not completely share in Mrs. Mallard's new feeling of freedom, because if Mrs. Mallard were African-American, she would be no more free after her husband's death than before.

Scott Johnson: A NEW HISTORICIST critic might use this passage to illustrate that every individual exists within a social context defined in part by relationships of power. Mrs. Mallard believes that she has discovered a kind of absolute freedom. It is significant, however, that she has to leave the presence of other people to express this feeling. Her sister and Richards both expect her to be utterly devastated by her husband's death. If she reveals the exhilaration she feels to the outside world, she knows that she will be criticized. In fact, the very cause of her exhilaration is social. Before, she had lived through her husband because she was expected to do so. After her husband's death, however, that particular social restriction would be lifted. What she doesn't seem to realize, however, is that other restrictions would come to take its place. A widow would be expected to act in certain ways, just as a married woman would. Her joy at her husband's death also reveals her to be upper-class, for it would be impossible for a woman without strong economic support to rejoice over the death of a husband. There were not, after all, many good jobs for women in the late nineteenth century. If Mrs. Mallard were from the working class and were left to fend for herself economically, she might well be chained to a sewing machine for sixteen hours at a stretch, making barely enough to survive. If Louise is free at all, then, it is in large part because she is free from being a worker during an extremely oppressive period in American history—a period in which relations of power were quite important.

10. *"Her fancy was running riot along those days ahead of her. Spring days, and summer days, and all sorts of days that would be her own. She breathed a quick prayer that life might be long. It was only yesterday that she had thought with a shudder that life might be long."*

Kathleen B. Durrer: A FORMALIST might respond to this passage by first noting how effectively it contributes to the form of the story. A powerful meaning is conveyed in a relatively short, simple paragraph. Then the critic might note the irony in the passage, especially since it suggests that Brently's death has given Louise the will to live. Finally, a formalist might look at the words themselves in an effort to discover the story's complex meaning. For example, a formalist might examine the use of the word "fancy" and note that as a noun "fancy" comes from the middle English word for "fantasy." This use might imply that Louise's perception of freedom is (as the reader finds out in the end) only a fantasy, a creation of her imagination. Then a formalist might look at the words that follow, especially "running riot," and point out that the word "riot" may imply indulging in revelry, wantonness, or profligate behavior. This sentence might then be viewed as implying Louise's intent to flaunt the standards of society and focus only on her own pleasure. Such close analysis would continue until all the significant words in the passage had been analyzed. Then the formalist would attempt to bring the results of such analysis together to formulate a harmonious but complex interpretation of the work. **Barbara Larson**: A FORMALIST critic might respond to this passage by concentrating on its language, paying relatively little attention to the story's social or cultural contexts. Chopin's words can be taken to imply rebirth and an exciting new life for Mrs. Mallard; the reference to "her fancy," for instance, suggests that she is limited only by the limits to her imagination. Chopin encourages the reader to accompany Mrs. Mallard on her fanciful rebirth by continually repeating the word "days," modifying it first with "spring" (suggesting new birth), then with "summer" (implying mature vitality and satisfaction), and finally with "all sorts" (again implying limitless possibilities). The words "would be her own" confirm Mrs. Mallard's transformation from dependence on her husband to independence, while in the next two sentences words such as "quick," "prayer," and "shudder," along with the repetition of "long," remind the reader of the life/death pattern that permeates and helps organize the story. **Dianne Russell**: A FORMALIST critic would appreciate this passage because of its use of implication, subtlety, and irony. All three qualities are especially present in the final sentence.

Kathleen B. Durrer: A TRADITIONAL HISTORICAL CRITIC might respond to this passage by relating it to social developments occurring at the time the story was written. It was a period of unprecedented change in the opportunities available to women. For the first time in history women were being admitted into universities and being allowed to participate in professions such as medicine. For the first time in history many women had significant choices beyond marriage and spinsterhood. For a woman such as Louise (an intelligent woman who felt repressed) the sudden release from the role of wife might seem to offer the opportunity to sample many of these new opportunities. For the first time in the history of women, these opportunities were now available to her.

Barbara Larson: A **FEMINIST** critic might feel some conflict in responding to this passage. On the one hand, such a critic might note and appreciate the description of a woman relishing the idea of independence. On the other hand, such a critic might feel uneasy at the somewhat flippant language ("fancy," "running riot") used to describe this reaction. Such language, after all, might contribute to the stereotype of the frivolous female. The contrasting diction might be interpreted as reinforcing this stereotype by implying the fickle nature often attributed to women.

Kathleen B. Durrer: **LONGINUS** might react to this passage by admiring how quickly and effectively Chopin conveys Louise's ecstatic reaction to her new freedom. Longinus distinguished between rhetorical amplification (which he associated with an abundance of words) and sublimity (which is often comprised in a single thought). Chopin excels in presenting an extremely complex experience in concise yet beautiful language. Here, for instance, she describes Louise's sudden transformation from despair to hope. Longinus compares sublimity to a lightning bolt that scatters everything before it, and something of that effect is certainly achieved here. **Barbara Larson**: Although **LONGINUS** might value the slightly elevated diction of this passage, he most certainly would applaud Chopin for using language to make the audience share the powerful emotions of the character. Like the formalist, for instance, Longinus would appreciate the hypnotic repetition of the word "days" to emphasize the emotion of the character and enthrall the audience. **Amanda Higgins**: **LONGINUS** might contend that the heightened, passionate nature of the language here allows the reader to associate Mrs. Mallard's new-found freedom with a victory over death (although that victory is ironically short-lived in her case).

Kathleen B. Durrer: A **MARXIST** critic might respond to this passage by noting how it implies the class interests of Kate Chopin. Here as elsewhere in the story, Chopin seems to challenge the subordinate role of women while nevertheless accepting the larger social structure. In this particular passage, for example, Louise voices no financial worries. Clearly she is of the upper class. This position allows her to revel in the possibilities of her situation, while a widow of a lower social class (such as the wife of the peddler mentioned earlier) would face the prospect of a life of poverty and struggle. However, a feminist Marxist might note that Louise has finally found freedom from the repressive relationship of husband

and wife which subordinates and demeans women. **Barbara Larson**: A MARXIST critic might note the phrasing that suggests the character's class privileges. A "fancy" capable of "running riot" can develop most easily within comfortable environs. The description of Louise's future as "days that would be her own" places her firmly in a privileged society. Her changing attitude toward the "long" life ahead of her may reflect a self-centeredness rooted in whim rather than a worry anchored in poverty.

Kathleen B. Durrer: An ARCHETYPAL critic might respond to this passage in several ways. First, she might focus on the use of "spring days, and summer days" as images suggesting birth and harvest. Spring is typically seen as a season of new beginnings, and Louise is contemplating a rebirth from a life of repression to one of freedom. Summer is often viewed as a time of abundance, a time when labor comes to full fruition. Louise is looking ahead to enjoying the results of her rebirth. From another archetypal perspective, however, Louise herself might be seen as a symbol of the Jungian "anima"—a female invested with unusual power. Louise might here be seen as archetypally symbolizing life and vitality of soul, without which any person would feel dead.

Kathleen B. Durrer: PLATO would probably be distressed by "The Story of an Hour" and particularly by this passage. Plato believed that human emotions must be controlled because they interfere with the search for the truth about reality, a search that can only be successful if guided by facts and reason. "The Story of an Hour" is a story of emotions. This passage, for instance, not only expresses Louise's exhilaration in her freedom but also encourages an emotional response from readers.

11. *"When the doctors came they said she had died of heart disease—of joy that kills."*

Kathleen B. Durrer: ARISTOTLE might respond to this final sentence of "The Story of an Hour" with great appreciation. Aristotle viewed tragedy as "an imitation not only of a complete action, but of events terrible and pitiful." He felt that such events are best presented so that they "come on us by surprise." In these last words, the story of Louise's short freedom is complete. The ending is unarguably surprising. Yet when the reader stops to analyze what has occurred, she discovers that the events are not improbable. Mrs. Mallard's weak heart is mentioned in the first line of the story and thus provides a logical cause for the tragic surprise at the end. Aristotle felt that the element of surprise was strengthened when it, like everything else in a work, had a necessary connection to the rest of the work. In the closing words of her story, Chopin achieves a surprise that does not violate the work's unity but instead strengthens it. **Barbara Larson:** ARISTOTLE might note that the story has depicted a change in fortune and that this final ironic twist, although surprising, is completely consistent with the story's very first words. **Amanda Higgins:** ARISTOTLE might appreciate the fact that this short sentence wastes no words but is completely efficient in bringing the work to an intricate, complex conclusion. **Dianne Russell:** ARISTOTLE would value this sentence because it epitomizes the complex unity of the story. He would also applaud the sentence because it exemplifies his assertion that recognition and reversal are most effective when they coincide. Here we learn of Mrs. Mallard's death (reversal) at precisely the moment that we recognize the inadequacy and irony of the doctors' explanations.

Kathleen Durrer: HORACE might have responded to the final sentence in "The Story of an Hour" by advising Chopin to moderate the shocking impact of the sudden closure. In discussing every element of the literary text, Horace advised the writer to consider its potential impact on the audience. For this reason, Horace tended to counsel moderation in presenting a story. He advised writers to avoid taking risks that might shock or repel the audience. Chopin's story challenged the conventions of her society. This final sentence conveys an especially shocking meaning (that death may be preferable to life as a married woman), and that message would have been seen by many as almost revolutionary in the 1890s. Horace would have frowned upon the use of literature as a tool of social reform. Such reforms are often unpopular, and since Horace emphasized the writer's need to please an audience, he would have been reluctant to advise the writer to offend them. However, the final judge in Horace's theory of literature is always the audience. Perhaps this fact would help redeem Chopin in Horace's opinion, since "The Story of an Hour" is now viewed as a classic model of the short story. In other words, it has won audience approval. **Barbara Larson:** HORACE might commend Chopin for the simplicity with which she depicts Mrs. Mallard's tragic end. The irony of the phrase "the joy that kills" is moderate enough to please an audience rather than confusing them, and the ironic twist shows a desire to please and amuse them. **Amanda Higgins:**

HORACE might appreciate the final sentence because it affects the audience; it packs a powerful punch. He would praise Chopin's efficient use of language, and although she violates stereotypes of female behavior by showing Mrs. Mallard's happiness at her husband's death, Chopin does so in moderation (for instance, by stressing Louise's appreciation of Brently). Horace would admire this restraint.

Kathleen B. Durrer: A FEMINIST critic might applaud the tremendous irony in the final words of "The Story of an Hour." The irony results because the reader knows that Louise's death occurs not from joy but from the horrible realization that she has lost the freedom she thought she had achieved. Louise's death emphasizes the oppression she has suffered, for she dies not "of joy that kills" but because, having once captured a brief glimpse of freedom, she refuses to return to a life of repression. **Lara Bridger**: A FEMINIST critic might be disturbed by the implications of this conclusion, preferring instead an ending that affirmed the possibility of female empowerment. **Amanda Higgins**: A FEMINIST critic might consider it tragic not only that Mrs. Mallard never lived the freedom she desired, but also that no one ever knew her brief happiness. **Foster Dickson**: A FEMINIST critic might find it ironically fitting that her husband's mere presence kills her at her moment of greatest triumph. It is almost as if a free woman must die. **Barbara Larson**: Because the "doctors" are not identified explicitly as feminine and are therefore presumably males, a FEMINIST critic might note their patriarchal assumption that Mrs. Mallard would die from joy at seeing her husband again. Feminists might see the doctors' response as typically condescending and ignorant.

Kathleen B. Durrer: A READER-RESPONSE critic might respond to this sentence by arguing that different audiences would interpret it differently. Both feminists and formalists, for instance, might admire the irony of this conclusion, but for varying reasons. Also, a reader-response critic might note that reactions to Chopin's ending would probably have been different in 1894 than in 1994. **Barbara Larson**: A READER-RESPONSE theorist might note the multitude of possible responses that even one word of this passage—"doctors" —might evoke in different readers. Different readers might imagine the doctors, variously, as caring or pompous or solicitous or skilled or inept or any number of other possibilities. **Lara Bridger**: A READER-RESPONSE critic might observe, for instance, that while a conservative male reader might take some satisfaction in Louise's end, a sympathetic feminist might lament her tragic demise.

Kathleen B. Durrer: A Freudian **PSYCHOANALYTIC** critic might respond to this sentence by arguing that Louise's death was caused by her tremendous guilt at the pleasure she had experienced at the news of her husband's death. All of Louise's repressed desires had emerged and had been recognized and embraced. When Louise is confronted with her living husband, all of society's conventions return to her mind, and she feels extreme guilt for her earlier thoughts. Louise cannot balance her inner feelings with the conventions of society and marriage. Instead of continuing to live a life wracked by guilt, she therefore chooses death. **Amanda Higgins:** A Freudian **PSYCHOANALYTIC** critic might argue that Louise dies from the realization that she would never be able to live a life that would fulfill the desires of her id and the needs of her ego. A Freudian might argue that she died not from literal heart disease but from psychic conflict. **Mary Mechler:** A Freudian **PSYCHOANALYTIC** critic might contend that Mrs. Mallard's death demonstrates the destructiveness of the repression forced upon her all her life by social conventions.

Kathleen B. Durrer: A **DIALOGICAL** critic might respond to this sentence by noting that in the final line of the story the narrator intrudes upon the form of the work by relating Louise's death in an emotionless voice. Readers are thus closed off from Louise's direct final thoughts and must form their own interpretations of what has occurred. **Amanda Higgins:** A **DIALOGICAL** critic might note how the doctors ultimately speak for Mrs. Mallard, telling her story and in effect having the last word. Such a critic might find the absence of Mrs. Mallard's voice the most intriguing part of this passage, since it links her death and her life. Mrs. Mallard is as voiceless in death as she had been while alive—an ironic illustration of one way that dialogue does define life and literature for the dialogical critic. **Mary Mechler:** A **DIALOGICAL** critic might appreciate this passage since it concludes a secret dialogue with the reader. Although the surviving characters in the story believe that Mrs. Mallard died from the joy of realizing that her husband was still alive, the reader knows a secret to which the other characters have not been privy. **Lara Bridger:** A **DIALOGICAL** critic might note how even the phrase "heart disease" can express two divergent voices or points of view; in more ways than one, perhaps,

Mrs. Mallard dies of a disease of the heart. The words of the doctors are truthful in ways the doctors do not realize.

Index of Critical Approaches

prepared by John Burdett

Archetypal Criticism: Bow 5; Fau 22; Fit 19; Hem 19, 27; Jac 5; Jew 4, 8; Law 7, 8, 17; Lon 3, 9, 11; Oat 2, 10; Poe 8; Wel 3, 6

Aristotle: Cra 4; Joy 3; Law 5, 14; Lon 6; O'CFl 16; OCFr 5; Ste 1

Deconstruction: Fau 13; Haw 4, 20, 21; Jew 7; Joy 21; Lon 10; O'CFl 18; Poe 17; Twa 7

Dialogical Criticism: Cra 8; Fau 17, 23; Joy 16, 19; O'CFl 3, 10, 22; Ols 4

Feminist Criticism: Cat 5; Fau 1, 7, 14, 29, 34; Gil 2–9; Haw 1; Hem 2, 28; Jac 5, 8, 10; Jam 9; Jew 1, 5, 8; Joy 12, 19, 22; Ols 3, 4, 5; Poe 17; Por 15, 16, 17; Ste 2, 4, 8; Upd 4; Wal 5, 8, 10, 11

Formalist Criticism ("New Criticism"): Bea 3–8; Bie 1, 3, 5–9; Bow 1, 3, 6, 7; Cat 1, 3, 5, 11–13; Cra 1, 3–6, 8, 9; Fau 1, 2, 7, 8, 11, 12, 16–19, 21, 23, 26–28, 31, 33, 35, 37, 39; Fit 1, 2, 5–8, 10, 13–16, 18–24, 26; Gil 9; Haw 2, 10, 12, 17, 22–23; Hem 2–5, 7, 9–12, 14, 15, 18–28; Jac 1, 3, 6, 9, 13; Jam 3, 5, 6, 8, 9, 12–14; Jew 2, 3, 6, 9, 10; Joy 4, 10, 17, 18, 23, 24; Law 1, 3–5, 10, 13, 14, 18; Lon 5, 9, 10; Mel 5–7, 9, 11, 12, 14; O'CFl 1, 6, 7, 10, 14, 17, 19, 24, 31, 33, 35; O'CFr 1, 2, 4–7, 11–13; Ols 2, 4, 7, 8; Poe 2, 3, 7, 8, 10, 11, 13, 21, 22; Por 1, 9–12, 14; Ste 2, 5, 6; Twa 2–6, 8, 9, 11; Upd 2, 3, 5, 8–10; Wal 3; Wel 1, 2, 7

Historical Criticism: Bea 1, 2, 8; Bie 2, 4, 7, 8; Bow 3; Cat 1–4, 7, 8, 10–13; Cra 1, 2, 5, 9; Fau 3, 9–11, 13, 15, 19, 20, 26, 27, 30–32; Fit 1, 4, 5, 9, 10, 12–15, 17–19, 23, 26; Gil 1–7, 9; Haw 7, 8, 11, 13, 16–17, 20, 23; Hem 1, 3, 6, 8, 9, 12, 14–16, 17, 18, 23, 26, 27; Jac 4, 7, 10, 11; Jam 7, 10; Jew 5; Joy 1–3, 7, 11–13, 15, 16, 22, 24; Law 4, 15, 18; Lon 1, 4, 5, 11; Mel 1–5, 10, 12, 13, 15, 16; Oat 1–4, 6–8; O'CFl 15, 16, 20, 24, 25, 30, 34, 36; O'CFr 2, 3, 10, 11; Ols 5; Poe 1, 3, 6, 7, 10–15, 19, 20, 23, 24; Por 3, 5, 6–8, 14; Ste 2, 7, 9–10; Twa 1, 4, 5, 8–11; Upd 6, 11; Wal 7, 8; Wel 3, 4, 7, 11

Index of Topics

prepared by John Burdett

10, 13; O'CFl 9; Poe 11, 23; Por 2; Ste 2, 7; Twa 9; Upd 2, 7, 11

sacrifice Cra 1; Fau 6; Gil 1; Haw 1; Jac 9; Joy 15; Law 17; Oat 9; O'CFl 27; Ste 6

safety Bow 1, 2; Cra 1; Mel 2; Oat 3

salvation Fit 25; Gil 1; Haw 16, 17; Hem 24; Joy 18; O'CFl 2, 8, 21; Por 9; Wal 2

Satan Fau 11, 12, 19, 31; Haw 11, 12, 14; Jew 5; Oat 1, 2, 11, 12; O'CFl 15

satire Fau 31; O'CFl 1, 6; Twa 4, 11

schizophrenia Cat 4; Mel 3, 5, 12

science Cra 1; Haw 2, 6, 8, 9; Jam 11; Oat 14

secret(s) Bea 1; Cat 8; Fau 31; Fit 7; Jam 3, 11; Oat 5; O'CFr 10; Por 12

security Bow 1; Fit 19; Mel 11

seeing Bie 9; Bow 4; Cat 11; Cra 2; Fau 27; Gil 8; Haw 14, 21, 23; Hem 18, 20; Joy 20; O'CFl 11; Poe 18

self Bea 8; Bie 3, 9; Cat 2, 5, 6, 11–13; Fau 1, 3, 11, 12, 17, 28, 31; Fit 15–18, 27; Haw 5, 16; Hem 6, 12, 22, 23, 26; Jam 2, 5, 7, 9, 11, 15; Jew 1–3, 6; Joy 2, 8, 12, 13, 15, 16, 20, 22; Law 2, 6, 8, 15, 17; Lon 3, 7, 10; Mel 2, 4, 12, 13; Oat 3, 14; O'CFl 1, 4, 6, 9, 14, 18, 22, 23, 27, 28, 33, 35; Poe 4, 15, 17, 22, 23; Por 16, 19; Ste 3, 7, 9; Twa 4, 5, 7; Upd 3, 7, 8, 11; Wal 2, 11; Wel 10

self-awareness O'CFl 28; Por 19; Wal 2

self-consciousness Jew 6; Joy 20; O'CFl 4

self-control Fit 16; Poe 22

self-deception Fau 17; Jam 5; O'CFl 33

self-pity Fit 17; Upd 7

self-possession Fau 31; Joy 2

sense Bie 4, 5, 11; Bea 4, 7; Bow 4, 6; Cat 3, 8, 12; Cra 1; Fau 1, 3, 6, 11, 24, 25, 27, 34, 36; Fit 14, 23, 27; Haw 11; Hem 13, 18, 25; Jac 1, 14; Jam 10; Joy 1, 3, 4, 8, 15, 16, 18, 20; Law 9, 10, 16; Lon 5, 10, 11; Mel 2, 15; Oat 3; O'CFl 1, 2, 12, 18, 24, 31; O'CFr 1; Ols 4, 6, 8; Poe 15, 16; Por 1, 2, 4, 8, 10, 19; Ste 9; Twa 3, 7; Upd 5, 9, 10; Wal 1, 10, 11

sensitivity Hem 25; Jew 5; Upd 8; Wal 10

sensory Bie 3, 4; Haw 7; Hem 18

sensuality Fau 16; Fit 1; Haw 14; Poe 15

sentiment O'CFr 13; Poe 7

sentimentality Bie 6, 9; Cat 13; Cra 6; Fit 24; Hem 24; Joy 4; Law 10; Oat 3; O'CFl 1, 3, 6, 36; O'CFr 6, 12; Upd 2, 5, 7, 10;

separation Cat 11; Jew 1, 7; Ols 4, 6

setting Bie 8; Bow 1; Haw 5; Hem 14; Jac 11, 14; Jam 12; Jew 1, 8; Lon 6; Oat 13; O'CFr 1; Poe 1, 3, 7, 13, 24; Ste 10; Wel 1, 6

sex Bow 7; Cat 5; Gil 1; Haw 8; Jam 11; Jew 3; Oat 1, 9, 14; Por 4, 12; Ste 3, 6

sexuality Cat 8, 10; Fau 25, 34; Fit 1; Gil 4, 6; Haw 3, 7, 8, 14, 22; Jac 10; Jam 9; Jew 3; Joy 11; Law 4; Oat 10, 12, 14; Ste 4, 7, 8

silence Bea 6; Bie 5; Fau 23; Fit 4; Jew 4; Joy 19; Mel 5; O'CFl 10; Ols 5; Poe 9; Wel 5, 10

sin Fau 3; Fit 2, 7; Haw 6, 12, 14, 16, 22; Jam 11; O'CFl 8, 14, 15; Poe 9; Por 12, 13

sinister Bow 2; Jac 6; Poe 17

sister Fit 20, 25, 26; Haw 7; Joy 2, 5, 6, 8, 9, 11; Oat 3, 14; O'CFl 9, 26; Ols 6; Poe 14, 16, 17; Wal 6; Wel 9

Index of Critics

prepared by John Burdett

Hansot, Elisabeth, Jam 4
Harris, Janice Hubbard, Law 6
Harris, Kathryn M., Poe 3
Hayden, Mary H., Joy 5
Hays, Peter L., Fau 30
Healey, James, Oat 4
Hedges, Elaine R., Gil 4
Hedrick, Joan D., Lon 4
Heilman, Robert B., Jac 6
Held, George, Jew 5
Heller, Terry, Jew 6
Hendin, Josephine, O'CFl 12
Hendricks, King, Lon 5
Herndon, Jerry A., Hem 22
Hiles, Jane, Fau 9
Hill, John S., Poe 16
Hoefel, Rosanne, Por 16
Hoeveler, Diane Long, Poe 17
Hoffman, Daniel, Poe 4
Holland, Norman N., Law 7
Hollister, Michael, Wal 9
Hopkins, Mary Frances, O'CFl 29
Hostetler, Norman H., Haw 17
Hughes, Douglas A., Bow 6
Hughes, R. S., Ste 1, 2
Hume, Beverly A., Gil 5
Humphreys, A. R., Mel 8
Hurley, C. Harold, Oat 5; Upd 6
Hurley, D. F., Oat 6
Hutton, Virgil, Hem 8

Iyer, Pico, Bea 5

Jackson, Shirley B., Jac 7
Jacobus, Mary, Gil 6
Jauss, David, O'CFl 30
Johnson, E. Shirley, Por 2
Johnson, Greg, Gil 7
Johnston, Kenneth G., Fau 10; Hem 23
Jones, Diane Brown, Fau 11, 31
Junkins, Donald, Law 8

Kain, Richard M., Joy 9
Kamel, Rose, Ols 5
Kane, Patricia, Wal 6

Kaplan, Louise, Poe 18
Kasmer, Lisa, Gil 8
Kavanaugh, Patrick, O'CFr 6
Kelchner, Heidi, Jew 7
Kelly, Margot Anne, Wal 7
Kendall, Lyle H., Jr., Poe 19
Kerner, David, Jam 5
Kissane, Leedice, Cra 5
Kloss, Robert J., Ols 6
Knights, L. C., Jam 6
Koban, Charles, Law 9
Korenmann, Joan S., Wal 8
Kosenko, Peter, Jac 8
Krause, S. J., Twa 4
Kuehl, John F., Fit 7, 22

Labor, Earle, Lon 5, 6
LaFrance, Marston, Cra 6
Laman, Barbara, Por 17
Lamson, Roy, Law 10
Lassner, Phyllis, Bow 7
Lavers, Norman, Por 3
Lawrence, D. H., Poe 20
Lawrence, Robert G., Law 11
Leonard, Garry M., Joy 8
Levenson, Michael, Joy 16
Levy, Leo B., Haw 18
Lewis, Thomas N., Wel 4
Lieberman, Michael, O'CFr 7
Lindholdt, Paul J., Jam 7
Linkin, Harriet Kramer, Bie 5
Logan, F. J., Bie 6
Loomis, C. C., Jr., Joy 17
Luscher, Robert M., Upd 7
Lynn, Kenneth S., Twa 5
Lytle, Andrew, Joy 18

Maclean, Hugh, Law 10
Maglaner, Marvin, Joy 9
Maida, Patricia Dinneen, O'CFl 31
Male, Roy, Fit 23; Haw 6, 19
Malin, Irving, Fit 8
Mangum, Bryant, Fit 24
Marcus, Mordecai, Ste 3
Marks, W. S., III, Law 12
Martin, Carter W., O'CFl 13